The Bishop's Utopia

THE EARLY MODERN AMERICAS

Peter C. Mancall, Series Editor

Volumes in the series explore neglected aspects of early modern history in the
western hemisphere. Interdisciplinary in character, and with a special emphasis
on the Atlantic World from 1450 to 1850, the series is published in partnership
with the USC-Huntington Early Modern Studies Institute.

The Bishop's Utopia

Envisioning Improvement in Colonial Peru

Emily Berquist Soule

PENN

UNIVERSITY OF PENNSYLVANIA PRESS

PHILADELPHIA

ART HISTORY
PUBLICATION INITIATIVE

This book is made possible by a collaborative grant
from the Andrew W. Mellon Foundation.

GOBIERNO   MINISTERIO   SECRETARÍA
DE ESPAÑA DE EDUCACIÓN, CULTURA DE ESTADO
           Y DEPORTE   DE CULTURA

Publication of this volume was assisted by funding
from the Spanish Ministry of Education, Culture and Sports.

Published by
University of Pennsylvania Press
Philadelphia, Pennsylvania 19104-4112
www.upenn.edu/pennpress

Printed in the United States of America on acid-free paper
10 9 8 7 6 5 4 3 2 1

Library of Congress Cataloging-in-Publication Data

Soule, Emily Berquist, 1975–
The bishop's utopia : envisioning improvement in colonial Peru / Emily Berquist Soule. — 1st ed.
p. cm. — (The early modern Americas)
Includes bibliographical references and index.
ISBN 978-0-8122-4591-2 (hardcover : alk. paper)
1. Martínez Compañón y Bujanda, Baltasar Jaime, 1735–1797. 2. Martínez Compañón y Bujanda,
Baltasar Jaime, 1735–1797. Trujillo del Perú a fines del siglo XVIII. 3. Indians of South America—
Material culture—Peru—Trujillo (La Libertad) 4. Indians of South America—Ethnobotany—
Peru—Trujillo (La Libertad) 5. Indians of South America—Peru—Trujillo (La Libertad)—Social
conditions—18th century. 6. Social planning—Peru—Trujillo (La Libertad)—History—18th century.
7. Utopias—Peru—Trujillo (La Libertad)—History—18th century. 8. Natural history—Peru—Trujillo
(La Libertad) 9. Material culture in art. I. Title. II. Series: Early modern Americas.
F3611.T8S68 2014
985'.033—dc23   2013035999

For Zoey

A map of the world that does not include Utopia is not worth even glancing at, for it leaves out the one country at which Humanity is always landing. And when Humanity lands there, it looks out, and, seeing a better country, sets sail.
—Oscar Wilde

This trip was longer than I had thought, because there was something to do everywhere I went . . . and it was not easy.
—Martínez Compañón to Viceroy Croix, 1786

CONTENTS

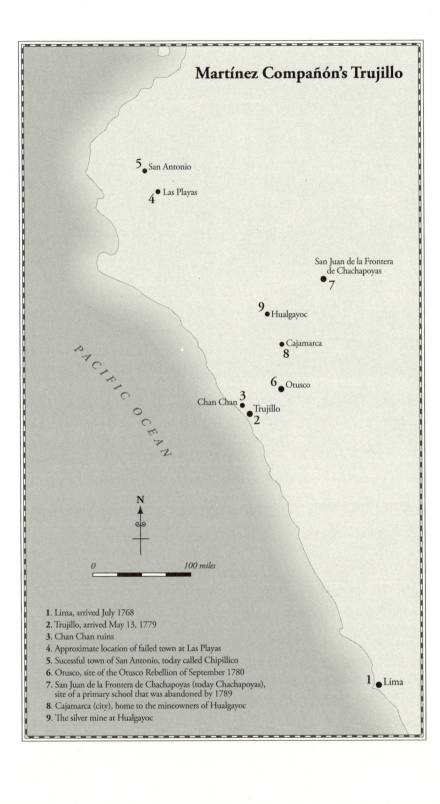

Martínez Compañón's Trujillo

5. San Antonio

4. Las Playas

San Juan de la Frontera
de Chachapoyas
7

9. Hualgayoc

Cajamarca
8

6. Otusco

Chan Chan 3
Trujillo
2

PACIFIC OCEAN

N

0   100 miles

1. Lima

1. Lima, arrived July 1768
2. Trujillo, arrived May 13, 1779
3. Chan Chan ruins
4. Approximate location of failed town at Las Playas
5. Sucessful town of San Antonio, today called Chipillico
6. Otusco, site of the Otusco Rebellion of September 1780
7. San Juan de la Frontera de Chachapoyas (today Chachapoyas),
   site of a primary school that was abandoned by 1789
8. Cajamarca (city), home to the mineowners of Hualgayoc
9. The silver mine at Hualgayoc

Utopias in the New World

From the moment the Spanish set foot in what would soon be known as the "New World," they were seeking mineral wealth, neophyte Catholics, free labor, natural resources, and wondrous marvels. But above all, the first Europeans to cross the Atlantic ventured to the other side of the world in search of dreams. They envisioned shining cities of gold and palaces overflowing with jewels and silver. They dreamed of forests where rainbow-hued birds fluttered overhead. They imagined becoming little monarchs with their own kingdoms and vassals. They dreamed of their epic deeds being immortalized in history books. And some of them believed that with all this behind them, they would return to Europe and claim the international dominance that they were convinced was the destiny of Spain.

What happened to those dreams—the civil wars between brothers, the capture and execution of kings, and the decimation of an estimated 90–95 percent of America's original peoples—has fascinated readers for centuries. These stories of darkness and depravity are an inseparable part of the history of the Spanish in America. Gripping as they are, they are not the only stories. Though the history of Spanish America is darkened by figures such as Bishop Diego de Landa of Yucatán, who in just three months arrested and tortured 4,500 Mayans on suspicion of idolatry, and Juan Ginés de Sepúlveda, a Spanish legal theorist who tried his best to prove that the Indians of America were natural slaves who benefited from captivity, these are not the only figures from the colonial period worth remembering. They lived alongside others less notorious—men who believed in harmony, prosperity, and exchange. Although these men also struggled with paternalism, orthodoxy, and even aggression, they held fast to their visions of a more perfect world in America.[1]

One such man is the subject of this book. Sent from Spain to the north of Peru in the final third of the eighteenth century, Baltasar Jaime Martínez Compañón dreamed of refashioning the rich natural environment and diverse peoples of Trujillo into a veritable utopia. He imagined a dreamlike world where Catholic morality and Spanish propriety would flourish in European-style towns. Indian children would attend primary schools to learn the basic reading and writing skills that would assist them in their future work as tradesmen or agriculturalists. Even the haphazard settlements outside Peru's notoriously abusive silver mines were sites for his vision of industry, order, and peace. Under Martínez Compañón, Trujillo became a laboratory for improvement where local communities participated in engineering their own futures, deciding for themselves the meaning of utopia and their place in it.

But the Bishop's utopia in colonial Peru was not only centered on the lives of natives; it also depended upon the natural world around them. Trujillo's environment was an Edenic paradise replete with exquisite flowers, exotic fruits, strange marine species, and fantastical animals. The Indians' ancestral knowledge was the key to observing, cataloging, and unlocking the vast potential of these riches. So the Bishop invited the natives of Trujillo to be his collaborators in a decade-long natural history project that cataloged the people, plants, animals, and past of the province. During almost three years of travels throughout his territory, he collected from locals in each district "a sample of all the specimens that are not found in other [towns]."[2] Ultimately, this effort produced a natural history collection composed of thirty crates of local specimens, including carefully inventoried native antiquities, dried plants, soil samples, and local manufactures. The boxes were remitted to Spain in 1788 and 1790, where some of the archaeological artifacts still survive in Madrid's Museum of America.[3]

As he traveled throughout the mountains, deserts, and jungles of Trujillo gathering his collection, Martínez Compañón kept careful notes of all that he saw, hoping one day to compile them into a "Historical, Scientific, Political, and Social Museum of the Bishopric of Trujillo del Perú."[4] He died before he was able to begin writing, so scholars can only fantasize about the treasures that such a book might have held. But as he worked on his collection and his notes, the Bishop also asked local illustrators to produce almost 1,400 exquisite hand-painted watercolor images depicting the world around them. After his promotion to the archbishopric of Bogotá, he compiled these into a "paper museum" in the style of the early modern visual compendiums by Athanasius Kircher, Cassiano dal Pazzo, and Federico Borromeo. The Bishop organized his "museum" into nine separate volumes depicting cities and towns, people, botanical specimens, animal, bird, and marine life, and native antiquities. They were edged in gold gilt, hand-bound in red Moroccan leather, and titled simply *Trujillo del Perú*.[5]

Received most enthusiastically by Crown and Church functionaries throughout the viceroyalty, the books offered a world in miniature. Volume 1 told the story of what Martínez Compañón had accomplished in Trujillo, beginning with a detailed topographical map of the diocese, as seen in Plate 1—particularly timely because just four years earlier, imperial officials had issued a frantic call for maps of the colonial provinces.[6] The Bishop also used the book to display the vast array of reform projects that he had enacted or begun during his time in Trujillo. By his own calculations, these included fifty-four primary schools, thirty-nine churches built "from their foundations," twenty towns, six new roads, and three irrigation channels. The volume also included a painted procession of Trujillo's bishops, their lace chalices and thick black cassocks accented by ornate jewelry. Nestled among them were two portraits of Martínez Compañón himself. The first shows a younger man clasping a Bible to his chest in deep contemplation. The second portrait features a sterner man whose face wears the signs of his advancing age.

Volume 2, depicting quotidian life, opens with a series of "type" images of Indians, mestizos, Spaniards, and people of African descent, echoing the contemporary craze for ethnographic portraiture.[7] More impressive than the Trujillans' various intricate costumes, however, was the industriousness that marked their daily lives. The images showed them at work raising sheep, harvesting wheat, hunting animals, and manufacturing textiles. Even in their free time, they behaved like obedient, loyal subjects—like the two Indians playing cards in Plate 2. Not only was this couple supporting the profitable Crown monopoly on playing cards; they were also virtuously declining to gamble with actual money, choosing instead to use feathers.[8] Like the majority of the native peoples shown in the volumes, these Indians have fair complexions and light hair, optimistically indicating that the Bishop's efforts to Hispanicize them had been so successful that their very flesh had begun to lighten.

The watercolors in the remaining seven books depicted natural items and man-made objects. Volumes 3, 4, and 5 showed a dazzling array of medicinal herbs, trees, shrubs, and other plants that Indians used in their daily lives, many of which held useful cures for sickness and disease. Volume 6 contained images of monkeys, llamas, lizards, and even an anteater. This was followed by a book of birds, one of marine life, and an exquisite collection of archaeological drawings.

Such a comprehensive natural history was intended to bring Bishop Martínez Compañón praise in the metropolis. Even today, botanists, archaeologists, and ethnomusicologists recognize his research as one of the most complete sources of information on northern Peru in the colonial period. The Bishop hoped that the impact of his work would extend beyond museums and cabinets of curiosities. By surveying Trujillo's natural resources and deciding how best to utilize them, he planned to transform his corner of the Spanish world into an orderly, profit-producing slice of empire. He trusted that studying such subjects as "geography, metallurgy, mineralogy and botany" would be useful for "industry and commerce" because the data could be employed for financial gain and because pursuing such knowledge would help to "distract my diocesans from laziness," as he put it.[9]

Yet, as he looked back at his specimens and illustrations, Martínez Compañón worried that his natural history was "a bit vulgar and common"[10] and perhaps "not all organized as well as it should be."[11] He may have guessed that his work would have one distinct problem in the eyes of the Madrid establishment: it did not conform to the contemporary parameters of natural history research, which privileged the Latin-based binomial classification system and called for technical natural history illustrations that could be analyzed and utilized by trained experts throughout the European scientific community. In the *Trujillo* natural history, in contrast, specimens were named either in the local Peruvian tongue of Quechua or in Castilian. The descriptions in the Bishop's collection inventory did not provide the proper Latin name and discuss the species and variety of the item in question. Instead, they focused on the geographical location of the plant, whether the climate of its provenance was "hot" or "cold," and how the locals prepared the specimen for medicine or food. The botanical images themselves were also problematic: rather than portraying their subjects in the most "objective" manner possible, they were impressionistic, focusing on details that their illustrators deemed most important instead of depicting the plants' reproductive organs, which most interested European-trained botanists.

The locally based view of nature that dominates the Bishop's utopia exemplifies an American-born scientific epistemology that was linked to—but, in many ways, differed from—the dominant scientific epistemologies of the Enlightenment. Though European scientific observers privileged data that could easily be plugged into "universal" systems of knowledge—mainly the binomial classification system developed by Karl Linnaeus—a smaller, competing scientific methodology flourished on the ground in America. This privileged native languages, scientific traditions, and ways of understanding the local environment. As a small but dedicated group of Creole scientists in Lima sponsored studies and wrote books defending scientific data generated from Indian informants in Peru, from Trujillo, Martínez Compañón and his local collaborators made their own contributions. The watercolor images and the natural history collection that they produced aggregated and displayed local knowledge of the natural world. Their work did not follow the standards of natural history illustration prescribed by academies in the metropolis, and it did not use the Linnaean system of classification that the Spanish government had made standard for naturalists working in America since 1752. Instead, the Trujillo information privileged local names, classifications, and uses, and it produced images that centered on basic description rather than parsing specimen components, as European standards suggested. Though Martínez Compañón hoped that his scientific work would be of use—or, at the very least, of interest—to bureaucrats and naturalists in Madrid, he held fast to his vision of a local utopia in Trujillo, recording, preserving, and displaying a vision of the natural world that proved that the Indians were, as he put it, "men given a rational soul just like ours."[12]

Back in Spain, the experts at the Royal Pharmacy, Royal Botanical Garden, and the Royal Natural History Cabinet were uninterested in such rhetoric; they seem to have viewed the watercolors and the collection as inferior, rustic, and essentially useless. They made no effort to publish any of the *Trujillo* work or to use it as an exemplar for similar projects.[13] The inventory was ferreted away in royal archives, the collection promptly disassembled, and its parts disseminated without being cataloged. The nine volumes of watercolors were relegated to the dusty shelves of the royal library. The utopia that Martínez Compañón had struggled to create and depict was mostly forgotten—until now.

The Bishop's Utopia returns this encyclopedic natural history to the ideological center of Martínez Compañón's time in Trujillo. It combines analysis of the visual data and the collection inventory with extensive archival research conducted over ten years in order to confirm that all this was mainly about one thing: the Indians. As Martínez Compañón wrote to King Charles III, it was the Indians of America who had populated his dreams as a young man in Spain. In 1786, the Bishop admitted that, like many learned Spaniards, he had "read and heard about the misfortunes and disgraces of the Indians of America, and believed that their luck was unhappy in general." But what he had imagined, he admitted, could not begin to compare with the tragedy that he had witnessed during his twenty-three years in Peru. His time there, he wrote, had shown him that the majority of the Indians of Trujillo were "a miserable people . . . wherever one looks." He believed that the Indians' unhappiness was in many ways the fault of the Spanish, who had failed to properly instruct them in Catholic spirituality and European sociability. This neglect was manifest "in their souls" because "in their profound ignorance, they have no idea of good, bad, or virtue." Equally upsetting was the physical misery that the Indians endured. "In sickness and in health," he wrote, "[they] are treated with positive indolence, inhumanity, and cruelty. . . . [They receive] no help when they ask for it—not even that commonly given to beasts."[14] Yet he also knew that despite the abuses and misfortunes that they had endured, it was the Indians of America who could provide the labor necessary to revive the empire's finances. In fact, Martínez Compañón's utopia in colonial Peru was altogether predicated upon the Indians. He imagined how to improve the Indians' financial, social, and religious lives through his schools, towns, and mining reforms. He also wanted to capitalize on their knowledge of local plant and animal life in order to bring the Spanish Crown, viceregal administrators, and the Indians themselves a financial windfall.

Improving the Indians was the Bishop's foremost concern over the almost twelve years he served in Trujillo, but they were by no means the only inhabitants of Trujillo; the bishopric was also home to large populations of mestizos and people of African descent, but it was the Indians whom the Bishop repeatedly singled out as the focus of his reform efforts.[15] He spent almost three years traveling the deserts, mountains, and rainforests of his bishopric, meeting them and assessing what their communities needed most. He found them living in dispersed settlements with no communal support. So he worked with them to establish twenty new towns that would dot the landscape with neat plazas, town councils, and parish churches. When he saw that Indian children could not learn basic reading and writing because Trujillo's rural areas lacked primary schools, he ordered the construction of fifty-four schoolhouses, two Indian colleges, and even a school just for girls. When he discovered the horrific conditions that Indian laborers endured working at the Hualgayoc silver mine in Cajamarca, he imagined an extraordinary plan to help them, one based on a utopian mining town where workers would be given free land and farm implements in exchange for their labor underground.

Although this agenda of socioeconomic reforms marks Martínez Compañón as a classic reforming prelate of the Bourbon period, it also reveals him to be an iconoclast who promoted an expansive, innovative vision of improvement that was fundamentally utopian. The utopia that he imagined in Trujillo was a real-time contribution to the debate over the New World, one that used local initiative and natural resources to construct a program of improvement demonstrating how the people and nature of Peru were useful and productive. In Trujillo, Martínez Compañón used native knowledge and manpower to construct a utopia based on local circumstance. He fostered an agenda of social improvement and gathered a body of natural history data that offered locally calibrated solutions to economic and social problems while simultaneously demonstrating that the Indians of Trujillo were capable of becoming the very sort of useful subjects the Spanish Crown sought.

Like all other utopias that came before his and followed it, this grand vision of an idealized life never materialized as the Bishop had imagined it. But utopias would not be utopias if they existed in the material world: they are dreams, imaginings, hopes for a better future. In *The Bishop's Utopia*, Martínez Compañón becomes an eloquent guide on an intellectual journey through the eighteenth-century culture of reform in the Spanish Atlantic world. The boundaries and parameters of what he imagined were marked by European reform culture and referenced past efforts of improvement in America; but ultimately, they were the product of the time and place and situation in the north of the Viceroyalty of Peru in the late eighteenth century.

Because Martínez Compañón's imagined utopia was so inextricably linked to local context, it provides a unique opportunity to examine how the rhetoric of reform was adapted and promoted on the ground by colonial communities. Instead of reacting against the Bourbon reform agendas with violence, the people of Trujillo absorbed the discourse of reform and refashioned it into a locally based vision of improvement that would better suit their needs. With Martínez Compañón's assistance, they imagined their own utopia in a distant corner of the Spanish Empire. They willingly adopted the rhetoric of urbane civility, public happiness, and economic utility, using it to envision how to improve their own local communities in the ways they would benefit from the most. They initiated projects to incorporate their settlements into towns and to build local primary schools. In so doing, they learned how to manage complex bureaucratic processes, how to gather and distribute information in ways that bureaucrats would accept, and how to ask for what they wanted in terms that would appeal to elites.

The Bishop's efforts were meant to improve the lives of Trujillo's Indians, helping them become the very sort of useful subjects that reformers in Madrid hoped to make of plebeians throughout the empire. But at an even deeper level, this agenda of social engineering and the Trujillo natural history project made an ideological statement about who the Indians were. Seeking to counter European detractors who characterized them as underdeveloped and backward, Martínez Compañón vividly displayed the Indians' ability to produce useful knowledge, their conformance to Catholic morality and Spanish behavior, and their capacity for hard work that would enrich the state. Though it operated in real time, not on the written page, the Bishop's utopia in Trujillo was his own contribution to the much-contested matter of whether the people and the environment of America were inherently inferior to Europe's. In his utopia, the people of Trujillo would work with him to improve their own future, standing as a shining testament to his conviction that Indians were "equal, or very little different to the other men" around them. *The Bishop's Utopia* tells the story of his struggle to make this a reality in his own little corner of the vast Spanish empire.[16]

Visual Culture as Historical Documentation

Central to the story told here is that which Martínez Compañón himself wished to tell—the one that he left behind in the nine volumes of watercolors, *Trujillo del Perú*. The 1,372 images that constituted this "paper museum" were organized into different books, each with its own narrative in pictures. The first held maps, city plans, architectural drawings, and portraits of leading local officials, secular and ecclesiastic. The Bishop had ingeniously designed it to preface his work in Trujillo and familiarize imperial bureaucrats with the people and places that had been key to his accomplishments. The second volume, depicting quotidian life in Trujillo, portrayed a universe in miniature with Spaniards, Indians, mestizos, and mixed-race *castas* engaged in their daily lives; sharing meals and music, plowing fields and harvesting wheat, tending sheep and spinning thread. Green was the predominant hue of the botanical illustrations of trees, herbs, plants, flowers, and shrubs that made up volumes 3, 4, and 5. A menagerie of animals, from the comical anteater, its tongue replete with shiny black ants (see Plate 3) to the fetchingly large-eyed guanaco camelid, filled the pages of volume 6. Birds and marine life each merited a separate volume, and the set closed with intricate archaeological illustrations of local ruins, burial sites, and ceramics. Had it ever been completed in the way that the Bishop had hoped, the "Historical, Scientific, Political, and Social Museum of the Bishopric of Trujillo del Perú" would have carefully situated each specimen within its proper scientific category, proudly naming it for posterity and for the benefit of the broader European scientific community. Unfortunately, Martínez Compañón was unable to begin writing the manuscript before his death in 1797.[17]

However, the great repository for colonial Spanish American documents, Seville's General Archive of the Indies, holds a valuable document that allows the dedicated researcher to begin piecing together how the project may have developed. The Bishop and his staff completed the "File About the Remission of 24 Crates of Curiosities of Nature and of Art, Collected by the Bishop of Trujillo [today archbishop of Santa Fé], and Sent by the Viceroy of Lima, Arrived on the Frigate Rosa" in 1788. This was an inventory that accompanied the immense natural history collection sent to the king of Spain that same year. It painstakingly described the botanical specimens, taxidermied animals, pre-Hispanic artifacts, and local manufactures packed in the crates. The anteater shown in volume 5 of the watercolors was included, its tongue carefully preserved, wrapped in paper and nestled alongside its body. The inventory described the ingenious way the so-called *oso hormiguero*, or "anting bear," used its tongue to eat: "arriving at an ant hole, it probes it with its tongue," the description read, "and sticking it all the way out, holds it steady until it is quite full of ants. Once it is, it recoils it and swallows them." Whoever had observed the anteater knew even more about the species: "it is calm if not chased and harassed," the informant claimed. "But once threatened, it gives enough fight to kill the man or dog that pursues it." Yet this was the last surviving information about the animal that the Bishop and his informants had found so intriguing. Like the vast majority of natural history items remitted from the overseas kingdoms in the early modern period, the anteater's body, tongue, and the other elements of the collection were parsed up and dispersed to the appropriate metropolitan institutions, including the Royal Museum of Natural History, the Royal Pharmacy, and the Royal Botanical Garden. In the end, most were discarded, lost, or their provenance obscured by categorization and re-categorization, transfers and moves.[18] So the watercolor illustrations and the written inventory were all that remained of the Bishop's animals, birds, and fish, great and small, rare and mundane.

Despite these losses, the textual and visual record of the Bishop's natural history research still stands as one of the most intricately detailed natural history sources of its day. Remarkably, Martínez Compañón at no time benefited from any official patronage or financial support for his work as a naturalist, yet he managed to produce one of the most thorough visual and material compendiums of the colonial period in Peru. In order to incorporate this extraordinary body of information into my historical analysis, I analyzed the visual documents like textual ones; drawing contrasts and comparisons, looking for what was there as well as what was absent, keeping in mind the creators and the context, and looking for the multiplicity of meanings that one image can hold. Often these clues were exceedingly subtle and took multiple viewings to catch, such as the tiny inkwells hidden in the student tables in the illustration of the school at San Juan de la Frontera de Chachapoyas (see analysis in Chapter 4 and Plate 4), which signified that the school's plans were too elaborate for local reality and local pocketbooks; or the small leafy green plant held in the left hand of the "hill Indian" (see Plate 5), who was depicted in the very act of gathering plants for the Trujillo collection. In other cases, my work with the images became a sort of cross-reading with the documents, a methodology best exemplified by the analysis of the "mestizo scarred by *uta*" image that opens Chapter 6 (see Plate 6). By pairing the image with corresponding documentation and supplementing with detailed research into regional ethnobotany, I uncovered more about native epidemiological knowledge in the colonial period than I thought possible using "just" an image and a few sentences of a document.

The visual information that the Bishop commissioned left a source so rich and varied that my main challenge was in choosing which portions of it were the most relevant; yet sometimes, I faced the opposite problem: a decided lack of information. Writing a book that dwells on a central character that revealed so little about himself, his motivations, or his understanding of his place in the world was no simple task. Perhaps Martínez Compañón's self-pitying quip that "before I was bishop, everyone wrote to me, but afterward, I don't get letters from anyone"[19] was not far from the truth because his archival trail contains frustratingly little personal correspondence. Unlike the New England Puritans who so conveniently bestowed upon researchers a wealth of diaries detailing their spiritual progress and their experiences in the material realm, the early modern Spanish had no tradition of diary writing or public commentary on their interior lives. Church and state archives contain caches of personal correspondence only in the rarest of cases: my work in no fewer than twenty archives and special collections in nine cities of four countries turned up only one set of personal documents from Martínez Compañón.

The Hermenegildo family of Lima had saved the Bishop's letters to Antonio Hermenegildo de Querejazu and Agustín Hermenegildo de Querejazu, a father and son who became his friends, confidants, and collaborators. The 250 letters that he wrote to them twice a month over a fourteen-year period reveal how he worried about his health, doubted the skills of physicians, and loved to dispense advice about family life. They show Martínez Compañón to be a curious student of the natural world, a dedicated follower of imperial politics, and a loyal friend.

While the letters shed light on one set of the Bishop's friendships with other men of privilege, it was difficult to integrate these glimpses of his interior dialogue with his ceaseless activities in Trujillo, about which he once commented that "day or night I have hardly stopped running around like a crazy person."[20] I needed to show how he came to develop such an ambitious program of improvement for his bishopric, to understand what had prompted him to imagine how a mining camp of exploited Indian laborers could become a plebeian utopia, or how shoeless and illiterate Indian children might one day learn to read, write, and practice trades so successfully that they, too, might achieve the privileged title of *don*. What about his time in Peru inspired him to combine his contemporaries' ideas of assisting the Indians, improving the plebeians, and mapping the natural world into one massive project to create a better future? Simply telling the story of his life and his influences as a way to explain his motivation would be insufficient. I wanted to give a sense of a mind, a time, and a world. So I followed the example of other historians who have experimented with integrating historical analysis with narrative techniques, including Rhys Isaac, John Demos, and Peter Mancall. The resulting scenes re-create conditions on the ground in real time at pivotal points in Martínez Compañón's life: as a young man on the docks of Cádiz, eagerly waiting for his ship to depart for the New World; traveling on foot from Montevideo to Lima; a new bishop entering his cathedral city for the first time. Documents indicate that these events actually took place, although they do not elaborate on contextualizing details. To extrapolate, I began with whatever archival records were available, matching dates and details as closely as I could. I supplemented these data with reports by historical contemporaries who visited the same locations in the late eighteenth century, as well as historical maps, newspaper accounts and official documentation produced by the massive bureaucratic machinery that hummed at the heart of the Spanish Empire in America. I read widely in secondary sources for additional texturizing details—as in the case of the San Francisco church in Bogotá, one of the sites of several of the funeral services held in honor of Martínez Compañón. These scenes became not only opportunities to make the Bishop more real but also chances to immerse myself—and, I hope, my readers—in the sights, smells, and sounds of the world in which he lived.

American Utopias

By the time Martínez Compañón arrived in Trujillo, Europeans had been dreaming about America and its potential for almost three hundred years. The very first reports from the Indies depicted lush tropical gardens with peaceful, accommodating natives. Calling the island of Hispaniola a "wonder," Christopher Columbus insisted that "there are six or eight kinds of palm trees . . . and fruits and herbs . . . marvelous pine groves . . . honey, and many kinds of birds, and very diverse fruits . . . many mines and an immeasurable number of people." He breathlessly reported to his benefactors in Spain that "the hills and mountains and the plains and countryside and the earth [are] so beautiful and fertile." Not only was Hispaniola's natural world richly fecund, he wrote, but its people were also ideal vassals. Columbus reported that they lived in spacious, orderly towns, with competent, forthright officials who oversaw their most precious resource: gold. Even better, the "Indians," as Columbus called them, were inherently generous. "Whatever thing they have, if you ask them for it they would never say no," he insisted. Although they were not yet Catholic, "they do not know idolatry; rather, they believe with certainty that all strength, all power, and all good exists in the sky." Conveniently for Columbus and his crew, the Indians were convinced "that I have come down from that highest mansion with my ships and my sailors." Perhaps this was why they were so "inclined to the love and service of Their Majesties [the Catholic Kings of Spain] and of the whole Castilian nation."[21]

Since Columbus wrote these words at the end of the fifteenth century, generations of readers have tirelessly scanned them for hyperbole, inaccuracy, and outright fabrication. His disastrous career as governor of Hispaniola only cemented his reputation as a selfish charlatan: he was condemned as a ruthless tyrant and brought back to Spain a prisoner, where he lived his last days in shame and poverty. He, with his invented tales of an American utopia, died lonely and humiliated. But such debacle aside, there was something utterly compelling about his letters, both now and in the early modern period. Renaissance Europeans were so drawn to his lavish descriptions of the wealth and prosperity awaiting them in America that they printed his first letter eighteen times within four years of its appearance, making it available in Latin, Italian, Spanish, and German. Columbus's writings soon inspired others to produce similar accounts—so many that by 1597, a Venetian bibliographer estimated that the first letter from the Americas had inspired twenty-nine other titles about the Indies. Although a generation previously, Europeans had wondered whether the world beyond them teemed with monstrous Cyclops, vicious Amazons, and dog-headed humans, Columbus's reports from the Indies confirmed that in some ways, America was much more familiar than they had guessed.[22]

This fascination with a newfound world engendered a veritable a rush toward utopias in the literary culture of the Renaissance, one that included such popular books as Thomas More's *Utopia* (1516), Tomasso Campanella's *City of the Sun* (1623), and Francis Bacon's *New Atlantis* (1627). These works imagined idealized states where educated, peaceful people wanted for nothing. Some scholars have suggested that the utopia genre was so popular because it offered a momentary escape from the religious wars and economic dislocation that plagued early modern Europeans' everyday lives. But escapism was not the only reason readers scanned their library shelves for tales of faraway lands of perfection. Utopias were also comfortably familiar because they appealed to some of the most fundamental beliefs of Christianity. Paradise in the New World could easily be equated to the abundant Garden of Eden, the perfect afterlife in the celestial heavens, and the longed-for millennial end of times that would save the souls of the converted during the resurrection of Jesus Christ. The New World utopia could also be conveniently slotted into popular tropes of classical mythology, such as the idyllic pastoral state of Arcadia or the mythical continent of Atlantis, which seventeenth-century Jesuit polymath Athanasius Kircher even went so far as to map in his *Mundus Subterraneus*.[23]

In 1515, when Thomas More was writing about the original fictional utopia, his imagined society of Bensalem, from the dark streets of London, he certainly had America on his mind. The book's narrator claims that its stories are based on the experiences of a young man called Raphael Hythloday, who "took service with Amerigo Vespucci" and "after much persuasion and expostulation . . . got Amerigo's permission to be one of the twenty-four men who were left in a fort at the farthest point of the last voyages." This fictitious narrator described Utopia as an island of cities "identical in language, customs, institutions, and laws" as well as in their physical appearance, since all had been erected "on the same plan." The walls surrounding the towns contained public hospitals and primary schools, and priests were the citizens revered over all others.[24]

Scholars have long recognized that More was inspired by the encounter between America and Europe, an interaction that was, at that time, indubitably dominated by the Spanish.[25] By 1515, the Spanish could already claim that Columbus had completed his four voyages under their flag; the pope had divided the world in two, to be shared between them and the Portuguese; and Diego de Velázquez had conquered Cuba. They had also seen five years of "success" at their first permanent settlement in the Western Hemisphere: Santa María in the territory that would later be known as Panama.

As the words of *Utopia* emerged on the paper before him, More may have thought of how America was not the only place where the Spanish were enjoying unprecedented predominance. Charles I's ascension to the throne of Spain in 1516 and his designation as Holy Roman emperor three years later meant that his territory now encompassed Burgundy, the Low Countries, parts of Germany and Austria, the Iberian Peninsula, Naples, Sicily, Sardinia, the Spanish Indies, and even outposts in North Africa. Never one for modesty, Charles immediately began a campaign to make over Spain's imperial image in a manner befitting its burgeoning global dominance. He ordered that the front of the Spanish eight-real coin (see Plate 7) be emblazoned with an emblem that he commissioned to reflect Spain's new role at the center of a rapidly expanding world. It featured two pillars towering above ocean waves, with the motto *plus ultra* (more beyond) on a banderole flag, and later, a Spanish crown floating above it. The king and his contemporaries would have recognized the columns as the Pillars of Hercules, which the mythical hero erected at the known boundaries of Europe and North Africa. Beyond these pillars, the legend told, lay the great mysteries of the unknown. By designing an emblem that claimed this untapped potential as part of Spain's imperial destiny, Charles permanently and publicly marked what he imagined would be a glorious future of Spanish expansion in the New World and beyond.[26]

But for all his enthusiasm, Charles was well aware that remaking the myth of Hercules required a bit of revision. The symbol needed to convey a sense of emboldening, not fear of what lurked in the vast "out there" where man had yet to venture. So he enlisted Spanish historian Pedro Sarmiento de Gamboa to do a key bit of public relations. In his popular *History of the Incas*, Sarmiento reworked the myth of Hercules and the pillars, claiming that though Hercules had originally inscribed the columns with *Ultra Gades nil*, or "there is nothing beyond Cádiz," after the discovery of America, Charles sent workers to correct the inscription accordingly. According to Sarmiento, the king ordered *Gades* (Latin for Cádiz) and *nil* ("nothing") removed, replacing them with a new inscription: *ne plus ultra*, which Sarmiento translated as "farther beyond there are many lands." Placing this symbol on the Atlantic's most commonly circulated coin was an obvious claiming of Spain's leading role in the ever-expanding universe of man's consciousness. It reflected the emperor and empire's wildly optimistic hopes for the immeasurable potential of Spain's "New World." It was a tactile reflection of a utopian moment when the world seemed full of promise and possibility.[27]

Politically and economically, the so-called Spanish Conquest certainly delivered. In just forty-one years, the Spanish had "discovered" the Indies and conquered the great Aztec and Inca nations. They captured staggering amounts of gold and silver, which they piled onto treasure fleets that cut across the ocean waves, relentlessly pursued by pirates and buccaneers. Columbus's prognostications about the vast untapped resources of America—especially the mineral ones—seemed thrillingly prophetic. A land with so much wealth in gold and silver could readily become a utopia like those that the Renaissance authors had imagined.

Yet amid such fabulous wealth and excess, a small minority of Spaniards was starting to realize that in the everyday lives of most people in colonial Spanish America, utopia was very far from reality. In his *Brief Account of the Destruction of the Indies*, first published in Seville in 1552, conquistador-turned-Dominican-friar Bartolomé de Las Casas vividly recalled the atrocities of Spanish behavior toward the Indians, describing how Spaniards "smilingly" maimed, tortured, and enslaved innocent natives.[28] It was not long before the rest of Europe caught wind of Las Casas's accounts, and by the end of the century, his work had been republished and translated so many times that it was accessible in some form to "nearly anyone literate in his own language." In the seventeenth century, Dutch printer Theodor de Bry published ten more lavish editions of the *Brief Account* with woodcut engravings featuring sensational images of Las Casas's most vivid scenes, such as a Spaniard dashing an Indian baby against a rock and an Indian chief being burned at the stake. These lurid images helped make the book an "unquestioned commercial and propagandistic success" that would ultimately become the "cornerstone" of the Black Legend of Spain's singular cruelty in the New World.[29]

Even if Las Casas's work was purposely provocative, he reported on the grim reality of the encounter between the old world and the new in America.

But as he might well have imagined, the horrors of the early conquest soon gave way to less shocking—but equally insidious—injustices to native peoples. The imagined utopia slipped further from reach as an Indian slave trade flourished in the first half of the sixteenth century in Central America, with Spaniards exporting chattel slaves to Panama and Peru. Once the idea was first articulated in the 1512 Laws of Burgos, Indian family and kinship groups were periodically broken up and relocated into settlements called *reducciones*, where the Spanish imagined that they could be more easily monitored for "correct" behavior—and forced to pay tribute and labor duties. Natives were also bound to the Spanish through the *encomienda* system, which rewarded Spanish conquistadores for their service to the Crown by giving them Indian vassals to use as laborers. Spanish legislators reasoned that as vassals, the Indians owed tribute, in the form of cash, goods, or labor, for the "privilege" of being governed by Spaniards. Some met these duties through a practice known as the *mita* in Peru and the *repartimiento de Indios* in New Spain, wherein they were forced to work in rotational labor drafts in fields, workshops, or mines for two to four months out of the year.[30]

By the 1530s, the injustices against the Indians had multiplied so many times that Spanish bureaucrat Vasco de Quiroga penned a treatise about the legal and ethical wrongs of Indian treatment in New Spain and sent it off to Madrid. In addition to listing countless injustices, Quiroga's *Information on the Law* provided a blueprint for how the Crown might raise an improved society from the ashes of destruction in America. To conceive of this new colony, Quiroga drew on one of the visionary works of his day: Thomas More's *Utopia*. Like More, he imagined a society composed of extended families that shared community property. Children would receive free primary education, as well as instruction in farming techniques and Christian doctrine. The towns that he would create for the Indians would feature free hospitals to care for the elderly and infirm. They would be overseen by just Spanish officials and priests. The Indians who came to reside in his so-called *pueblo-hospitales* had to contribute to the communal lifestyle by working in trades, crafts, or agriculture. They were even given rights over their property, so they were able to pass it on to their children. Quiroga had faith in his agenda because he was convinced that the Indians were a childlike, uncorrupted race whose souls could be carefully molded—like "soft wax"—through evangelization and proper socialization.[31]

To make his utopian vision a reality, Quiroga purchased portions of the land that he needed and requested that local landowners donate the rest. He relied on the Indians themselves to help erect the settlements: they would build the thatched huts that would be their homes, they would adorn the churches where they would worship, and they would farm the fields that would provide them with sustenance. To further entice them, he offered baptisms and hosted games and activities for children. Soon Indians who had no prior sustained contact with Spaniards were voluntarily arriving at Santa Fé de México, Santa Fé de Laguna, and Santa Fé del Rio—and choosing to stay. Quiroga ensured that the towns and the hospitals would have a steady supply of Spanish priests when he founded the College of San Nicolás in Pátzcuaro, which would train clerics in native languages. By 1534, news of his efforts had reached Madrid, and Charles signed a royal decree granting his projects official approval. Two years later, he was rewarded when he was promoted to become bishop of Michoacán. Quiroga's utopia enjoyed the support of the Crown, administrators in America, and the townspeople themselves. The hospitals operated for thirty years. By 1570, the town of Santa Fé de México was home to around 500 Indians. Their descendants still live nearby.[32]

Although Quiroga's utopia flourished, it failed to inspire a more systematic improvement in the way Indians were treated in colonial Spanish America. Labor drafts, special taxes, seizure of communal land, and violent persecution of native customs continued. By the mid-eighteenth century, Spanish ministers were forced to recognize that though their financial and political problems extended beyond America, revamping colonial policy—and especially its treatment of the Indians—was Spain's best hope at reversing its downward spiral. In 1743, Spanish minister José del Campillo y Cossío submitted to King Philip V a comprehensive plan for economic reform in the Indies, called the *New System of Economic Government for America*. Campillo suggested that Spain follow the lead of the French and the English in reconceiving its colonies. The Americas, he argued, should no longer be viewed as "overseas kingdoms" or portions of Spain that happened to lie an ocean away. Rather, they should have their own laws and statutes that reflected their status as colonies whose purpose was to provide Spain with raw materials and a market for finished commercial goods.[33] Campillo argued that the legal and administrative structure that Spain had erected in America was essentially unworkable. Looking to the French Bourbon system, he suggested that the corrupt regional administrators called *corregidores* be replaced with Crown-appointed bureaucrats known as intendants. They would gather valuable data about their districts, which administrators would use to design social and economic reforms. Campillo further maintained that people would become more productive if they lived in town settlements rather than in rural areas. He even thought to intervene in church administration, suggesting that many bishoprics were too large to adequately administer to the faithful or oversee the clergy, who had fallen into a state of disastrous disorder. His ideas became the basis of the eighteenth-century Spanish reform agenda known as the Bourbon reforms. Along with similar movements in Portugal, France, and Austria, these focused on gathering useful information that could be used to improve the populace and thereby enrich and empower the state. In the Spanish Empire, they reached their peak under the rule of King Charles III in the 1770s and 1780s—the very time when Martínez Compañón found himself in Peru.

While the central concepts of the Bourbon reforms were applied throughout the Spanish Empire, the program had a special focus in America. There, it rested largely on Campillo's assertion that it was "the Indians" who were the "true Indies and the richest mine of the world." Their labor, purchasing power, and knowledge of the American environment held vast untapped potential, and he recommended that Spanish reformers focus their efforts accordingly. They were to "reduce the Indians to civil life, and treat them with kindness and sweetness; [and] pique their interest in industry, and in this way make them useful vassals and Spaniards." Campillo suggested that the king send the Peninsula's most adept thinkers to America, where they would observe the treatment of Indians and file reports about their status. Then they would help to teach Indians about which crops were the most profitable. They should arrange for them to be given land to cultivate, along with the accompanying rights so that they might pass this land down to their children. Campillo argued that the Indians should learn to speak Spanish fluently. Indian leaders should be encouraged to dress like Spanish plebeians so that they might inspire their communities to do the same. Overall, Campillo's plan for economic government was a pragmatic eighteenth-century vision of a colonial utopia that rested on the backs of natives who behaved like Spanish plebeians. Like the utopias that had come before it, it was a best-case scenario, a dream of what the Spanish *could* do in America. Forty years later, when Martínez Compañón dared to imagine how he might implement a similar project of improvement in his own jurisdiction of the vast Kingdom of Peru in the wake of the largest Indian rebellion the Spanish had ever faced in America, he had Campillo's blueprint to guide him but a much more complex reality to contend with.

CHAPTER I

The Books of a Bishop

By December 1767, twenty-nine-year-old Baltasar Jaime Martínez Compañón had likely grown tired of waiting to begin the journey to distant Peru and his new life in Spanish America. Earlier that year King Charles III had called him to serve the Spanish Crown and the Catholic Church as *chantre*, or musical director, of Lima's metropolitan cathedral. In the meantime, he had completed his duties as a consultant to the Inquisition in Madrid and had prepared for departure. By June, his license to cross the Atlantic was in order. Yet almost half a year later, he still found himself waiting. At least some of the delay must have been meteorological: 1767 was one of the most active years for North Atlantic hurricanes, and October and November were prime storm season. At that time of year, ships making the crossing from Cádiz to the southern ports of Spanish America had to take particular care not to find themselves stranded in the windless equatorial region or battered by ferocious winds with nicknames like the "bellowing forty" that lurked below thirty degrees latitude.[1]

Though waiting for the weather to improve was the most prudent course, such inaction must have been all the more difficult, considering that Cádiz was a city built around voyages. In 1717, it became the center of Spanish trade with the American colonies when the Crown pronounced it the monopoly port on the Peninsula because its wide harbor better accommodated the larger ships of the eighteenth century. Situated on a narrow isthmus a few miles off the mainland, the city stood on rocky, sandy terrain surrounded by the Atlantic Ocean. Arriving vessels passed through the intimidating La Candelaria Fortress, with its breakwaters and cannons, before reaching the protected Santa María port. As the fourth-largest city in Spain, Cádiz in 1750 was home to 60,000 people, making it comparable in size with other large European cities such as Dresden and Stockholm. Many of its inhabitants were from merchant families whose affluent, cosmopolitan lifestyle marked it as a fashion and culture center second only to Madrid. The city was also famous for its merchant neighborhood, the so-called City of the Hundred Palaces, as well as its cathedral, which, when construction was complete, would feature grandiose towers as high as those of the famous Giralda of Seville.[2]

The ocean air and bustling streets of Cádiz were strikingly different from the cool, verdant valleys of Navarre that the Bishop's family called home. Baltasar Jaime Martínez Compañón was born on January 6, 1737, in the town of Cabredo, Navarre. Located in the Pyrenees region of northeastern Spain, Navarre was its own kingdom and held special *fueros*, or local legal privileges, including an independent viceroy and ruling Cortes. Shared culture, language, and social systems linked Navarre and the rest of Spanish Basque country (Alava, Guipúzcoa, and Vizcaya) with the French Basque provinces of Basse Navarre, Labourd, and Soule. Martínez Compañón's father, Mateo, worked as a customs officer to provide for his wife, María Martínez de Bujanda, and their family. Though there are no images of him as a child, Martínez Compañón as an adult was thin and of average stature, with pale skin and black hair. He had thick, dark eyebrows, prominent cheekbones, and a long Romanesque nose. His portrait (see Plate 8) highlights his curious eyes and penetrating, determined gaze.

Martínez Compañón began his education studying Latin in the nearby town of Quintana, continuing in La Merced Convent in Calatayud (Aragón), where he studied philosophy. He completed his first university training in canon law at the Universities of Huesca and Zaragoza, also in Aragón. He earned his degree in canon law in 1759 at the College of the Holy Spirit at the University of Oñate in Guipúzcoa. This course of study would have included grammar (or reading, writing, and Latin); rhetoric (dealing with classical works in Spanish and Latin, and learning persuasive speaking and writing techniques); and philosophy (which covered logic, physics, mathematics, and moral philosophy). It was designed to prepare the student to think on his feet and argue convincingly while referencing the most important classical scholarship—essential skills for a successful ecclesiastical career. After serving as a chancellor at the University of Oñate, Martínez Compañón was ordained as a Catholic priest in 1761 in the town of Vitoria. Two years later, still at Oñate, he earned his doctorate in theology and canon law. This advanced degree allowed him entry into the highest echelons of church bureaucracy. In 1766, he was called to serve as an adviser to the Inquisition, an appointment that brought him into the orbit of high-level Church and Crown officials and likely factored in his subsequent career successes. One year later, his hard work was rewarded when he was presented to King Charles III as a potential canon of Lima's cathedral.[3]

During the few months' delay before his departure, the young prelate would have had ample time to get to know the two men who would accompany him to America. Pedro de Echevarri, his personal servant, was twenty years old with dark hair and eyes. His face was dotted with smallpox scars. Also Basque, he came from Oñate.[4] Echevarri served Martínez Compañón in Lima, and became his secretary once the young canon was promoted to bishop. He attended him on his grueling *visita* through the mountains, jungles, and deserts of Trujillo and later followed the newly promoted archbishop of Santa Fé north to Bogotá, New Granada. As Martínez Compañón's personal secretary, Echevarri patiently penned the thousands of pages of official correspondence that his employer dictated. His handwriting is legible and pleasing to the eye—especially when compared with that of his superior, which is gnarled, small, and hurried. It appears to be Echevarri's hand that transcribed the hundreds of names on the images of the watercolors of *Trujillo del Perú*, and it was he who wrote out the collection inventory. Without Echevarri's careful cataloging of the Bishop's papers and his insistence that Martínez Compañón's natural history be sent to Spain after his death, much of the Bishop's life's work might have been lost. In many ways, Echevarri is one of the most important, yet least audible, characters in the story of the Bishop, the Indians, and Trujillo.[5]

Documents reveal almost nothing about the second servant who accompanied Martínez Compañón. Ceferino Manuel de Isla, a native of Santander, was eighteen years old in 1767, with a dark complexion and thick eyebrows that set off his brown eyes. He was to travel independently to Peru, overseeing the prelate's luggage on a separate ship that would sail south around Cape Horn and up the Pacific coast to Lima. This route typically took about four months—at least one month longer than arriving directly at Montevideo or Buenos Aires. The longer journey was the only way to handle large amounts of heavy cargo that could not be moved across the Andes Mountains on foot. In this case, the cargo that Ceferino supervised was perhaps the most precious thing that Martínez Compañón brought to Peru: crates and crates of his beloved books. These constituted one of the largest private libraries in the entire viceroyalty, with more than two thousand volumes inventoried upon his arrival in Trujillo. The Bishop had tracts by scientists, ecclesiastics, and government reformers in Spanish, Latin, Italian, and French. His library inventory reveals that he was intimately familiar with the dictates of European political economy reform, the early modern methods of making natural histories, and the most influential scholarship on the native peoples of the New World. These books were both inspiration and reference for his campaign to create a utopia in Trujillo that would become a real-time contribution to one of the most contentious debates of his day: whether the people and the nature of the New World were inherently inferior to those of the Old. Martínez Compañón brought from Europe practical guidebooks that he and his priests could use to help local communities improve agricultural techniques and develop local trade networks. He carried several texts explaining how to create local histories, how to study native cultures, and how to teach painting and illustration to students. And he kept a thorough selection of works that explained who the Indians were and how they had been treated since the Spanish had arrived in the New World. The books that the Bishop brought to help him build his utopia vividly demonstrated his belief that the Indians, plants, and animals of Trujillo were not feeble, unhealthy, or weak, as so many of his European contemporaries insisted.[6]

Like any ecclesiastic, Martínez Compañón had a full complement of religious texts. Along with his assortment of Bibles, he owned copies of Saint Augustine's *City of God*, the collected works of Sor Juana, and the popular *Moral Philosophy*, by the eighteenth-century Spanish Benedictine polymath Benito Feijoo. The bishop-to-be also owned works by Dom Jean Mabillon, a seventeenth-century French cleric who branched off from his Benedictine brothers to form a splinter sect known as the Maurists, who dedicated themselves to collecting, editing, and publishing historical documents. Mabillon also wrote about his frequent scientific journeys—Martínez Compañón referred to these as *itinerarios* (itineraries)—wherein he would visit local monasteries and look through their archives as well as investigate nearby catacombs, relics, and archaeological sites.[7]

Mabillon's work explained how to collect historical materials; *Sacred Painting* (by sixteenth-century Italian Cardinal Federico Borromeo), a book that Martínez Compañón requested to borrow in 1788, described how students should be taught to paint images that might accompany such a collection. Borromeo's central premise was that paintings could represent historical truth if their field of composition truly matched the subject that they depicted. He advocated the use of saturated colors, pointing out that "colors are like words: once the eyes see them they sink into the mind just as do words heard by the ears." Artwork, he maintained, was most valuable for representing nature. The Bishop must have admired the group of Milanese institutions that Borromeo founded: a library in 1607, a drawing academy in 1613, and a museum in 1618.[8]

Martínez Compañón owned Alonso Montenegro's *Itinerary for Indian Parishes*, one of the most widely used field manuals for priests and vicars in eighteenth-century Spanish America. This five-volume set, written by a sixteenth-century bishop of Quito, discussed the obligations of clerics toward their parishes. Its second volume, "Nature and Customs of the Indians," stressed how easy it was for the devil to erect "his tyrannical empire" among these uneducated and gullible people who most commonly committed idolatry by accident because they could not grasp the ideological divide between Catholic devotion and heretical idolatry. Montenegro drew liberally from Heinrich Kramer's ubiquitous *Malleus Maleficarum* to answer vexing quandaries such as "if he who has been cursed can legally ask the *hechicero* [who cursed him] if he can remove the curses." (The appropriately puzzling answer to this question was yes, but only if the curse could be removed without casting another spell. Any spell—even one meant to undo a previous curse—was heretical, so if the *hechicero* had no other method, the victim of the curse would simply have to bear his sour destiny in this life rather than risk eternal damnation in the next.)[9]

The Bishop's library revealed his interest in the natural world: among his many scientific tracts were Isaac Newton's *Natural Philosophy* and various works by Robert Boyle and Francis Bacon. He had a copy of Athanasius Kircher's *Mundus Subterraneus*, a delightful seventeenth-century publication that discussed the German Jesuit's expeditions to Mount Vesuvius under the midnight moon. Kircher's exploits might have crossed Martínez Compañón's mind during his journey from Lima to Trujillo as he passed near Peru's Sabancaya volcanoes. Some of his guides might have told tall tales of the devastating Huaynaputina eruption in 1600, which shrouded the city of Arequipa in ashen rain while aftershocks continued for weeks, convincing many locals that the end of days had finally arrived. While there were no such catastrophic incidents in the eighteenth century, the Sabancaya volcanoes did erupt several times between 1750 and 1784.[10]

Though Kircher's book on volcanoes was largely pleasure reading, Martínez Compañón's library showed more than a passing interest in matters of science, as well as matters of state. He was well-read in contemporary theories of society, economy, and governance. This familiarity with eighteenth-century political economy reform would later help him conceive one of colonial Spanish America's most expansive plans for improvement. The books that guided him included Jerónimo Ustariz's *Theory and Practice of Commerce and Maritime Affairs*, which argued that the Spanish should focus on manufacture and commodity trade, not simply exchange silver for goods. He had several works by leading reformer Pedro Campomanes, including *Discourse on Popular Industry*, which proposed that Spain could save its economy through encouraging economic productivity in the home. He also brought various agricultural manuals, such as Alonso de Herrera's *Agricultura General*. First published in 1513, this book was still in use over 200 years later, highly valued for its practical suggestions about how to cultivate everything from bees to cotton to onions. Carefully stored with the books were several collections of prints, including Otto van Veen's *Moral Theater of Human Life*, which featured woodcut engravings of voluptuous men and women in allegorical situations. One depicted a disgruntled farmer leaning against a tree with his arms crossed, while an industrious compatriot led a team of oxen plowing a field in the background. The caption reads, "He who does not begin does not finish." Such books would have helped him to imagine his own reform agendas and also served as references for communicating specific mandates to parish priests, who would be directly responsible for implementing these programs of improvement with the local population.[11]

Though we have no exact notice of which day the Bishop last stepped on Spanish soil—in his old age in America, he finally sought (but was never given) a see at home in Spain—documents indicate that his vessel left Cádiz sometime before the New Year, and he assumed his post in the cathedral on July 17, 1768. Presuming that he traveled the typical route for ships sailing from Cádiz, he would have first touched American ground at the Atlantic shores of Montevideo, and then traveled overland to Lima. This trek was likely the same as the one immortalized in the popular picaresque travel narrative *Lazarillo de ciegos caminantes* (Lazarus of the Walking Blind), published in Lima in 1775. It began with the short voyage across the River Plate to Buenos Aires, depicted in *Lazarillo* as a city with wide, straight streets; fragrant peach trees and grapevines; and happy dogs "so fat they can hardly move" because, like most of the city's inhabitants, they frequently dined on meat, chicken, and eggs. The next stop was typically Córdoba, which lay approximately 435 miles northwest of Buenos Aires. To reach it, Martínez Compañón and his party would have had to cross the river Tercero, known for its turbulent waters and bountiful fish. From there, they would have continued north on foot, stopping at the base of the Andes in the smaller city of Salta before heading up the mountains to 13,000 feet above sea level. This was the location of one of the world's highest cities, the snowy and windy mining center of Potosí, which the Cerro Rico mine had made into the most densely populated city in the world by 1650—although by the time Martínez Compañón may have been there in 1768, silver deposits were diminishing and the city was in decline.[12] Next was a short stop in the city of Chuquisaca before the long march along the Andes foothills. This route straddled the main Peruvian volcanic region to the east. To the west was the highest navigable lake in the world, the frigid and glassy Lake Titicaca, which sits at 12,500 feet. Then the party would probably have continued to Cuzco, the former Inca capital known for its beautiful cathedral that some insisted was every bit as striking as its counterparts in Europe. From Cuzco, they would have descended the Andes into the coastal desert of Lima, finding the city damp, cold, and shrouded in the typical *garúa* mist of the winter months.[13]

Though his books were likely still making their way up the Pacific Coast, they must have been on the future bishop's mind as the sterile, hard earth of the altiplano crunched beneath his feet. As he passed through the ancestral lands of the Tiwanaku empire, with its stone megaliths, ceremonial *puerta de la luna* (door to the moon), and sunken temples, he might have heard that the areas surrounding these sites were sparsely inhabited, by just a few remaining Indians. He likely would have remembered what he had read about these people in popular chronicles by Pedro Cieza de León, Bernabé Cobo, and Garcilasco de la Vega. Almost universally, they depicted the surviving natives of the Tiwanaku region as a dispossessed, pathetic, and unfriendly people who had lost all vestiges of their former glory. Perhaps such ruminating on their fate compelled the young prelate to turn over in his mind the "many things he had read and heard about the calamities and misfortunes of the Indians of America"[14] and how they had suffered since the arrival of the Spanish. No work on this subject was as vivid or horrifying as Bartolomé de Las Casas's *Brief Account of the Destruction of the Indies*, which the Bishop owned. Las Casas infamously characterized the early Spanish settlers on Hispaniola as "most cruel tygers, wolves, and lions" who took bets as to who would be able to slice a hapless Indian in two with one swipe of a sword, dashed babies' heads against rocks, and murdered Indians by roasting them to death like meat on a spit. Such lurid details made Las Casas a favorite of foreigners hoping to vilify the actions of the Spaniards in America. For idealists like Martínez Compañón, they were vivid examples of the abuses that their reforms sought to correct.[15]

The Bishop also had a copy of Gregorio García's *Origin of the Indians of the New World*, which considered the theological and scientific conundrum of how men came to inhabit America, a part of the world that was not known to classical scholars or mentioned in the Bible. García discussed the most popular contemporary solutions to this problem: that Noah's ark was shipwrecked in America, leaving behind a group of early Christians; that Christians crossed from Europe to America via the Asian landmass; and that they traveled there by boat across the ocean.[16] These questions may have seemed academic compared with the very real matters of Indian exploitation and poverty that Martínez Compañón would confront in Trujillo; but in the eighteenth century, the matter of Indian provenance was central to contentions over their place in the Spanish Empire. Scholarship showing that the Indians were descendants of Adam, Eve, and Noah was important because it insisted that Indians were men (however flawed)—and not half-wits who were natural slaves, as purported by Las Casas's nemesis Juan Ginés de Sepúlveda. It also linked them to ancient Christians, giving them a special protective status, meaning that they were to be treated as children, not animals.

As a treatise of intellectual inquiry, García's work was a useful reference, but its philosophical bent offered no suggestion toward a methodology for Martínez Compañón's self-designated task of studying "the arts, society, and culture of the Indians of Peru."[17] For that, he could have turned to his copy of the French Jesuit Joseph Lafitau's *Customs of the American Indians*. This two-volume work was a comprehensive account of Iroquois life, detailing everything from methods of warfare to gender relationships, food preparation, and religious beliefs. Though it dealt with an entirely different group of native people, it appears to have been influential in how the Bishop approached learning about the Indians. Lafitau's innovative comparative methodology used contemporary research to draw conclusions about the nature and past of the Indians. For instance, he described at length how Iroquois women heated grains of corn in ash and then ground it by hand to make a simple gruel called *sagamite*. He compared this with how the ancient Romans and Greeks prepared their own grains, also roasting first, grinding by hand, and simply adding water. To Lafitau, this similarity in the method of preparing and consuming grain was critical evidence that the Indians of America had common ancestors with Europeans. Most important, it implied that they were original Christians who had forgotten their true religious heritage but could be retaught correct behaviors and attitudes.[18]

Lafitau was convinced that he could help the Indians by learning about them and imparting knowledge of their culture. It is no mere coincidence that his work shares a number of similarities with that of Martínez Compañón; they stood on the same side of the great debate over the Indians that so divided early modern Europeans. Both asserted that contemporary Indians were not just the bedraggled remnants of their advanced ancestors (as many of their detractors argued). Accordingly, their work dealt simultaneously with contemporary and ancient Indian cultures: while Lafitau paired the data he collected living among the Iroquois with past accounts of their culture, Martínez Compañón worked with Indian communities throughout his bishopric and referenced and examined Peru's pre-Hispanic past through collecting and studying artifacts, burial mounds, Indian ruins, and pottery. Both men believed that the Indians themselves could provide valuable scientific and ethnographic information that was useful to society. Their studies drew on information gathered from native informants. When Lafitau's work with the Iroquois led him to "discover" ginseng in North America (it was native to the region and used regularly by Iroquois herbalists), he immediately imagined how to make it commercially viable in global markets by linking it to the Tartary ginseng plant that was sold as an aphrodisiac in China. Likewise, Martínez Compañón's botanical research with native communities outlined scores of plants that were commonly used by Trujillo's Indians and could become potential profit generators for the Spanish Empire.

Finally, the research of the French Jesuit and the Spanish bishop shared a similar fate. Lafitau's work sold well and was popularly acclaimed, but he was dismissed by the major French thinkers of the period who disdained his comparative ethnographic approach. Expert naturalists in Spain rejected Martínez Compañón's work when they parsed up his collection and relegated the nine volumes of watercolors to a dusty shelf in the Royal Palace Library. In the end, contemporaries of both men failed to recognize the value of their ethnographic, botanical, and historical investigations. To begin to understand why, we must look more carefully at the discourse surrounding Indians and nature in the eighteenth-century Atlantic world.[19]

Writing the History of Peoples Without History

The neglect that Lafitau and Martínez Compañón faced was, in many ways, related to a much bigger controversy about the history of America's Indians and how it should be written. In proposing an innovative historical method that combined face-to-face experience with written histories, Lafitau forged a radical departure from the older Baconian method of factual compilation.

He instead paired existing studies with his own research, using "reliable" (presumably elite, Europeanized) modern Indians as informants. As the work of Jorge Cañizares-Esguerra has so elegantly demonstrated, the epistemological shift that his work exemplifies had broad implications for the history of America and its native peoples, especially in the Spanish Empire. Eighteenth-century Europeans' mounting distrust of eyewitness accounts and first-person histories meant that the oft-used "chronicles" penned by the first generation of Spaniards in America no longer served as accurate sources of data on native cultures. Likewise, suspicion of non-alphabetic writing systems eliminated Indian codices and manuscripts from the list of potential sources for historical studies. The tested ways of making history were no longer deemed trustworthy.[20]

Responding to (or perhaps anticipating) such upheaval, the Spanish Crown founded its first official historical institution, the Royal Academy of History, in Madrid in 1755. Following the Bourbon agenda that stressed generating more profits from overseas, the academy then promptly declared its priority to be writing histories of the natural world of Spanish America. In keeping with current methodological fashion, these were to employ sources other than eyewitness accounts and existing historical studies. Scholars were to rely on data that were more readily verified, many of which were, in fact, material: paintings, buildings, hieroglyphs, and collections of natural history objects. By turning a critical eye upon their own history making, Spanish academicians actually anticipated the same critiques that European detractors would later use against them.[21]

While the Spanish could assert relative control over who wrote what history of America within the empire, the Crown had no say in what was published about Spanish America elsewhere in the Atlantic world. Foreign travelers decried continental Spain as backward, destitute, and "loaded with political evils"; but in Spanish America, their attack began with the environment itself. The theory that American nature was inherently weak, degenerate, and corrupt was most infamously articulated by Louis LeClerc Buffon, director of France's Royal Botanical Garden, in his seminal 1747 *Natural History*. Despite never having visited America, Buffon claimed that the American landmass was newer than the continents in the Eastern Hemisphere and therefore retained too much water and humidity. In its deleterious climate, bugs and venomous creatures flourished, but quadrupeds, birds, and other species useful to man did not develop the diversity or physical strength of their counterparts in Europe. Furthermore, Buffon insisted that when European mammals were transferred to those American environments, they, too, would deterio-rate in the unlucky climate.[22]

Twenty years later, Cornelius de Pauw revived these theories of climatic determinism in his wildly popular *Philosophical Researches About the Ameri-cans* (1768). Pauw concurred with Buffon's assertions about the unhealthy nature of the American climate, describing "air stagnated in immense forests," massive swamps, and "noxious vapours from standing waters." He reasoned that this detrimental environment weakened animal life, arguing, for instance, that the "lion" of America (the puma) was so timid that he never grew a mane. But Pauw broke new ground when he proposed that this same discourse of degeneracy also applied to human beings. People from colder climates in the Northern Hemisphere, he argued, had faced greater challenges to basic survival and therefore became more industrious. Individuals from tropical zones, in contrast, had to work very little in order to survive and therefore were naturally lazy and corrupt.[23]

This discourse further soured with Guillaume-Thomas de Raynal's *Philo-sophical and Political History of the . . . Indies*, published in installments from 1770 through 1781. Raynal dismissed the majority of the native Peruvians as "a set of naked and wandering men." He mocked their *quipu* (knotted cords of string used for accounting) as a laughably deficient data storage system. Even worse, he insisted that the Spanish chronicles detailing the enormous building and engineering projects of the Inca were nothing more than hyperbolic fan-tasy that the Spanish had projected onto sad little "heaps of ruins." He main-tained that the Spanish exaggerated their prowess by claiming to have conquered sophisticated societies with dazzlingly large urban centers, trade networks, and civic buildings. "We must, therefore consider," he cautioned his reader, "fabu-lous the report of that prodigious multitude of towns built with so much labor and experience. If there were so many superb cities in Peru," he reasoned, "why do none exist except Cuzco and Quito?"[24] Taking a different approach, William Robertson's *History of America* (1777) dismissed the Indians as effemi-nate and weak because of their lack of facial hair and their "feebleness of con-stitution," which was "characteristic of the species." While he proposed a variation on Buffon's original argument by maintaining that men were less af-fected by climatic degradation than animals and plants were, he still posited that American natives were naturally lazy because the "spontaneous produc-tions of nature" around them allowed them to flourish with almost no effort.[25]

Though aware of this vitriol, the Spanish Royal Academy of History was rife with internal discord and busywork that kept it from mounting a focused counterattack to defend the nature and natives of its American kingdoms. Instead, its members had determined that Mexico, Peru, the Philippines, and the Caribbean merited no fewer than three natural histories and four civil histories each—a task that left them far too busy to defend the people, nature, and history of Spanish America.[26] Instead, Spaniards living in America came to their own defense with local histories that responded to European detractors by celebrating the environment, culture, and inhabitants of Spanish America. In his *Ancient History of Mexico* (1780–1781), Francisco Clavijero, a Jesuit expelled from New Spain, refuted Buffon's claims that American animals were puny and weak. He proposed instead that the relative smallness and gentleness of New World mammals signified the "softness" of the American climate. He listed multitudes of plant and animal species that could be found in New Spain but not in Europe. But perhaps most important, he insisted, "the souls of Americans are not at all inferior to those of the Europeans." Citing Indian codices and manuscripts, he insisted that Aztec pictographs were, in fact, a system of writing, "not just simply images of objects."[27] Similarly, Jesuit Juan Ignacio Molina dismissed the work of "Paw" and Europeans like him as "weird" and uninformed: not only had Pauw never been to America, he pointed out, but it also appeared that he read only those accounts that suited his purposes of degrading it. Molina insisted that America's Indians were healthy and productive and that their own "documents"—*quipu*, manuscripts, and codices—served as a good basis for a history of Chile.[28] Writing from exile about his native Ecuador, Juan de Velasco focused most of his *History of the Kingdom of Quito* (1789) on pre-Hispanic Indian history. He wrote about Inca rulers such as Huayna Capac as if they were heroes, praising their laws, government, and civic buildings. Velasco especially valued the "mechanical arts" practiced by Quito's Indians and mestizos, individuals whom he found talented and naturally inclined to crafts and trades.[29]

Had Martínez Compañón been able to finish writing the "Historical, Scientific, Political, and Social Museum of the Bishopric of Trujillo del Perú," which he had been working on for many years but which remained in the research stage at the time of his death, he may well have been recognized as one of the Spanish clerics who wrote in defense of America's nature and people. But even without the text to narrate it, his utopian project in Trujillo was designed as a living, breathing declaration of the utility of its natural world and the capacity of its human inhabitants. His reform agenda and his natural history research were intricate variations on the classic eighteenth-century defenses of the New World and its peoples. When he collaborated with natives and plebeians to develop and implement political economy reform, local communities became engineers of their own improvement. When they requested his help to build new towns in more socially and commercially advantageous locations, and then worked with him to secure the necessary permissions, land, and financial backing, the people of Trujillo were not just passively receiving reform ideas born in European capitals. Instead, they were actively participating in creating their own future while displaying their ability to improve their own situation. Similarly, the agendas to found Indian colleges and local primary schools throughout Trujillo were driven by local requests, initiative, and manpower. Despite their physical and geographical distance from large European-style "lettered cities," local communities understood the social capital that literacy provided and were willing to work hard to obtain it. Taken together, these initiatives were living evidence of Martínez Compañón's conviction that if properly guided, the Indians of northern Peru could be transformed into ideal vassals. They would work with ecclesiastic and secular officials to design and implement a program for their own improvement. These reform agendas drew their inspiration from European precedent but were specifically designed to meet local needs. In this vision for Trujillo's future, the peoples' dedication to these efforts would demonstrate their ability to engineer their own improvement, providing incontrovertible evidence that they were useful vassals and fully contributing members of Spanish society. There was no better way to defend their usefulness than having the Indians serve as evidence of their own abilities.[30]

Improving the financial and social situation of Trujillo was not the only way to contribute to the debate over the New World. In addition to creating a living laboratory of reform in Trujillo, Martínez Compañón and his local collaborators amassed a staggering amount of natural history data that demonstrated the intellectual ability of native Peruvians and the richness of their physical environment. The hundreds of illustrations of plant and animal species that came to be the nine volumes of watercolors of *Trujillo del Perú* were direct evidence of the rich and diverse climate there. Trujillo's animal kingdom included useful animals such as llamas, guanacos, and other camelids, which could transport goods long distances over difficult terrain and also provide valuable wool. Northern Peru was home to vibrantly colored exotic birds, various types of large cats, and a dazzling array of marine species. Their diversity was a far cry from the fragility and deformity that New World detractors were so convinced of. Trujillo's botanical world offered an even more comprehensive set of data to prove that its environment was a fabulous resource awaiting discovery. Its many herbs, bushes, and trees offered cures for endemic disease and common illness. They included plants that had commercial value as dyestuffs, food items, and even valuable import substitutes for items such as cacao or silk.

While the data served to defend Trujillo's natural world, the provenance of the information—which was all gathered from local and native informants— was an even more sophisticated mode of contributing to what one scholar recently called "the eighteenth-century great debate."[31] All of Martínez Compañón's data were culled from area informants and depicted in watercolors by local artisans. Their participation in the botanical research not only provided valuable facts; it also demonstrated that they were fully able to cultivate and retain the sort of useful knowledge that royal scientific expeditions pursued throughout the Spanish Empire. Finally, the archaeological drawings of ruins, pottery, tombs, and other artifacts celebrated the accomplishments of northern Peru's pre-Hispanic peoples. When it depicted how the Chimú and Mochica cultures of Peru's northern coast constructed great urban settlements, managed large-scale projects of public engineering, and expertly elaborated pottery, jugs, and other artifacts, Martínez Compañón's natural history vividly displayed the intelligence and civilization of Trujillo's natives.

In addition to defending the Indians through his socioeconomic reforms and his natural history investigations, the Bishop wrote more directly about his views on the great epistemological debate of the eighteenth century. Referring to the way men like Pauw and Raynal characterized them as naturally degraded, he asserted that "the Indians are not [really] like those stupid men want to portray them."[32] His efforts to teach them reading and writing, to use them as natural history informants, to move their towns to more commercially advantageous locations, to teach them useful trades, and even to award them with titles of nobility were all predicated on his view that the Indians were "men given a rational soul just like ours, and that they live in the same environment as we do, and what proceeds from that is that they have the same natural dispositions of body and soul as we do." This was the same argument that Clavijero, Molina, and Velasco promoted in their written studies.[33]

Paradoxically, despite its defense of Indian intellectual capacity, this statement demonstrates that, like most learned men of his time, Martínez Compañón accepted the mainstream theory of climatic determinism. However, he used it to prove the virility of the American environment, not its degeneracy. In a 1785 letter to the parish priest of Chachapoyas, he outlined his stance on how environment affected human beings. "Diverse influences correspond to diverse climates," the Bishop argued, and these differences explained the "great natural diversity that is seen among men of different regions." He did not venture that this external difference was indicative of intellectual or spiritual ability, but he did believe that it accounted for differences in skin color and other external characteristics such as facial hair. It also explained the great variance in size of human beings, including why "some men are giant like those of the Patagonian coast . . . and others pygmies, like the Japanese."[34]

It was no coincidence that the Bishop chose to discuss Patagonian giants as an example of how men could grow inordinately large in certain climates. Martínez Compañón was, in fact, somewhat of a giant enthusiast. The questionnaire that he remitted to his dioceses prior to leaving on his *visita* in 1782 asked respondents "if at any time they have found any huge bones that seem to be human . . . whether they have any [local] tradition that in some time there might have been giants, and in the places where they might have had them, for what time, when did they become extinct and for what reason, and what support the people have for the said legend."[35] He received at least some material evidence of giants unearthed in a field outside Santiago de Chuco, in the Huamachuco province of Trujillo. These specimens were deemed important enough to be carefully wrapped, packaged in the crates of his collection, and sent back to Spain. They included a "top of a femur bone that seems to be of a giant, already half petrified," a "molar, also half-petrified that seems to be of a giant, found in the same place," and "part of a sacrum bone with the same circumstances and provenance."[36] Although the title does not confirm it, a giant may also appear in this image of "Indian boys playing jai alai" (see Plate 9). The figure in the orange jacket is almost three times as big as the boys who play around him, and his body is significantly too large to fit through the door of the building behind him. The individual is shown bending over and supporting his body weight on his knees, a position that highlights his severely humped back, likely a symptom of the osteoporosis that is a common side effect of gigantism.[37]

The Bishop's obsession with giants was no mere caprice—in providing visual, material, and anecdotal evidence of their existence in Trujillo, he was actually participating in the debate over the natural world of America and the men who lived in it. Spanish American scholars regularly discussed giants—especially those of southern Spanish America—implying that they evidenced the natural abundance of the local environment. For instance, the *Mercurio Peruano,* Lima's Enlightenment periodical, reported on a giant named Basilio

Huaylas, who, at twenty-four years old, stood seven feet tall when he was brought to Lima from the coastal town of Ica. Pedro O'Crouley's 1774 *Description of the Kingdom of New Spain* mentioned giant bones and teeth in its chapters on curiosities. Even Archbishop Francisco Lorenzana of Mexico stored in his library some of the giant human bones unearthed at Culhuacán. Giant bones even became a popular collectors' item throughout America in the eighteenth century because any evidence of giants was striking disproof of the argument that American mammals were smaller and weaker than those of Old World origin. That is why men like Robertson and Pauw were so insistent that giants were fabrications of desperate Spaniards in America. Robertson's *History of America* was blatantly skeptical about South America's famed giants, maintaining that the existence of giants and fossil evidence of them was "seemingly inconsistent with what reason and experience have discovered." Years later, historian Antonello Gerbi wrote of Pauw that "giants would have brought down his whole thesis on the weakness of the nature of America."[38] Martínez Compañón's own interest in giants, therefore, was a small-scale manifestation of his broader agenda to defend the nature, plants, animals, and people of Trujillo through engineering and depicting a living utopia in the north of Peru.

Martínez Compañón in the City of Kings

After his journey through the Andes, Martínez Compañón finally arrived in the most important Spanish city in South America: Lima, the so-called City of Kings. Despite its notoriously damp climate and cloudy skies, Lima was a commercial, intellectual, and administrative capital that was densely populated for the time (52,627 inhabitants in 1793). Francisco Pizarro chose the city site for its easy access to the nearby port of Callao, its flat terrain, and its climate, which, despite the humidity, was much milder than the highland population centers favored by the Inca. Visitors to colonial Lima tended to remark on the elaborate dress of its inhabitants and its multitude of churches, monasteries, and convents. It was recognized for the impressive baroque mansions that surrounded the city center, such as the Torre Tagle palace, built in the early eighteenth century for a Spanish marquis, celebrated for its typical carved stone portico and Moorish-style enclosed wooden balconies. Lima was also known for its lavish festivals: the Spanish technocrats Jorge Juan and Antonio Ulloa (who traveled throughout Spanish America from 1735 to 1746) were especially impressed with the pageantry surrounding Lima's viceroy. They reported that Antonio de Mendoza had a personal militia of 210 men: 160 cavalry who wore blue and red uniforms with silver accents, and fifty Spanish troops dressed in blue suits and waistcoats made of crimson velvet with gold trim. On the day the viceroy made his official entrance into the city, the streets were hung with vibrant tapestries, and local artisans erected an impressive triumphal arch over the Rimac River. Next to it, municipal workers built a special grandstand so that the highest dignitaries could enjoy a parade featuring local militia troops, secondary school and university students, and civil servants. The parade route ended at Lima's cathedral, where the new viceroy would meet the archbishop and cathedral canons and receive a ceremonial golden key to the city.[39]

He was not greeted with such pomp, but when Martínez Compañón stepped into Lima's *plaza mayor* for the first time, he found himself in the symbolic and cultural center of Spanish life in Peru. The plaza was home to the cathedral, the viceregal palace, and a famous fountain featuring eight lions with water trumpeting from their mouths. His eyes would have fixed on the cathedral's elaborate façade, featuring delicate Corinthian columns made of stone imported from Panama. He would have entered the cathedral for the first time through the main of the three doors facing the plaza—the so-called *portada del perdón*, or door of pardon. Looking up, he would have seen the soaring Gothic arches that supported the weight of the roof. Plated in gold, these intersected in a crossed design that recalled the starry night sky.

When Martínez Compañón—or Limeños, for that matter—tired of liturgical celebrations, their city also offered many venues for proper European-style amusements. These included theaters, where comedic productions were reputedly "as good as what you see in Madrid or Naples"; a cockfighting coliseum, a circular amphitheater with nine grades of spectator seating; and lively cafés where city dwellers could enjoy coffee, tea, chocolate, traditional yerba maté, and even games of billiards. A cathedral canon was unlikely to attend comedies or cockfights or to play billiards; but like many Limeños, Martínez Compañón may have frequented the city's cafés, especially to enjoy a cup of his favorite beverage: hot chocolate prepared in the typical style of the late eighteenth century, with chocolate shavings flavored with sugar and cinnamon.[40]

While chocolate was one of the few earthly pleasures that the Bishop enjoyed, he likely would have been far more interested in Lima's vibrant intellectual life. The city was home to the University of San Marcos—the oldest in South America—as well as more innovative institutions such as the Convictorio Carolino, where students learned experimental science, and the Colegio de San Carlos, where Newtonian physics found a place on the curriculum the same year that Martínez Compañón arrived in Peru. Lima also had a growing community of naturalists. Cosme Bueno published his yearly almanac, *Conocimiento de los tiempos*, there. The city was the home of Hipólito Unanue, a naturalist who proposed that cultivating commerce based on Peru's rich natural resources could benefit the viceroyalty. Another local scientist, José Eusebio Llano Zapata, sent a manuscript detailing the natural resources of Peru, titled *Memorias histórico, físicas, crítico, apologéticas de la América Meridional*, to the king in 1761. In 1787, Lima's first Spanish-style economic society was founded. This same group would later become the Sociedad de Amantes del País (Lovers of the Country) and publish the *Mercurio Peruano* (1791–1794), which frequently commented on scientific matters. In 1792, Padre Francisco González Laguna oversaw the founding of Lima's own botanical garden.[41]

Although all this surrounded Martínez Compañón, his chances for engagement would have been limited by his duties inside the walls of the cathedral. As *chantre*, or musical director, he was one of the most important members of the *cabildo* or cathedral chapter of dignitaries. These men met directly with the archbishop on a regular basis, exercised power on his behalf in his absence, and oversaw religious services. Martínez Compañón was responsible for supervising the musical accompaniments to liturgy, including chanting, singing, and instrumental music. Much of his work would have taken place in or near the cathedral's impressive choir stall, one of the oldest and best preserved in all Peru. Built in the early seventeenth century, this large wooden structure features ornate chairs for each choir member. Situated at ground level alongside the cathedral's main altar, the severe wooden seats are dominated by the carved relief figures of saints that stand behind them.[42]

Though records reveal nothing further about Martínez Compañón's duties as *chantre* in Lima, we know that during his *visita*, the Bishop taught Gregorian chant to seminary students in Piura, Lambayeque, and Cajamarca. He also recorded musical notations and lyrics when visiting communities throughout Chachapoyas, Otusco, and Cajamarca. The songs he collected ranged from Christmas carols to music for a Chimú dance performed with violin accompaniment. As with the illustrations that made up the nine volumes of watercolors, he gathered these songs from vernacular sources; they were mostly "simple" folk songs dismissed as such. Today, ethnomusicologists praise the entire collection, especially the "Chimú tune," which is the only known surviving musical notation in the Mochica language (extinct today and, even in 1644, spoken by only forty thousand people). The Bishop thought to preserve several musical instruments in his collection, including a "copper tambourine with seven jingle bells, a little hen, and four Indians dancing," in which one of the human figures carried "in his hand an axe like those that . . . the Indians use to dance [with today]."[43] Likewise, many of the watercolor images include musical instruments or people playing them, especially during Carnival.

In addition to his musical duties in the cathedral, Martínez Compañón was tasked with compiling a master list of chaplaincies and charitable endowments. The two massive volumes that resulted were an early indication of his organizational abilities: indexed like a modern-day address book with tabs separating the letters, the *capellanías* books listed by surname the individuals who had made the bequests, and for what purpose. He recorded that Miss Maria Theodora, for instance, had in 1740 established a chaplaincy based on the value of her country home outside Lima. With these funds, she supported a licentiate named Lorenzo de Azogue.[44]

In Lima, Martínez Compañón cultivated a close relationship with Archbishop Antonio de Parada, who soon thereafter rewarded him with additional responsibilities. By 1770, Parada had named him rector of Lima's Saint Toribio Seminary, a position that he retained until his departure for Trujillo in 1779. Although the majority of the documents from his time there are lost, we do know that while at the seminary, Martínez Compañón worked tirelessly to organize and improve, soliciting permission and funding for several structural improvements to the building, including more student rooms and easier access to water in the cooking area. Years later, when he was founding his own seminary in Trujillo, he hoped for the boys there to wear purple sashes similar to those that the Lima students had worn.[45]

In 1772 and 1773, the cathedral hosted the Sixth Provincial Church Council of Peru, in which canons, bishops, and the archbishop debated how they would implement Charles III's modernizing ecclesiastical reforms and how they would handle the aftermath of the expulsion of the Jesuits from Peru five years earlier. Martínez Compañón was named consultant, canon, and secretary of the council. He would have observed and perhaps even participated in heated discussions about the preparation of primary school teachers (they had to be well trained in Catholic precepts), the importance of repetition in teaching doctrine to Indians (adults were to study every Monday and Friday;

children were to study every day), and the necessity of teaching Indians to speak fluent Spanish, so that "they will be more easily and better taught in the subjects of religion and of the state."[46] Many of these same ideas about Indian education were later incorporated into the reform agenda that the Bishop imagined for Trujillo.

In 1773, Martínez Compañón became a member of the Real Sociedad Bascongada de los Amigos del País, or the Basque Friends of the Country Society, a social organization dedicated to improvement and reform that would likewise prove influential in his future imaginings of utopia in Trujillo. Founded in the Basque town of Vergara in 1765, this was the first of scores of economic societies established throughout Spain and America in the late eighteenth century. Although an ocean and a continent separated him from Vergara, Martínez Compañón's membership in the Basque society was not an anomaly: the majority of the society's nobles, government officials, academics, and clergy were men of Basque origin pursuing careers in other parts of the empire. Their original manifesto outlined their goal as "the socialization of progress [and] collective improvement . . . [of the] labor of groups and institutions." Their many publications provided suggestions for improvement that Martínez Compañón later planned to implement in Trujillo: cultivating alfalfa and flax, promoting agriculture and industry, building town primary schools, and educating women. They suggested that students' improvement be rewarded with prizes, and they thought contests useful for promoting technological advancement. In its 1780 ordinances, the Basque Society promoted the study of the arts, particularly drawing, which it decreed "useful to all types of people," since it was "the basis of the liberal arts, the soul of many branches of commerce" and "a universal language that can benefit everyone."[47]

Martínez Compañón carried these ideas with him when, on February 25, 1778, he was promoted to become the next bishop of Trujillo, in the north of Peru, near Ecuador. Reforming the Indians, promoting primary education, and pairing religious and social goals would become the foundations of his utopian agenda there. When complete, his successes would make plain to the rest of Peru, the Spanish Empire, and the world beyond that the Indians were fully capable members of society. Yet even with such a vast array of improvement strategies at his disposal, there were inevitable reservations. Being assigned to a post that was comparatively poor and isolated may have been somewhat of a disappointment. He subtly revealed these feelings in a letter from 1790 in which he wrote about how much he had loved Trujillo, "even though it was not Lima."[48] Regardless of any doubts he might have had, in

1778 he was scheduled to be confirmed as bishop the following June. When the necessary decrees finally arrived, he learned that, like all bishops in America, he was responsible for obeying the laws of the Indies and ensuring that all ecclesiastical income was to be shared with the Crown. From Lima that March, he confirmed: "I swear I will guard and comply with our king with all corresponding faith, observing all the laws of the *patronato real* [royal patronage of the Church], and that I will not contradict anything contained in them in any way."[49] After filing the paperwork and journeying 500 miles up the coast to Trujillo, he was confirmed as bishop on May 13, 1779.[50] He was forty-two years old.

CHAPTER 2

Parish Priests and Useful Information

On May 13, 1779, the new Bishop of Trujillo made his first official entrance into what was now his cathedral city. The journey from Lima would have taken him on the King's Road, or Camino Real, the thoroughfare that hugged Peru's Pacific Coast. Coming from the south, he would have entered the city from the New Huaman gate and preceded up what is today Francisco Pizarro Street, named for the conquistador who founded it in 1535. To honor this occasion, he might have chosen some of his most luxurious clothing—perhaps one of his fine Dutch silk shirts and gold lamé vestments bordered with gold thread, with the ensemble finished with British stockings and a bracelet with a large emerald surrounded by pink diamonds.[1] To the left side of the road lay Trujillo's Jesuit College, empty of the Saint Ignatius order since its 1767 expulsion from the Spanish territories. Several blocks north, the modest seventeenth-century Santo Domingo Convent and Church came into view. Once the carriage crossed the street that is today named for Pizarro's friend-turned-foe Diego de Almagro, Martínez Compañón's gaze would have landed on Trujillo's pristine, perfectly square *plaza mayor*. It was significantly smaller than that of Lima but nonetheless home to the necessary buildings of state and church administration, including the municipal *cabildo*, the jail, the cathedral, and the Bishop's palace, which would be his official home for the next eleven years. The brightly painted *casona* mansions of Trujillo's well-to-do merchants and agronomists overtook the remaining lots around the plaza. Behind the wooden screens shading their traditional Moorish balconies, appropriately demure young ladies could observe the goings-on of the city without exposing themselves to public view. The houses' high walls concealed rear private gardens resplendent with vibrant fuchsia bougainvillea and purple morning glories.

Even in the midst of such beauty, many of central Trujillo's buildings were crumbling or stood empty. Much of the city had yet to rebuild from the earthquakes that struck the north coast in 1729 and 1759. One such unlucky structure was the city's cathedral, which had been badly damaged in the last tremor. Furthermore, the same gentle ocean breezes that wafted through the city carried with them sand from the Pacific beaches three miles away—so much sand that sometimes pedestrians waded through knee-deep drifts to cross city streets. Outside the city walls, the poor mestizos, mulattos, and other mixed-race *castas* occupied the former Indian ghettos called *rancherías*, which, by the 1780s, had become slumlike.[2]

Of his visit to Trujillo over twenty years later, Alexander Humboldt dismissively wrote that "it is necessary to be familiar with Peruvian cities to find any beauty in a city like Trujillo."[3] Yet sandy streets and unattractive buildings were the least of Martínez Compañón's concerns. Even before he left Spain for America, he had dreamed of learning about and helping the Indians; when he arrived in Trujillo, he found himself responsible for 118,324 of them. In a 1783 circular letter to "My Beloved Children, the Indians of this Bishopric of Trujillo," he promised that "since I have arrived in these kingdoms . . . I have not forgone any occasion . . . to be useful to you, and to help you to know with my words, and my deeds, all that I have been able to do for your true well-being."[4] Happily, some of the Indians living in Trujillo city already seemed to be the hardworking plebeians whom the Bishop and other reformers of the eighteenth century tried to cultivate; they spoke fluent Castilian, wore Spanish-style clothes, and worked as artisans or manual laborers. But in provincial areas of the bishopric, many lived in poor, rural communities. They made meager wages as porters, farmers, or fishermen, often living in simple reed *choza* huts. Others resided on the outskirts of local haciendas, where they ceaselessly worked small plots of land in vain attempts to repay their debts to wealthy landlords. The situation was even direr in the Amazonian jungle regions, where some natives existed entirely outside the Spanish sphere of influence, such as the "infidel" Indians of Hibitos and Cholones, in the extreme eastern territory of the bishopric (see Plates 10 and 18). These "infidels" might have been the very men and women who kept Martínez Compañón awake on certain nights; their total isolation from European society and Catholic morals was a harsh reminder of the collective inability of the Crown and the Church to penetrate the deepest reaches of northern Peru.

Trujillo's Indians would soon become the almost singular focus of Martínez Compañón's utopian reform agenda, but in actuality his bishopric was much more diverse. His own demographic calculations listed the ecclesiastical province of Trujillo as the home of 118,324 Indians; 79,043 mestizos; 21,980 Spanish (including Creoles born in America); 16,630 *pardos* (mixed-race of African descent); and 4,486 blacks. The *pardos* and blacks were the smallest groups; but when combined, their total population rivaled that of the Spanish and made the city home to the viceroyalty's second-largest black population. Though many were slaves who had been brought to the coastal regions through Panama to work on area sugar plantations, the majority were free, lived in urban areas, and worked in skilled trades such as masonry and carpentry. Some, such as Master Architect Tomás Rodríguez, even collaborated with the Bishop on important projects, including rebuilding the towers of Trujillo's cathedral and rehabilitating the damaged church at Ferreñafe, northeast of Chiclayo. Paradoxically, although people of African descent constituted such a significant part of Trujillo's population, Martínez Compañón never imagined how they might be incorporated into his utopian vision. In this, he was similar to other reformers of the Spanish eighteenth century, who focused on generating a productive plebeian class of poor Spaniards, mestizos, and Indians while relegating people of African descent to the category of slaves, marking them as easily replaceable beings unworthy of improvement.[5]

In terms of market forces, the fate of slavery was tied to the broader fiscal well-being of Trujillo. Bourbon economic restructuring meant that while Trujillo's hacendados had been previously able to purchase African slaves from Panama, they could now do so only by way of Buenos Aires and secondary markets in Chile and Lima. As a result, slaves were suddenly more expensive and scarcer, driving up labor costs. At the same time, cheaper Brazilian sugar was flooding the Peruvian market. By 1784, the situation was so bad that Crown-appointed *visitador* Jorge Escobedo, who spent six years in Peru acting on behalf of the powerful minister of the Indies José de Gálvez, met with local officials to discuss the matter. In response to their complaints, he proposed that Brazilian sugar be prohibited in Spanish territory and that slaves be made available for purchase in Panama. His suggestion fell on characteristically deaf royal ears.[6]

Slaves aside, the situation in Trujillo was so dismal that in 1763, Corregidor Don Miguel Feyjoo concluded that "it seems that the same appreciable advantages for human happiness have turned into ruin and desolation. Not only . . . the many Spanish who have come to Peru, but also . . . the . . . natural children of the country [the Indians] find themselves notably diminished."[7]

There seemed to be an almost endless need for improvement in Trujillo. Martínez Compañón would dedicate himself to it with an intensity reflected—but not equaled—by his colleagues among the bishops and archbishops of America, marking himself as an iconoclast among reforming prelates. To accomplish such a far-reaching agenda for change, he relied on the clergy to become foot soldiers working to foster public happiness and improvement at the farthest corners of the bishopric. He tasked them with promoting the agricultural, economic, and educational development that was the foundation of his utopian vision. At the same time, they would act as collaborators in his natural history research, sharing invaluable data on local resources, traditions, and customs. Although Martínez Compañón employed the time-tested information-gathering techniques of questionnaires and a *visita* to learn about his bishopric, he still needed local clergy to function as his eyes on the ground. It was only with their dedicated assistance that Trujillo could move forward toward its idealized future.

A Bourbon Bishop in Trujillo

When Martínez Compañón was named bishop of Trujillo, he became a member of the so-called Bourbon prelates: high-level ecclesiastics of the eighteenth century who functioned as "a kind of religious civil service, closely identified with the task of national improvement."[8] These archbishops, bishops, and cathedral canons were secular clergy who were ideologically and politically tied to the Spanish Crown, often having been handpicked by Charles III himself. As the king's representatives in America, they were responsible for implementing his vision of reform for the Catholic Church. They oversaw the campaign to "secularize" Indian parishes by replacing the friars who administered them with secular parish priests. To avoid past abuses, they monitored these priests closely, scrutinizing their physical residences in their parishes, cataloging the sacraments they performed, and limiting their involvement with local judicial matters. The Bourbon prelates also managed a broad campaign of parish finance reform, closely examining religious brotherhood dues and *arancel* income from the collection of fees charged for sacraments. They targeted convents where nuns enjoyed lavish dowries, personal servants, and opulent costumes that flouted the Bourbon calls for austerity in religious devotion. In worship, they championed a return to private piety by discouraging the baroque tradition of overwhelming the senses with lavish architecture, self-flagellation, and opulent church décor.[9]

Many Bourbon prelates were involved in political economy projects that meant to improve the social and economic lives of their constituents. In Ecuador, Bishop José Pérez Calama opened a road connecting the jungles of Esmeraldas with their rich production of fruit and cloth to the commercial center of Quito. In New Granada, Archbishop Antonio Caballero y Góngora collaborated with scientist José Mutis to improve public health by promoting the newly invented smallpox vaccine. Many prelates worked to improve education: Bishop Francisco Fabián y Fuero, for instance, supported a literature academy and endowed university professorships in Puebla. Some even gathered natural history data about the Americas, with Pérez Calama contributing articles to the *Mercurio Peruano* journal, Caballero y Góngora supporting the Royal Botanical Expedition in New Granada, and Archbishop Francisco Lorenzana publishing a new edition of Hernán Cortés's letters from Mexico, elaborated with his own reports on local nature and society, as well as newly commissioned illustrations and maps.

Though Lorenzana's *Historia de Nueva España* is well known, scholars are less familiar with his 1768 manuscript, "Instructions for Making Indians Content in Spiritual and Material Things." In keeping with what Spanish reformer José Campillo had called for twenty-five years earlier, Lorenzana mandated renewed efforts toward the spiritual and "material" education of Indians. Properly educated, he believed, the Indians would become more closely integrated into Spanish society. Therefore, priests and ecclesiastics should help them to engage in commerce, learn new agricultural techniques, and practice Spanish-style social norms, such as maintaining separate bedrooms for parents and male and female children. Despite such good intentions, Lorenzana was careful not to threaten the strict social hierarchy of the colonies, never suggesting that the Indians deserved to enjoy the social, racial, and economic advantages carefully guarded by Spaniards and Creoles. Other reforming prelates constructed similarly paradoxical campaigns that purported to benefit the Indians while ensuring their social inferiority. For instance, Archbishop Manuel José Rubio y Salinas sought to help the natives of Mexico by creating 237 primary schools for them; but he planned to use the schools to extinguish indigenous languages by forcing students to speak only Castilian. He also spent twenty-five years actively blocking an attempt to create a seminary for Indian boys just north of Mexico City.[10]

In Trujillo, Martínez Compañón did not display such paternalistic disdain for America's native population. Instead, he referred to the Indians as "my beloved children" and placed them at the center of the utopia he envisioned. In addition to promoting their welfare and improvement in spiritual and temporal matters, he thought to afford them ideological advantages that would enhance their positions in colonial society. As we shall see, he suggested to King Charles III that deserving Indians be allowed to dress in the silken finery that was officially reserved for Spaniards. He believed that those Indians who most excelled in school should be honored with burial plots within their churches, just like Spanish elites. He even ventured that they be allowed to use the noble titles *don* or *doña* in their public lives, and be addressed with the supplicatory second-person title of *vos* in municipal government and at church. Although he, too, promoted the use of Castilian in primary schools, his careful cataloging of Quechua names for plants and animals, as well as the 344-word "Chart of 43 Castilian Words Translated to the Eight Languages That the Indians of the Coast, Sierra, and Mountains of the Bishopric of Trujillo Speak," demonstrates that he sought to value and preserve the native languages of the Andes, rather than simply erasing them from existence. Instead of blocking a seminary for Indian students, as Rubio y Salinas had, in Trujillo the Bishop created his own body of itinerant priests' assistants drawn from native communities. Such daringly egalitarian rhetoric not only reinforced his position in the debate over the inferiority of the New World; it also made him radically different from many of his peers. He was fully ensconced in the highest echelons of the Church hierarchy in America, yet he was wholeheartedly involved in secular reform, deeply engaged in scientific research, and, to a much greater degree than his compatriots, completely dedicated to the cause that mattered most to him: improving the Indians.[11]

Martínez Compañón's plans to assist the Indians must have been swirling in his head ever since he had learned of his promotion; but before he could focus on these matters, he had to attend to his duties as an ecclesiastical administrator in the capital. Rebuilding the demolished tabernacle, sacristy, and towers of Trujillo's cathedral was paramount. He imagined a new neoclassical façade for the building—the same one that still adorns it today. He ordered a crypt constructed on the south patio to alleviate the foul odors resulting from the old practice of burying the city's dead within the church itself. His drafting plans feature a window that allowed breezes to circulate, individual tombs one yard wide and two and a quarter yards long, and brick

overlay on the limestone walls. In the new *cabildo* room that he commissioned for the cathedral, the Bishop gathered portraits of his thirty predecessors, compiling along with them a historical document detailing the major
deeds of each.[12]

In addition to these matters of *fábrica*—church structure, materials, and
decoration—the Bishop made changes to ecclesiastical education in Trujillo.
He knew that seminaries were of special importance to Charles III and his
ministers, who wished to submit ecclesiastical education to empire-wide regu-
lations. They were particularly interested in secular conciliar seminaries that
would teach aspirants to the priesthood standardized courses of doctrine,
grammar, rhetoric, geometry, and art. The Lima Provincial Church Council
of 1772 also stressed the importance of seminaries, arguing that reforming the
manners and behavior of priests was the best way to ensure proper behavior
among the populace. Martínez Compañón must have had these decrees in
mind when, upon his arrival in Trujillo, he found that the city's San Carlos
Conciliar Seminary was no longer operational. He set to work almost immediately, and, under his watch, the first repairs were complete as early as
November 1781. He planned for the seminary to educate forty-eight students,
half of whom would pay full price and half of whom would be Indian scholarship students.[13]

But the Bishop's vision for seminaries in Trujillo involved more than the
traditional elite aspirants to the priesthood studying in the provincial capital.
As Vasco de Quiroga had done with his own utopia in New Spain centuries
earlier, Martínez Compañón was already imagining how seminary students in
rural areas of Trujillo would become foot soldiers for his agenda of reform. Following the precedent of groups such as the Operarios del Salvador del Mundo
and the Sacred Congregation of Propaganda (Propaganda Fide), first created in
seventeenth-century Rome to recapture the faithful from Protestants, he
planned four such missionary schools in the cities of Trujillo, Lambayeque,
Piura, and Cajamarca. Priests, community members, and day students would
study there, as well as young Indians who would learn Spanish, Christian doctrine, and basic literacy. The students, known as *operarios eclesiásticos*, or ecclesiastical workers, would make annual excursions into the countryside, where
they would busy themselves "confessing the parishioners, visiting and consol-
ing the sick, fixing disagreements and private discord . . . and leaving . . .
rules of healthy governance."[14] They were to become, in essence, a native clergy
of Creoles, mestizos, and Indians that could better reach people in sparsely

populated areas distant from Spanish centers of control. The *operarios* would help to ensure that the people of rural Trujillo would behave as obedient subjects and proper Catholics, even when there were no parish priests or municipal officials close by to monitor them. Because they came from provincial communities themselves, local Indians, mestizos, and people of African descent would more readily accept them. They could stand in for civil government in areas where this often seemed entirely absent. With the *operarios* constantly reinforcing and spreading their mission, the seminaries would become vital support systems for the improved future of the bishopric. Like the preceding institutions and clergy who inspired them, the *operarios* would become foot soldiers of a future utopia.

Martínez Compañón imagined that of the four schools, Trujillo's Seminario de Operarios del Salvador would hold jurisdiction over the other three. It opened its doors in September 1785, with the accompanying fanfare of a ceremony he later described as lengthy and well attended.[15] In June of the following year, the seminary was confirmed by a royal decree. But official approval was never secured for the remaining three seminaries. Later referring to the attempt to found one in Cajamarca, Martínez Compañón worried about "the distrust of the town to be able to form an institution that it does not know, and has no experience with." There was also the ubiquitous problem of lack of funds. The Bishop hoped to raise money for the seminaries through redistributing *cofradía* religious brotherhood income and selecting parish priests to serve in vacant parishes in Trujillo, so that they might hold Mass regularly and generate more tithe income. He also hoped that, since Indian children were welcome to be educated at the seminaries, native communities would make small annual donations for their operation costs. But none of these measures worked. When he found himself still unable to raise adequate finances for the *seminarios* by 1788, the Bishop turned to the ecclesiastical *cabildo* of Trujillo—which also denied the support that he needed to sustain the schools. The Spanish, mestizo, and Indian *operarios* would not become the foot soldiers of reform he had imagined they could be.[16]

While it must have been disappointing, the community's general lack of interest in the seminaries had ample historical precedent: early attempts to allow Indians into the priesthood in sixteenth-century Mexico were promptly squashed with a 1555 Provincial Council ban—a prohibition that was first iterated in Peru in 1551 and again in 1567. As the career of archbishop Rubio y Salinas demonstrates, even in mid-eighteenth-century Mexico, a plan to found a seminary for Indian students was rejected, largely because of prejudice toward allowing Indians into higher education as well as fears about taking positions away from Spanish and mestizo priests.[17]

Although the seminaries that Martínez Compañón envisioned were not successful, Trujillo did not generally lack for religious figures. The bishopric was home to twenty-one monasteries and three convents, with the majority of the regular clergy being Franciscans, Mercederians, and Bethlehemites who lived in monasteries in the main population areas. As regulars, they were bound to follow the rules of their own orders; but the remaining priests and assistants who made up the secular clergy of Trujillo were directly subject to Martínez Compañón's rule. Many of these were *curas* administering to the Spaniards, mestizos, and people of African descent who belonged to their own parishes, known as *curatos*, often located in the most densely settled coastal regions of the province. The less educated priests (often mestizos) who administered to the *doctrinas*, or Indian parishes, were known as *curas doctrineros*. Most often, their work brought them to the sierra towns where the largest groups of natives lived. In even more rural areas, traveling priests staffed ancillary churches called *añejos*. Especially in the jungle and the sierra, *añejos* were often located far from the communities they were meant to serve, limiting access to sacraments and worship.[18]

This isolation was even more problematic because in rural areas, priests and their assistants were sometimes the only Spaniards or mestizos of authority closely involved in daily life. Recognizing this, Martínez Compañón reminded Trujillo's parish priests that one of their most important duties was to "reduce the Indians to civil life in town" by ensuring that all their charges lived "within the sound of the bell," meaning that they could literally as well as figuratively be reached by their priest and their church. They were also to ensure adherence to the sacraments of communion, marriage, confession, and extreme unction. They should carefully record all births, deaths, marriages, and baptisms in their parishes, and keep meticulous tallies of all church income. They were to oversee proper behavior in the home, ensuring that parents married and that male and female children were properly clothed and that they slept in bedrooms separated by sex. With adults, they were to discourage drunkenness and adultery and to forbid men and women from bathing together in the same place.

While typical, such spiritual and moral directives were far from the only responsibilities Martínez Compañón gave to his parish priests. He also intended for them to participate in his vision of economic development, relying on them to share technological innovation, moral support, and organizational skills with the people. He told them to "speak lovingly of the fields" where the Indians worked, to explain which crops were best cultivated there, to show how to weed the soil, and to discuss how to grow fruit trees. He mandated that priests support young Indian women in their parishes by reallocating *cofradía* funds to buy them spinning wheels or pairs of oxen that would help supplement their household income. He also sought their help in building primary schools in his territory, as we will explore in greater detail in Chapter 4. In the Bishop's utopia, priests were essential collaborators who would use their daily interactions with the local population to gather the data that he needed to construct his vision of reform for Trujillo.[19]

While promoting agricultural improvement and primary education might have been some of their most enjoyable responsibilities, priests in Trujillo also oversaw *policía*, or general orderliness in their parishes—a task that occasionally proved quite trying. In 1786, Francisco Simeón de Polo reported on a striking episode of unruliness from Saña, north of Trujillo. It began one night when two mestizos and a mulatto (who happened to be mute) were rehearsing for a play celebrating the feast of the Virgin of Guadalupe and decided to partake in some unsanctioned merrymaking. Breaking into the local church, they pulled the statue of Mary from its display and headed for the room where the Augustinian brothers stored their religious garb. One mestizo donned a white ecclesiastical garment and a choir member's cape, while the other found a frock with an image of San Francisco. Their mute mulatto companion dressed in the traditional black, long-sleeved habit of the Augustinian monks. The three proceeded to "make a scene . . . yelling as if they were preaching" to lampoon the strict Augustinian brothers (the documents do not suggest how a mute could have joined in this parody). The townspeople who had gathered nearby to enjoy a bonfire joined in their mockery until the wee hours of the morning, leaving the priest to report that, had he been there, "he would have instituted a remedy to avoid such excess and irreverence." Later, he got his wish, as only one month after the incident was first drawn to Martínez Compañón's attention, the Bishop decreed Polo to be a priest of "discernment, virtue, and discretion" who could conduct an investigation into the matter on his own. Leaving the matter to the priest's discretion demonstrates how much the Bishop relied on his priests to maintain order and decorum at the local level. It was impossible for Martínez Compañón to personally ensure that his orders were followed, so he had to trust his priests to enforce proper decorum in the church and its environs. But this responsibility was only one aspect of a much bigger, and more innovative, role that he had planned for them in helping to build a utopia in Trujillo.[20]

Priests as Informants

Once the Bishop's duties in the provincial capital were well under way, he turned to tasks elsewhere in his bishopric. To start, Martínez Compañón knew that he needed a thorough understanding of the 93,205 square miles of extreme geographic diversity that made up Trujillo, and he planned to obtain it by personally visiting as much of it as possible. His task of assessing such a large area was not simple—in fact, no prelate had traveled extensively in northern Peru since Archbishop Toribio Alfonso de Mogrovejo of Lima in the late 1500s. But eighteenth-century reform culture promoted the pastoral *visita* as the most efficient and thorough method of gathering data to promote reform at the provincial level. Charles III was so convinced of the *visita*'s utility that in 1776, he mandated that all American prelates make thorough visitations of their territories and remit the data to the Council of the Indies.[21] Martínez Compañón readily accepted this duty. He hoped that his *visita* would help him gather the information he needed "to complete [a project] that His Majesty might review with his own eyes, or [to] be informed of . . . the different qualities of the lands, of the provinces of this bishopric, and its principal fruits and manufactures of its inhabitants." Above all, he planned to gather information about the population of Trujillo, "so that this report might contribute to the prosperity of the towns of this bishopric and of the whole nation in general."[22] The parish priests would be key to this endeavor, as they had direct access to parishioners, who could assess the informants' testimony and who would gather the material and visual reports that the Bishop requested. Once compiled, their data would serve as a foundation from which the Bishop and the people would begin to build their utopia.

Martínez Compañón's words about prosperity are a reminder that even though he was first and foremost a man of the cloth, as a vassal of the king, a functionary of the state, and a citizen of the world, he was bound to improve the material and social situation of his diocesans. Accordingly, much of his work consisted of promoting one of the most important concepts of late eighteenth-century government: public happiness. The basis of this, according to Italian Catholic intellectual Ludovico Muratori (whose work Martínez Compañón owned) was charity—a principle made real only when it was executed in daily life.[23] The Bishop had likely begun imagining this charitable work while still in Spain, where he would have started reading about ecclesiastics who worked with the Indians of America. In fact, Spain is where Martínez Compañón acquired his copies of the collected works of Juan de Palafox, bishop of Puebla, New Spain (1640–1655). Palafox wrote that in order to truly grasp how the Indians' "nakedness, poverty, and work" enriched the state *and* the church, viceroys and bishops had to gather information from the parish priests who had daily contact with them. Like Martínez Compañón a century and a half later, Palafox was certain that once the Indians were properly understood and managed, they could become useful subjects. "They have a great facility to learn trades," he argued, "because in seeing painting, they very soon paint; in seeing work, they work; and with incredible quickness, they learn four or six trades."[24]

But before Martínez Compañón could seek the vital demographic, cultural, and socioeconomic data that would be the foundations of these improvements, he had to prepare for the long and difficult journey. In autumn 1782, his servants carefully folded his simple priest's gown and singlet with an amice (a square piece of linen with a cross in the middle). They might have also prepared his gold-tipped cane, useful to maintain steady footing on precipitous rural roads. Outside the Bishop's palace, stable hands might have been busy readying his sorrel horse and a small pack mule to carry other personal items.[25] As his assistants and servants bustled about, Martínez Compañón selected the team that would accompany him: his secretary Pedro de Echevarri, a missionary, a chaplain, a notary, a scribe, a Spaniard named Antonio de Narbona (who, strangely, does not reappear in the documentation), his nephew José Ignacio Lecuanda, and six slaves to service the group.[26] Perhaps one of these was Theodoro, a kitchen slave whom Martínez Compañón had purchased with the plan of granting him liberty in a few years (but as of the Bishop's promotion to Bogotá, the unfortunate Theodoro was "inventoried" as property of the Trujillo episcopate).[27]

Meanwhile, Martínez Compañón coordinated how local clergy would receive the group. In April, he had sent a pastoral letter that told parish priests to expect the *visita* party. But rather than demanding the lavish ceremony and ritual that would typically accompany a bishop's visit, he requested restraint and sobriety in their preparations. He cautioned that they were not to arrange for more than three dishes to be served at the midday meal, two at dinner, and one for dessert. In areas with no houses for his party's lodging, priests were forbidden to order the construction of any structures for their use. "I have decided," the Bishop wrote, "to bring a tent in which we will stay in those places."[28]

While the priests and their assistants were not to furnish any special creature comforts, they were asked to prepare for the Bishop's arrival by gathering answers to two questionnaires that they received along with the pastoral letter. The first of the questionnaires was directed to the priests themselves, but in the case of rural *doctrinas* or *añejos* that were irregularly staffed, it stipulated that provincial *corregidores* were to interview "the most learned landowners or city-dwellers," meaning well-to-do Spaniards or mestizos, and occasionally Indians.[29] These questions were to inform Martínez Compañón of standard ecclesiastical matters, such as whether the priests worked alone or with the assistance of a subordinate priest (often known as a *vicario*). This questionnaire (see Appendix 1 for a transcription) also asked for information on church finances, including whether the priests supported only themselves with their benefice, or if other family members lived from the same income as well. If the parish was home to any *cofradías*, or religious brotherhoods, the Bishop wanted information about them—specifically, what type of funding they received. He inquired about any additional income generated by religious festivals or *arancel* fees for religious sacraments. He also asked for information about the distance from *añejos* to their mother churches and the city of Trujillo. He sought to learn about the devotional practices of parishioners, wanting to know whether local parishes had any "image" or statue that they venerated and "whether the town was sick or healthy, and where one would go for medicines in case of sickness, and how much they would cost." Finally, he asked if the parish had any poor or infirm residents who could not work. Taken together, these data would help him assess how much local religious authorities would be able to contribute to his planned utopia in Trujillo. He could then employ the information to mobilize parish church resources, with priests at the helm.[30]

A Questionnaire for Useful Information

Martínez Compañón's request for information about local religious life and ecclesiastical administration was not atypical in an age of close scrutiny of church finances and management. Much more innovative was his plan to use his priests as informants who would help him to complete the research for his

"Historical, Scientific, Political, and Social Museum of the Bishopric of Trujillo del Perú" and its accompanying watercolor images and natural history collection. Therefore, they also received a second questionnaire that focused on temporal matters, particularly natural history and local resources. As he told them, he sent it because he believed "that within this diocese we have much more than what we imagine and that a distinct and thorough knowledge of it could be of great utility."[31] Such information, he was convinced, would serve not simply for "vain curiosity" but to promote "industry and commerce."[32]

In employing this second questionnaire to compile information, Martínez Compañón utilized a time-tested technique of gathering data on distant and unknown parts of the Spanish Empire. In sixteenth-century Mexico, Bernardino de Sahagún's *Florentine Codex* and Gonzalo Oviedo's *History of the Indies* were both derived from questionnaire responses. But the most widely distributed questionnaire in colonial Spanish America was developed by royal cosmographers Alonso de Santa Cruz and Juan López de Velasco in 1598 as part of Philip II's massive *Relaciones Geográficas* project to map the lands of the Spanish Empire. By asking respondents to answer specific questions about local history, the natural world, area economies, and geography, Santa Cruz and Velasco sought to gather sufficient knowledge for the Spanish king to rule the overseas territories that were too distant and dangerous for him to visit himself. Their method of inquiry—asking discrete questions to provoke short answers that could be later compiled and analyzed—signaled a major epistemological shift in European attempts to learn about the world, one that led scholars away from the discursive techniques of the past and toward the methodological inquiry of the future. Two hundred years later in the Spanish Empire, bureaucrats, naturalists, and ecclesiastics employed these same techniques of information gathering through written query and response, now standard throughout the Atlantic basin.[33]

The questionnaire that Martínez Compañón composed reveals that, like most administrators gathering systematic data about unfamiliar territories, he wanted to learn about the people of Trujillo as well as the natural world in which they lived. Without understanding local people, he could not adequately assess how they utilized the natural world around them and how this relationship could be improved. Useful information was the very foundation of reform culture—without it, officials had no way of knowing what needed to be done. For help in beginning such an important task, he turned again to his parish priests, asking for them to facilitate detailed answers from local informants on the following queries:

1. What is the character and natural inclination of the natives of this *doctrina*, and if they understand and speak Castilian. If they are applied to their work or not. If there is any noticeable difference between Indians, Spanish, and other *castas*, as much in this or in their customs. And if this is attributed to differences in their education, or to some other natural or accidental principle. And what is the education they usually give to their children.

2. If the weather and climate is beneficial, and if . . . the . . . [territories] . . . of your jurisdiction are reputed to be healthy or sick, and to what they attribute whichever of these two qualities . . . are prevalent. Which are the most common sicknesses, and their causes, and the common medicines used to cure them, and [what is] the age to which its inhabitants typically live.

3. If there might be news that any of the towns belonging to this *doctrina* have been abandoned, [have] disappeared, or moved to another place, and the cause of the one or the other.

4. At what age they usually marry . . . in this *doctrina*. By which hand they usually arrange marriages. If there are any celibates, and [where] this virtue is most frequently found, both in terms of the *castas* and in terms of the sexes.

5. If one finds increased or not the number of landowners and city residents, both in this capital and in its annexes, with respect to the information in the censuses and old books, or the traditions of the towns. And what is the total of this augmentation or diminution, and if it is of Indians or other *castas*, and to what cause they attribute it.

6. If either within this principal town or its annexes, or surrounding areas begin any sources [of water], if these are the waters that serve for the common use of the people, and if in these they might have noted any particular quality, and what it might be.

7. If a river runs through its land or its borders, what they call it, where it has its beginnings, if they make use of its waters, and if they are known to be healthy. If it is navigable and if it has a

bridge, and if not having a bridge if it would be possible to build one, and how much, more or less, its construction would cost.

8. What crops they harvest, and their quality, how much the fields produce, and what is the method, form, and season of doing their planting, cultivating, and harvesting.

9. If they keep any commerce . . . and of what kind, with towns or provinces, and what utilities it produces, and whether there might be some method or means of advancing it.

10. If there are any sugar plantations or refineries, cattle ranches, workshops, or agricultural estates, what are their profits, if tribute is given to them, how much they are given and how many workers they maintain. And if among them there are any *mitayos*, what salaries they pay them, and how they are paid.

11. If there are any minerals, which they are, how they mine them, and what they yield.

12. If there are any medicinal herbs, branches, or fruits, which they are, what are their shape, and the virtue of each one of them, and the mode of applying and using them.

13. If there are any mineral waters, and . . . if they are hot or temperate, sulfurous, nitrous, ferrous, or of another quality, what use they made of them, and to what effect.

14. If there are any resins or fragrant balsams, which they are, and what virtue they attribute to them.

15. If there are any strange birds or carnivorous animals, or any poisonous animals or insects, and if there are any of these, what precautions those who live around them take.

16. If there are any woods, their abundance, and qualities, the use they make of them, or might be able to make of them.

17. If there are any structures from the times before the conquest that are notable for their material, form, grandness, or any vestiges of that. If at any time they have found any huge bones that seem to be human. And whether they have any tradition that in some time there might have been giants, and in the places where they might have had them, for what time, when did they become extinct and for what reason, and what support the people have for the said legend.

18. If in the Indians one sees anything that smells of superstition, about what points and which are the reasons to distrust, or

believe it, and what methods would be the most effective
to extirpate them with respect to [the Indians'] character,
inclinations, ideas, and customs.[34]

A careful reading of the questionnaire suggests that the Bishop was already imagining how to draw the broad outlines of his utopia in Trujillo. Perhaps thinking of the Túpac Amaru Indian rebellion that had so recently threatened Spanish hegemony in the southern portions of the viceroyalty, the first section of the document sought details about "the character and natural inclination of the natives of this *doctrina*." This had several facets, most of which concerned how "Hispanicized" the Indians were. Martínez Compañón wanted to know whether they spoke Spanish, a central indicator of previous meaningful interaction they had with church and state authorities. He also inquired whether there was any "noticeable difference" between the local Indians' places in society and that of the Spanish or other *castas* who lived nearby. This would reveal whether they had fared well under Spanish colonial authorities, or whether they had become a permanent underclass that would have little motivation and few resources with which to support his reform agenda. Another factor that would signify a group receptive to his plans was whether "they are applied to their work or not," as he put it. In response to this query, he must have hoped that he would not hear stereotypically negative comments such as those that would appear in Carrio's *Lazarillo* a few years later, which claimed that Peru's Indians had "no objective other than that of drunkenness" and that they were so lazy that they "would let themselves be eaten by lice" rather than work.[35]

Given his experience as rector of the Saint Toribio Seminary in Lima and his plans to extend primary education throughout the bishopric, Martínez Compañón inquired as to whether area children attended school, likely understanding that "differences . . . in education" for Indian and white children might explain why the Indians were not known for industriousness or facility with the Spanish language. If local people assumed that differences between Spaniards and Indians were based on inherent deficiencies in native bodies and minds, the Bishop needed to know about the "natural or accidental principle" to which they attributed this difference.

Assuming that the Indians in question did work, Martínez Compañón wanted to gather more specific details about how they did so. He wanted to know if the community in question had any established commercial networks, and where these were. He hoped that the priest might suggest, if he could, "whether there might be some method or means of advancing [such commercial activity]." The Bishop knew that the people might also work in agriculture or mills, or perhaps in small workshops known as *obrajes,* if they did so, he wondered whether it was in order to meet their tribute duties or to earn money for themselves. He inquired as to how large these commercial operations were, including how many employees they had and whether any were assigned *mita* laborers. Such information would help him imagine how to improve each—perhaps through facilitating transportation along trade routes, sharing innovative agricultural techniques, or seeking updated machinery that might increase production in mills or *obrajes.*

While work and productivity were key to the present and future potential of Trujillo's Indian communities, Martínez Compañón—like most administrators in Spain's overseas territories (as Chapter 3 will illustrate)—believed that communal living in cities or towns was also key to development. He knew that with the exception of larger population centers such as Trujillo, Piura, Cajamarca, and Chachapoyas, many miles of Trujillo were isolated and rural, with no towns to speak of. He therefore inquired if the area in question had been home to any previous urban settlements that had "been abandoned, [have] disappeared, or moved to another place." A related question was about local population statistics: over time, had the population of Indians and *castas* increased or fallen in the area? This would provide valuable clues as to whether the land was rich enough to sustain a sizable population. The questionnaire asked if local census records, town traditions, and archival records (or "old books," as he called them) showed how many city dwellers owned the land on which they lived.

Although the first questionnaire had thoroughly covered local religious practices, Martínez Compañón saw fit to ask about them in this second one as well. He inquired whether there was "anything that smells of superstition" in the local Indian population. If so, he wondered if the priests had any suggestions for how to most effectively eradicate these beliefs, specifically "with respect to [the Indians'] character, inclinations, ideas, and customs." While this was written in the tone of a dedicated extirpator, the Bishop's questionnaire in fact showed him to be slightly skeptical of the harsh charges of "idolatry" that Indians often faced. Before condemning any such behavior in the local population, he wanted to know "the reasons to distrust, or believe it." This attitude of levelheadedness toward potentially inflammatory Indian behavior would resurface throughout his time in Trujillo, helping him to maintain an air of careful detachment when observing the customs and traditions of the Indians around him.

Almost as important as verifying that the Indians behaved like good Catholic subjects was learning whether they followed the European social norms that would signify their status as upstanding vassals of the Spanish Crown. In the questionnaire, this had to do mainly with the institution of marriage: at what age it typically happened and how it was arranged. In asking about marriage, the Bishop was quietly inquiring whether communities fostered upstanding marriages sanctified by the Church, or if they followed traditional Andean customs of trial marriage, or *pantanacuy*, in which young couples were encouraged to informally cohabitate before marriage. Martínez Compañón also wanted to know if his bishopric had many inhabitants who had specifically chosen celibacy, and what racial group was most likely to do so.[36]

In addition to investigating the present state of social relations in Trujillo, the questionnaire inquired about the area's past. Peru's north coast was rich in ruins from the "gentile," or pre-Hispanic Moche and Chimú, peoples. Martínez Compañón therefore asked the priests to report "if there are any structures from the times before the conquest that are notable for their material, form, grandness, or any vestiges of that." Regarding the people of the past, he wondered whether the priests might have heard of local people finding "any huge bones that seem to be human." As we saw in Chapter 1, these were the giant bones that would serve as evidence to help prove that the natives of Peru were not physically weak and inferior.

While a good deal of Martínez Compañón's questionnaire focused on the social resources, or the people of Trujillo, he also inquired about the natural world in which they lived. Although these questions were focused on "geography, metallurgy, mineralogy, and botany," as the Bishop put it, they were just as important in determining how to build his utopian vision of improvement. Recall that, like most early modern Europeans, Martínez Compañón believed in climatic determinism, or the idea that the Earth and the heavens that surrounded it inevitably influenced men. The second item on the questionnaire asked priests to inform him "if the weather and climate is beneficial" in their area of jurisdiction. Accordingly, he wanted to know if people there were more likely to be healthy, or to be ill much of the time. If they did suffer from repeated illnesses, he asked "which are the most common sicknesses, and their causes, and the common medicines used to cure them."

This question directly led to another farther down the list: if "there are any medicinal herbs, branches, or fruits, which they are, what are their shape, and the virtue of each one of them, and the mode of applying and using them." As Chapter 6 will show, these answers formed the basis of the impressive collection of botanical information that the Bishop gathered from local informants throughout his time in Trujillo: three volumes of watercolor images showing 488 individual portraits of plants, trees, and bushes (many of which were medicinal); and ten crates of his natural history collection, half of which held exclusively plant matter and half of which mixed it with other specimens. In a related matter, question fourteen asked "if there are any resins or fragrant balsams, which they are, and what virtue they attribute to them." Balsams, derived from the aromatic resin of trees and shrubs, had been seen as valuable medicines even before Dioscorides, and since the 1520s, the Spanish had sought new balsams in American nature. Along with botanical medicines, they had vast potential as commercial trade items throughout the Atlantic world.[37]

But Martínez Compañón also wanted to know what local natural resources might affect the health of his diocesans. He inquired as to whether "there are any mineral waters, and if there are if they are hot or temperate, sulfurous, nitrous, ferrous, or of another quality, what use they made of them, and to what effect." It is possible that one response he received to this query is depicted in volume 2 of the watercolors, in an image that shows a "woman with leprosy bathing" (see Plate 11). In the late colonial period, Lima had its own hospital dedicated to lepers (named for their patron saint, Lazarus), and the viceroy endorsed projects to develop leprosy remedies based on balsams and ointments.[38] The image shown here suggests that the waters from this mountain stream in Trujillo might have served the same purpose. Along with potential cures for endemic disease, the Bishop inquired about "any poisonous animals or insects" and what might be done about these. He asked for notice of "any strange birds or carnivorous animals," many of which must have been those depicted in volume 6 of the watercolors.

Plant and animal life was central to understanding the local environment; and in a bishopric that held vast expanses of arid desert and rocky mountains, water was an even more essential resource. So Martínez Compañón inquired if there were any water sources in each area. Perhaps having been warned that water disputes were rampant in Trujillo (as they were in much of the Andes and still are today), he wanted to know whether these were "for the common use of the people" or if they were held privately. At the same time, water was essential to transporting commercial goods and crops. So the Bishop inquired about any local rivers, their sources and tributaries, and their navigability. In addition, he wanted to know whether each river in question had a bridge and, if not, "if it would be possible to build one, and

how much, more or less, its construction would cost." Bridges would become
a central part of the Bishop's reform agenda, especially in the watery eastern
portions of Trujillo, where he managed a campaign to build a bridge over the
San Antonio River in the province of Luya and Chillaos.[39]

Once water was secured both for irrigation and transport, the Bishop
could turn to local agricultural production. He wanted to know what crops
were farmed in each area, how productive the fields were, and "the method,
form, and season of doing their planting, cultivating, and harvesting." While
agricultural crops provided both local comestibles and material for trade,
Martínez Compañón realized that American woods were even more potentially profitable, largely because of their high demand in European markets.
Of these, he wanted to know about not only "their abundance, and qualities"
but also "the use they make of them, or might be able to make of them."[40]

Finally, like most anyone who had any knowledge of the Indies, Martínez Compañón knew that the Spanish were still looking for the very
substance that had made their earliest ventures in America so fantastically
successful. He asked simply, "if there are any minerals, what they are, how
they mine them, and what they produce." These would have complemented
the great silver mine at Hualgayoc in Cajamarca, which was closely linked to the
economic future of the entire province. As Chapter 5 will demonstrate, his
reform work there would be some of the most thoughtful and innovative of
his efforts in the bishopric.[41]

In the end, the questionnaire presaged what Martínez Compañón's
broader reform agenda would ultimately entail. His blueprint for reform was
clear: he first needed to teach the people proper Spanish language skills, manners, and work habits. To do so, he would use local primary schools. He wanted
to be sure that the bishopric was sufficiently populated and that people lived
healthy lives; this was why he sought demographic information. Once the
people were healthy, he would ensure that they had stable family structures
based on strong Catholic marriages. With all this in place, the people needed
to live together in orderly towns. They could then promote the infrastruc-
tural improvements—such as roads and irrigation ditches—that they needed
to develop for agricultural and commercial growth. Mining was also an important economic factor, but the Bishop was concerned about indigenous
laborers being harshly exploited—both underground in silver pits and
aboveground on haciendas and in obrajes. In addition to wanting to improve
the social and economic well-being of his diocesans, Martínez Compañón's
questionnaire demonstrates that he also sought to learn about "the arts, society,

and culture of the Indians of Peru."[42] He inquired about their knowledge of materia medica, or botanical medicines, balsams, and any antidotes they might use against the bites of poisonous animals. He wanted to know about their antiquities and whether they had abandoned their idolatrous practices. Once it was received and compiled, this information would help him to construct his living utopia in Trujillo. He could also employ it as evidence in his ongoing campaign to demonstrate the Indians' intellectual capacity.

Had the responses to these questionnaires survived in municipal or state archives, they would have formed an unbelievably fecund source for scholarship on local life in northern Peru in the late colonial period. Unfortunately, years of research in Peru, Colombia, and Spain produced almost no evidence of responses. But this does not mean that they were never written; Viceroy Croix's report on his term in office clearly describes how Martínez Compañón gave him "an exact and prolific document with reports of priests, subdelegates, and Indian officials . . . everything with the corresponding documentation." Convinced that the reform agenda that they meant to support was "of utmost importance," Croix shared the reports with the Ministerio Fiscal in Lima. By June 1786, the viceroy had seen that the files were sent to Fernando Saavedra, the intendant of Trujillo. From there, they disappeared from the archival record.[43]

The *Visita*

After such an effort preparing the questionnaire, organizing his team, and packing for what was sure to be a lengthy expedition, Martínez Compañón finally set out on the cool, clear Southern Hemisphere winter morning of June 21, 1782. That day, he began designing and implementing his utopian agenda for Trujillo. The *visita* would allow him a bird's-eye view of his territory. He would meet local authority figures and personally assess the challenges faced by provinces and municipalities. He would learn about the region's natural resources and come to understand its best chances for improvement. Perhaps most important, he could spread news of his utopian vision, gathering support for his plans and inspiring local communities to begin the challenging but rewarding process of reforming their own futures. First he traveled north from Trujillo along the Camino Real through the pale sands and crescent-shaped dunes of the Sechura Desert and into the sunny, verdant Chicama Valley. After a brief stop at the seaside town of Chicama, he headed up into the

Cajamarca sierra, where he visited several small towns, including Contumazá, Trinidad, and Gusmango, which he reached on June 25. He continued northeast through the sierra to Celendín, a sparsely populated area where
Indians lived scattered on distant haciendas. Here he conducted a thorough
inspection of the local clergy, cautioning priests to carefully record names,
dates, and the socioeconomic status of townspeople who presented themselves
for baptism, marriage, and other sacraments.[44] He commissioned a map of the
pre-Hispanic Moche irrigation canals that bifurcated the local landscape.[45]
Here he also made his first attempt at founding a new town—something that
the local hacienda workers requested he assist them with. As the next chapter
shows, his efforts to establish Amalia de Celendín were successful—a 1794
letter from the local priest revealed that there were already two hundred
houses built there, and in 1802, the Crown officially bestowed upon Celendín
the title of *villa*, meaning that it was now an official Spanish settlement, with
a population of two thousand to four thousand inhabitants.[46]

From Celendín, the Bishop and his sorrel mare, along with Echevarri
and the rest of the party, headed down the sierra toward the Marañón Valley
and the Amazonian province of Moyobamba. Although it was the largest of
the ecclesiastical provinces of Trujillo, it had only one significant town—also
named Moyobamba. The *Trujillo* watercolors include a map that shows the
province to be "in the mountains," sparsely settled except for along the Moyobamba, Negro, and Tonchima Rivers. It stood surrounded by jungle forests
and was an arduous eight-day mule journey from the nearest population
center. This Amazonian lowland terrain was the most difficult to travel of the
bishopric, with frighteningly precipitous roads and rivers that swelled past
their banks during the rainy season, making the entire region impassable.
The thick jungle vegetation teemed with dangerous animals, many of which
are depicted in the *Trujillo del Perú* volumes, such as the ferocious mountain
lion, red and black *tapa machacuai* rattlesnakes, and deadly scorpions. Here
in the middle of the wilderness, the Bishop founded another new town,
Santo Toribio de la Nueva Rioja, named after the great defender of the Indians he eventually had recognized as the patron saint of Trujillo.[47]

By September, after almost three months on the road, the team headed
back west toward Chachapoyas province. Strategically located between jungle and sierra, its main city (also Chachapoyas) was the vital commercial and
transport link between these two regions. The Bishop planned to found a
primary school there. In their free moments, he and his team spent several
afternoons observing the embroidery and sewing work of local women, famed

throughout the bishopric. Next, the party headed along the coast to Paita, and then to the city of Piura. They stayed there for several months, using it as a home base from which to make shorter trips, including one to San Miguel de Piura, one of the towns in which Martínez Compañón hoped (but was ultimately unable) to found a seminary of ecclesiastical workers. The people of Piura also requested their prelate's help to found new towns, so that they could live more independently on lands owned by hacendados, enjoying regular access to priests, schools, and communal support. The story of what happened with two proposed towns in their province is retold in Chapter 3.

From there, the party traveled back down through the sierra, reaching the town of Sechura by late May of 1783. Here the Bishop ordered a new *reta-blo*, or decorative altar, built for the parish church. Quick stops in Monsefú and Reque were followed by a visit to the town of Saña, the burial place of Archbishop Santo Toribio. It might have been here that Martínez Compañón acquired what would be his parting gift to the Trujillo cathedral seven years later: a holy relic of Toribio that he placed in a gold reliquary encrusted with nineteen pearls and forty-four diamonds.[48] The party's next stop was Lambayeque, the most important town in the region. The city map that they produced was extensive, illustrating the cathedral, four churches, and hospital within its city limits, as well as the extensive canal that rounded the city, separating it from the outlying agricultural fields. Here the Bishop tried to found another *seminario de operarios* and build an underground crypt like the one he had completed in Trujillo's cathedral.[49] In his free moments, he instructed his assistants to gather samples of local cascarilla (also known as *quina*, the bark that was the basis of malaria-combating quinine), and bought or acquired a locally manufactured black hat made of vicuña wool, which he later added to the crates of his collection of the manufactured goods of Trujillo.[50]

Finally, the *visita* brought the team back into the Andes, south of Lambayeque. On October 23, 1783, they arrived at the Hualgayoc silver mines, situated outside Cajamarca at over 13,000 feet above sea level. They went there with a purpose: the local miners' guild had requested the Bishop's help to improve their economic situation. After meeting with them, he developed a proposal to found a new town called Los Dos Carlos, which would provide volunteer workers with free land and the implements to work it. As Chapter 5 will demonstrate, this became an idealistic microcosm of his broader vision of improvement for his bishopric.

After quick stops at the *doctrinas* of San Pablo and Contumazá, the Bishop headed to the villa of Cajamarca, the site of the fateful first meeting between

Pizarro and the Inca Atahualpa in 1532. Cajamarca was the second most important city in the bishopric, home to the miners and merchants who had made their fortunes at the Hualgayoc Mountain. One of these was Miguel Espinach, who owned mines and a hacienda and served as a colonel in the local militia. Espinach would later work with the Bishop on the Hualgayoc mining reforms, ingeniously portraying himself as a vital collaborator while simultaneously managing to privilege his own interest over that of the local community. It was also here that the Bishop forged a close relationship with Indian cacique Don Patricio Astopilco, who petitioned for assistance in founding local schools for natives and donated some of his ancestral land for the projects. In the surrounding areas of Cajamarca province, Martínez Compañón gave the sacrament of confirmation to 40,398 people—a significant portion of the total 162,600 souls he confirmed throughout the entire journey.

As his *visita* drew to a close, the Bishop began to realize that for much of it, he had been beset by seemingly constant illness: headaches, fevers, and failing eyes were among his most frequent complaints. He admitted that "every day I feel more and more the effects of my pilgrimage; sometimes my limbs hurt so much that I want to stop the suffering."[51] But before he could return to the Bishop's palace in Trujillo, he made a final stop in the beachside town of Santiago de Cao, where compiled the results of his *visita* into one single document, the "Edicts of the Visitation to Santiago de Cao." These 120 points constitute the agendas of the entire *visita*, summarizing the time when, as the Bishop put it, he "hardly stopped running around like a crazy man day and night." He had spent two years, eight months, and seven days of his life at this endeavor, mobilizing local resources to gather the useful information that he needed to fashion a veritable utopia in his faraway corner of the great empire of Spain in the distant Kingdom of Peru.[52]

CHAPTER 3

Imagining Towns in Trujillo

Three miles outside the city of Trujillo lies what Martínez Compañón called "the ruins of a town of the Chimú kings," a UNESCO world heritage site today known as Chan Chan. The Chimú people who built it predominated on Peru's north coast from the tenth century until the arrival of the Inca in the 1460s. At the height of their power, they controlled a vast territory stretching from Peru's border with Ecuador to the Chillón Valley, north of Lima. Chan Chan was in its day the largest city in all the Andes, with a population thought to have reached 40,000 at its height. By the late eighteenth century, the ruins were most notable for their crumbling *huacas*, or burial mounds, looming in the distance. Their dusty walls were scarred with holes that were the handiwork of the infamous grave robbers known as *huaqueros*. Pilfering precious metals, ceremonial costumes, and other artifacts from native burial sites was big business in colonial Peru: in the sixteenth century, one individual reportedly unearthed almost 300,000 castellanos' worth of gold and silver from just one *huaca*; in 1602, an enterprising group of men from Trujillo tried to divert the Moche River directly into the path of the pyramid at the Huaca del Sol so that water would cause it to cave in and expose the gold inside. But the most valuable find at Chan Chan was made in 1558–1559, when a down-on-his-luck townsman named Antonio Zarco unearthed treasures so brilliant that they set off a looting fever that eventually produced 700,000 castellanos worth of gold pieces and even more disagreement about who had rightful dominion over the wealth.[1]

Although these early missions were more focused on plunder than on archaeological investigation, more academically minded Europeans soon followed their avaricious predecessors to the pre-Hispanic ruins of the northern Andes. As early as 1631, Antonio de la Calancha investigated the nearby Moche sites of Huaca del Sol and Huaca de la Luna. By the eighteenth century, archaeological notations had become almost de rigueur in travelers' reports from northern Peru. Frenchman Charles Marie de La Condamine and Spanish bureaucrats Jorge Juan and Antonio Ulloa wrote about and mapped the Inca ruins at Hatun Cañar near Cuenca, Ecuador. Spanish botanists Hipólito Ruiz and José Pavón devoted portions of their Crown-sponsored botanical expedition to archaeological investigation. Their work was not anomalous: as the Spanish sought visual and material data that could be shared with experts throughout the Atlantic world, they increasingly came to value archaeological research as a method of understanding cultures that almost three hundred years after contact remained, for the most part, impenetrably foreign. Physical samples of pottery and tools, as well as maps of buildings and engineered changes to the environment were useful data that could be transported great distances and shared with the broader scientific community. Such research was part of a broader Spanish Bourbon fever for surveying ancient sites that began during Charles III's time in Naples (1735–1759), when scholars excavated the great ash-covered cities of Herculaneum and Pompeii. By 1777, the Crown was so intrigued by ancient sites that the Royal Cabinet of Curiosities in Madrid put out an official call for antiquities taken from pre-Hispanic tombs and ruins in America.[2]

Although the only written records of Martínez Compañón's participation in the archaeological craze of the Bourbon Spanish empire are the inventories of archaeological objects that he sent to Spain in 1788 and 1790, a detailed map of Chan Chan (see Plate 12) in volume 9 of his *Trujillo* watercolors indicates that he and his assistants spent a good deal of time at this important site, carefully demarcating the foundations of buildings and the location of tombs, as well as houses, piles of metal scraps, the walls that separated the complex from the desert around it, and even an underground tunnel that ran to the hills in the distance.[3]

Contemporary visitors to Chan Chan find a site that is quite similar to what late eighteenth-century archaeologists would have encountered. Hand-molded walls of golden *cascajo* (gravel and mud) adobe are shaped into sophisticated high-relief patterns where stylized pelicans, fish, and monkeys play alongside ocean waves. The air within the compound is fresh and cool despite the exterior temperature; the walls ingeniously channel the cooling sea breezes from the nearby Pacific Ocean. In many places, the contours have softened from the torrential rains that torment the region in years of heavy rainfall, wearing away the corners. But still visible are the fading outlines of the delicately spined spondylus shells carved into the wall by Indian craftsmen. The Chimú celebrated these shells as a demonstration of their imperial prowess—the spondylus were harvested in the distant north of their kingdom, in what is now Ecuador, and carried south to Peru.

At the height of Chan Chan's power, the interior of the city was dominated by the remnants of eleven structures that the Bishop later dubbed "palaces." Today scholars refer to them as *ciudadelas*, or citadels, because of the high walls that once surrounded their interior courts and a burial structure. Although up close, they look like little more than crumbling mud walls, these barriers originally stood over thirty feet high. The *ciudadelas* lay among thirty-five separate housing complexes for Chimú elites, interspersed with other structures called *barrios* that housed commoners, their workshops, and the crafts they produced. At one time, these storage areas must have held mountains of the characteristic gray-black or rosy pink Chimú ceramics, many of which were already removed or destroyed by looters by the time the Bishop and his team would have visited.[4] But they might have been able to salvage some specimens, such as the whistling pot that Martínez Compañón poignantly described in the collection inventory: "figure of a female Indian with her eyes, mouth, and nostrils gilded in gold; with a nun's habit and three openings, one at the neck below the chin, and two near the breasts. Painted pottery of pink-red and white. This piece, if it is blown [in] without water sounds like a sad and melancholy flute. If water is added, the little Indian begins to give her groan[ing sounds]. If after adding the correct proportion of water, so that the vase takes air, and it is tilted toward the side with the little Indian, the groan increases, like when the Indians cry in their greatest despair. If the vase is turned to the opposite side, so it catches its breath with force, it returns to release the flood of tears."[5]

This was just one piece of the Moche, Chimú, and Inca artifacts that made up the Bishop's extensive collection, which he scrupulously detailed in its accompanying inventory. He also had items such as the figure of "two little Indians in their little *totora* reed boat perched atop a fish, in black ceramic" and a drinking cup engraved with figures of long-legged egrets. He preserved several pots for the *aguardiente* liquor "that here the natives call Pisco"[6] and a black ceramic whistle "in the shape of an Indian, who has in each hand a monkey [held] above his head." Several small figures were anthropomorphic or fantastical, such as a monster with the body of a human and the head of a barn owl; and a pink pottery dog-headed figure that sat cross-legged and played the drum with human hands. The collection even included items that might have aroused suspicions of idolatry, such as the "figurine of an Indian crowned with a half moon fastened beneath his beard," which Martínez Compañón admitted "might be an idol." But, the Bishop explained, this statue showing classic attributes of Inca royalty could just as well be a "toy for children because it is not a vessel that would serve for drinking, or for anything else."[7]

To scholars who promoted the intellectual capabilities of indigenous Americans, such artifacts were tangible evidence of the sophistication of the pre-Hispanic peoples of the northern Peruvian coast. By displaying the former achievements of Trujillo's native peoples, Martínez Compañón hoped to convince the king, his ministers, and the viceregal authorities that with the proper improvement, the current inhabitants of his bishopric might be able to accomplish equally sophisticated tasks. Accordingly, the Bishop put out an official call for archaeological information in 1782 when he requested that parish priests inform him of "any structures from the time before the conquest," especially those that were "notable for their material, form, grandness, or any vestiges thereof." Any evidence he received in response would help him to counter the dismissive stance that many European thinkers assumed toward native peoples of the Americas.[8]

The information that his parish priests remitted helped determine which local archaeological sites were depicted in volume 9 of his *Trujillo* watercolors, which was devoted exclusively to ruins, ceramics, and other pre-Hispanic crafts. In addition to the plans for Chan Chan, these images feature a unique stratigraphic cutaway view of the *Huaca* Tantalluc in Cajamarca (see Plate 13), a site first written about by *corregidor* Miguel Feyjoo in 1764. The letters on the image indicate the various layers of soil, coal, ash, and rock hidden in the mountain, at the bottom of which lay a cavity holding "many pieces of diverse figures of gold, and some of copper." Another illustration portrayed Marcahuamachuco, a ceremonial site and burial ground built ca. AD 400–1000 atop an isolated plateau outside the city of Cajamarca. Equally fascinating were the large-scale pre-Hispanic engineering projects of the region, including the Chimú irrigation canals, which were almost destroyed by the time Martínez Compañón arrived in Trujillo but which are seen today as evidence of a "hydraulic and surveying expertise [that] points to a most advanced technological society." Other watercolors depicted Inca ruins: the remnants of a building outside Saña; and portions of the Inca highway between Saña and Jequetepeque. Volume 9 also contained eight images from burial sites throughout the bishopric. Taken as a whole, Martínez Compañón's archaeological research showed that the Indians' ancestors had maintained a complex cultural landscape with highly developed urban life, sophisticated burial traditions, and extensive manipulation of the environment.[9]

Though modern scholars praise the Bishop's work on the archaeological history of Trujillo, calling him "the founder of Peruvian archaeology" and agreeing that his documentation of the Chan Chan site remained unsurpassed until the 1970s Harvard Chan Chan–Moche Valley Project, some of his contemporaries did not share his appreciation for Peru's pre-Hispanic past. A 1791 commentator in the *Mercurio Peruano* dismissed the Indians of pre-Columbian Peru as obsessed with "delirious traditions" and "very ridiculous and degrading superstitions." Outside the Spanish Empire, the debasement was even worse: recall how Guillaume-Thomas de Raynal derisively referred to Inca building projects as "heaps of ruins" and insisted that, with the exceptions of Cuzco and Quito, the pre-Hispanic architecture of South America had never amounted to much. William Robertson went so far as to say that the Inca did not deserve to be considered a "civilized" nation. Cornelius de Pauw, Amédée Frezier, and Comte de Buffon all concurred.[10]

Such arguments about the inferiority of pre-Hispanic material culture mirrored broader European discourses about the inferiority of the American natural world. As we saw in Chapter 1 these claimed that its too-humid climate hindered the growth and diversity of animal species and even the Indians themselves, whose New World origins doomed them to remain weak, effeminate, and lazy. Recall how Spanish Americans and Spaniards residing in America—including Jesuits Francisco Clavijero, Juan Ignacio Molina, and Juan de Velasco—rose to their defense, writing lavish histories that praised the people and nature of Spanish America. These men also took care to defend pre-Hispanic architecture and material culture. Although they did so less directly, Martínez Compañón's maps and plans of archaeological sites, depictions of burials, and collections of pottery, textiles, and other pre-Hispanic objects served the same rhetorical purpose. Recording the Indians' facility with building, ornamentation, and craftsmanship was yet another way to defend them against European detractors. After all, Raynal had dismissed Peru's pre-Hispanic peoples by degrading their building sites as pathetic piles of crumbled structures. By demonstrating the complexity and artistry of Chimú builders and craftsmen, Martínez Compañón's archaeological investigations attempted to prove the opposite.

Like the rest of his natural history work, the Bishop's archaeological research celebrating pre-Hispanic Peru was tied to how he imagined his reform agenda for the Indians who lived all around him. Mapping Chan Chan, portraying intricate ceramics, and surveying the impressive Inca road system in northern Peru demonstrated that the Indians of Trujillo had once been a great society. If the people of Trujillo had been so highly civilized in the past, forging their place in the new utopia was a much more realistic task. With such illustrious achievements behind them, it would undoubtedly be easier for contemporary Trujillans to flourish within the dictates of eighteenth-century Spanish politics, culture, and religious tradition.

Like the generations of Spaniards who had come before him, Martínez Compañón believed that urban settlements were central to the Spanish mission of colonizing (or recolonizing, as it were) rural Spanish America. But in the Bishop's utopia, Spanish notions of colonization through urbanization would not simply be transplanted onto local communities. Instead, he would collaborate with the people to found new urban settlements that would address local needs, rely on community initiative, and promote the prosperity of the people they served. In this chapter, two case studies of town foundation projects—one successful and one failed—demonstrate how local people absorbed the dominant discourse of reform through urban settlement and sought to use it to promote their own well-being. Both studies demonstrate how the vision for Trujillo's utopia was hotly contested on all sides. Local communities, elites and bureaucrats, and Martínez Compañón himself all had their own convictions of what Trujillo's best possible future would look like. Understanding how they attempted to negotiate these visions and what factors determined their success or failure reveals broader trends about local reform initiatives in late eighteenth-century Spanish America.

Town Foundation in Colonial Spanish America

To anyone who cared to look, the ruins in Trujillo were striking proof of the complex urban society that the Chimú had developed on the north coast. Evidence of such urbanity should have been meaningful for the Spanish: throughout their history in Europe and overseas, they had successfully employed the urban settlement as the essential conqueror's tool. Drawing on the writings of Aristotle and Saint Augustine, they conceived of the city both as polis, a place that fostered civilization among individuals; and as a *civitas*, a Christian republic that promoted a mutual citizenship through public events, civic buildings, shared histories, and charitable foundations. Cities and towns were also sites of *policía*, where manners and refinement befitting proper Spanish vassals would flourish. The notion of the city as a civilizing entity was all the more important in the American wilderness, as urban settlements reminded the colonists of their superiority to and separation from the "uncivilized" natives who lurked outside the city limits.[11]

By the end of the sixteenth century, the Spanish so valued their formula for urban settlement that they ordered it officially transcribed and disseminated. The 1573 "Royal Ordinances for New Towns" carefully stipulated that each Spanish town in the New World was to be built in a healthy location with good elevation, fresh water, wood for building, and land for farming. Each settlement would center on a *plaza mayor* that was to be of a rectangular shape, "as this size is the best for celebrations in which horses are used." The main religious and civil structures, including the cathedral, the courthouse, and the *cabildo*, or municipal government building, were to be erected around the perimeter of the plaza. After finishing the center of the city, settlers were to attend to their agriculture and husbandry duties first, and then erect their own houses, taking "great care . . . to build them with good foundations and walls."[12]

The town ordinances were careful to note that the plaza was to be the perfect embodiment of Spanish order, law, and economic dominance in each city or town. For full dramatic effect, settlers were cautioned to refrain from interactions with the Indians until the city center was complete "and the houses built so that when the Indians see them they shall . . . understand that the Spaniards settle there for good . . . and fear them." Once the Indians were sufficiently intimidated by these cities in the wilderness, the real work of winning them over—or taking them by force—could begin. The settlers were instructed to "maintain friendship with . . . [the Indians] and . . . teach them to live in a civilized manner . . . [and] to know God." Should the natives prove to be less than willing converts, they had orders to attack their settlements but with the ironic caveat that they should not do the Indians "other hurt than what may be necessary for the defense of the settlers and so that the town should [not] be molested."[13]

Moral turpitude aside, this agenda for colonization proved to be a smashing success. Throughout America, the Spanish managed to build European-style cities and to accost, intimidate, or otherwise coerce the Indians into becoming the subservient class of manual laborers, servants, and artisans who would sustain their own designs at greatness. This strategy of colonization through urbanization was perfectly encapsulated in the settlements known as *reducciones*, where groups of Indians lived and worked under the paternalistic guidance of Spaniards who oversaw their social and religious development while teaching them the "proper" Spanish work ethic. Although the *reducciones* purported to have the Indians' best interests in mind, many were populated only after Indians were forcibly uprooted from their ancestral lands and marched to their new settlements, conveniently located near the mines, workshops, or farms where they would now work.[14]

Despite the economic and social "success" of the *reducciones*, even in the eighteenth century, many colonists still huddled in their great hacienda houses while vast swaths of wilderness pulsed all around them. In rural areas, plebeians had regular contact with a very limited segment of the Spanish population—mainly hacendados and their families. While such an equation was immensely profitable for the hacendados who rented land in return for labor, Spanish administrators and Catholic officials worried that hacendados neglected their duty to instruct the Indians in Spanish laws, morals, and customs.

In Trujillo, Martínez Compañón embraced the less insidious aspects of Spanish city building, planning to found new towns and relocate isolated households to more urbanized areas. Although he never advocated forcibly removing local people to towns or cities, he was certain that urban settlements could promote economic activity, social interaction, and Christian behavior, becoming sites that reproduced in miniature his broader utopian vision for Trujillo. Conveniently for him, this initiative dovetailed with a main concern of the Catholic Church in Peru. In 1772, the Lima Provincial Council had ruled that rural parishes should be redivided so that priests could more easily reach the faithful. Since parishes had to be tied to a population of adequate size living in rural areas, individual families had to be moved or new settlements erected. Once they were congregated together, the people would have churches with resident priests and the all-important access to confession, communion, and the sacraments that marked the Catholic life.[15]

Martínez Compañón knew that if he wanted to strengthen Trujillo's rural economy, he would have to request more priests and churches in these underserved areas. They would bring with them the creation of new towns where the people could assist and inspire one another. In this way, his secular reform work would complement the broader agenda of the Archdiocese of Lima and the Catholic Church in Spanish America. By appealing to religious goals, he could mobilize church resources—especially the influence that parish priests and their assistants had in rural areas—while simultaneously pursuing temporal reforms. He used the resources of his see to advance his conviction that urban settlements "would awaken and excite love of work among . . . townspeople . . . promote industry, [and] . . . facilitate the payment of . . . rent" because people would not have to travel such great distances in order to work. He was also sure that a town would offer people "a new social and civil life" with "more equity, humanity, and justice," so they would be less inclined toward disorderly behavior. Although he did not say it explicitly, he must have known that if the rural laborers were able to provide one another mutual assistance, their economic situations would undoubtedly improve. Through living in communities instead of isolated households, Trujillo's native and poor mestizo workers would be able to begin shaping their own communal utopias in the wilderness.[16]

With this in mind, the Bishop consulted his parishioners and began erecting new settlements throughout Trujillo, ultimately submitting plans for seventeen relocations of existing settlements and twenty new towns. All these had a religious component: each new town would feature a parish, or *doctrina*, that would be more accessible for people currently living in underpopulated areas served only by distant *añejo* churches. The Bishop stipulated that once they received official authorization from viceregal authorities, the settlements would establish the *cabildos* necessary for their governance. For their part, the people had to agree to build a local primary school, erect a new church building, and build separate sleeping quarters for the male and female children in their homes. Since the town foundations received no financial benefits from viceregal authorities, Martínez Compañón imagined that they would be funded by a combination of parish collections, contributions from native communities, and his own salary. For the land for the new towns, he relied on the largesse of local landlords. Unsurprisingly, securing land to use for the new towns would become one of the biggest challenges of his urban settlement projects.[17]

While most of the relocations of existing settlements happened in the Amazonian provinces of Moyobamba and Chachapoyas, the towns built from their foundations up were more often located in the bishopric's northernmost province of Piura. Nestled between the Pacific Ocean and the Andes Mountains, this district's rich soil was fed by the Chira, Piura, and Olmos Rivers. By Martínez Compañón's count, the area supported thirty-five agricultural haciendas and cattle estancias that generated almost 95 percent of provincial wealth. Although the peons who lived on these haciendas were not slaves, they typically survived as semi-destitute tenant farmers subject to the whims of their landlords, who paid them so stingily that they could barely eat after covering rent, taxes, and tribute.[18]

The hacendados were well aware that exploitation of renters supported their lavish lifestyles; accordingly, they sought to maintain them in feudal conditions. Often this meant that instead of building workers' houses in centralized locations, they preferred their workers to live "in great dispersion, scattered about the mountains and fields,"[19] where they would be less able to band together to demand fairer treatment. But for Martínez Compañón, bringing the impoverished and the underprivileged into urbanized settlements was the surest route to "civilize them, maintain their liberty, and help them with everything . . . so they become vassals useful to themselves, to commerce, to good order, and to the growth of the Royal Treasury."[20] His vision of little urban utopias was built on contemporary ideas of "civilization" through city building but featured invitation and collaboration rather than the coercion that characterized the mainstream Spanish tradition of building town settlements in the wilderness. By guiding local people to create better futures for their own communities, the Bishop refashioned the Spanish discourse of domination through urbanization, transforming it into an idealized vision of a better future.

Although these new and improved urban settlements were not always successful, they nonetheless highlight the entrenched social hierarchies and bureaucratic inefficiencies that plagued local reform agendas throughout late colonial Spanish America. The first case of the failed town at Las Playas demonstrates how when local elites made the correct alliances with viceregal bureaucrats, they could unite to preserve their own interests and destroy the vision of reform that the Bishop and the plebeians promoted. In contrast, the town at San Antonio was ultimately successful, but the story of how it came to be also highlights the importance of power networks and elite alliances. Here the implacable landlord who tried everything he could to stop the people of his hacienda from founding their own town ultimately failed in his campaign because he made the fatal error of working against local church officials. Despite these differences, both case studies highlight how the town settlements became a site of fiercely disputed visions of utopia. The local communities, area elites, viceregal administrators, and even the Bishop all had their own unique plan for how the new towns would contribute to the utopia in Trujillo.

In the end, these ideological conflicts were one of the biggest factors hindering the foundation of the new towns.

The Failed Town at Las Playas

One of the central tenets of Martínez Compañón's plans to create a living utopia in Trujillo was incorporating local ideas and initiative. In fact, all his agendas in founding towns, building schools, and improving the conditions of mine work began with initial requests from individual communities. The people who wanted to build new towns wrote to their bishop requesting his help to so that they too might enjoy the mutual support, social interaction, local government, and easier access to Catholic religious practice that came with a communal lifestyle. In a scenario that mirrors what would happen with the education and mining reforms, their initial petitions were followed by reports from local officials that confirmed the conditions they described and provided additional information on geography and demography. Martínez Compañón then intervened with local landowners and bureaucrats, attempting to gather the necessary permissions so that the people could make the new towns a reality. As is the case with so many reform efforts of the early modern period, a majority of the town projects ultimately failed. Yet a closer examination of how their fate was decided highlights the dissemination of reform rhetoric in late colonial Spanish America, showing how ideas of civilized urbanity that had their origin in European city building were disseminated to and embraced by rural populations in Spanish America. It also exemplifies the importance of power alliances in blocking or promoting projects. But most overwhelmingly, these stories recall that although planning for utopia sounds harmonious and romantic, local players of every social group were loath to cede power or influence to those they viewed as their opposition.

The story of the town at Las Playas incorporates these same divisive challenges. It began in May of 1783, when Martínez Compañón received a letter from Eusebio Palacios, Francisco Montero, Vicente Palacios, and thirteen other mestizos and *castas*. They all lived and worked on the lands of the hacienda Tambogrande, situated along the banks of the Piura River amid the thickest concentration of agricultural estates in the province of Piura. They began their request with a plaintive appeal to their spiritual leader: "neither we, nor our children, are able to achieve a way of living that is healthful for the spirit," they told him. Their letter explained how with the nearest priest and church located forty-five miles away, they were effectively unable to worship the saints, donate alms, receive the sacraments, or take communion on a regular basis. To make matters worse, their isolated position meant that they were unable to build a school or find "an old lady to cure our ailments, or even a barber for the repair of the accidents that need the quick attention of his instruments." They were certain that the only remedy for their situation was "to build . . . a town, and a church, with its own priest." They hoped that their bishop would help them secure the land that they needed, since hacendados owned all the surrounding territory—even the land that stood empty. The people guessed that the local landowners, who were notorious for having "little charity," would not look kindly on their request. So they turned to the Bishop to help smooth the way in founding a new town on the land known as Las Playas, a town that the Bishop later suggested they call "La Luisiana."[21]

The leading men of the local *cabildo de naturales,* or Indian town council, also composed a letter to Martínez Compañón, which he received on the same day. Tomás Gulachi, José Carmen, and Antonio Rentero shared the mestizos' vision of how the new town could improve their lives. They asked the Bishop, their "true father," to help build a church and secure land for their resettlement. The Indians described the hardships they faced worshiping in an empty chapel in the wilderness that was far from their homes. On fiesta days, when an itinerant priest arrived to give sacraments, many of their neighbors had to walk at least three and a half miles to find a place to spend the night. To rectify this situation, they, too, imagined founding a new town. It would be a veritable utopia where neighbors would be able to help one another in their labor, making it easier for the entire community to meet tribute duties. They believed that it would even promote peace among the races because aligning with mestizo and poor Spaniard neighbors "would provide . . . a great assistance and defense against the extortions of outsiders," while offering a good model of civic and Christian life. Like the mestizos and *castas* who would share their proposed town, the Indians promised to follow the Bishop's plans for their settlement by complying with the dictates he had laid out during his *visita,* including building their houses around the church and ensuring that all their houses had separate bedrooms for parents, male children, and female children. They hoped that making these promises would persuade the Bishop to assist them in building the town so that they could enjoy the benefit of their own parish priest, one who would "confess us, administer the sacraments when we are dying," and just "help us a bit . . . rescuing us from the cowardice that comes from a wild life."[22]

In June, José Luis Freyre Orbegoso, the senior priest of the area, wrote to the Bishop confirming the isolation that the petitioners had spoken of, clarifying that some had to travel over 165 miles to visit the nearest priest. He added that creating the new town was "absolutely necessary for the good order of the Indian parish, and to avoid the irreligiosity . . . and rebellion" in which these people had always lived.[23] The city council of Piura also supported the towns that the Bishop proposed to found in the area, telling him that the plan was, in their opinion, "one of the best, and most useful," and it would "fill this city with happiness."[24] The community clearly enjoyed the support of area religious and municipal government authorities, but that was not enough. They needed local landowners to give permission for them to move and to donate or sell the land on which they would build their towns.

Accordingly, Martínez Compañón assumed the leading role in the sensitive negotiations with the hacendados who held the rights to the workers and the land. He first approached the Castillo family, who owned the hacienda Tambo- grande, where the petitioners worked, and therefore held the rights to their labor. Without their permission, the people could not relocate to their new town. The Bishop tried to assuage their presumed fears of losing control of their labor force by explaining that living more closely together in towns would ac- tually encourage the people to work more, because they would observe their neighbors laboring all around them. "It would promote industry that they do not know today in a thousand ways," he promised. Most important, this mu- tual inspiration and communal support would make it easier for the people to pay the rents they owed to the family. He reasoned that a healthy and happy population would produce more and become the foundation of a stronger local economy.[25]

For their part, the Castillos—Silvestre, Diego, Miguel, and their sister Mariana—were not so readily convinced. They agreed that the renters who proposed to settle the new town were acting in "good faith," but they were concerned that "these people [were] motivated only by a spirit of novelty and restlessness" and, even worse, driven by "the firm belief . . . that they will come to be owners, and legitimate possessors of this, our said hacienda of Tambo- grande." Like landowners throughout the bishopric, the Castillos feared that sharing jurisdiction over workers or land could jeopardize their captive labor force. As they were already benefiting from current social and economic hier- archies, they had no interest in promoting any efforts that might endanger their positions of privilege.

Despite their reservations, the Castillos wrote that they agreed to the proposal of the Bishop and the workers. Perhaps they did so out of a sense of equity, or duty to their bishop and their church. They might have realized that their simple acquiescence in no way meant that the project would proceed unhampered by other factors. Whatever their reasoning, the family recognized that by building up four or six blocks of urban settlement around the chapel in the wilderness, the people could "create a very comfortable city" but one that would nevertheless be "subject to the following conditions." The Castillos mandated that the land and the houses that the people would build on it would ultimately be the property of the hacienda, not the people themselves. They stipulated that the inhabitants of the new town could not raise any type of cattle, and they could not make use of the hills and riverbanks surrounding the town for pasturing or cultivation; nor could they use any fallow fields on the property. The Castillos retained the right to dismiss any townsperson from the settlement at any time for any reason, and if the people abandoned their houses and town of their own accord, they had to sell their houses or buy them themselves—that way, the family's rent payments would not be interrupted.

In the end, such a complex series of caveats compromised what seems at first glance to be a magnanimous acceptance of the plan. In the Castillos' vision of the future town at Las Playas, the townspeople would not own the houses that they had built with their own hands. They would be forced to continue their work as paid laborers because they were prohibited from owning their own cattle or farming their own fields. If they should somehow displease the hacendados, they could be shut out from their new town at any moment, for any reason. If they ever decided to move, they would be compelled to pay for the houses that they had never actually owned in the first place. The Castillos' vision was certainly far from the plebeian utopia that Eusebio Palacios and the others had imagined in their first requests. In Martínez Compañón's mind, though, it was still preferable to the current situation and was thus worth further effort.[26]

Once he had secured permission for the workers to move, the Bishop needed rights to the land that these 689 people proposed to use so that they might come "to live in a civil and Christian way."[27] The unoccupied acreage that they had their eye on was part of the neighboring Tangarará hacienda, owned by the Marqués de Salinas, a bureaucrat in Lima. Likely assuming that Salinas would be loath to part with a portion of his territory, Martínez Compañón decided to go over his head and contact Viceroy Croix directly to determine "what is most appropriate in this matter." He explained how the people planned to build their houses with separate bedrooms and to set up "a good Church for the common use of all." But even more important, he pointed out, in the process they would be able to "establish and maintain good order."[28]

It was not until almost a year later that Martínez Compañón wrote directly to the landowner Salinas. After explaining what he and the people envisioned for the Las Playas lands, he obsequiously told him, "I never wished in any way that Your Illustriousness would experience the smallest harm."[29] The following month, the Bishop got his response from his viceroy. It was one that he might have anticipated but probably not the one he had been waiting for. "When [the files regarding the project] . . . are examined and surveyed by me with the attention they demand," Croix wrote, "I will command for each matter what it merits, and I will advise Your Illustriousness of the results."[30] It was a typically vague viceregal commitment to a promise of action at some undefined future junction.

In contrast to Croix's bureaucratic stonewalling, Salinas responded almost immediately, likely fearing what he could have seen as an attempted land grab. He began by telling the Bishop that Tangarará was actually owned by his son, who was conveniently away in Madrid. Though he claimed to find the Bishop's plan "most agreeable," he noted that he himself was ill suited to make any such decisions about the land because it was not his, and he had never been there himself. The only person who could determine the fate of the new town would be his son. Thus he was conveniently able to both appear agreeable and leave a valuable exit strategy for the family and his son, all the while keeping the status quo intact. It was the sort of ingenious calculation that helped powerbrokers hold on to what was theirs.[31]

Since it was impossible to secure permission from the Salinas family within any reasonable time frame, Martínez Compañón had no choice but to wait for Croix's response. All he heard from the capital was a resounding silence; so in December 1789, he tried another route: contacting Intendant Saavedra to see if there had been any progress on the matter. He implored Saavedra to use his "respect, constancy, and prudence" to overcome "whatever difficulties might oppose the execution of the project." He stressed that he hoped Saavedra would be able to convince the hacendados that they were mistaken in the notion that "the said foundations will come to be the ruin of their interests."[32]

Although the intendant's response took only four days, it must have been disappointing. After praising the aim of the projects, Saavedra told Martínez Compañón that his grand vision was likely to have little success. He noted that the problem with implementing the plans for the towns was the "bad climate" of the area (he did not specify whether he referred to the meteorological climate or the sociopolitical one) and the "little, or entire lack of desire [the Indians] have of fulfilling these offers," or meeting the strict conditions that the Castillos had laid out. He concluded with the pessimistic but insightful statement that "this kingdom, as Your Illustriousness knows, has the disgrace that no one does anything, except for his particular interest."[33]

This is the last that the record shows of the plan to found a town at Las Playas. Although the Bishop, the townspeople, and the local authorities tried their hardest to persuade both the hacendados and viceregal administrators to support their project, the town never came to be. A closer look reveals several structural problems that help explain its failure. First, the renters of Tambogrande proposed that all the work involved in the new houses, church, and land donation be done to benefit a relatively small group of only 689 people. The petitioners were also in somewhat of a quandary when it came to patronage for their new town. They knew that their bishop was their strongest advocate and that stressing their need for a church and a priest was most likely to capture his ideological and financial support. What they seem not to have known is that, despite his illustrious reputation, Martínez Compañón was limited in his ability to help them. A church official had little influence over the actions of landowners and civic officials, and he had only limited funds to donate—indeed, with all his town projects, any money Martínez Compañón contributed came directly from his own salary.[34]

Most important, what the people were asking for stood in direct opposition to the interests of the landed elites of the area. The latter group recognized this immediately: the Castillo family feared losing control of their labor force and their territory. They also realized that in a land of such vast distances, it would be exceedingly difficult to monitor whether townspeople stole cattle or misused land. Even worse, once gathered together in a town settlement, workers would be in ready contact with one another and therefore much more able to band together against them. So the hacendados laid out a series of "conditions" that appeared amenable to the town foundation but in reality twisted the contours of the project so much that it was almost unrecognizable. As for the Marqués de Salinas's missing son, if Viceroy Croix ever did bother to show him the files about the proposal (the record does not say), he most certainly would have wondered why he should give up his own family's land to be used by peons who were supposed to be laboring on the estate of the Castillos.

It turned out that, in many ways, Saavedra was right. Las Playas was just one of sixteen town foundation projects that failed. While it was never built, other towns that made it through the building stage and that began functioning eventually failed, as well. For instance, the new town of San Carlos, founded in the jungles of Chachapoyas in 1782, faced difficulty from the beginning. Just two years after its establishment, the indigenous mayor Bernardino Cuccha wrote to his bishop with his concerns. Despondent about how the project was unfolding, he claimed that the local Indians despised him because of his attempts to monitor their behavior and temper their drunkenness. He reported that instead of living permanently in San Carlos, the Indians would inhabit their new homes for only three or four months at a time because the land was sterile and they could not farm there. The Indians also told him that they could not attend Mass because their houses were too far away from the center of the town; they feared that if they abandoned them, vagrants would invade.[35] The desperate tone of his letter suggests that the plans for San Carlos may not have been entirely appropriate to local reality. The location offered no way to earn a living and was ultimately unattractive to those it had been intended for. Perhaps this was an alternate strategy of an intractable landlord: instead of complex deferral and evasion, one could simply offer land that was unsuitable for permanent habitation. All these techniques contained the benefits of seeming to comply with the magnanimous intentions of the Bishop while effectively blocking any change.

The Successful Town at San Antonio

Although a disappointing outcome of failure seems to have been the rule for most of the attempted town foundations, Trujillo has several exceptions where new towns did develop and even flourish. When the renters of the hacienda Chipillico, which stood along the Chira River, slightly northwest of Tambogrande, approached Martínez Compañón in spring 1783 with a request to build a town called San Antonio, they might reasonably have assumed that, like most others, their query was futile. Familiarity with their landlord, the unpredictable and vengeful Vicente Fernández Otero, may have given them the greatest pause: they might very well have guessed how he would fight their project to the end in an epic episode of accusation, intimidation, and brutality. Yet the outcome of his battle demonstrates that he chose poorly when orchestrating his efforts; by challenging local religious figures, he turned Martínez Compañón against him and ultimately doomed his cause.

Fernández Otero was a notorious troublemaker whose hotheaded behavior makes him one of the more memorable figures in late eighteenth-century Trujillo. Surely, his reputation preceded him in the case of the town foundation at San Antonio; yet Don Miguel Sarmiento, Juan Manuel Rodríguez, Antonio de García, and the other Spaniards, mestizos, and *pardos* of the hacienda Chipillico believed enough in the advantages that a town would bring that they thought it worthwhile to try to form a new settlement outside his control. They explained to Martínez Compañón how their community suffered from "the fatal effects of savage life." Most detrimental were "the isolation of the people, the sickness of its airs, the lack of food," and the general "lack of comforts." They noted that the community had many times mourned the death of a member without the proper administration of last rites because priests rarely visited. Furthermore, in such a rural setting, they wrote, "we do not have the teachers who would discipline us, or our children" in primary schools. For these reasons, they requested to be able to build their houses (with the proper separate bedrooms for boys and girls) in a centralized settlement with a church. There was just one problem: their landlord, Don Vicente Fernández Otero, already owned the only available land.[36]

Although Sarmiento hoped that some "justice and Christianity" in Fernández Otero would prompt him to approve their proposal, they quickly learned that he would do no such thing. Instead, Fernández Otero immediately seized on the myriad of "pernicious consequences" that the proposed town of San Antonio would effect. Incensed by the mere proposition, he quickly penned a letter to his bishop. This set off a flurry of heated correspondence between Piura, Trujillo, and Lima, engendering a highly controversial episode with an unexpected ending. The letter revealed in great detail how Fernández Otero was concerned with losing control over both his land and its resources. First, although the land that the people proposed to use was fertile and easily irrigated, the hacendado deemed it entirely unsuitable for the project, pointing out that the new town would deprive him of this excellent land—even if he had no need for it previously. He also thought that the new town's livestock would decimate the pastures that he needed for his cattle. Furthermore, the proposed site was much too near his sugarcane fields, from which he worried that "many boys and servants, because they were young and troublesome," would inevitably pilfer. Like the Castillos, he feared the loss of rents if the people of San Antonio suddenly decided to move away and abandon their houses. He simply could not be persuaded to altruistically give up a tiny piece of his territory for the good of those who worked for him. As a final deathblow to the proposal, he maintained that the people's signatures on the original letter of request had been "forged." He explained that "the priest's assistant . . . forced . . . [the people] to sign, without explaining the context of the request" or telling them that the proposal would basically create a "den of thieves" where they would have an even more difficult time obtaining the religious guidance and civil services. In his mind, this invalidated the entire project, which he hoped would simply be called off.[37]

Meanwhile, in Piura, priest Freyre Orbegoso caught word of the accusations against his assistant. Hoping to reason with the hacendado, Freyre Orbegoso journeyed to his house to persuade him to retract his condemnation. After two such visits, it became apparent that the priest's entreaties were falling on deaf ears, and Fernández Otero instead raised the stakes even higher. He enlisted his brother-in-law, Don Baltasar Ruiz, to knock on the doors of the renters who had signed the original petition. When they failed to respond to his initial threats, he barged uninvited into their houses, demanding the retraction of their signatures under threat of raised rents or total expulsion from the hacienda. While Ruiz was busy being the strongman, Fernández Otero devoted himself to composing a threatening letter to Apolinario Herrera, the priest's assistant whom he had accused of inventing the petition. This letter stonily warned him that establishing the town would be "very difficult" and that "only divine piety can make happen what Your Illustriousness wishes."[38]

Apparently, Ruiz's invasions of the renters' households were effective because soon thereafter, a second letter from the Chipillico tenants arrived on Martínez Compañón's desk. He must have been shocked to learn that they were reversing their request for his assistance. Their letter stated: "it has come to our notice that a document in our name asking the permission to form a town" had been submitted. They had not willingly affixed their names to such a document, the people now claimed. Instead, the priest's assistant Herrera had made them sign it, without explaining the various ways the new town would actually hurt them. The retraction letter reasoned that if they relocated to San Antonio, their cattle would be lost when they inevitably mixed with those of their owner, or the herd would eat all the available grass on the hacienda. They also worried that if they relocated, their new settlement would be vulnerable should they ever have to leave it behind in the hands of only women and children. They ended their letter by confirming their belief that "there is no place for the attempted town on the Chipillico hacienda." Fernández Otero's fear campaign had been so effective that the people had given up on the dream of their own town.[39]

But Herrera, the young priest's assistant at the center of the controversy, was not so easily swayed. Angered by the accusations against him and confident that he had acted in good faith, he sought to clear his name by writing to his superior, Freyre Orbegoso. He concluded that the people of Chipillico had been so frightened by Baltasar Ruiz's threats that they "told me it would be impossible to build the chapel and houses" that they had wanted.[40] A few weeks later, he sent another letter to Martínez Compañón, in which he insisted it was simply untrue that "the renters had presented the [original] request against their will." He had carefully explained the benefits of the new settlement to the people, he claimed. The forgery accusation had been concocted by the angry hacendado, who "only seems to want a priest who . . . tears apart his sheep, without trying to protect [them] or remedy [the situation]." He insisted that Fernández Otero had forced the people to write the retraction against their will.[41]

By this point, Martínez Compañón had had enough. Not only had Fernández Otero thwarted the town foundation project; he had sullied the name of local ecclesiastics in the process, going so far as to claim that they had intimidated and blackmailed their parishioners in the name of the Bishop's reform agenda. Although Martínez Compañón risked negative attention for his pet project of founding towns in Piura, his anger at Fernández Otero's slander compelled him to inform Viceroy Croix of what was happening on the Chipillico hacienda. He forwarded a copy of the file from Piura on September 22, 1783. The matter then dropped out of the documentary record until June 1785, when Pedro Castillo, the alcalde of Chipillico, wrote a mild letter to Fernández Otero, imploring him to "carry out . . . the excellent ideas that inspire the venerable prelate" by allowing the town foundation to proceed.[42] His meek plea did little to impress the hacendado, who responded with a letter detailing the negative results of two similar such experiments. Fernández Otero explained how the *dueño* of the nearby Pacaipampa hacienda had lost his property when he was unable to defend it from robberies and attacks after all his renters had moved away. An even worse case was in the recently founded town of Corocotillo. There, "they do not obey the rules of justice," Fernández Otero claimed; angry settlers once almost killed the Piura alcalde. The town was notorious for "robberies, stabbings, deaths, murders, and public whippings," and cattle stealing was endemic. Neither the priest's assistant nor the assistant *corregidor* had any control over what was going on, and "the provincial mayor cannot do anything, either," because he did not want to risk losing his own life. Fernández Otero tried his best to make it seem as though the town foundation projects were breeding the opposite of civility. He clearly believed—or tried to make others believe—that if the local plebeians were extended more autonomy and independence, they would devolve into a mess of lawless infidels, threatening stability and good order. What he depicted was the opposite of utopia. Instead of evoking the rhetoric of reform, he threateningly envisioned the new town as a dystopia.

Despite such outrageous claims, something must have made the hacendado reconsider his position because later on in the letter, Fernández Otero conceded that the subintendant and the intendant were ultimately the "bosses of my will" and that he would leave it up to them to decide whether "the town is established, or not." But if it was, he asserted, each person who lived there would be obligated to pay him two pesos a year as rent for their use of the land for houses, pastures for cattle, and fields for farming. He also wanted to ensure that he and his relatives would be able to maintain their residency in the hacienda houses "because these are our own houses that we live in with our own families and servants." Although it is impossible to know what exactly persuaded Fernández Otero to change his mind and allow the settlement, the concluding paragraph of his letter offers a clue. It appears that once the civil authorities were involved on behalf of the Bishop, he had no choice but to accept the seriousness of what he had done. Summarily making enemies of the local clergy, the Bishop, and viceregal bureaucrats would severely hamper his future business and social dealings. Therefore, he sought to make amends as well as he knew how. "To obtain the blessing of His Majesty," he promised, "I am ready to give 4,000 pesos to his royal treasury . . . for the holy will of your Illustriousness."[43] Although this offer was generous, it could not completely disguise the fact that the terms he proposed delineated a new "town" that seemed little different from the current living situation. The people would still pay "rent" for land, houses, and agricultural pursuits.

Even under these strict conditions, the hacendado had given in. His own missteps with the priest's assistant had cast him as the manipulative landlord. In response, Martínez Compañón muscled all available resources to see that the town foundation project could proceed. With the matter finally settled, the Bishop wrote a letter to Viceroy Croix the following December. He proudly told him that the new town that would sit on the lands of Fernández Otero's Chipillico hacienda would be home to 943 souls. Living together, the people would have an easier time attending church services, and they could build a school. They would enjoy the support of a community. Most important, they would feel a sense of belonging that would inspire them to work harder, ultimately producing more agricultural goods and raising more cattle. This would benefit everyone involved. Looking back on what had been a difficult episode, he concluded, "I think that Fernández Otero, and the other landlords, will receive . . . more benefit from the foundation of the said towns, than the renters themselves."[44] Throughout the travails in San Antonio, the Bishop had held fast to his belief that his utopian new town balanced the interests of all parties involved: it gave the local people a true stake in their homes and their land and afforded them the advantages of municipal government, a local church, and the mutual support of communal living. At the same time, he was confident that the hacendados would be pleased with the outcome because happier tenants with a vested interest in their own communities would inevitably work harder.

In the end, Fernández Otero's opposition was all for naught. Perhaps it even worked in favor of the renters, by garnering support for their cause from local clergy and bureaucrats. The renters moved to San Antonio, built their new houses, and their town thrived. Today it has reassumed the name of the hacienda from which it was originally wrested: it is called Chipillico. It is not the only lasting success of the town foundations in Trujillo. One report indicated that although Santo Toribio in Moyobamba had not yet received official decree from Lima, by April 1783, local Indians had already relocated to the site, built their church and most of their houses, and prepared their fields for agriculture. The same letter confirmed that the town of Santa Rosa in the jungle province of Chillaos was prospering. Although the town of San Carlos in Chachapoyas was struggling somewhat, the local Indians continued to express enthusiasm for the plan.[45]

Years later, when Martínez Compañón prepared for his departure from Trujillo by compiling statistics on his accomplishments, he listed twenty new towns that were still in existence or in various phases of development. Of those, scholars have archival evidence that at least three survived until the present day. One is El Príncipe, carved out from the lands of the Castillo family haciendas, which was run by an Indian town council until 1823. Today El Príncipe is called Sullana. A second town founded on the hacienda Tambogrande lands also survived; like Chipillico, it is named for the original hacienda. Finally, Amalia de Celendín, which was established in Piura in 1785, weathered the difficulties of foundation. It had the straight city blocks, main plaza, church, and cemetery that the Bishop envisioned for all his towns. A 1794 letter from the local priest informed Martínez Compañón that there were already two hundred houses built there. By 1802, Celendín received the title of *villa*. There, at least, Martínez Compañón had definitively accomplished his goal of "reducing to town life many thousands of men who lived a misanthropic life in the countryside." Celendín stood as a testament to the accomplishments of the Bishop and his diocesans, a place where they had created a laboratory of utopia in the hardscrabble sierra of northern Peru.[46]

Assessing the Town Foundations

Although San Antonio was successful while the town at Las Playas failed to progress, the examples share connections. In both cases, local groups requested assistance in founding new communities. In so doing, they built on a classic Spanish notion of colonization through city building. But their city building was not based on conquering and intimidation, as the early Spanish town foundations in America had been. The people of Trujillo sought to collaborate with their bishop and to apply their own effort and initiative to create their own local versions of utopia that would best meet the needs of their communities.

Close examination of the two cases demonstrates how both agendas were caught up in the highly complex colonial bureaucracy, with correspondence, documents, and permissions slowly making their way from the place of their inception to Trujillo, then Lima, and back. Both agendas were subjected to the time-tested bureaucratic technique of deferral. They were hampered by the institutional change from *corregidores* to intendants, which further clogged the bureaucratic channels when the local authority who had been engaged with the project was suddenly usurped by an outsider with scant familiarity with the local situation.

Finally, the stories of Las Playas and San Antonio evidence how elites could achieve their goals or unwittingly destroy them, based on which alliances they chose. The landowners of Las Playas—the Castillos and the Marqués de Salinas—relied on their strategic alliances in Lima and Madrid to help them in blocking the town. Perhaps even more important was that they did not choose to tamper with local ecclesiastics. When Fernández Otero slandered Apolinario Herrera and repeatedly refused to comply with Freyre Orbegoso's requests, he made an enemy of the Catholic Church in Piura. With the powerful

Bishop and intendant turned against him, he risked displeasing even the viceroy—the most powerful person in all Peru. He was therefore left with no choice but to support the town foundation—and to donate money to Martínez Compañón for good measure.

The reticence of the landlords to affect what Martínez Compañón was convinced were highly advantageous improvements highlights the divergent visions of utopia that plagued the project. The Indians, mestizos, and poor Spanish who requested the Bishop's assistance in the first place imagined that these new towns would give them autonomy in their daily lives, offering places where they might go home to their own houses that they had built with their own hands. They hoped that the settlements would foster social networks of mutual assistance and camaraderie. Even more important, they saw the towns as places where they could assume their rightful status as vassals of the Spanish king, places where they would be entitled to access municipal officials, houses of worship, and educational opportunities. Martínez Compañón's vision was similar in how he promoted mutual aid, religious community, and autonomous households, but he, too, brought his own agenda to the project. In addition to the original petitions for assistance, he insisted that the townspeople conform to religious dictates by living near the church and attending regularly, as well as providing for seminaries of religious workers. He requested that they support primary schools at both the local and provincial level. And he demanded that the people manage their households according to European cultural norms—above all, by ensuring that male and female children did not share a bedroom. Inevitably, these additions stretched already-scarce finances, as well as any available time that the people had to build their houses, schools, churches, or new bedrooms.

While the people's and the Bishop's idea of utopia may have been close enough to be reconcilable, deep-rooted difficulties arose when it became apparent that the most powerful figures in the equation—the hacendados who owned the land and the labor of the workers—had an entirely separate vision. Seeking to preserve their increasingly perilous positions in the northern Peruvian economy, they fretted that plebeians granted any new freedoms would soon be knocking at their doors requesting more. The Castillos, the Marqués de Salinas, and Fernández Otero all feared that workers allowed autonomy in their living situations would become more intractable in the fields; abandoning their duties, failing to pay their rents, or even going so far as to assault authority figures. At the same time, the elites were even more concerned that allowing their workers to live independently might give their subordinates a strong case to argue that they held more than the usufruct property rights that they had been given. Such a scenario could easily endanger family dynasties built upon possessing valuable agricultural terrain.

While the utopian new towns were therefore a vision of a future contested from three sides, they also evince at least one aspect of development that all parties seemed to agree upon. The plebeians, Martínez Compañón, and the hacendados were all keenly aware of the power of urban settlements. They all recognized how cities and towns had helped the Spanish to conquer and control immense portions of the Western Hemisphere. They knew how cities had become sites of Spanish cultural reproduction, of religious cohesion, of commerce and industry, and of general civility. The cases of Las Playas and San Antonio demonstrate how the people believed in the power of city life and town settlements. They were willing to conform to the modified Spanish lifestyle dictates that Martínez Compañón insisted on because they saw how cities and towns were the key to fashioning their own spaces in the fast-approaching society of the future.

CHAPTER 4

Improvement Through Education

Once the Bishop and his team had departed the city of Trujillo to begin their *visita* in June 1782, they began working on the hundreds of watercolor images that would later be compiled into the nine volumes called *Trujillo del Perú*. These illustrations recalled the many places that they had visited, intricately portraying the natural and human environments of northern Peru in the eighteenth century. Over the almost three years of travel, they had observed creatures great and small—from the rotund *quinde* hummingbird alighting on a bush with red flowers to a delicate seahorse and spiny sea urchins. The images they created included a *gato montés*, or mountain lion, a fearsome cat with treacherous claws, snarling fangs, and evil red eyes. They had seen people of all types, from Spaniards in military regalia mounted on muscled white horses to African slaves laboring in the fields. Taken together, the hundreds of hand-drawn and painted illustrations presented Trujillo as a veritable utopia with a wondrous multitude of animals, plants, landscapes, and people, each of which served a unique purpose.

Although the illustrations offered an encyclopedic view of Trujillo, they also portrayed how Martínez Compañón himself envisioned the utopia that he was building there. Like other social reformers from the late eighteenth century, the Bishop believed that people were the foundation of improvement. Accordingly, the images show them hard at work, building the utopia of their future. They occupy themselves shoeing cattle, cultivating fields, and fishing in coastal waters. They shear sheep, card wool, dye it, and spin thread. The "shepherdess Indian giving birth" (see Plate 14) is so dedicated to tending sheep and spinning yarn that when her labor starts, she squats in the lush green fields and delivers her baby under the bright blue sky. By depicting Trujillo's Indians as ideal vassals, the watercolors demonstrated that, as Martínez Compañón had argued, the Indians were "men endowed with a rational soul like ours and that they live in the same environment in which we live, from which proceeds that they have the same natural dispositions of body and soul that we have."[1] The images in the nine volumes were yet another way Martínez Compañón defended the Indians from their detractors.

A striking example of this visual idealism is "Indians playing cards" (see Plate 2), which shows a native man and woman seated beneath a reed shelter. Though their lack of shoes and stockings marks them as humble, these Indians are wearing European-style dress—the man even has a long coat with buttons. Their cards are piled up between them, demonstrating that they, too, could amuse themselves like civilized Europeans, meeting at what scholars later would call "the great altar of sociability," with all its accompanying rituals of civility and decorum. Their pastime contributed to imperial economic growth: in the colonial period, the Spanish Crown held profitable monopolies on luxury items such as playing cards, tobacco, alcohol, and paper. The image carefully details the feathers that they are using to make their wagers. By betting with feathers instead of actual currency, the Indians are following the Bishop's utilitarian recommendation that they play cards with "imaginary coins" rather than risking their hard-earned cash. The artisan who witnessed this scene portrayed the two Indians as white-skinned and fair-haired, a visual trope repeated throughout the watercolors. Depicting Indians who "looked white" was an artistic method of implying that Trujillo's natives were so receptive to Martínez Compañón's reform efforts that their very bodies were becoming more and more Hispanic, their skin lighter and their hair more blond.[2]

Similarly, the watercolors depicting children were particularly striking evidence of the Bishop's assertion that through education, young Indians could become colonial subjects "more useful to God, to themselves, and to the state."[3] Instead of playing games, two Indian boys work in the fields with their fathers, learning to plow with a miniature implement attached to a pair of dogs. They were practicing the hard work and obedience that would make them into what they should be: diligent vassals who were "the true treasure of the state," as reformer José Campillo had put it in 1743.[4] To the Bishop and other reformers who were interested in early childhood education, their youth made them the ideal subjects for such formation. Like Vasco de Quiroga, the visionary bishop who had worked with Indian children in Mexico 250 years before him, Martínez Compañón believed that "in our early childhood we are like soft wax. . . . First impressions form images . . . so profound in our souls that they come to be the roots of our judgments and operations in the entire course of our lives."[5]

His agenda for reforming Trujillo would build on the notion of childhood as a foundation for future success, by creating schools for all children of the bishopric, including Indians. The Bishop's utopia featured a detailed plan for two Indian colleges in Trujillo that would cultivate a privileged class of indigenous community leaders. His reform agenda imagined that communities would assume leadership in their own town primary schools that would educate children throughout the bishopric.

In both these initiatives, Martínez Compañón pushed the boundaries of contemporary reform culture by closely collaborating with local inhabitants, especially Indians. By involving the people in conceiving, planning, funding, and building the schools that would serve their communities, the Bishop ensured that they would be willing participants in learning Spanish-style reading and writing. At the same time, they would practice Spanish social mores, work ethics, and spending habits, providing the colony with an economic boost that matched their social improvement. Native schools would also benefit local elites and the Spanish Crown because hardworking natives inculcated into Spanish material culture and social life would purchase Spanish-made goods and help sustain a more peaceable environment where they could enjoy them. This venture to dot Trujillo's landscape with primary schools for the common people looks all the more innovative—radical, even—when examined within the context of what had taken place in Peru just a few months earlier. Imperial authorities had responded to the Túpac Amaru, Tomás Katari, and Túpac Katari rebellions—the most serious threats to their hegemony in the entire colonial period—with capital punishment, cultural censorship, and a fiercely renewed interest in putting Indians in their proper (subordinated) place.

Indian Policy After the Túpac Amaru Rebellion

On November 4, 1780—less than two years after Martínez Compañón's arrival in Trujillo—outside the southern Peruvian town of Tinta, an Indian cacique named José Gabriel Condorcanqui kidnapped the local *corregidor*, changing the course of Peruvian history. Claiming that Antonio de Arriaga had overcharged natives in business dealings, Condorcanqui held the bureaucrat and several of his aides prisoners for five days while he summoned Indian leaders to the nearby town of Tungasuca. Speaking before throngs of locals gathered in the plaza on November 10, he claimed that, as a descendant of Túpac Amaru, the last Inca leader executed by Viceroy Toledo in 1572, he was the rightful ruler of Peru. He assumed his ancestor's name, calling himself Túpac Amaru II. He boldly announced that the king had personally instructed him to abolish the *alcabala* sales tax, end the Potosí *mita* labor draft, and execute Antonio de Arriaga. Túpac Amaru II had Arriaga dressed in the shameful clothing of a penitent and hanged. The anxious townspeople gossiped about whether the rebel leader planned to find and murder six more *corregidores* and destroy the local textile mills where many Indians were forced to work under slave-like conditions.

No one could have foreseen that Túpac Amaru II's challenge to Spanish rule would quickly engender a large-scale rebellion that, by some estimates, included as many as 50,000 Indian, mestizo, and *casta* combatants at its height of popularity. After a series of successful offensives (including a bloody massacre of Spanish troops sheltered in a church for the night), the rebel army mounted an attack on Cuzco, the most important Spanish city in the Peruvian highlands. But after only two days of fighting, the rebels were outnumbered by royalist troops and they retreated. By mid-April, the Spanish regained the upper hand, capturing Túpac Amaru II and his closest advisers. On May 18, 1781, they were executed and dismembered in a gruesome ceremony in the center of Cuzco. Spanish *visitador* Antonio de Areche shipped various heads, arms, and legs throughout the viceroyalty in an attempt to "prevent the spread of various ideas that have been extended throughout the nation of Indians."[6]

The Cuzco uprising was frightening enough on its own, but the Spanish also faced unrest in the Chayanta region of Upper Peru (today Bolivia), where Tomás Katari had begun rebelling against the colonial government in mid-1777. After his capture and execution in January 1781, another rebel leader named Túpac Katari replaced him and sustained the movement until his death the following November. In Upper Peru, the rebels' rhetoric was harsher: they called for removing all nonindigenous peoples, including mestizos, from the Andes. When combined with the Túpac Amaru rebellion, these uprisings resulted in four years of direct challenge to Spanish hegemony—the most unequivocal menace that the Spanish faced in their American kingdoms prior to the wars for independence.[7]

Although debate continues as to whether the movements were protonationalist or racially motivated, scholars agree that the Indian rebels were unsatisfied with local governance, particularly the recent effects of the Bourbon reforms. The problems had begun when Spanish administrators revised tax rolls to include more Indians who had previously only paid tribute.

Simultaneously, the Spanish legalized the *reparto*, or forced sale of goods, to Indians. This meant that natives were often forced to pay double or triple fair-market price for items that they sometimes did not want or need, such as razors, eyeglasses, and silk stockings. *Alcabala* rates also went up, and essential items that were not taxed previously—such as coca leaves and hot *ají* peppers—were added to the list. But most onerous of all was the Potosí *mita*, the forced labor draft system that provided workers for the most notorious silver mine in South America. Amid so many causes for discontent, the rebel leaders successfully tapped in to the resulting political instability, social discord, and financial turmoil.[8]

Some scholars estimate that throughout the years of Indian rebellion, 100,000 people died in the conflicts. Afterward, Spanish authorities scrambled to recalibrate official policy toward Indians, whom they viewed as the unmistakable source of the revolts. Foremost on their minds was preventing another such episode. So they replaced the much hated *corregidores* with better-regulated intendants, Crown-appointed bureaucrats who were paid a higher salary and therefore theoretically less inclined toward corruption. The king outlawed the *reparto*, although in practice it was impossible to completely eliminate. The Crown then turned toward social reform, emphasizing the need to "Hispanicize" the Indians. Fearing that their native tongue helped foster conspiracy and cultural difference, Areche and other Spanish officials determined that Indians should be forced to dress, work, and behave more like Europeans, which would help to integrate them into the Spanish world. Areche insisted that Indians learn to speak Castilian (or improve their limited knowledge thereof). Four years of education in Spanish-language schools, he reasoned, should suffice for them "to speak fluently or at least . . . to explain themselves in Castilian." He also censored cultural expressions of native ancestry. While previously, Indians had been encouraged to mark their cultural distinction by incorporating items such as the *unco* tunic, the *yacolla* shawl, and the *maskapaycha* headdress into their costumes on ceremonial occasions, now the law prohibited the use of such "pagan clothes." Portraits of Inca royalty, a popular genre found in many Peruvian households, were also outlawed, as they might inspire loyalty to the former kings of Tawatinsuyo.[9]

Almost 700 miles to the north, in Trujillo, the situation was nowhere near as dire. Instead of organizing en masse and threatening Spanish rule, local Indians mounted several spontaneous small-scale uprisings against local officials between 1780 and 1800. The most well known happened in the cold sierra town of Otusco less than four months after Martínez Compañón had assumed his post. At midnight on September 10, 1780, Indians rose up against local officials, angry that the new census bid them to pay individual tribute. They threatened violence against the alcaldes who enforced it. As soon as he heard of the uprising, Martínez Compañón contacted the local priest, Bernabé Antonio Caballero, imploring him to resolve the dispute without military intervention. The Bishop recommended that he employ a convincing, paternal tone rather than the heavy-handedness with which Areche had responded to the Túpac Amaru rebellion. He encouraged the priest to reason with the angry Indians by explaining the role of taxation in government and likening the king's relationship with his subjects to that of a father and his children. He suggested that Caballero remind the Indians how the Spanish kings gave them benevolent guidance and that, in return, they were bidden to submit to his governance.[10] When compared with the extensive list of prohibitions and decrees that Areche had made in the wake of the Túpac Amaru rebellion, his negotiated solution seems both logical and pacific. He attempted to reason with the local Indians instead of dominate them. In this case, the milder solution proved effective. Ultimately, the rebellion dissipated, and the town of Otusco caused no more difficulties for the Bishop. Martínez Compañón had suggested that his priest respond to the Indians of Otusco on the terms that they themselves had laid out: as Spanish vassals whose customary rights had been violated. Although his tone was admittedly paternalistic, he still negotiated with the Indians, treating them as members of the same society.

Even though this episode had ended well, the Otusco rebellion must have been on Martínez Compañón's mind as he prepared to leave for his *visita* almost two years later. The Indians there had not followed through with any violent acts, but they had certainly made known their distaste for Spanish rule. In considering how to prevent another similar situation, the Bishop may have remembered Areche's insistence that Indians be forced to attend Spanish language schools to "free themselves from the hatred that they have conceived against the Spaniards."[11] Such notions were far from unusual at the time. King Charles had decreed in 1770 that all Indians should be taught to speak Spanish fluently so that they would be better able to participate in Spanish social, economic, and religious life. He decided that ecclesiastical officials should be responsible for encouraging Indians to use Castilian at church and in daily life. Eight years later, he declared that primary schools should be set up in Indian towns and that the salary of the teachers who would instruct the children in Spanish, reading, and writing be paid both from royal taxes and community savings. In 1782, he ordered principal towns throughout Spanish America to build Indian schools and suggested that one way to pay a teacher's salary was for the community to cultivate a specific plot of communal land, or for Indians to contribute heads of cattle. He noted that parents should be persuaded to send their children to school "by the softest methods, without any coercion." He thought that bishops and archbishops were the ideal figures to oversee these efforts, likely because they could mobilize the priests who had the most interaction with Indian communities.[12]

Though these decrees promoting Indian education must have been partially motivated by the fear of rebellion spreading throughout America, the idea of formally educating Indians had enjoyed renewed interest since the beginning of the Bourbon era. In 1743, reformer José Campillo had argued that the "true treasure" of the Indies was no longer silver or tobacco but the men, or the indigenous plebeians of Spanish America. It was they who would rescue the fiscal future of the empire by farming the fields, manufacturing the cloth, and building the cities that were the vision of peninsular reformers. But none of this could happen, Campillo wrote, unless the Spanish were able to "reduce the Indians to civil life, to treat them with kindness and sweetness, to introduce them to industry, and in this way make of them useful vassals and Spaniards." In his view, this could be accomplished by tasking Indian caciques with teaching the Spanish language and customs. He also pointed out that priests could help the Indians by "raising them from laziness, drunkenness, and the other vices that limit their progress." Finally, Campillo thought that knowledgeable Indians or Spaniards should teach students about agriculture according to the "best rules and concepts that are followed in Europe."[13]

On the ground in America, reformers refashioned Campillo's agrarian classes into primary education for all children, including Indians. Some scholars estimate that in late eighteenth-century New Spain, there were more than a thousand primary schools in Indian towns, which served Indian, *casta*, and even white students. The majority of these were financed from community funds, and some were even staffed with native teachers. For his part, Martínez Compañón was confident that properly educated Indian children could be "the glory of their parents, their household, and their republic."[14] Building on the optimistic reform rhetoric of his contemporaries, he planned that Trujillo's primary schools and Indian colleges would be vehicles of improvement for Indian children. Inculcated in European lifestyles and work habits, they would return to their homes at night and share their learning with their parents, effecting change in the adults much more efficiently than heavy-handed administrators or ecclesiastics ever could. Educated, these children would be walking examples of the benefits of learning the Spanish language, under-standing catechism, and knowing the customs and manners of the Europe-ans. In the eyes of the rest of the world, they would be shining examples of the benevolence and diligence of the Spanish Crown and the Catholic Church. Some, he imagined, could even become distinguished community leaders who had access to some of the same trappings of noble status that elite Span-iards enjoyed. But in a post–Túpac Amaru world, where many Spaniards turned to suppression and domination to manage the Indians, Martínez Compa-ñón's vision could be viewed as frighteningly radical. Ultimately, Spanish administrators appear to have been less concerned with helping Indians ad-vance in society than with ensuring that they remained in their proper place in the social hierarchy. Again, the Bishop would find his utopian ideas con-tested.[15]

Colleges for Indians

As we shall see, although Martínez Compañón's vision of an educational uto-pia in Trujillo would prove to be too radical for popular tastes; he was not alone in envisioning the reforming potential of elementary education. Begin-ning in the second half of the eighteenth century, bureaucrats and adminis-trators throughout the empire stressed the importance of basic education for plebeian youth. This typically included basic literacy, math skills, and reli-gious instruction. In America, where so much of the population was indig-enous, royal and ecclesiastical officials ordered that Spanish language classes be added to the curriculum. The 1772 Lima Provincial Church Council, for instance, recommended establishing primary schools in local towns and sug-gested that these institutions teach Spanish to Indian children so that they would be "more easily and better taught in the subjects of religion and of the state and political government."[16] This was all the more important because in most of America, there was very little primary education in the late colonial period. The same was true in Trujillo: many of the few schools that did exist had not yet been repaired from the damage they sustained during the earth-quake of 1759, or they had remained closed since the expulsion of the Jesuits in 1767. There were almost no opportunities for primary education that did not involve sending boys to expensive boarding schools in Lima.[17]

After his travels throughout his bishopric, Martínez Compañón reached the same conclusion as the leaders of the council on which he had served ten years earlier: the people, especially the Indians, needed schools. Educating young children was central to his utopia because properly taught youth would have their entire lifetime to behave like ideal vassals, and they would serve as role models for their parents, other community members, and their own children. From Piura in April 1783, he sent an impassioned plea on the matter to the parish priests of Trujillo. After gently describing the "unfortunate state" of the Indian communities that he had seen throughout his bishopric, he assessed their overall condition as one of "general ignorance and poverty, and lack of faith." However, instead of blaming this on innate Indian inferiority (as did so many of his contemporaries), Martínez Compañón insisted that these problems were due to the "lack of application and zeal for instruction, direction, and reform" in Indian towns. To remedy the wrongs of past generations of Spaniards secular and ecclesiastic, he suggested that "wherever possible," towns erect primary schools and hire teachers who would be supervised by parish priests. Additionally, he proposed the foundation of two Indian colleges in Trujillo: in one, boys would learn doctrine, basic literacy, and trade skills; in the other, Indian girls would be instructed in basic literacy and the "duties and skills appropriate to their sex and condition." Like reformers in Spain and the canons of the Lima cathedral, he was confident that this plan would prove that "well raised and taught, the Indians could become different men who would be more useful for God, for themselves, and for the state."[18] But in contrast to the dominant paradigm of imposing reform initiatives on reluctant natives, Martínez Compañón's plans to educate Indians relied on inviting them to participate and become fully vested participants in their own improvement.

The Bishop's letter was distributed to parishes via the royal mail. A few weeks later, Pedro José Buque, the priest of Ferreñafe, gathered together the Indians of his parish to share it. The indigenous mayors Domingo Trino and Benicio de la Cruz were present, as was Basilio Capitán, who acted as the *procurador*, or legal representative, of the Indian town council. Even the local *forasteros*—Indians who had arrived in Ferreñafe from other destinations, leaving behind their ancestral communities and land rights—were represented by Isidro Soto. The letter from the Bishop began with a serious tone: "Listen with attention to what I am about to say," he wrote. "It is a matter of great importance for your life in the next world and this one." He went on to detail how he believed that the Indians lived "hidden in part in the night of ignorance, and otherwise submerged in an abyss of poverty and misery," wherein only a very few "have understood what it truly means to be a man, and much less a

Christian, or a member of society." Nevertheless, the letter assured them that the Bishop believed in the possibilities of the Indians. He had traveled throughout their territory, and his experiences had proved to him that they were "as much men, as much Christians, as much members and parts of the state, as much married men, as much the heads of families, and even as much ministers of justice, and public persons," who were fully capable of fulfilling the obligations of their roles in civil society.

The letter moved on to discuss the men's roles as fathers. The most important of their obligations was to feed and dress their children, to teach them a useful skill or trade, to instruct them in Christian doctrine, and instill in them "the love of virtue." He reminded them that the best way to accomplish these goals was to set a good example for their children by "correcting them" and exhorting them to leave behind "superstition, prideful behavior . . . laziness, irreligiosity, drunkenness, sensuality, [and] prejudice." After "the most serious reflection," their Bishop had formulated an agenda that would help eliminate these roadblocks to their advancement. This entailed "two houses of education in the Capital of Trujillo, one for the Indian boys and one for the Indian girls of all the bishopric."

With the exception of the prestigious San Borja college in Cuzco, which educated Indian boys throughout the eighteenth century, Martínez Compañón's proposal for Indian colleges in Trujillo was unprecedented in the viceroyalty.[19] In Trujillo, the boys' school would be sponsored by the Spanish Crown and run by the bishopric. It would accommodate about 225 students from seven to nine years old who would be chosen via lottery from all the cities, villas, and towns of Trujillo. Once arrived in the city, they would learn Christian doctrine and "to read, write, and count to perfection." At the same time, they would be instructed in a skill or trade of their choosing. Several years later, Martínez Compañón elaborated on a list of preferred occupations: "mason, carpenter, sculptor, painter, musician . . . brass-worker, potter, chair-maker, mill grinder, bread-maker, barber, bleeder, surgeon, poultice-maker, tailor, shoemaker, butcher, driller, hatmaker, tanner, [and] dyer."[20] Every year, the students would be brought before a committee of local dignitaries and officials to face exams in religious doctrine, Spanish language, and agricultural skills. The boy who most excelled at this public display of learning would be rewarded with a mule or twenty-five pesos, which he could collect upon graduation. When it was time to return to his hometown, each student would be given "the instruments of his trade, and a little capital to make it possible that he could begin to practice it, or open a little store." The school would provide room, board, and anything the children would need during their stay. These details imply that Martínez Compañón hoped that the boys would leave the school as young men who could read, write, and count with ease, and that these skills would help them understand Catholic doctrine. He also planned for them to become proficient in a profitable skilled trade that would benefit not only their own families but also their communities at large by developing commercial networks and promoting local industry. It was a major step toward creating a self-sustaining utopia.

The letter went on to describe a similar girls' school in which 120 students would reside under the supervision of a mother superior who would be an "elderly, learned, and virtuous woman." A schoolmistress would instruct them in doctrine, writing, reading, and counting—just like their counterparts in the boys' school. However, instead of learning trades, the female students would learn to "weave, sew, embroider, and the other skills appropriate to their sex." Like the boys, they would come from communities throughout Trujillo, but they would arrive one year earlier, between six and eight years of age. Their annual exams, held inside the school, would focus on "the obligations and skills of a married woman, and a mother toward her husband and children and servants." The girl who dominated the exam would receive a prize of twenty-five pesos. When they returned to their homes at the age of sixteen, the girls would all bring with them a spinning wheel, sewing and weaving implements, and a dowry "of at least 25 pesos in silver," something that would enable them to marry well and become the foundations of strong families in their towns, promoting the morality and sociable behavior to properly complement the economic productivity of their male counterparts.

Martínez Compañón's letter revealed that he had already considered how communities would respond to such an extensive proposal. "I imagine that every one of you is saying to himself," he leveled, " 'what our prelate proposes is good, is well thought out, will be very useful. . . . But at the same time, we cannot but see that these two schools . . . would require a large endowment and foundation, and that it would be impossible to construct . . . sustain, or maintain them without great expenses and fees.' " Nevertheless, Martínez Compañón reassured them that "there is no reason to faint, or to be discouraged by this." He promised a thousand pesos a year of his own money toward the schools, and he hoped that each household could add an annual contribution of six reales—a moderate amount that roughly matched the daily earnings of a skilled worker at a Peruvian silver mine. Unless they were desperately poor, Trujillo's Indians should have been able to make this payment.[21]

While it was forward-thinking to promote Indian involvement in skilled trades and education for girls, these were not the most radical parts of Martínez Compañón's education agenda. In keeping with his conviction that "the Indians are equal, or very little different from the other men of their *calidad*, or quality,"[22] Martínez Compañón went so far as to venture that several of the most visible markers of social superiority be extended to the students who did the best at their annual exams. After they were married and had children, he proposed, these former students should be referred to with the honorary title *don* and the supplicatory second-person usage of *vos*—two of the most commonly encountered markers of social status in such a strictly hierarchical society.[23] He even suggested that after their death, the most deserving Indian students and their spouses be honored with privileged tomb locations closest to the presbyteries in their home churches, permanently signifying how their achievements in the temporal world brought them closer to God. He proposed flouting the imperial sumptuary laws that prohibited Indians from wearing the fine silk clothes that were reserved for noble Spanish men and women. In an age when viceregal authorities were concentrating on removing markers of "Indianness" through censorship and monitoring, a program like this, which took the opposite approach and invited certain Indians to become more Spanish, was particularly groundbreaking. Instead of enforcing visible markers of social difference, the Bishop planned to use cultural assimilation to encourage appropriate behavior.[24]

While Viceroy Areche and other Spaniards around him were busy orchestrating unprecedented attacks on Indian communities in the wake of their treasonous behavior, Martínez Compañón's notions of extending elite social status to deserving natives instead relied on promoting "inclination [toward] and love for the Spanish." He was confident that by offering such highly prized status symbols to a select group of educated Indians, he could bring "many great advantages to the management and good order of the towns." He believed that when other Indians observed their friends and neighbors being spoken to with deference and honorific titles and dressing like high-status Europeans, they, too, would want to "apply themselves to work" so that they could enjoy the same advantages. This would have the added benefit of growing the Spanish export sector in America because fabric and trim for upscale clothing had to be imported from the Peninsula. If these proposed status rewards were used and received in the way Martínez Compañón imagined, they would feed into the most important agendas of his utopia in Trujillo: improving the Indians *and* growing the imperial economy. This approach was remarkable because it mandated that the Indians become personally invested in the increasingly capitalistic economy, rather than proposing to increase profits by better managing the old methods of tribute and labor turns. It was a program based on incentive rather than extraction.

But such questions of rewards would have to wait. After Indian communities received the original proposal for the two Indian colleges in Trujillo, they had eight days to report to their parish priests with news of their support for or their opposition to the projects. The Bishop entreated the parish priests to remind their flocks that although the Indian colleges were the focal point of this fund-raising campaign, the money would be split three ways, also going toward town primary schools and the missionary seminaries that he planned to found in Piura and Cajamarca. He concluded his instructions by reminding the priests to ensure that if the Indians did agree, they did so unreservedly, with even wives giving their consent.

Judging from the Indians' responses that the parish priests forwarded to the Bishop, it seems that he had little cause for concern that they might reject the projects. The people of Cajabamba responded that they found themselves "submerged in retreat, terror, and without society . . . poor, naked, and needy." Yet they had been sufficiently swayed by the Bishop's rhetoric to admit that they found the Indian colleges "beneficial in every way to our nation, the king, the public, to ourselves, to our fathers, our families, and our towns." They could see how "if we come to achieve the establishment of these two schools . . . [our youth] will learn politics, urbanity, and the best method to work and grow."[25] Along with such ideological approval came promises for requested funding. The people of Monsefú and Etén wrote that they would reallocate *cofradía* money toward the schools. An official from Guancabamba reported that the people of his community would contribute to the colleges. Other Indians wrote through their local priests, agreeing that they could contribute six reales per person annually.[26] Overall, the response was so positive that in March 1785, Martínez Compañón carefully recorded that, of the communities he had so far contacted, "each, and every one . . . concurred about the said establishments, obligating themselves to contribute."[27]

The next step was one that had concerned Martínez Compañón since the inception of the project. He had to secure the necessary funding for the schools and was well aware that even if the Indian communities could afford the agreed-upon six reales per year per household, his education agenda would still need financial assistance. Their promised contributions reached an impressive 7,000 pesos a year. Yet even after Martínez Compañón doubled his proposed donation to 2,000, the schools would still need more. Approaching the financially strapped Spanish Crown to make up the difference was not an option. So the Bishop imagined a number of alternative methods of raising money, including renting out empty land, asking for donations during the Easter season, and imposing a tax on alcohol. These possibilities were more exacting and innovative than the usual stipulations that Indian schools be sponsored by indeterminate "community funds" or by donations from families.[28]

Regardless of whatever inventive fund-raising schemes he proposed, the Indian schools could not open without the appropriate royal license, which required another cycle of bureaucratic process. The Bishop composed the long letter explaining the colleges to the king, but the correspondence had to be remitted to Spain via the proper channel: Viceroy Croix himself. By October 30, 1785, the letters had reached the viceregal palace in Lima. In January 1786, Croix praised "the laudable and indefatigable zeal" with which Martínez Compañón "dedicated himself to everything that promotes the improvement . . . and benefit of these kingdoms." As to his decision on what to do with the proposed Indian colleges, he simply wrote: "I have decided to remit the file subject matter to the Lord Intendant Governor of this province."[29] He offered no explanation as to why he thought it unworthy of royal consideration. By February, the files had reached Saavedra—back in Trujillo, where they began. The following month, the intendant reached his decision: to pass the matter on to the care of his subdelegate, Juan de Guizla Larrea. Perhaps Guizla did not appreciate the project, because the documentation tells nothing more of what happened to the Indian colleges. There are no archival indications that the Indian colleges ever operated.

In retrospect, although there were many factors that might have impeded the schools' advancement—most notably, the lack of funding and Martínez Compañón's impending departure from Trujillo—there were also decided ideological roadblocks to the program. At first glance, the colleges seem to be the crowning achievements of the Indian utopia that the Bishop planned to build in Trujillo. Their graduates would be hardworking, upstanding citizens who understood and propagated Christian doctrine, Spanish language, and European customs—theoretically, the kind of young people who would make the Bishop and colonial administrators proud. Yet other Spaniards may not have felt so generous about building special schools to cultivate "Hispanicized" youth, especially in the tumultuous political climate of the 1780s. James Axtell has shown how support for similar Indian education efforts in colonial New England waned in the wake of conflict between the English and the natives. In Martínez Compañón's Peru, the earth-shattering Indian rebellions of the early decade were only a few years past, and with this in mind, perhaps Croix, Saavedra, and other bureaucrats were less inclined to support schools for the very social group that had caused them so much concern. Even more important, these Spanish officials may not have been the only constituents who found the Indian college proposals less than satisfying. It is possible that although their letters said otherwise, the Indians themselves saw little sense in paying to send their children away so that they could be further indoctrinated into the language, religion, and customs of the Spanish, potentially becoming cultural outsiders once they returned to their own communities. Perhaps they astutely realized that the Indian colleges were mostly part of Martínez Compañón's imagined utopia in Trujillo, not the one that they envisioned when they thought of their own future and that of their children and grandchildren.[30]

Town Primary Schools

With the Indian colleges, Martínez Compañón's best efforts to carefully lay out the plans, gather local support, amass funding, and solicit the necessary permissions seemed to go largely unacknowledged. Native communities and viceregal officials paid lip service to the agenda but ultimately proved unwilling to stand behind it, perhaps sensing that the colleges did not match their narrower vision of improvement. Yet somehow, these same communities offered an outpouring of support for local primary schools that they were informed about only in the most oblique terms. The instructions accompanying the pastoral letter detailing the colleges told the priests that "in the towns where it was possible," the Bishop hoped to build primary schools. Other than stipulating that parish priests should oversee them, he offered no specifics about what the schools would be like, who would attend them, or how they would be managed. It would be up to local communities to garner sufficient funding "to maintain a teacher of learning, virtue, and zeal." Just as with the Indian colleges, the people were then given eight days to consider whether they would support a primary school in their town. In the end, it seems that local primary schools were more easily incorporated into the utopias that the people of Trujillo wanted to build. Most obviously, while the Indian colleges would lie miles away in the distant provincial capital, primary schools in their own towns could be more easily monitored and directed to best suit local interests.

Most local communities, as Governor Gabriel Carillo and the Spanish officials of Etén put it, "recognized the great utility and advantages that having a schoolteacher in our town would bring."[31] They wrote effusive praise for the projects that were still undefined but that they found full of promise nevertheless. The members of the Chachapoyas *cabildo* responded that they "did not know how to thank the said Lord Bishop for the honors and rewards with which he favors this poor city." They were confident that a primary school for local girls and boys would, in a few years, rescue their community "from the backwardness in which it is today submerged." They promised that if the Bishop could help them secure land for the schoolhouse, they would be able to contribute one to two reales per month from each family.[32] The governor, alcaldes, and secretary of Morrope wrote on behalf of their constituents and "the community of natives" that the people recognized "the many advantages that would result to this town and to every one of its townspeople if they were to establish a school in which our children would be educated."[33] The Indian alcaldes of Santa Cruz thought that the schools would help their children learn "Christian doctrine, good manners, and the fundamentals of religion."[34] Eventually, 124 of their townspeople signed a letter in support of the school foundation. News of the schools even traveled on the ground—Don Pedro Llontop, the cacique of Chiclayo, reported that "our brothers"—the Indians of Lambayeque, Motupe, and Ferreñafe—had told him good things about the school foundations there. He therefore endorsed the plan to educate Indian girls and boys in a primary school where they would learn "the Holy fear of God," along with "reading, writing, and counting—with all care and perfection."[35] These overwhelmingly positive responses are striking evidence of just how engaged native and plebeian communities were with education as part of the eighteenth-century discourse of improvement.

In many cases, locals both native and Spanish were so enthusiastic about the possibility of building a primary school that they offered various strategies for funding even before learning how the schools would operate—a clear indication of their support for local educational efforts. They imagined agendas based on their own financial situations and their traditional methods of raising money. In the jungle town of Lamas, married Spaniards and mestizos would contribute four reales annually, while unmarried men would be responsible for just two. The Indians, meanwhile, turned to traditional collective strategies and offered to farm one field of wheat and one of corn that would be put toward the teacher's salary. While the natives of Ferreñafe were sufficiently wealthy to promise two reales "each person, without exception," their counterparts from Pacora could offer only to build a shed where classes might be held. Leftover *cofradía* funds were another source of financing—the Indians of Morrope figured that they could contribute a hundred pesos a year from these monies. The natives of San Pedro de Lloc offered two reales a year for each person but were careful to note that this would be possible only after they finished the necessary renovations to their local church.[36] Perhaps imagining a more thorough education for male students that would be more valuable, the people of Guancabamba promised to pay two reales a month for each child who learned to read in school and four for those who were practicing writing.[37]

Such a multitude of strategies for covering the costs of primary education suggests that local communities believed that their children and their towns would benefit from the schools. Perhaps they saw that, unlike the colleges that would remove their children from native culture and parental guidance, local primary schools would allow their children to remain within their familial and communal networks. Even while they were taught to practice the Catholic religion, speak in Spanish, and generally behave "like Spaniards" during the day, their parents would still oversee their behavior once they returned home from school. Parents also likely realized that it would be more difficult for untrustworthy teachers or administrators to exploit their offspring by forcing them to work on the school's behalf.

But once the people had agreed that they wanted to found schools in their communities, they needed to locate land on which to build them. Priest José Urteaga suggested that the Chachapoyas school be built on empty land held by the church.[38] His colleague Gregorio Guinea, in charge of the church with the land in question, responded that even though he had orders not to part with any vacant land, he would be able to donate the lot for the school under the guise of "meeting the needs of the poor."[39]

After a location for the school was secured, the next step for communities was to write to their bishop requesting "ordinances and rules that would seem . . . most opportune for the best direction and government of the school."[40] Never short on ideas, Martínez Compañón responded quickly. He mandated that from Monday through Saturday, boys aged five to ten and girls aged four to eight would attend school from seven to eleven in the morning and from two to five in the afternoon, with a break to return home for lunch. On Thursday mornings and Saturday afternoons, they were to dedicate their studies to

Christian doctrine, and they would attend Mass every day. Students had to arrive at school "washed and with their hair combed and shirt buttoned." Boys should wear a *chupa*, or long-sleeved coat with four tails, the type of garment depicted in Plate 15, which shows two proper young students in European-style coats playing in a schoolyard. The use of such attire was essential, Martínez Compañón claimed, because "the exterior of the man indicates his interior." He thought that such proper dress would replace the "dishevelment" and "dirtiness" of many children with "cleanliness and culture," which would "without a doubt contribute to the good health of the body." He mandated that students attend class regularly and stipulated that it would be the teacher's duty to reprimand parents who did not send their students to school every day. Those who failed to meet these obligations were to be disciplined with "the punishment they deserved," which was often corporal. Teachers were to disregard complaints from any parents who disagreed with such harsh treatment of their offspring.[41]

Martínez Compañón stipulated that students in all the primary schools be taught from the same set of books. Many of the texts that he recommended were religious in nature: Thomas Kempis's *Imitation of Christ* was a devotional manual that encouraged readers to meditate on the life of Jesus. In a chapter likely to have been unpopular with children, "Of Superfluous Talking," Kempis declared that "much conversation on secular business, however innocently managed, greatly retards the progress of spiritual life."[42] Martínez Compañón insisted that students were to become familiar with the work of Spanish Dominican theologian Luis de Granada. His *Sinner's Guide* explained why Catholics were duty-bound to serve God. Perhaps for some diversion with their lessons, the Bishop recommended that students read Aesop's fables, as well as Granada's *Introduction to the Symbol of Faith*, which explained various questions of natural history pertaining to plant cultivation, the human body, and the animal kingdom. He reminded teachers that unidentified books that "were not edifying, or of good doctrine" were strictly forbidden.[43]

While Martínez Compañón's ordinances do not appear to have caused controversy with local communities, the most important factor of how a school would be run—the person running it—proved more contentious. The Bishop had a clear vision of the ideal primary school teacher: he should be a "prudent and zealous expert" who could see to it that "from the time they opened their eyes, children would learn their trades, and duties toward God, their king, themselves, and other men."[44] The teachers' good skills were particularly important in Peru, the Bishop decided, because the "docile and easily susceptible" children there "usually follow the example of their teachers."[45] Teachers were to be adequately prepared with the skills that they would need: they had to know how to read, write, and count. They were to be "well instructed" in Christian doctrine and to live "free of vices, especially drunkenness." Additionally, teachers should have good manners, be prudent, brave, and likeable.[46] Along with all the things teachers were exhorted to do, there were certain things they should avoid. They could not, under any circumstances, have children work in their fields or assist in their private economic ventures. If a teacher's living quarters were adjacent to the schoolroom, he had to ensure that students were not permitted to enter his private rooms because of the "inconveniences . . . that might result" from such informality.[47] Teachers had to take care to deliver lessons (especially those pertaining to Catholic dogma) in the proper fashion, being sure that students understood the material and did not simply "learn doctrine by memory, like parrots."[48]

Martínez Compañón believed that he and the future bishops of Trujillo should be responsible for choosing teachers, something that would eliminate the "differences and disagreements" that could result from open competition for the positions. The people of Chiclayo confirmed that he would be best equipped to make the decision, but other towns wanted the right to choose for themselves. In these cases, the Bishop recommended that they proceed with "impartiality," choosing the best of the applicants without considering the "flesh or blood" (race or social status) of the teacher.[49] Regardless of what communities wanted, viceregal officials looked none too kindly on ecclesiastical control over what should have been Crown institutions. In May 1786, Martínez Compañón received a letter from Lima reminding him that bishops could not be responsible for choosing teachers, nor could priests help to collect community contributions toward teachers' salaries.[50]

Once a teacher had been decided on, it was up to Martínez Compañón to request official approval for the schools, which had to come from Lima. He first contacted the archbishopric's financial adviser there, who gave his blessing, calling the program a "radical experiment" that would be useful for the entire viceroyalty. But the real coup was the letter he received from Viceroy Jáuregui in March 1783. This expressed official approval for the three schools in Chachapoyas, Lamas, and Tarapoto, along with "due thanks" for the Bishop's work in the area. The next step involved sending the file back to the local level, specifically to the *corregidor* and *ayuntamiento* of Chachapoyas, who would be responsible for executing it. The project seemed set up for success; even before he heard of Jáuregui's approval, *corregidor* Pinillos reported that almost 200 local boys were already attending the three schools.[51] Overall, the primary school agenda for Trujillo was modestly successful. Of the fifty-four primary schools that Martínez Compañón hoped to found, thirty-seven received official approval from Viceroy Croix in June 1786—an accomplishment in itself.[52] Several of these functioned well into the nineteenth century: as of 1809, the school in Santo Toribio de Rioja remained open (although it no longer served native children). The school in Chiclayo lasted until 1813, and that of Otusco for three years longer.[53]

Even these achievements cannot explain the fate of the project in its entirety. Seventeen schools were never approved or were abandoned before reaching that stage. An attempt to found a separate school just for female students in Huamachuco also failed.[54] In part, their fate must have been tied to the massive bureaucratic upheaval that Peru faced in the late eighteenth century. In April 1784, Viceroy Jáuregui, a fellow Navarese who seemed enthusiastic about the Bishop's reform agenda, was replaced by Teodoro de Croix, a man rumored to have a "low opinion" of all Indians, even those who had submitted to Spanish rule.[55] Almost immediately, Croix began implementing the Ordinance of Intendants, replacing corrupt local *corregidores* with royally appointed (and theoretically more upstanding) intendants. Most confoundingly, all matters of viceregal business previously submitted to the *corregidores* had to be reissued to the intendants. It was amid such transformations that Martínez Compañón approached Croix for help with the education projects.[56] After a year passed, Viceroy Croix replied that he had seen the files regarding the school foundations and had examined them with "the reflection and carefulness they merit." Yet when Martínez Compañón received his promotion to become archbishop of Bogotá, the matter was left unresolved. Around that same time, independent reports confirmed that the Chachapoyas schools had been abandoned. Francisco Paula Collantes reported that the school was "today completely closed," and Alvaro Llanos Valdes noted that the plan for the school "never had stability: I do not know the motive or cause."[57]

Perhaps we might look to an image in the *Trujillo* watercolors for clues about the problems with the Chachapoyas education project. Closer examination of the sketch or "plan for the primary school in the city of San Juan de la Frontera de Chachapoyas" (see Plate 4) indicates several potential difficulties with the school design. Rather than holding classes in an existing structure or even in the teacher's house, as was often done in New Spain, the plans called for an entirely new building with an ornate neoclassical façade. Instead of using inexpensive benches with no desks, the school would have nine tables to accommodate students. The painstakingly drawn tiny inkwells indicate that not only would the students have desks but would be provided with ink and pens—a far cry from the leaves of the *duco* tree that the children of the remote town of Jaén scratched on to practice their alphabets.[58] The school was to have separate rooms for beginning students, advanced students, and female students. It would also feature a teacher's office and sleeping quarters and a kitchen. Although impressive, these relative luxuries were not essential to the basic mission of the school, and attempting to arrange for them may have caused yet another distraction from the project.

While such structural problems could have hampered the school foundations, ideological conflicts over their mission were likely even more damaging. These highlight how even when they were closely calibrated to local circumstance, visions of utopian reform could be rife with contention. Spaniards and elites seem to have considered the school projects as chances to make financial contributions demonstrating their largesse toward the local community. Indian groups, in contrast, saw precious opportunities to give their own children the same advantages that more affluent Spanish and mestizo children had. Martínez Compañón likewise had his own agenda. Because he was trying to accomplish so many aspects of "improvement" during his brief visits to the towns in his bishopric, he linked his initial school proposals to other changes that he wanted in local communities: he requested that Indians living in rural areas relocate to town centers, that families create separate sleeping areas for female and male children, and that communities needing irrigation ditches dig them and grow cotton and other crops likely to produce profits. With so many tasks to accomplish simultaneously, it is easy to see how the financially overburdened townspeople were overwhelmed to the point of despair.[59]

By 1790, Martínez Compañón indicated that the monies that the Indian communities had promised never materialized. He admitted that, regarding the fields that they alternately agreed to farm in order to raise the money for the schools, "even this they did not comply with."[60] Nevertheless, the school projects highlight how improvement through education was a circuitous path to utopia in late eighteenth-century Peru. With their vision colored by the Túpac Amaru rebellion, Spanish authorities envisioned a future that was largely based on social control. Through education and improvement, Indians would learn to speak, behave, dress, and work like Spaniards. In the process, they would inevitably become more loyal to the Spanish Crown, viceregal authorities, and local bureaucrats. While some adult Indians had already proved themselves intractable when faced with this foreign vision of their ideal futures, children could be readily transformed into the ideal vessels of improvement. Not only were they more impressionable and easily controlled; they would return to their families and communities as ambassadors of the happy state of cultural conversion that the Spanish sought. Thus for viceregal administrators, children became instruments of social coercion.

But like his town foundation plans, Martínez Compañón's vision of utopia was not so strictly based on force. Instead, he imagined incorporating Trujillo's native peoples into his vision of improvement and reform. He would encourage communities to participate and invite children to join. In his mind, the schools provided good press for the Spanish Empire because every Indian, casta, or mestizo who attended proved that the people of Spanish America were better off under the paternal gaze of the Crown. Every boy who neatly combed his hair, washed his face, and put on his coat with tails every morning and every girl who sang the correct religious verses when she passed a Spanish authority figure proved that the "Black Legend" of Spain's cruelty in America was no more. They provided a form of moral capital, a public demonstration of how America's Indians and plebeians were intelligent and useful enough to become willing and grateful participants in Spain's imperial venture, and how benevolent the Spaniards were to transform them in this way.[61]

*   *   *

Years later, visitors to the Royal Palace Library could find the *Trujillo del Perú* illustrations capturing the activities and pastimes of the people whom the Bishop had worked so diligently to reform in Trujillo. Flourishing with a renewed industriousness, Trujillans labored together to sell their local products at regional markets, plant alfalfa, and defend their fields from hungry deer. They maintained their own iron workshops and operated the silver mines at Hualgayoc. In their spare time, they staged elaborate dances for Carnival season, with musical accompaniment and intricate costumes. However, among the traditional devil, lion, and bear costumes that marked the annual festivities in the Andes, the watercolor illustrations featured several dances that were unmistakably different. In the "Chimú dance" (see Plate 16), two dancers perform in traditional Inca costume—*unku* tunics, ceremonial axes, and even *suntur paqwar* headdresses. All these items had been expressly outlawed in the wake of the Túpac Amaru rebellions, yet the *Trujillo* images still depicted them. But these were nowhere near as controversial as a pair of images called

"dance of the decapitation of the Inca." The first shows an actor costumed as
the last Inca king, Atahualpa, with his gold tunic, crown, and staff of office
adorned with the sun—the traditional symbol of Inca royalty. He is seated
on a golden throne and surrounded by his court. The following image, Plate
17, shows that the throne has been moved outside. Six Spaniards have appeared in black hats, long coats, shoes, and stockings. Atahualpa's lifeless
body lies next to his throne, a Spaniard in a red coat grasping his decapitated
head by the hair while another prepares a platter on which to carry it.

An astute contemporary of the Bishop would have readily seen what modern observers will have to deduce about this image: it does not show a "dance"
at all. It actually depicts one of the "conquest plays" that were performed
throughout colonial Spanish America to commemorate some of the most
memorable events of the first meetings between the Old World and the New.
But these had also been outlawed in the post–Túpac Amaru crackdown, when
the Spaniards feared that Indians would use them as anti-Spanish propaganda.
Why, then, did Martínez Compañón choose to include them in a selection of
images that he dearly hoped would one day sit before the very king of Spain
himself? Allowing a potentially treasonous image to be presented to the king
was no mere caprice. In contrast, it suggests that the Bishop was so confident
in his efforts of improvement in Trujillo that to him the image did not signal
forbidden insubordination but rather showed how the Indians of his bishopric were able to engage in these cultural displays of their heritage while remaining loyal to the Spanish Crown. While in Martínez Compañón's utopia,
Indians occasionally dressed like Inca and performed in plays or dances that
evoked their power, these were just ceremonies. The real Indians of Trujillo,
the ones the Bishop knew and loved and worked to help, were best represented by the Indians depicted laboring in the fields, slaving over their looms,
and playing cards—but not betting—in their free time.[62]

Promoting his accomplishments in Trujillo was not the only intention of
the nine volumes bound in red leather. Like any visual report from the New
World, the books were meant to illustrate what had already happened; and
they were also an essential part of his continued request for patronage. They
were a gift meant to please, and, at the same time, they were a reminder and
a request. While they conveyed Trujillo's many successes in becoming a productive outpost of empire, they reminded their patron that there was more
work to be done. Nowhere was this clearer than with the three images that
close volume 2. After 201 images of proper, obedient subjects, three watercolors of "infidel Indians" suddenly appear, cutting a stark contrast to the

earlier illustrations. The savage-looking man wears an impressive feather head-dress almost overshadowed by the long stick threaded through his pierced lower lip (see Plate 18). He carries two instruments of war: a heavy wooden club; and a large bow and arrow. His female counterpart refuses to cover her naked breasts or to wrap her infant in anything other than a banana leaf. The final image, "infidel Indians in canoe," (see Plate 10) shows ten naked, grimy, smug Indians piled into a boat fashioned from tree bark. They seem to be laughing as they paddle deeper into the wilderness and farther from the reaches of the Catholic Church and the Spanish Crown. They would remain blissfully barbaric until Martínez Compañón—or another figure equally as enterprising and connected—could somehow reach them.

CHAPTER 5

The Hualgayoc Silver Mine

Situated at 13,000 feet above sea level, Trujillo's great silver mines at Cajamarca stood at the same elevation as the distant snowy land of Tibet that Jesuit scientist Athanasius Kircher had written about in his epic *China Illustrata*. But this was no fantastical kingdom—the disheveled mining camp of Micuypampa, the gateway to the Hualgayoc silver mine of Cajamarca, was an inhospitable place about which a visitor once remarked that "water freezes indoors, at night, during a great part of the year."[1] In addition to the disagreeable climate, the area was not renowned for natural beauty. The terrain was marred by sloping mine shafts hammered from the frigid soil, hung with simple ladders made of boards and thin leather straps hooked to the earthen walls dug around them. The ladders featured strategically placed wide planks meant to provide rest for the *capacheros*, or basket carriers, who ascended the shaft carrying loads of silver ore weighing almost as much as a grown man strapped to their brown backs.[2]

The inside of colonial silver mines was an intensely alien part of Trujillo that bore no resemblance to the densely verdant jungles of the Amazon basin. There were no yellow flowers with purple centers dangling from the delicate branches of the Saint Thomas tree. Instead of the symphony of hoots and howls made by the monkeys of the Amazonian rainforest, the only sounds were the sharp smashing of iron instruments against the earth. In this lunar world, nature's abundance was turned on itself; rocks, dirt, and mud proliferated. The only signs of life were the small rivulets of sweaty water that dripped down the bare mud walls, pooling into puddles. As they labored, the Indian, mestizo, and Afro-Peruvian mine workers hoped that these trickles would not one day become streams or even small rivers that would flood the shaft, causing it to cave in and entomb them as they struggled for breath. To counter this danger, the men known as *desagüadores*, or drainers, periodically inspected active sites, examining the small water flows and diverting them in order to prevent a possibly fatal collapse, like the one at the Huancavelica mercury mine in central Peru that would kill two hundred workers in 1786.[3]

The most numerous mine workers in colonial Spanish America were the *barreteros*, or pick men, who were responsible for the heaviest labor. They carried with them twenty-pound hammers to smash the silver ore out from the walls of the deposit, and twenty-five-pound crowbars with which to pry it loose. As they worked, heaps of loose dirt and rock piled up at their feet. They filled their baskets with what some of the Indian workers called *killa sut'u*—the tears of the moon, the ancient Andean term for silver. Typically, the mine shafts where they worked were barely reinforced with rickety wooden supports; most miners in Peru were too poor to invest in such vital infrastructure. This endangered their laborers and made their commitment to deposits much more fickle: when a certain vein became too difficult to work, they would often simply rent it or sell it to the highest bidder, who would then set to work at an even more arduous and risky task. After learning about working conditions at Hualgayoc on a visit to the site, Martínez Compañón decided that people should not be forced into what he later called such "dark and difficult" labor.[4] His opposition to the *mita* forced labor draft confirmed what the jurist and mining reformer Francisco Xavier Gamboa had written fifteen years earlier about New Spain's silver mines: "mining, in short, is attended . . . with every pain which hell itself can inflict."[5]

Few of Gamboa's contemporaries would have ventured to question him; the abuses and discomforts facing those who labored underground were notorious throughout the Americas. Silver had long been the most spectacular economic sector in the Spanish Empire—at one point accounting for up to 90 percent of American exports to Seville—and the Spanish Crown and the mine owners had shaped a system of labor accordingly. In Peru's *mita*, native workers were forced to travel great distances over inhospitable terrain so that they might toil in the cold dark for up to twelve months at a time. The slight compensation that they were given did not make their backbreaking work worthwhile. Since newly imported slaves from Africa were not acclimatized to work at dizzyingly high altitudes, the fate of indigenous workers in Peru's silver mines seemed inalterable.[6]

The *mita* had, by Martínez Compañón's time, been outlawed everywhere in the viceroyalty but the Huancavelica mercury mine in southern Peru. (It also still operated at the Cerro Rico of Potosí, which had been transferred to

Río de la Plata when the new viceroyalty was created in 1776.) Even with forced labor being outlawed, miners continued to insist on the necessity of conscripted workers, and those of Hualgayoc proved no different: they envisioned a mercantilist closed-market system in which they would be the main beneficiaries of forced labor, monopoly contracts, and price fixing. Like their counterparts throughout colonial Spanish America, they were some of the most powerful and wealthy men in the colony. Those who dared to thwart their desires faced potentially disastrous retribution. At the same time, it was well known that one of the main complaints of the Túpac Amaru rebels had been the Potosí *mita*. Such difficult labor in such deleterious conditions for so little pay jeopardized the peaceful order of the kingdom. Accordingly, Martínez Compañón believed that there was ample historical precedent to oppose the *mita*, which contradicted the true aims of the Spanish Crown in America. As he later told Viceroy Croix, he was certain that "it would not be proper to impose the *mita* in the kingdom of the most religious and pious monarch on earth."[7]

It was with this in mind that the Bishop began a protracted struggle for the future of the Indians and castas who worked at Hualgayoc. Instead of advocating an exploitive economic model based on forced labor, Martínez Compañón turned to the ideas of community, sociability, and industry that had been the hallmark of his other attempts at reform in Trujillo. Though his plan to revamp the mining industry was unprecedented, he was not alone in advocating the potential benefits of liberal economic and social policy in mining regions. In 1761, Gamboa had argued that urban settlements should be built at mining camps. "Towns promote the civilization and reduction of the Indians," he insisted. "Then follows consumption, industry, taxes, and many other consequences of the greatest importance to religion and the state."[8] For his part, Martínez Compañón imagined a utopian town at Hualgayoc, an ideal location where mine workers could settle with their families and split their time between work underground and in the fields. He was confident that after arriving in the utopian town that he proposed to build at Hualgayoc, the settlers would find that "in a short time they will be able to fulfill, and maybe even exceed, the sum of their tribute, [and] this will make them more civilized . . . [and] then they will introduce the necessary order and good government."[9]

Of course, the episode did not unfold so simply. The Bishop's radical vision for a plebeian utopia that promoted workers' rights and benefits, a free market, and an independent laboring class stood in stark contrast to what the mine owners wanted. They saw the Bishop's visit to their area as a moment of opportunity, a chance for them to improve their fortunes by shoring up their access to a captive workforce. What they did not foresee was that Martínez Compañón also viewed his trip to Cajamarca as a chance to promote his own vision of utopia. A similar line of demarcation had been drawn with the Bishop's other reform projects in Trujillo, when the people requested independent towns but landlords feared the insubordination that would result; and when local communities supported primary schools but ultimately failed to produce the funding necessary to run them. This battle of wills played out again and again throughout the Americas when reformers proposed agendas of improvement. What was different this time was just how far Martínez Compañón was willing to go to create a workers' utopia at the mine.[10]

The Meeting with the Miners' Guild

On October 28, 1783, the Bishop met with the Hualgayoc miners' guild on the Chala estate near the Hualgayoc mine. The miners had already asked him to serve as "director and protector" of their guild—a telling sign of their faith in the general influence of a man with no actual experience in the business of mining, and of their hopes for how far flattery might get them. A prelate visiting a mine and its environs was not unheard of; Archbishop Luis Francisco Romero of Sucre traveled to South America's most famous mining town, Potosí, in 1727, but his concerns were inspecting the religious orders and stopping the "lascivious" activities that occupied so many of Potosí's inhabitants.[11] The miners of Cajamarca, in contrast, were not interested in censorship of their private or religious lives. Instead, they sought the Bishop's expertise as an improver and a reformer. In their minds, the new towns, primary schools, and seminaries that he had founded throughout Trujillo evidenced his accomplishments and made him an attractive candidate for the position. Hoping to gain his favor, the miners praised him as "the most strong proponent of moving forward the business of mining," a man whose "capacity, prudence, and outstanding well-known talents enlighten whatever he attempts." But what they really wanted was for the Bishop to help them foster a closed economic system at the mine. They sought a draft of forced labor, a monopoly contract for mercury, and a royal bank that would purchase their silver at prearranged prices and make loans of capital. They requested permission to pay their workers in kind, not in cash, and the right to be the sole vendors of material goods and comestibles at the mines. To them, the ideal Hualgayoc silver mine of the future looked barely different from how it did today—with the exception of its profit margins, of course.[12]

Documents reveal that on the morning that the Bishop and the guild met, the session began when guild deputy Joseph Costales Estrada stood up and introduced himself, then read aloud the thirty-two reform ideas that the miners had already presented to the Bishop in a written treatise. In composing them, they had drawn on their own experiences and utilized an official royal inquiry into the state of the mine made five years earlier, when in 1778, *visitador* Areche had instructed local bureaucrat Francisco Uralde to inspect Hualgayoc and file a report explaining why the mine was becoming less and less profitable by the minute. Uralde was also to suggest "the methods that might be employed to make it flourish." Areche was desperate to know how the mine had fallen into such a dismal state only a few years after enthusiasts had breathlessly claimed that it "exceeded Potosí in riches and advantages."[13]

Uralde's investigations revealed that Chota and Cajamarca—the nearest towns to the mine—lay twenty-eight and forty miles away, respectively. Because there was no way to travel such a great distance each day, workers lived nearby in haphazard mining camps, where straw huts provided scant protection from the almost constant wind and rain. Uralde estimated that the surrounding environs had only about 1,500 inhabitants, half of whom were men eligible to work in the mine. As a result, the few who were available could demand higher salaries, further imperiling the mine owners' profits. The dearth of workers also meant that miners could typically place only about ten workers in a single pit. Because this protracted process resulted in high transportation and labor costs, the miners could not afford the technology and machinery that would help them extract ore more efficiently. They might have wished for a barrel-refining machine (in which silver, mercury, and the other ingredients of the refining process were placed in an automatically ro-tated barrel) like the one built by Huamachuco miner Ignacio Amoroto, which was carefully detailed in volume 2 of the *Trujillo* images. But at Hual-gayoc, no one seemed to have such ingenuity or the capital to back it up. In all, the situation was so poor that Uralde saw only one possible remedy: "the *mita* of Indians is the only and effective method to populate the mines with workers," he baldly told Areche. Along with this, he recommended a royal *asiento* monopoly contract, through which the Crown would provide the miners with the mercury they needed for refining.[14]

This arrangement addressed another common complaint of American miners: the scarcity of mercury, an indispensable component of the refining process. Spain had only one source in all of South America—the Huancavelica mine in Upper Peru. Any additional mercury had to be shipped from Europe. To make matters worse, frequent Spanish-British conflicts endangered the transatlantic shipping channels for Spanish mercury mined at Almadén (Spain). But that was not the end of the difficulties; once the silver was prepared, miners were still challenged to find local merchants willing to buy it at a fair price. Uralde hoped that the Crown could purchase the refined silver and provide the miners with capital for loans. In turn, the miners would agree to sell only to the Crown, and at slightly lower prices. This partnership would increase royal profits, standardize buying and selling, provide a ready market for silver bars, and offer the miners access to loan capital.[15]

In the five years that had passed since Uralde's report was filed, the miners' guild had yet to receive official word on the matter. This may have been partly due to the sour relations between Areche and Peru's then-viceroy, Agustín de Jáuregui, who quarreled over many matters, including appointing officials at Hualgayoc. By 1783, the miners had decided to create another set of reforms—and to ask Martínez Compañón to assist in implementing them. Like Uralde, they thought that Hualgayoc's biggest problem was the lack of workers. They also cited the distance that workers had to travel to the mines and the discomfort that they endured in the mining camps (although, as the Bishop likely knew, their sympathy had its limits). So they recommended moving the mining camps nearer to the mine, where the people would live in a new settlement called Los Dos Carlos (named after King Charles and his heir apparent, Charles IV). The Bishop concurred with this aspect of the guild's plan, as he described the standing settlements of Micuypampa, La Punta, and the aptly named Purgatorio (purgatory) as having "their houses, stores, and *pulperías* (food stalls and taverns) uncomfortably stacked right up against one another . . . so that they seem more like . . . dens of thieves than buildings for rational, honest men." He and the miners agreed that the lack of order gave unscrupulous workers ample opportunity to conceal and sell stolen silver.[16]

The miners' report suggested that the land for Los Dos Carlos would be purchased from local hacendados and would feature an orderly settlement that would be the opposite of the disarray of most mining centers. Their plan cleverly appealed to the dominant reform rhetoric of the era by proposing a

town with religious and state institutions that would ensure good behavior
from the townspeople. Los Dos Carlos would include a church, a dormitory
for priests, a house for the alcaldes who would oversee mining operations,
and a jail for counterfeiters, thieves, and other criminals—one "with all the
necessary security," Estrada promised. The streets would cut across the town
in neat straight lines, and each miner would be given a lot for his house in
town. In addition, the miners would build *rancherías*, or housing for workers
outside of town, near their mines, where they would live alongside their workers and supervisors. This would not only ensure "good" social behavior from
the mine workers; it would also help prevent the inevitable siphoning of silver
destined for the contraband trade, which some scholars have estimated equaled
30–50 percent of officially registered silver production.[17]

The miners' use of the language of improvement suggests that, like the
Castillos of Chapter 3, who had given permission for their workers to relocate
to a new town that they knew could never be founded, the guild recognized
the benefit of agreement. If they appeared to be aligned with the culture of
improvement that their Bishop promoted, they would gain his goodwill and
likely that of other important provincial officials as well. At the same time,
because implementing such large-scale projects was notoriously difficult, they
could be reasonably sure that their operations could continue unimpeded.
This was a simple yet ingenious technique of managing colonial bureaucracy.
By appearing to concede and then simply waiting for events that would most
likely never take place, the Hualgayoc mine owners could game the system
and come out on top.[18]

While proposing to settle an orderly town was an obvious way to curry
favor with the Bishop, the miners' thirty-two points revealed that they had
more immediate concerns in mind. As it stood, the very process of extracting,
refining, and selling the silver limited their profits. They were forced to use
mules to transport their ore down the mountain to Chota, where it was pul-
verized and ground in mills, then mixed with salt and water in an open-air
patio before the refining process began. Once workers mixed it with mercury,
the silver was washed and sent to Trujillo, where it was made into bars. Finally, the miners had to find local silver merchants willing to purchase their
bullion at a fair price. Because the silver merchants knew that the capital-poor
miners had to sell quickly to keep their operations running, they offered sub-
par prices. The entire process involved an extensive outlay of capital on which
they would see no return for ten to eighteen months.[19]

Though the poverty of miners was especially notorious in Peru—it cost 10–20 percent more to produce a marco (an eight-ounce measurement used for silver) there than it did in New Spain—miners' dismal finances provoked much commentary throughout Spanish America in the late colonial period. In his *New System for Economic Government*, Campillo wrote that "there are so many taxes and frauds practiced . . . with the poor miners . . . that it is a miracle there would be anyone interested in this business." He outlined how their perpetual poverty made it impossible for the miners to "undertake [the] expensive projects that would make the mines more productive, such as opening new [veins of silver], draining those known to be rich [with deposits, and] bringing useful experts and well-designed machines from Europe." Without such opportunities for advancement, he bemoaned, "things will remain in their same current state of imperfection."[20]

Accordingly, the Cajamarca miners sought to improve their financial situation through a Crown-sponsored silver exchange bank, or *caja de rescate*. They hoped that the bank would purchase each marco at the fixed price of seven pesos, one real. This was more than what private silver merchants typically offered.[21] The miners also envisioned the *caja* offering loans as needed. They planned that the bank would retain two reales out of every sum of seven pesos, one real that they earned, which would pay the salary of various officials and become loan capital for purchasing machinery, improving mine shafts, or paying workers if necessary. The bank would become a sort of insurance for the miners, guaranteeing that they could sell their silver. It was a central component of their vision of a closed economic system that would benefit their own interests. Martínez Compañón would later disagree with this controlled vision of the mine's financial future. In response to the idea of the bank, he contended that it would "inhibit . . . the growth of . . . [the mine's] profits through free commerce." The bank would become a flash point for the differing visions of the mine and its place in Trujillo's economy.[22]

The disagreement over the bank could not begin to compare with the contrast between the Bishop's and the guild's visions of the workforce underground. Point 17 of the miners' proposal baldly asserted that "the falling behind of the mine comes mostly from the lack of *mitayos*," or forced laborers. To remedy this problem, Estrada and the miners sought a thousand *mita* laborers. They wanted to round up four thousand mestizos and free *quinteros* (Indians who had left their communal lands and instead worked as day laborers on others' estates) from Cajamarca, a quarter of whom would work in the mines at any given time. For good measure, the miners added that most of these men were "inclined toward laziness and vice"—thereby implying that they were useless subjects who would actually benefit from being forced into productivity.[23]

Despite their careful arguments, Martínez Compañón maintained that, no matter how it was executed, the *mita* was the root of myriad "grievous problems." But it seems that some of the miners had anticipated his opposition because on paper, they agreed that workers in the mines should be treated according to the "humane" standards that eighteenth-century reformers promoted: for instance, from now on, they would labor only from sunrise to sundown. Those who chose to work extra hours would be paid up to four times their regular daytime salary. They promised to keep the mine technologically up to date by sponsoring a yearly contest for innovations. Finally, the guild sweetened the deal by offering to contribute two thousand pesos annually toward the Bishop's Indian colleges or "whatever other pious work within the bishopric" he wished. This thinly veiled attempt to buy Martínez Compañón's favor seems to have had no effect. Although two thousand pesos was no small sum, it was only a tiny fraction of the estimated 62,000 that was the projected annual operating cost of the schools. Paying to educate a small group of Indians was scant compensation for periodically enslaving four thousand of them. The Bishop made no further mention of the miners' offer to contribute to his projects.

In addition to converting local plebeians into a captive labor force, the guild proposed making them into a captive market. They sought exclusive rights to sell whatever food, clothes, liquor, and trade goods that their workers would need. In this capacity, they would be acting as *habilitadores*, or financiers who profited from offering goods on credit. They promised to settle on a fixed scale of prices to alleviate the price gouging that was so common in cash-rich goods-poor mining towns. Though they claimed that such transactions would help the workers by giving them ready access to manufactures and foodstuffs, the miners were well aware that selling high-priced goods to their workers—often on advance—would place some laborers into debt, forcing them to work all the harder. To further codify this exploitation, the miners insisted that they pay salaries not in silver but rather in "cash, clothes, or food." They likely reasoned that workers who could not legally possess silver would be more easily discovered in the process of stealing it. Finally, they agreed on standard rates of compensation for payment in cash or in kind: four reales a day for the *barreteros* who extracted the ore from the mine, three for the *capacheros* who carried it up the shaft in baskets (see Plate 19), and two for the less specialized workers who handled other tasks on the mountain.[24]

In concluding their statements, the miners turned again to flattery, pronouncing Martínez Compañón a man clearly "concerned with public good," one who possessed "correct and knowledgeable opinions." Though such public praise from powerful men was complimentary, Martínez Compañón would not agree to many of the miners' proposals, and he would attempt to alter others so that they fit within his utopian agenda rather than contradicting it. The situation at Hualgayoc was the polar opposite of the utopian civil society of Indians that he had been working so hard to create in Trujillo. He began his response to the miners' points by telling them of his conviction that "in this mine, scarcely anything was in its place . . . [and] almost everything was all mixed up." He had no choice but to directly challenge them. But how could he persuade the miners to admit the central role that they played in the mine's problems? Relying on the tools of discourse that he had honed in his university classes on rhetoric, he compared the problems at Hualgayoc to "a cancer," one mostly caused by "paralysis or laziness in the miners' guild." He was confident that "if the cancer is not cut out, it will keep growing every day until it does away with all the other parts of the body."

As if to compensate for such harsh rhetoric, he next reminded the miners that "bishops, because they are bishops, cannot stop being vassals of their kings and functionaries of their states, nor are they exempt from practicing with all those around them (especially with their diocesans) works of mercy—physically as well as spiritually—as much as they see fit and according to their respective talents, wealth, and powers." He loosely quoted one of his favorite Roman politicians and philosophers, Marcus Aurelius, who had written in his *Meditations*: " 'you are a man, you are a citizen of the world.' In addition to this," the Bishop continued, "you must be agreeable in your other relations and ties; they deserve to be maintained well . . . [because] through these relationships, you are building your dignity. You are a son, or a father of the family, or a husband. Think well about what these titles oblige you to, and do not dishonor any of them."[25] By appealing to the *patria chica* of their own families and households, the Bishop hoped to remind the miners to maintain the same sense of fealty to their local communities and to the Spanish Empire. In his utopia, powerful men kept the best interests of their workers and their Crown at heart, working together across social divisions to increase social harmony and economic productivity.

Theoretically, the Bishop did not oppose greater flow of capital or worker availability. But in reality, he did not consider forced labor an acceptable solution to the mine's problems. Instead, he argued that *mita* labor would damage the local economy more than help it because the indigenous and mixed-race men whom the miners wanted to force into work mostly made their living as farmers. If they were taken away from their fields for months at a time, local food supplies would dwindle. Even more important for a man of the cloth, the *mita* directly countered the stated designs of the Spanish kings and the Catholic Church in America. Idealistically, the Bishop believed that "since the beginning of the conquest, the kings of Spain have tried to keep their consciences clear in these lands and have wanted to be known for their holiness, manners, and zeal." When they had no choice but to force native peoples into labor, they did so—but only "under very difficult situations," he reasoned, "and maybe they might never have done so if they had seen [the *mita* draft] with their own eyes." In his mind, periodically enslaving the Indians contradicted the entire project of Spanish colonization in America. He was so overwhelmingly opposed to it that as the episode unfolded, he failed to recognize how his workers' utopia seemed more and more like a direct challenge to the economic core of Cajamarca.[26]

Martínez Compañón envisioned how he might refashion the miners' proposed town to make it fit with his utopian vision of improvement. He imagined a veritable city upon a mountain, a place where the infamous discord and chaos of colonial mining towns would be transformed into a shining example of civic order and productive labor. Rather than forcing Indians and mulatos to operate the mines, the Bishop thought that the town could attract workers by offering free land in exchange for labor. This was an unconventional suggestion, especially in an industry that had for so long relied on holding its workforce in pseudo-slavery status. He thought that if the workers were given their own plots of land, as well as cattle "and the tools they would need to work their fields," the town could function on a free-labor basis. They would be assigned alternate weeks in the mines and at home in their own fields, so that they could provide sustenance and additional income for their families. When they worked underground, they would do so only from sunrise to sundown, and in a mine near where they lived. In this way, the Bishop reasoned, "in sickness and in health, they would have the help of their homes and the solace that brings." They would also receive mules, which they were to use to bring metal to the refineries in Chota one day each week. To ensure a supply of meat and wool, the town would select several individuals to work as shepherds in common pastures, something that "has been done with much success in the most orderly towns in Spain," he commented. The towns would be run, the Bishop imagined, not by bureaucrats but by priests, "so that . . . [the people] might be better directed and governed." Martínez Compañón was confident that with this plan, current business at Hualgayoc would not suffer and that "the mine could be better improved than it ever would be through the *mita*."[27] Reshaped in this way, the mining community could become a plebeian utopia, a shining example of what goodwill and hard work could accomplish in the most improbable of places. The Bishop elaborated his own plan down to the last tiny detail. As we shall see, what he had not counted on was that the enthusiasm with which it was initially received would soon fade in the face of opposition from the miners themselves.

Planning the Mining Town

Before the buildings could be built, the tools and cattle purchased, the priests selected, and the workers summoned, there was much to be done. So Martínez Compañón began as he had with his town and school foundations, turning to local elites and officials for assistance and guidance. While some willingly collaborated, others took advantage of his reliance upon them to promote their own economic, social, and political interests.

The first order of business was deciding where exactly Los Dos Carlos should be situated; Martínez Compañón called this "one of the most serious and pressing points of the entire matter."[28] The location needed sufficient water to operate the *ingenio* mills for refining and water for irrigating the agricultural fields that would feed the townspeople. The town should have enough flat land for a road that would be "open and comfortable to travel on" and one "on which it would be possible to transport goods in all sorts of weather." The area needed nearby forests to fuel the smelting furnaces. Preferably, the Bishop thought, the town should have the correct type of soil "to make [the] adobe, tiles, or bricks" that would be used for the buildings. The town's cattle, horses, and sheep needed ample pastures for grazing.[29]

Finding out which land near the mine was best suited to the project was, as usual, a collaborative process. To make this decision, Martínez Compañón relied most heavily on two individuals with extensive mining experience. The first was Juan de Azereto, a miner who had previously served as a mining official in Caylloma, a small mine in southern Peru near Arequipa.[30] Azereto was particularly excited about the invited settler idea, calling it a "truly great project . . . for the public good." To work alongside him, the Bishop contracted miner and militia captain Miguel Espinach, one of the most powerful elites of Cajamarca. Espinach held a multitude of properties, mining investments, and social contacts in the area that could have benefited from an appropriately designed plan for the new town. At one point, he owned seven mining pits in which he employed 167 workers and eighteen overseers. In contrast, Azereto appears to have been a more detached informant; though he had economic interests in mines in Peru, his ties to Cajamarca were not particularly strong. Throughout the episode, the men behaved congruently with their personal situations. Azereto supported a free-market economy at the mine, similar to what Martínez Compañón advocated. Espinach, in contrast, promoted a closed system, from which he would undoubtedly see greater profits.[31]

Despite their particular concerns, both men were tasked with investigating the feasibility of the Bishop's proposal and reporting their findings. Azereto sent his report first. It recommended purchasing Manuel Martínez Infante's Lanacancha hacienda as the site for the future town. Martínez's land lay on the plain of Bambamarca, only seven miles from the mines. It had good agricultural fields, two refineries, and a large house on the property. Nearby were ample pastures for two hundred sheep, two hundred cows, and one hundred horses. Furthermore, Infante was offering the whole complex at what Azereto deemed a very fair price: 1,600 pesos (though the rest of the land would have to be secured from other parties). Azereto reasoned that building Los Dos Carlos on these lands so near the mines would attract workers without resorting to the *mita* draft. He was certain that such a plan of voluntary settlement and labor would be infinitely "less uncomfortable for the Indians."[32]

Soon after he received Azereto's report, Martínez Compañón passed it on to Miguel Espinach, who, in his own deposition, would express no such concern for local Indians. In fact, he recommended buying the communal lands of the Chota Indians, reasoning that they had "plenty of wood, grasses, and good [soil] for growing potatoes." He thought that these agricultural lands should be paired with a site for the mining town on the nearby plain of Pascapuquio, in a location that featured "a hill, with some mountains on both sides." It stood near Infante's Lanacancha hacienda, which Espinach thought would be better suited for agricultural use. He also recommended purchasing the neighboring Los Negrillos cattle ranch, owned by a local group of Bethlehemite fathers. With his suggestions, he included a detailed map (now lost to the historical record), as well as calculations estimating that the total cost of land would run about 36,950 pesos.[33]

Within four days of receiving the initial reports, the Bishop wrote to both men, asking for more information. In addition to advice on where the town should be located, he requested suggestions on who would live there and how they should be governed. He wanted to know who the best settlers would be: "original Indians [those who had remained on their ancestral land], *quinteros* [landless Indians], or mestizos." He sought Azereto's and Espinach's opinions about his idea to give each worker two mules that he would use to carry metals down to the refineries every week. The rest of his inquiries had to do with how daily life would unfold in Los Dos Carlos. Would it be possible, he wondered, to place "at the head of the town a priest . . . especially in the early years, for its better direction and governance?" He inquired whether the lands in question would support community pastures and if the attached agricultural fields would be adequate. Could they afford to supply the *colonos*, or settlers, with the instruments and tools they would need for their labor in their fields and in the mines? Would these be able to work alternately one week in the mines and one week at home, growing their own food? And could town officials enforce more humane working hours, so that those who worked mine shifts during the day could rest at night? Ultimately, the Bishop hoped to confirm that the proposed settlement "could better achieve the reform of the said mine, rather than [using] the *mita* that the miners' guild requests."[34]

Espinach's response arrived first, on September 10, 1784. He answered that the landless *quintero* Indians—especially young men over twenty—would be the most appropriate settlers for Los Dos Carlos because "they seem more suited for the work in mines and refineries . . . [and] because they have stronger constitutions." A more practical consideration that he failed to mention was that since they did not own agricultural land, removing these men from their homes would not directly threaten northern Peru's food supply.[35] Espinach agreed with the Bishop's proposals to ameliorate work schedules in the mine and calculated that providing each settler with "two mules, two oxen, a plough, [and] and an ax" would run about fifty pesos per man, with a total cost of 60,000 pesos. This time, he did not mention where the town should be located.[36]

Again, Martínez Compañón requested further information. Another eighteen days passed before the second report from Azereto reached the Bishop's hands. Now the entire affair became even more complex. In addition to proposing a different location for Los Dos Carlos, Azereto disagreed with Espinach on several key points. First, he thought that much of the land that his counterpart proposed to buy was not suited to the project. The hacienda Negritos, for instance, had poor-quality soil that would produce "only a few potatoes and onions, without the hope of any other grains or seeds." The Tallamarca ranch was not ideal, either; its lands were "all hilly and unpopulated." Regarding Espinach's idea to buy the communal land of the Chota Indians, Azereto stayed true to his conviction that a free-market economy was better for the mine, writing that "it would not be wise to strip . . . [them] of their lands" because they could just as easily be persuaded to work in the mines on a free-labor basis—if offered appropriate compensation. He also challenged the figure that Espinach had put forward for buying the eight estates in question, saying that instead of the 24,000 pesos Espinach cited, the land was actually worth 25,000. Finally, he thought that rather than the 1,500 workers Espinach suggested, Los Dos Carlos would need two thousand, so that these could have more free time to provide for their own upkeep. Their disagreements over the site of the future town highlight the tension between mine's two possible economic futures: a controlled, mercantilist system that would benefit the mine owners, versus a more open economy in which workers as well as owners could have the chance to get ahead.[37]

Regardless of where the workers would actually go, the Bishop and his collaborators could not proceed with founding Los Dos Carlos in any location until the owners of the lands in question agreed to sell. After hearing the request of their Bishop, most local landowners were readily convinced of "the most advantageous utility that this project would bring, not only to this Villa [of Cajamarca] and its province, but to the entire kingdom, and even to the Crown."[38] For Antonio Bernal, who owned mines and the Santa Ana hacienda in Cajamarca, agreeing to sell his land for a fair price was an easy decision because he knew that the "happiness of these provinces"—and likely the very success of his own finances—was reliant upon the profits of the Hualgayoc mine. He stipulated only that his cattle should remain on the grasslands that they currently inhabited "because of the risk of getting lost and dying if they were moved to other pastures."[39] Marcelo Hernández, the militia captain who owned the Lanacancha hacienda, wrote of "the desire I have as a vassal to cooperate with the holy intentions" of the Bishop, agreeing to sell the lands he had inherited from his parents. This was an essential contribution, as Lanacancha included pastures, irrigation ditches, and a refinery for grinding silver. He estimated all this to be worth approximately a thousand pesos.[40] Even Xavier de Villanueva, the chaplain of Lanacancha, offered to sell his corner of the estate, which included several houses, a small chapel, and "two bells that cost me 200 pesos." He suggested a price of 1,700 pesos for the lot, even though the sale "will deprive me of the only sure *capellanía* [religious endowment] that I have."[41] The hilly pastures of the Chugur ranch were owned by five men who wrote to the Bishop that "there is no doubt . . . that the idea [of Los Dos Carlos] is one of the most useful that might contribute to the progress of the mine." They knew that the coal and wood that could be extracted from their property was essential to the functioning of the town, so despite their poverty, they "begged that [the Bishop] deign to accept our offer to hand over . . . our *ranchería*."[42] Other of the lands in question belonged to the Indians of Chota. The local cacique, Marcos Carhuajulca, agreed to turn them over to the Los Dos Carlos project for the price of five thousand pesos. Unsurprisingly, the documentation fails to reveal whether he did so under duress or whether he truly believed in participating in the project.[43]

Although they were offered fair prices for their lands, the question still remains as to why these individuals would so enthusiastically rush to part with the ranches, farms, cattle, and refineries that provided them with financial security. One clue comes from Santa Ana hacienda owner Antonio Bernal, who somewhat offhandedly wrote that he was "one of the interested parties and a miner of the mountain of Hualgayoc."[44] When he agreed to turn over his land, Bernal may have known of a customary loophole that was mutually beneficial to both these investment sectors: though it was officially prohibited, holders of agricultural or cattle ranches that had allotments of *mita* workers could transfer the workers to the mines if their property was sold, thereby repurposing them for the more productive mining industry. Though they did not say so directly, perhaps the other landowners knew this as well. This was yet another avenue for elites to appear supportive of the Bishop's agenda while promoting their own economic well-being.[45]

Martínez Compañón was either unaware of this subterfuge or chose not to acknowledge it because after receiving their correspondence, he reported to Viceroy Croix that the hacendados "unanimously" agreed "to offer their lands if they were necessary for the improvement of the mines." To hear Martínez Compañón tell it, the hacendados were so convinced of his plans to reform Hualgayoc that they "preferred the good of the public to that of their own personal benefit." In addition to highlighting their tendency to "act so generously," their willingness to contribute to the project "filled the entire

town with admiration," he later gushed. Though the actual selling and purchasing of the land never took place, the Bishop nevertheless rewarded Cajamarca's elite for their support. He helped them with their petition to elevate
their town's civic status from that of a *villa*, or smaller discrete urban settlement, to a *ciudad*, a much larger entity that had jurisdiction over nearby
territories as well. The matter was still pending when he left to assume his
new position as archbishop of Bogotá in 1790; on December 19, 1802, King
Charles IV finally decreed Cajamarca to be a city. The record does not say
whether the Bishop had advanced these favors in the hope that one day, the
landowners would return them. In the end, the elites got what they bar-
gained for: by agreeing to support Martínez Compañón's agenda to help the
workers at the mines, they had gained goodwill and public largesse. If the
plans succeeded, they could have moved their workers into the more profitable mining sector. When the project never materialized, they were able to
continue with the status quo. As for the mine workers, their fate remained
undecided, but the Bishop would continue envisioning how to help them, his
provisions veering into increasingly radical territory.[46]

A Workers' Utopia

As the Bishop's vision for a mining city on a silver mountain unfolded, he
imagined how to cultivate a critical mass of industrious, obedient plebeians.
He planned to do this by implementing a host of improvements that would
create general well-being in the community. As we shall see, some of these
improvements, such as the right to publicly own and bequeath land to heirs,
were unprecedented in the history of Spanish imperial policy toward Indians.
Others were less radical but equally important. He designed this program
with the workers' best interests in mind; but like any good Bourbon functionary, the Bishop knew that the workers' productivity would ultimately
contribute to the finances of the entire Spanish Empire. In the end, it seems
that he was so compelled by his radical vision of reform that he was unable to
foresee how it threatened the very foundations of Spanish colonialism in
America.

To promote his program, Martínez Compañón needed the approval of
mine owners and hacendados, as this was essential to securing funding,
moving through bureaucratic channels, and sustaining any project once it
had begun. He realized that one of the most frightening aspects of a mine

owner's work was the ever-present threat of debilitating illness that would keep him from overseeing day-to-day operations on his properties. Therefore, the Bishop decreed that a portion of profits from the mine should "be put toward helping . . . in case of sickness or unexpected accident." Miners also worried about the welfare of their families should they be unable to work. This surplus fund would help their next of kin: any widows and their children would receive five thousand marcos in assistance over the span of fifteen years. Upon reflection, the Bishop was convinced that such measures "would more efficiently induce men to attempt this profession, which should really be promoted."[47]

Although such provisions may seem unremarkable by modern standards, Martínez Compañón's plans to provide for the social welfare of mine owners and their families were groundbreaking for their time. Northern European guilds had offered protection for illness, death, or accident since the mid-seventeenth century, but such practices were slow to get off the ground in the Spanish world. The earliest true health or disability insurance measures were passed in the maritime industry to ensure the safe shipment of cargo, but they did not inspire similar measures in other industries. Later, the Spanish Crown offered a sort of disability pay and retirement options to mariners on royal ships, but the practice did not extend to other industries. Although Pedro Campomanes argued that "the aid of disabled sick people, widows, and orphans of the guilds is useful to the state because [this way] they do not become lazy or beg," his efforts to put such measures into place on the Spanish Peninsula met with resounding failure. Royal officials seemed deaf to his claims that providing such social assistance "is a way that the families of artisans propagate and people remain content in their jobs." In this context, the Bishop's plans to provide such support to the miners marked him as an outlier, even among other reformers. But no one had imagined such a proposal in the American context—much less in the high-stakes mining industry.[48]

While offering an early version of disability and life insurance for miners' families was in some ways a calculated pandering to the elite of Cajamarca, Martínez Compañón focused much more intently on how he might make the projected town more appealing to the plebeian laborers who would populate this utopia. Simply eliminating the most exploitative practices at the mine would not be enough. He needed to attract workers to his utopian colony—to make them see, as he put it, "how lucky they are compared with the other mestizos or Indians in the province and the bishopric." He guessed that what would appeal most to potential settlers was who they might become there: free laborers who earned their own living, largely on their own terms. This is the same rhetoric that he used to gather support for his new town foundations and his schools: by participating in their own improvement, men (and women, and even children) could provide for increased stability. At the same time, they would bring economic advantages to the province, the viceroyalty, and the Spanish Empire at large.

But Martínez Compañón's plan did not end there. He also declared his intention to reward the men who faithfully continued their work in the mines with official titles to their land and the right to pass these titles down to their heirs. In this way, he argued, the settlers at Los Dos Carlos could "enjoy the right of primogeniture, as is done in Spain." He must have known that this revolutionary provision signified a much larger departure from the history of Indian land ownership in the empire. Though Indians were allowed to hold and utilize land communally, the Spanish Crown legitimized their possession through the idea of *dominio útil*, which meant that pre-Hispanic occupation of their lands gave them the right of continued use. However, their legal classification as perpetual minors meant that Indians lacked absolute rights to their land.[49] By proposing a drastic change to this tradition—not unlike what Campillo had argued for in his *New System for Economic Government*—Martínez Compañón imagined remaking the plebeian mine workers into self-sufficient wage earners who could build wealth for their living and future relatives. He seems not to have considered that such a proposal ran counter to the very machinations of empire in America. Instead of marking and codifying difference between Indians and Spaniards, it provided an avenue to surmount these inequalities.[50]

Along with offering the mine workers an unprecedented chance at land ownership, Martínez Compañón hoped to further ensure their self-sufficiency by providing them with "one mule, ten sheep, one beef cow, one milk cow, one bull, one pig, six hens, and a rooster," as well as "one plough, one hoe, and one ax." With these implements, they could transport their silver ore as well as provide their families with beef, pork, chicken, dairy products, and various food crops. This was a starkly different vision from how most mining towns handled matters of commerce and comestibles: most often, mine workers were paid in credit, which they then used to purchase the food and household items at a company store owned by the mine owners, just as the Hualgayoc miners' guild had suggested. Unsurprisingly, such a process typically furthered the mine workers' debts and dependency.

In addition to imagining what would attract laborers to the mine, the Bishop considered what reservations they might have about the project. He guessed that Indians would be suspicious of whether the Los Dos Carlos settlement was an elaborate plan to entrap them in virtual slavery. So he mandated that administrative officials, miners, and overseers at Hualgayoc "agree to treat [the workers] with all humanity and tenderness." He also sought to implement structural changes that would make the work at the mines less onerous. The plan to move workers and their families nearer to the mine would help "keep them in the best possible health by getting them accustomed from childhood to the winds and the climate of the mine." Once the settlers were old enough to work underground, the Bishop wanted to ensure that they did so in safer conditions. He decreed that the miners should be forced to invest more in vital infrastructure, such as the wooden support beams that prevented the deadly cave-ins that were an almost constant threat. "The mine will never be fixed if this continues," he reasoned, because if the mine workers truly felt that their safety was in jeopardy, they would simply "go and work [the mine] in a different place," leaving the town abandoned and the mine owners without the workers they so dearly needed.

Also key to the well-being of the mine workers was allowing them sufficient rest. Martínez Compañón thought that they needed more than the customary half-hour breaks in the morning and evening, for workers to do "what they vulgarly call *coquear*" (to chew coca leaves, which the Indians believed gave them energy, quelled nausea, and abated hunger).[51] Instead, he proposed three solid hours of rest every day, which he was sure that they needed "because of the nature of the work and the weakness of their constitutions . . . in these environments." Finally, he hoped that night shifts in the mines could be eliminated, or else assigned only to volunteers who would be properly remunerated. Alternately, night shifts might be given to "those who deserve it as punishment, or are lazy, or vagabonds."[52] Taken together, these measures would vastly improve the workers' quality of life.

Though they may seem simplistic by modern standards, these precautions were revolutionary for their time. In fact, the most well-known analysis of the colonial mining industry, Gamboa's *Commentaries on the Mining Ordinances of New Spain*, touched on the deplorable conditions in the mines but made no specific suggestions as to how to improve the actual work. Similarly, the 1778 exposé of working conditions at Spain's Almadén mercury mine penned by Spanish doctor José Parés described the ailments that frequently plagued mine workers but made no exact recommendations on how to eliminate such problems. Martínez Compañón's vision for Hualgayoc, then, stands out all the more for its proposed on-the-ground improvements for daily life in the mines.[53]

At the same time, the Bishop realized that, like everyone else involved in silver mining, the laborers harbored dreams of building the prosperity that would enable their families to become self-sustaining subjects of the Spanish Crown. So he suggested that Los Dos Carlos guarantee the customary right of *polleos*, or the chance for the workers to enter the mines on their free day (typically, Saturdays) and extract ore for themselves, which they could then sell. Throughout Peru, many miners believed that this was "the only way to attract workers."[54] But at Hualgayoc, the guild wished to outlaw unrestricted *polleos* and impose a five-hundred-peso fine on any mine owners who allowed them to continue. They proposed instead that each Saturday after work, the *barreteros* and *capacheros* be allowed to take out one *capacho*—a basket that could hold about twenty to forty pounds of ore but "with the express condition and charge that . . . he sells it only to his mine owner."[55] In reality, such a tightly monitored scheme offered little to the mine worker. Martínez Compañón, in contrast, proposed that if the workers were properly paid and supervised, *polleos* would serve only to endear them more to the settlement at Los Dos Carlos.

The Bishop stipulated that those who served their supervisors at the mine "with happiness and love" for at least twelve years should be rewarded with a sort of retirement fund that would provide them with five hundred or a thousand pesos a year, paid in installments. "This provision would cost little," Martínez Compañón gently reminded Viceroy Croix, "and it would form some sort of hierarchy among the workers" so that "they would be more obedient to their supervisors, and they would all work so that they would one day be deserving of this award."[56]

Incentivizing obedience and productivity was a tactic that the Bishop had applied to his Indian schools, where he had wanted to reward the best students with titles of nobility and silken finery, reasoning that this would "appeal to the natural emulation . . . [that the Indians] have among themselves."[57] He was convinced that this same principle could function at Los Dos Carlos. But first, work at the mine needed to be monetized. This stood in contrast to the customary practice of paying workers in goods—something that the miners had explicitly argued for, claiming the right of each owner to "personally provide to his workers all that they need . . . for the sustenance of themselves and their families."[58] Martínez Compañón, in contrast, thought that acting as *habilitadores*, or loan agents, would "distract the miners from their job" while also being "unnecessarily expensive for the workers." Such coercion was sure to engender "a breeding ground of disagreement and distrust" between mine owners and laborers. Instead, he proposed that workers should be paid in cash and be able to spend that cash as they saw fit. Such an arrangement, he argued, would "incite [the laborers] to work to be able to afford [the] goods" that they coveted. He pointed out the added benefit of creating a conveniently captive market for Spanish wares. Furthermore, when the workers gathered at the market to make their purchases, "they would all have to act with decency to one another, which would invigorate commerce and make them want to work to be able to maintain themselves." Periodic markets would also help the workers to socialize within the context of their new and improved roles as consumers of Spanish goods. "They would continually deal with one another," the Bishop imagined, and "a shared understanding of one another's customs would grow between them . . . and some good marriages, or at least better marriages than they have been known to create while remaining only in their local villages."[59] The Bishop thought that the people of Los Dos Carlos might establish a regular weekly market day. All this was a classic liberal recipe for promoting individual initiative and free commerce. Martínez Compañón's city on a mountain would become a living laboratory for liberal eighteenth-century ideas of improvement, a tiny slice of utopia in Trujillo.

While the labor and financial measures would engender the structural improvements that the Bourbons sought for Trujillo's mining industry, the Bishop's plan for Hualgayoc featured intellectual components as well. He proposed the foundation of a mining college where students would learn "mineralogy, metallurgy, natural sciences, and the arts leading to the most perfect and efficacious mining, and use of metals."[60] He advocated the formation of a society to discuss matters of mining and propose innovations. He suggested contracting mining experts from Mexico who knew how to build modern refineries that used horses instead of men for heavy work. He wrote to Croix that he had heard that this new technology was so efficient that "in fifteen or twenty days," ten horses could do the work "formerly done by a hundred men in two months."[61] He promoted awarding innovative guild members with monetary prizes from the guild savings account and sponsoring annual contests about mining problems. The best entries would be rewarded with a medal that the Bishop thought might feature "the king's face on one side, and on the other side the inscription *Charles III—True Father of the Americas and*

Hualgayoc." He added afterward that alternate, simpler prizes could include a "silver inkstand" or a "little knife."[62] In the end, the silver inkstands, metallurgy classes, and imported experts all were meant to do one thing (in addition to improving profits at the mine, that is): by developing a culture of information exchange, academic rigor, and polite sociability, they would contribute to the civility and good order of the Hualgayoc settlement.

The Bishop knew that Los Dos Carlos, like any good city on a hill, would be built on a foundation of religious devotion and clerical supervision. During their transformation into productive plebeian workers, the Indian settlers would be guided by the "intelligent, virtuous, and well-educated" priests whom Martínez Compañón sought to place in charge of the town, at least during its early years. They would help remedy the sad state of religious devotion in the mining district, about which the Bishop complained that "there is not one church where the Holy Mass might be celebrated, or the word of God explained." He realized that this was partly due to the area's sparse population. If such conditions made it too difficult for priests to properly perform their duties, the Bishop thought that perhaps his *operarios eclesiásticos* might help in attending to the needs of the miners and mine workers. He imagined that every year, a group of these young men would make a visitation of the area, hearing confession from the faithful whenever they could. Under the watchful eye of priests and the *operarios*, Los Dos Carlos would instill order and discipline among the settlers. The Bishop knew that this was of the utmost importance in the workers' lives but also remembered the broader "service that this would do to humanity, agriculture, the miners' guild, and the state."

While Church authorities could oversee the settlers' proper behavior and religious observance, Martínez Compañón knew that they alone would not provide for all the town's needs. To be most effective, religious supervision had to be paired with secular authority, preferably in the form of a bureaucrat who could manage operations on the mountain and represent the miners in the viceregal capital. The Bishop proposed that the best person for this job would be a judicial figure who could keep Hualgayoc from becoming as unruly as Potosí, which was legendary for its "continuous barbarity" and "unnamed irredeemable homicides."[63] This man would be the ultimate overseer of "good order in everything." It would be his responsibility to "promote the work and economics of the mine," and he should see to the good treatment of the workers. At the same time, he would be careful to "not do injustice or harm with his actions and privileges." Martínez Compañón thought that when it came to dealing with unpaid loan debt, having a judge serve as head of the colony would be most useful; if necessary, he could withhold funds or even embargo silver deposits. At the same time, he was to ensure that "the workers . . . and their salaries should never be interfered with." The bank could oversee that the mine workers would "receive their salaries in cash on a daily or weekly basis." Running the bank in this way, the Bishop thought, would not only help the miners and the workers; it would also generate "improved consumption of supplies" because more money would circulate within the bishopric. The bank would have positive effects "for the general merchants of Castile and for the clothes that are made there."[64] The participation of religious and judicial authorities was central to the success of the settlement, perhaps all the more because the Bishop knew that his proposed town would stand as a marker of something that he cared dearly about but rarely spoke of directly: "my [own] reputation."

Martínez Compañón must have been well aware that the ways in which others responded to his vision of reform at the mine reflected on his broader agenda for Trujillo. Though as of late fall of 1784, there was still much to be done at the mine, the demands of his *visita* beckoned, and he had to leave Cajamarca behind. In his stead, he appointed Pedro Orbegoso, then Justicia Mayor of Cajamarca, as magistrate. "I consulted him because I knew he was just," the Bishop confided to Viceroy Croix years after his visit to the mine. "He had learned a lot by doing business in this mine for many years." Undoubtedly, Martínez Compañón also suggested Orbegoso because of how the latter advocated on behalf of the Indian mine workers. He had argued that the more skilled *barreteros* should be paid six reales of daily wages, and all other workers four—a significant increase over the two to four reales that Espinach and Azereto had recommended earlier. Orbegoso also concurred with the Bishop's plan to place a judge at the head of the mine. He wrote to his bishop explaining that the judge should be a gentleman and "of well-regarded behavior in commerce in the kingdom."[65] Orbegoso's correspondence does not indicate whether he was surprised when Martínez Compañón nominated him for the position.

Orbegoso was an attractive candidate because he endorsed the plan to create an exchange bank that would purchase silver and sell mercury, as well as a separate loan bank that would lend extra capital to the miners. Recall that Martínez Compañón's idea of two separate banks diverged from the miners' original proposal, which was for one bank managed and sponsored by the Spanish

Crown to handle exchanges as well as loans. The miners' vision of the bank fit with their own emphasis on creating a closed-market system at the mine. In the Bishop's mind, a single institution supported by the Crown would create more dependency in the mining sector. He proposed instead that the two functions should be handled separately. He imagined these banks as private institutions funded by merchants as well as a portion of the miners' profits.

When Martínez Compañón first turned to Orbegoso for his opinion on the bank, the latter knew that he could not make any final recommendations without investigating the matter. On September 16, 1784, the Justicia Mayor wrote to Martínez Compañón, explaining that he "would like to have a singular and well-researched report" on how much raw silver the mine produced and how much mercury the bank would need to supply the refineries. He also wanted to know exactly how much capital the miners' guild would need for the loan fund. In only one week, Orbegoso gathered the information he needed. He recommended that the fund contain 300,000 pesos provided by the Crown. He approved of the plan to purchase silver for the sum of six pesos, four reales per marco, with two reales of each selling price retained as an operating fund for the bank. Unlike the miners' guild, which had suggested that the alcalde run the bank, Orbegoso believed that a merchant company, one where all members would be "well-informed about the process of politics" and finance, would be better suited to administer the banks. The loan bank should offer loan capital to miners for a period of only six months, he thought, because otherwise, the rising price of silver would make their investments in the miners less profitable. The fact that the Bishop and Orbegoso seemed to be of the same mind about how the miners should be financed must have been reassuring. As Martínez Compañón's attempts to build new towns and primary schools had shown, in the colonies the success or failure of a project depended heavily on its ties to local power networks. Choosing the right collaborators and pleasing the proper authorities were essential.[66]

Utopia Versus Empire

After Martínez Compañón and Orbegoso agreed so readily on the bank, it was surprising that the latter took issue with several points of the Bishop's plan for Los Dos Carlos. Most disturbingly, after his appointment, Martínez Compañón reported that Orbegoso had boldly admitted that "he did not approve of moving the workers . . . [to the new town], as it would be contrary to the subordination in which they should live to the miners, and it would create discord and differences."[67] While Martínez Compañón sought to transform the workers into an independent free holding class, Orbegoso suddenly seemed set on maintaining their dependency. This point of contention highlighted the broader ideological conflicts surrounding the project: Martínez Compañón appears to have been the only one who imagined such a revolutionary change in the social order in Cajamarca. He failed to recognize that his concern for the workers had veered into radical territory and that it could easily be construed as threatening the social order of the area. But Orbegoso's reservations beg more questions: Did the reticence about the new town suggest a broader discomfort with the Bishop's plan? Who would the local elites side with? It was likely that the hacendados who had already agreed to sell their lands for the town would probably continue to support the project. They would still benefit from the wages of their workers—all the more because these would be transferred into the more profitable mining sector. But local elites who did not own any of the lands or mines in question did not stand to benefit from the project. For them, transforming disenfranchised Indians into landholding workers threatened to turn the whole world upside down.

Soon, other roadblocks to creating Los Dos Carlos emerged. Recall that the Bishop and the miners' guild had concurred on where it should be located: they had agreed that the lands of Bambamarca were best suited for the project, especially since they already possessed a "good, wide and deep ditch that has all the water . . . [the town] would ever need."[68] Furthermore, they had testimony from local mine owners confirming that "in Bambamarca, they would find all that was necessary: good climate, supplies to build the necessary buildings and to have fields and gardens, an open and passable road to the mine, and better proximity to the valleys, so that provisions could be brought to the mines."[69] Not everyone agreed with the Bishop and the guild. Azereto and Espinach had recommended the Lanacancha hacienda as the principal territory for the settlement, even though they disputed which adjoining lands should be purchased. But Martínez Compañón had also sought the opinion of the other miners who had been unable to attend the meeting with the Bishop. This splinter group claimed that Bambamarca had no water, so any settlement there would not be able to operate refineries—thus erasing the convenience and lessened travel time that were the basis of the entire project. Undeterred, Martínez Compañón visited the Bambamarca location, where he found water that "in addition to being very abundant . . . was of very good quality." It seems that the splinter group of miners had purposely tried to derail the project. Soon disagreements began to pile up. Most parties appeared intent on pursuing their own possible interests, and with so many individuals involved, a debilitating chaos seemed inevitable.

The five miners had further disagreements with the Los Dos Carlos project as well. They opposed the proposed salt contract, which stipulated that the *corregidores* of Lambayeque and Huamachuco would supply the mines with salt for refining at the price of four pesos, four reales per load. They thought that such a plan stood "against free commerce." They suggested that in addition to demolishing the existing buildings at the mining settlements of Micuypampa, Purgatorio, and La Punta, something that the miners' guild had proposed, all the refineries at the foot of the mountain should be destroyed—likely because it was too difficult to monitor them for fraud and theft. The five miners in particular seemed to see the situation at Hualgayoc as a zero-sum game: if the salt contract was too favorable for refiners, they would lose. If the refineries were too accessible, their own economic interests would suffer. This was the opposite of the collaborative notion of communal improvement that Martínez Compañón had envisioned. To try to change their minds, he cautioned against such large-scale destruction, reminding them that many of the owners involved were too poor to recover from such a blow and that if such destruction were inevitable, they should at least be fairly compensated for their losses.

Ultimately, the Bishop could not broach the differences between the guild and the five dissenting miners, so he decided that the matter would remain unresolved until a later date. "In the meantime," he suggested, "the miners and merchants can raise some financial support for the moving of the towns." Similarly, he had to beg off on the question of where exactly the town of Los Dos Carlos would be founded. He left it up to the miners' guild to decide whether Lanacancha or Bambamarca "would be best . . . [and] have the resources to solidify the good and prosperity of the guild, which would also benefit the province, and the state in general."[70] He was finding that despite their original receptivity toward the plan for Los Dos Carlos, now elites felt that it would be too costly to their own interests. Ultimately, they preferred the status quo—or, as the original thirty-two points that the guild had put forward exemplified, the status quo disguised in the eighteenth-century rhetoric of improvement. In hindsight, we can see that their attempts to manipulate the process by placing their own officials on the inside, their insistence on a controlled market situation, and their eagerness to employ the rhetoric of public improvement as a disguise for promoting their own economic interests were all signifiers of where their true allegiances lay. Concerned mainly for their own financial prospects, they refused to accept Martínez Compañón's vision of utopia as their own.

While such squabbles surely complicated the project, these were not the only limitations that the Bishop faced. The most serious obstruction was the most predictable one: finances. Orbegoso had calculated that the entire project would cost about 300,000 pesos, an untenable sum roughly approximate to the annual production of all Hualgayoc.[71] At first glance, such a discrepancy between profits and available funding makes the Bishop's proposal seem shockingly idealistic—even for him. Yet a closer look into the mine's finances suggests that Martínez Compañón was not entirely misguided.

The mines were, in fact, profitable—but the problem in accessing the funds ran much deeper than even the greed of the miners. Despite their protestations of poverty, studies of regional income levels in the viceroyalty indicate that Trujillo's finances improved dramatically after the discovery of the Hualgayoc mine. For instance, from 1760 to 1769, Trujillo brought in only 29,076 pesos. The only provincial treasury, or caja, with a smaller income in that period was Saña. But by the next decade, Trujillo had become the fourth-largest income generator in the viceroyalty when its revenues shot up to 117,278. In 1780 through 1789—Martínez Compañón's years in Trujillo—the local caja brought in 344,605 pesos, even more than Cuzco, which generated only 338,329 for that period. The statistics for regional mining profits tell a similar story: for the 1760s, Trujillo generated zero income in that sector; but by the following decade, it had become the third-largest mining producer. By 1790, mining in Trujillo had produced 112,110 pesos. Trade income also skyrocketed over the late colonial period: it went from 13,105 in the 1770s to 36,216 in the following decade. In fact, after 1770, Peru's northern region brought in about 6–9 percent of all revenues throughout the viceroyalty.[72]

Some scholars argue that Hualgayoc's production gains were due to increased investment in drainage tunnels and easier access to mercury. Whatever the reason for the jump in profits, understanding that the mines at Hualgayoc made the region one of the most financially critical parts of the viceroyalty in the late colonial period begs another question: If regional finances were so flush, why was there no funding available for Martínez Compañón's improvement agenda at the mine itself and elsewhere in Trujillo? Part of the explanation lies in Spanish economic policy, which decreed that any income of the local cajas was redirected to Lima, and then dispersed throughout the empire via a complex taxation instrument known as the *situado*. In late eighteenth-century Peru, this meant that a vast portion of silver profits—including those from Cajamarca—were reinvested in military matters: defending Peru's Pacific coast from pirate attacks by building garrisons and forts and supplying troops; and sponsoring the attacks against the Túpac Amaru rebels in southern Peru. Other amounts were frequently sent out of the viceroyalty; as early as 1770, surplus funds from Peru's silver mines were redirected south, to the viceroyalty of Río de la Plata to shore up defenses for the increasingly strategic commercial depot of Buenos Aires.[73] Later, Peruvian silver was also sent to Panama and Chile.[74] Although this practice of siphoning from the most profitable colonies to finance poorer ones had been standard in the empire since the mid-sixteenth century, the Bishop must have felt his patience tested when he watched how the successes of his little corner of the kingdom were repossessed and repositioned, leaving the local community no better off than when the project began. The community-based collaborative notion of improvement and prosperity that was the very center of his utopia was, it turned out, essentially incompatible with the economic infrastructure of the Spanish Empire.

In the end, the utopian mining town of Los Dos Carlos never came to be. The land was not purchased from the hacendados who had agreed to sell. The 60,000 pesos set aside for hoes, axes, and pairs of mules was not spent. The Indians did not journey to the settlement to receive their free plots of land, oxen, or mules. In fact, the situation at Hualgayoc remained mostly the same throughout the end of the colonial period. In June 1788, the miners found themselves mired in collective debt of 119,618 pesos despite the jump in profits.[75] In 1794, Martínez Compañón's nephew José Ignacio de Lecuanda commented that if the necessary reforms at Hualgayoc could be enacted, "it would be an abundant source [of income] for the state." More pessimistically, he added, "but it seems that the same wealth blinds us to reason, making us apply less effort to achieving it than coveting opulence."[76] As late as 1802, Alexander Humboldt reported from Cajamarca that conditions in the mine were substandard. Miners failed to maintain the various small veins of ore, choosing to rent or sell them when extraction became difficult, instead of investing in better infrastructure.[77]

If the Los Dos Carlos project died a slow death after Martínez Compañón's departure, does this mean that its only legacy is one of incompletion, bureaucratic backlog, and unrealistic finances? Even though the mining city on a hill never came to be, its plans were meaningful and influential. For instance, several key points of the plan for Los Dos Carlos later appeared elsewhere in Peru. Along the lines of the proposal for the Hualgayoc bank, mining communities throughout the viceroyalty requested their own banks: the miners of Pasco petitioned for one in 1786; and in 1788, the Cuzco miners wanted to open one there. In Cajamarca, nine years after the plan for the Hualgayoc bank was first articulated, an exchange bank opened at the mine. It operated successfully for two years, until Viceroy Gil had it inspected and closed down upon suspicion that officials were personally profiting from the venture. Almost simultaneously, the Hualgayoc miners were again petitioning for a separate loan bank, although this never came to be.[78]

The Bishop's proposal to arrange a visit of mining experts who "could bring many advantages to this mine" through their knowledge of modern machinery and refining technology was similarly unsuccessful during his time at Hualgayoc; later, similar ideas reverberated throughout the viceroyalty.[79] Under Escobedo's supervision, smelting expert José Coquet arrived in Peru in July 1785. He visited the mines at Huarochirí and Pasco before returning to Lima and enjoying a lengthy career as a bureaucrat in the mining industry, which included being named general director of mining in the kingdom, along with Limeño mining expert Santiago de Urquizu. Later in their careers, their main task was to oversee the imposition of the 1783 Mexican Mining Ordinances in Peru—something that Martínez Compañón had also recommended. In 1790, the Swedish mining expert Thaddeus von Nordenflicht arrived in Peru and immediately began experiments to determine whether barrel refining was a preferable method of processing silver.[80]

More important, the Bishop's plan to place a judge at the head of the mine appears to have succeeded. By August 1784, Francisco López Calderón had become a member of the Tribunal de Minería as well as the Judge of Mines of Trujillo. He recommended several specific measures that seem to be drawn directly from the pages of the Bishop's plans for Hualgayoc: paying workers in cash, allowing them to purchase the goods that they needed from whomever they wished (not just the operator of the mine in which they worked), improving working conditions in the mine, and calling for experts to visit Hualgayoc.[81]

Perhaps back in Trujillo, as he tended to *cabildo* business and celebrated Mass in the cathedral, Martínez Compañón might have looked on these changes to the Cajamarca mining industry and felt satisfied. Los Dos Carlos had not come to be, but profits at the mine continued to increase, mining banks were opening throughout the viceroyalty, experts visited other mines (if not Hualgayoc), and—undoubtedly, most important for him—the people of Trujillo were at least considering the welfare of the Indian workers. Cajamarca was faring better as well; a 1794 *Mercurio Peruano* article reported that commerce had proliferated throughout the region, and "all the poverty of the town has turned to opulence; their humble outfits are now ostentatious finery."[82]

Maybe sometimes, just for a moment, the Bishop felt satisfied with one other aspect of the plans: how even though Hualgayoc had not become the workers' utopia that he had envisioned, his plans to reform the mine generated praise from his superiors. In his official instructions to Fernando Saavedra, the first intendant of Trujillo, Jorge Escobedo, publicly praised "the carefulness with which the Illustrious Lord Bishop of that Diocese has tried to foster the reestablishment and arrangement of said [Hualgayoc] mine." He pointed out how the Bishop's proposals reminded everyone that the mine's main problems—"the lack of people, mules, and salt"—were "not unfixable."[83] But Martínez Compañón must have treasured even more a letter that arrived from Lima, dated June 20, 1786, from Viceroy Croix:

> I have read with singular pleasure and joy the letter from May 29 of this year that your Illustriousness sent to me, which accompanied the reports about the mines of Hualgayoc, the ruinous state in which they lie, and the means to reestablish them.
>
> I admire very much the wise conduct of their author, his zeal for the common good, and his wisdom and insight in knowing men and pressing them to remove themselves from their previous preoccupations, making them move ahead and understand their true interests. For all of this, I give to Your Illustriousness the most round and full thanks, and also for the certainty with which you work to promote the physical and spiritual good of this bishopric, sacrificing your own riches, time, and health. And I assure you that you should proceed with all confidence in this matter, treating it as you see fit.[84]

Though we have no notice of how the Bishop continued his work with Hualgayoc after this letter, he could not have accomplished too much. Just over two years later—on September 12, 1788—he received word of his promotion. As soon as he could get his affairs in order and arrange for his passage, the

Bishop of Trujillo was to become the Archbishop of Bogotá. Perhaps his mining city on a silver mountain, despite its failure, had played a part in enhancing his reputation and earning his promotion. Or, as the Bishop may have sometimes wondered in his darker moments, its liberal social provisions might have angered his superiors, who then sought a way to remove him from his beloved Trujillo. It was a question for which he would never find a definitive answer.

CHAPTER 6

Local Botany: The Products of Utopia

As the Bishop and his team made the final preparations for their departure to Bogotá, where he would assume his new post, we might imagine him surrounded by twenty-four large wooden crates, each numbered and marked with the letters *MD*, signifying their final destination of Madrid. While he prepared their contents to journey to Spain alongside Peru's outgoing Viceroy Croix, he surveyed the results of six years spent documenting what he called the "productions of nature" of Trujillo. As the largest intendancy and bishopric in Peru, Trujillo encompassed warm, pastel-hued agricultural valleys; steamy Amazonian forests full of the noises of strange creatures; the rocky, desolate terrain of the sierra; and the damp air and drifting sands of the coastal desert. Each of these climates was home to an astounding number of animals, plants, and native cultures, the majority of which were represented in this natural history collection. Martínez Compañón and his assistants would have carefully wrapped Indian masks; tools and instruments; minerals from Trujillo's mines; textiles; plant leaves, stems, and flowers; and taxidermied animals, including a *cahapi-curo* (porcupine), which they described as a "worm between thorns." Cases within boxes held snails and other small marine species. There were several more curious items, such as lizard butter (which, according to the Bishop, the Indians used to cure pain, buying it for two reales a pound), a rock in the shape of a cross, and the bones of a *rumihuma*, or "hard-headed" fish, used to treat urinary retention, ground and dissolved in a small amount of water.[1]

Although most naturalists had high hopes for their work, the Bishop nevertheless expressed reservations. His poor health and the concerns of his office had kept him from devoting as much time to it as he would have liked, and he was not yet finished compiling the painted images that were meant to form the accompanying "paper museum" depicting what the team had observed during their travels throughout the bishopric. Because of time constraints, he had yet to begin writing his natural, civil, and moral history of the bishopric of Trujillo; nor had he had time to rearrange the collection and the images so that their contents would correspond to what would be written in his book. He still hoped that one day this massive project would inspire other regional histories of provinces or bishoprics and that, taken together, these would serve to create a "perfect and complete" history of "these vast regions" called Peru.[2]

We can imagine that, as he hurriedly wrapped his precious objects, Martínez Compañón would have been keenly aware that time was of the essence: for now, the book and the illustrations would have to wait. The natural specimens were rapidly deteriorating in the humid coastal environment and soon would become unusable; the entire collection of birds (which, he boasted, contained a pair of almost every species in the bishopric) had molded and been ruined, a mishap that caused him "great pain and anguish." So he chose to send ahead the remaining items more quickly than he had planned. Certain specimens, such as a "lizard" that was almost ten feet long, did not fit into the boxes. Others, he cautioned, perhaps thinking of the simple *cuy*, or guinea pig, raised throughout the region, might seem inconsequential at first. But ultimately, as Martínez Compañón wrote to the Spanish minister of justice Antonio Porlier, he was confident that "in nature there is nothing as ridiculous or worthless as it might seem."[3]

In the eighteenth-century Spanish Atlantic world, this statement was most poignant with regard to plant specimens. From 1745 through 1819, no fewer than 335 natural history collections were shipped from Spain's overseas territories to Madrid. Approximately 87 percent of their materials were plant matter.[4] The immense value that governments, naturalists, and individuals placed on plant specimens is reflected by their dominance in the Bishop's collection. Thanks to the care with which Martínez Compañón recorded the materials, we know exactly what was contained in each of the twenty-four crates that the Bishop sent to Madrid. Of those, five crates—by far, the largest segment—were filled entirely with botanical matter. Crate eleven contained pressed and dried medicinal herbs, separated into four cases. These held specimens such as the *cuhillo-pico* plant, useful for treating burns, and the *floripondio* flowers, which were "good for sleeplessness" when left under one's pillow at night. Box twelve included various balsams from local trees and the *chinquisi* plant, whose pressed leaves produced oil similar to olive oil.

Crate fourteen featured the seventeen types of fever-combating cascarilla that grew in Trujillo, and box fifteen was composed of food plants such as cacao, coffee, sugar, and almonds. Fruits, vegetables, and spices, such as cinnamon, saffron, and beans, made up box sixteen. Five other crates included plant items such as tree bark and cotton from Chachapoyas. The collection inventory described them listing their Quechua names, followed by the Castilian translation if available, the climate of the area of origin, and the way the locals used the plant. *Cuhillo-pico*, for instance, translated as "monkey bird" in Spanish, grew in cold and temperate climates, was cooked in water to ease urine retention, or used as a powder to treat burns. "Rat's ear" (*venchaprinrin*, in Quechua) grew in muddy and cold areas and was useful for cleaning and healing wounds.

Though records show that the plant material was shipped to the Royal Botanical Garden, the specimens, including the rat's-ear and monkey-bird leaves, were not cataloged and presumably have long since been discarded. We know about them today because the inventory that painstakingly described the contents of the Bishop's collection was preserved in Seville's Archive of the Indies. Also surviving are the 1,372 watercolor illustrations that Martínez Compañón commissioned to visually represent his natural history research. As images on paper, they were key components of the Spanish efforts to make visible the rich natural world of the Spanish territories. In an age that lacked technological reproductions, drawings and illustrations—along with actual specimens—were the most objective and unadulterated of sources. They also had one distinct advantage over live or dried plant specimens: they were transportable and durable. Images of plants could be analyzed by experts in Madrid, Dresden, and beyond.[5]

Even a brief reading of the *Trujillo* volumes makes abundantly clear how Martínez Compañón and his informants found visual botanical information to be the most important aspect of Trujillo's natural world. Volumes 3, 4, and 5 of the watercolors—488 images in total—focus solely on plants, trees, shrubs, flowers, and herbs. These vibrantly colored and stylistically original illustrations show the bark, leaves, and stems of the *huambuquero* plant, the tree that produces the sweet sapote fruit; and the manzanilla (chamomile) flower, plucked from the ground to its roots. Other illustrations, such as that of the *algarrobo*, or carob tree—prized in Peru for its solid wood and the sweet syrup made from its fruit—depict the plant in parts, with the leaves and the seedpod shown separately alongside the tree. Intended to familiarize the viewer with the plant life native to the various microclimates of northern Peru, the illustrations include many of the plants that are most important in

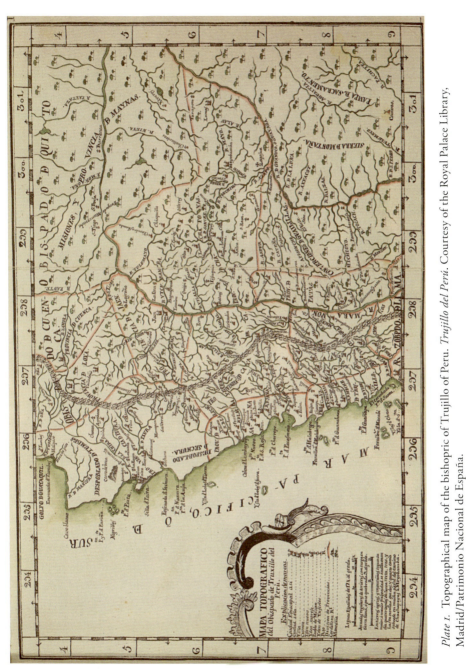

Plate 1. Topographical map of the bishopric of Trujillo of Peru. *Trujillo del Perú.* Courtesy of the Royal Palace Library, Madrid/Patrimonio Nacional de España.

Plate 2. Indians playing cards. *Trujillo del Perú.* Courtesy of the Royal Palace Library, Madrid/ Patrimonio Nacional de España.

Plate 3. Anteater. *Trujillo del Perú.* Courtesy of the Royal Palace Library, Madrid/ Patrimonio Nacional de España.

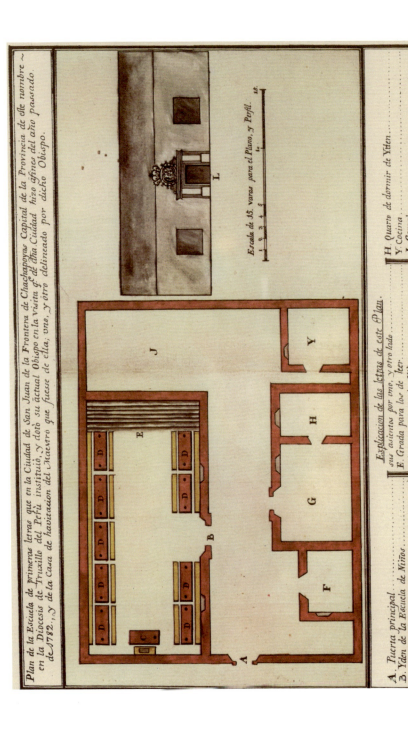

Plate 4. Plan for the primary school in the city of San Juan de la Frontera de Chachapoyas. *Trujillo del Perú.* Courtesy of the Royal Palace Library, Madrid/Patrimonio Nacional de España.

Plate 5. Hill Indian. *Trujillo del Perú.* Courtesy of the Royal Palace Library, Madrid/Patrimonio Nacional de España.

Plate 6. Mestizo scarred by *uta.* *Trujillo del Perú.* Courtesy of the Royal Palace Library, Madrid/ Patrimonio Nacional de España.

Plate 7. Eight-real coin, 1768. Photo by Bill Soule.

Plate 8. Baltasar Jaime Martínez Compañón y Bujanda, José Miguel Figueroa, ca. 1830. Copyright Museo Nacional de Colombia.

Plate 9. Indian boys playing jai alai. *Trujillo del Perú.* Courtesy of the Royal Palace Library, Madrid / Patrimonio Nacional de España.

Plate 10. Infidel Indians of the mountains in canoe. *Trujillo del Perú.* Courtesy of the
Royal Palace Library, Madrid/Patrimonio Nacional de España.

Plate 11. Woman with leprosy bathing. *Trujillo del Perú*. Courtesy of the Royal Palace Library, Madrid/Patrimonio Nacional de España.

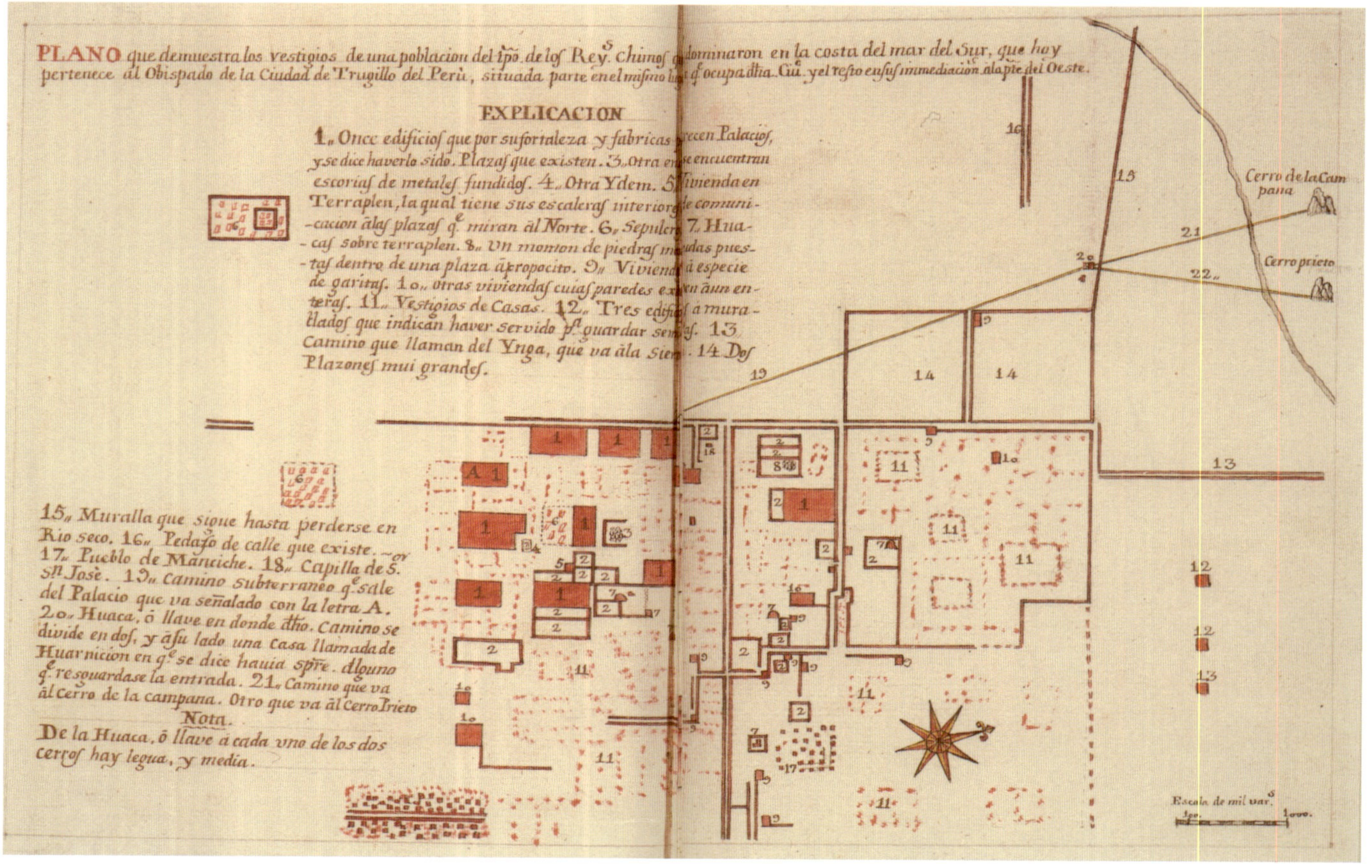

Plate 12. Map of the vestiges of a town of the time of the Chimú kings (Chan Chan). *Trujillo del Perú*. Courtesy of the Royal Palace Library, Madrid/Patrimonio Nacional de España.

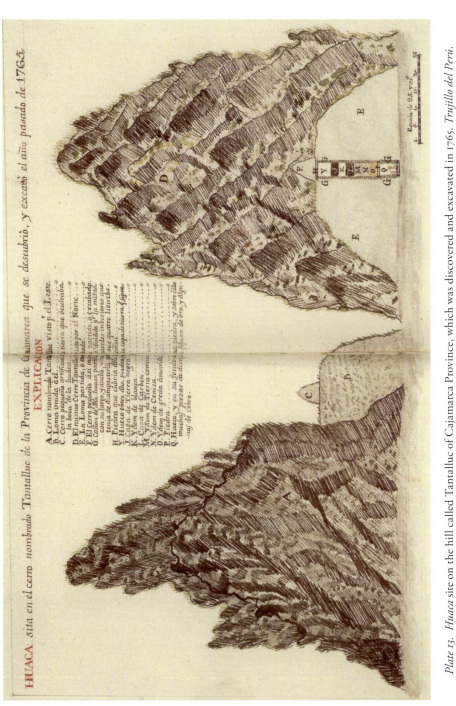

HUACA *sita en el cerro nombrado Tantalluc de la Provincia de Cajamarca que se descubrió, y excavó el año pasado de 1765.*

EXPLICACION

A. Cerro nombrado Tantalluc visto p.^r el Leste.
B. Loma unida á él.
C. Cerro pequeño artificial, y tierra que ocultaba la boca de la huaca.
D. El mismo Cerro Tantalluc visto por el Norte.
E. La Loma partida, ó Quebrada.
F. El Cerro pequeño así mismo partido, ó cavado.
G. Camino de la huaca partido, ó dividido á la mitad con su largo, y ancho. Y las paredes interiores que tenía de mampostería, en sus quatro tercios.
H. Piedra, que cubría dicha huaca.
Y. Hueco entre dha. piedra, la capa, ó tierra q.^e sigue.
J. Capa de Tierra negra.
K. Ydem de blanca.
L. Capa de Carbon.
M. Ydem de Tierra comun.
N. Ydem de Ceniza.
O. Ydem de greda amarilla.
P. Piedra.
Q. Hueco, y en su fondo, ó piedra, y sobre ella muchos pedazos ó piezas de diferentes figura de oro, y algunas de Cobre.

Escala de 28. var.^s

Plate 13. Huaca site on the hill called Tantalluc of Cajamarca Province, which was discovered and excavated in 1765. Trujillo del Perú.
Courtesy of the Royal Palace Library, Madrid/Patrimonio Nacional de España.

Plate 14. Indian shepherdess giving birth. *Trujillo del Perú.* Courtesy of the Royal Palace Library, Madrid/Patrimonio Nacional de España.

Plate 15. Indian boys playing with a top. *Trujillo del Perú.* Courtesy of the Royal Palace Library, Madrid/ Patrimonio Nacional de España.

Plate 16. Chimú dance. *Trujillo del Perú.* Courtesy of the Royal Palace Library, Madrid/ Patrimonio Nacional de España.

Plate 17. Dance of the decapitation of the Inca. *Trujillo del Perú*. Courtesy of the Royal Palace Library, Madrid/Patrimonio Nacional de España.

Plate 18. Infidel Indian
of the mountains.
Trujillo del Perú.
Courtesy of the
Royal Palace Library,
Madrid/Patrimonio
Nacional de España.

Plate 19. Capacheros
carrying metal.
Trujillo del Perú.
Courtesy of the
Royal Palace
Library, Madrid/
Patrimonio
Nacional de España.

Plate 20. Angusacha. Trujillo del Perú.
Courtesy of the Royal Palace Library,
Madrid/Patrimonio Nacional de
España.

Plate 21. Pumaparan or *ajonjoli. Trujillo del
Perú.* Courtesy of the Royal Palace Library,
Madrid/Patrimonio Nacional de España.

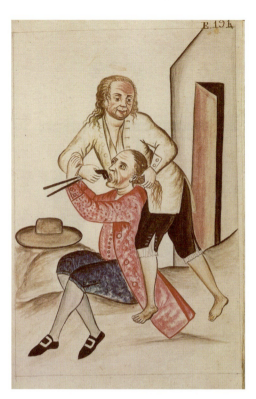

Plate 22. Indian having his molars removed. *Trujillo del Perú*. Courtesy of the Royal Palace Library, Madrid/ Patrimonio Nacional de España.

Plate 23. Omeco-machacuai. Trujillo del Perú. Courtesy of the Royal Palace Library, Madrid/Patrimonio Nacional de España.

Plate 24. Dance of the devils. *Trujillo del Perú.* Courtesy of the Royal Palace Library, Madrid/Patrimonio Nacional de España.

the region today: commercial crops such as cotton and boxwood; fruits such as the creamy cherimoya, the tart granadilla, and the almost saccharine *lucuma*; and staples such as yucca, lentils, and rice.

With broad outlines, saturated color, and flat perspective, at first glance most of the images appear to be straightforward (if stylistically unusual) representations of the plants to which they refer. Lacking any accompanying explanation, they can easily be dismissed as "pretty," if quaintly unsophisticated. However, Martínez Compañón was convinced that his natural history work had intrinsic value and would contribute "to the study and knowledge of the arts, society, and culture of the Indians of Peru."[6] This is why priests were to question their native parishioners and compile the information that they gave about the natural world. Because of historical convention—or their lack of literacy skills—the Bishop could not ask the Indians to speak in writing for themselves. Instead, they conveyed their knowledge in the oral testimony preserved in the collection inventory and in the images they painted. By having Indians illustrate and describe the natural world around them, the Bishop sought to make a social and political statement while he provided useful information to metropolitan authorities. He made visible the natural resources of his territory while simultaneously proving how its native peoples were valuable sources of useful information—not just bedraggled leftovers from formerly great civilizations, as so many Europeans claimed. Careful examination of the data that the Bishop and the Indians prepared confirms this when it produces unexpectedly exciting results, such as in the case of the *angusacha* plant (see Plate 20). According to the collection inventory, "*Angusacha*, from hot and warm places, [is] ground and applied like a paste [when] it is used to bring abscesses to a head. From its stalk pellets are made to put on the heads of them, because it is a purgative. *Angusacha*, which in Castilian means 'corrosive herb,' is also used as a powder to cure wounds, and *uta*."[7]

Read alone, this sounds like a regular ethno-pharmacological description not unlike the typical "vernacular" botanical research of the day. *Angusacha* and *uta* are both Quechua words. *Uta* was and is a popular Andean term for the skin disease leishmaniasis, an illness caused by the leishmania parasite that can be transmitted to people from sandflies or animals. Cutaneous leishmaniasis affects the skin and produces ulcers and a gray or blackish skin tone, most often on the face, and sometimes on the extremities. Mucutaneous leishmaniasis, the more severe form of the disease, affects the mouth and mucus membranes. Endemic to many parts of Latin America and three quarters of Peru, the disease was known to the pre-Incaic people of the north coast, whose pottery depicted its ravages to the human form. Leishmania is most prevalent in the northern region of the country: it has five separate strains in Peru, and four of these appear in Trujillo. Given the seriousness of the disease and its predominance in the area, it is only logical that Martínez Compañón included a plant that treated it in his collection and decided to represent that plant with an illustration in volume 3 of *Trujillo del Perú*.[8]

Without further explanation, it is difficult to understand the Bishop and the people's knowledge of the disease they called *uta*. However, combining the inventory description with images from the nine volumes produces unexpectedly rewarding results. The illustration identified as a "mestizo scarred by *uta*" (see Plate 6) clearly shows a man suffering from leishmaniasis lesions, mainly on the face. The illustrators' decision to depict a *man* suffering from the disease may have been in accordance with the way the disease still affects people: far more men than women contract it, likely because their occupations bring them into the wilderness more often. The subject has darkened skin on his nose area, suggesting that he suffers from the more serious form of the disease. He is seated on a tree in the sort of natural, wooded environment where one would likely contract leishmaniasis, and he purposefully holds a branch in his hand. Although it is smaller in scale, the plant depicted looks remarkably similar to the *angusacha* plant. A portion of his right forearm is smeared with a green paste, presumably made of the leaves of the *angusacha* plant, as the inventory indicates. Indeed, the effectiveness of this plant—officially called *mansoa standleyi*—in treating leishmaniasis was confirmed in a recent ethnopharmacological study in the nearby Loreto region of Peru.[9]

While modern confirmation of this eighteenth-century remedy is striking, even more remarkable is the abnormally oversize bug that appears in the middle right of the image. This is the sandfly that presumably transmitted the disease to the man. Today epidemiologists know that the sandfly vectors that transmit leishmaniasis in Peru are *lutzomyia peruensis* and *lutzyomyia tejadai*. These phlebotomine sandflies (which, ironically, are not found in sand) obtain the disease microbes when they feed on infected animals. The image in the Trujillo watercolor suggests that the artisans may have been depicting *lutzomyia peruensis*. It shows a fly with three sets of legs and wings that rest on an angle toward the back—the most notable characteristics of the *peruensis* fly. Taken together, the inclusion of the plant and the bug demonstrates a remarkably sophisticated understanding of epidemiology and of how to employ botanical resources: not only did the informants know that the *angusacha* plant could treat *uta*; they were also aware that the disease was spread through an insect vector. This indicates knowledge of vector-borne diseases that is far more advanced than that of the European medicinal establishment at that time. In fact, it was not until over one hundred years after the Trujillo research was completed that the work of Ronald Ross on malaria and Walter Reed on yellow fever confirmed that these two diseases were transmitted by mosquitoes. The *Trujillo* informants thus demonstrate a heretofore-unknown understanding of fly vector transmission, one that indicates a high degree of sophistication of indigenous medical knowledge, at least in the case of leishmaniasis. Though they had no opportunity to promote the medical and commercial utility of their ancestral plant-based medicine, it is a striking example of how the botanical expertise of local peoples could contribute to building a local utopia in Trujillo.[10]

Of the vast repertoire of local botanical cures, why did the informants focus on this one? Maybe Martínez Compañón realized that it had commercial potential and wanted to suggest it to the Spanish Crown as a product for exploitation. The disease most commonly affected recent immigrants to the area—mainly Europeans, because natives would have been exposed earlier in life and developed immunity. Perhaps the image meant to warn new arrivals to Trujillo about the potential harm caused by the sandfly and to demonstrate how they might begin to combat the disfiguring lesions using resources from the area's plant life. Simultaneously, it pointed out a plant resource with economic potential to cure a common disease—something that hundreds of naturalists around the globe sought every day. In this way, the image—and natural history research in general—served one of the Bishop's major goals: to enrich and empower the Spanish Empire using local manpower to make visible the resources of Trujillo's natural world. When he worked with local informants and illustrators to envision the *angusacha* plant and how it could treat endemic disease, the Bishop demonstrated how, through combining local knowledge and European commerce, a simple production of nature could be transformed into a marketable production of empire.

In imagining broader scientific, medicinal, and commercial uses for local specimens, Martínez Compañón was part of a broader trend of naturalists and intellectuals in Peru who sought to capitalize on local natural resources. Though their efforts are little known outside Peruvian history, they represented what scholars have called "Creole science," a local manifestation of eighteenth-century natural history that privileged data collected from local (often native) informants, utilized indigenous language terms for specimens, and publicized findings with local publications and institutions. In his 1757 work

on South American natural history, José Eusebio Llano Zapata used indigenous names to refer to plants and animals and wrote about how he observed
Indians using local plants. From his university position in Lima, Alonso
Huerta lobbied for all students of science to learn Quechua, a language that
he maintained was crucial to scientific investigations because the Peruvian
Indians had already done exhaustive studies of local plant life. Hipólito Unanue wrote the series *Political, Ecclesiastical, and Military Guides to the Viceroyalty of Peru* (published in five installments between 1793 and 1797), which
detailed the natural resources of the region. The elites who made up the Amantes del País (Lovers of the Country) society in Peru—the viceregal corollary
of the Spanish Amigos del País economic societies on the Peninsula—promoted
the discovery of natural resources that could benefit and enrich Peru. Like
Martínez Compañón's attempts to build a utopian society in Trujillo, these
efforts meant to produce useful information and to celebrate the richness of
Peru's natural world, proving that it was not a geographically inferior region
swollen with foul swamps and second-rate animals. Instead, their work demonstrated the spectacular climatic, biological, and historical diversity of Peru,
celebrating it for those at home, elsewhere in the empire, and throughout the
Atlantic world.[11]

 Although Martínez Compañón has not previously been recognized as a
part of this scientific trend, the scientific data in his nine volumes, particularly
the botanical information, mark him as an important proponent of locally based
science in late colonial Peru. His work offers a singular example of native
participation in natural history projects because its separation into scientific
illustrations and collection inventory entries enables modern scholars to observe the creation of local scientific data in heretofore-unseen ways. The Trujillo case offers an extended example of two of the most important techniques
of early modern colonial science: the generation of scientific data via a questionnaire distributed throughout rural areas; and the use of an extended
network of informants, collaborators, and arbiters who generated and refined
local scientific knowledge, and then began introducing it to the scientific establishment in the metropolis. Martínez Compañón's scientific investigations strayed from the norm in their refusal to censor or cover up certain
Indian traditions that made use of plants in ways that the Spanish officially
prohibited. Yet his botanical research exemplifies one of the driving forces in
colonial natural science: the possibility of transforming heretofore-unknown
natural resources into profitable commodities that would benefit the empire.

More significant, it provides an unprecedented opportunity to examine how the dynamics of ethnic identity and social class influenced the making of scientific data in the New World.

The Hidden History of Natural History

In imagining how to use American natural knowledge to benefit the empire, Martínez Compañón was in decidedly good company. Almost immediately after arriving in the Western Hemisphere, the Spanish began searching for valuable products in nature; to gather this information, they needed help from natives. Although the early modern Spanish were accomplished at studying plants, botanists could rely only so much on their European university training when they confronted an entirely new botanical lexicon that they did not know how to identify, prepare, or employ. Understanding local plant life was most important when it came to medicine: uncovering the medicinal uses of American plants was often a matter of life or death. Many of the diseases and illnesses that Spaniards experienced in the New World differed from common afflictions in Europe, and much of the materia medica that they would have brought with them would not have survived the transatlantic crossing. They also needed information about food crops, what to plant where, which plants were poisonous, and which wood could be used to build houses. Since their classical texts offered no orientation to this new universe, the Spanish had little choice but to try to collaborate with native peoples to create new bases of knowledge.

The first documented instance of Spaniards gathering botanical information from native informants was the work of the twelve Franciscans who arrived in New Spain in the 1520s and almost immediately sought knowledge of medicinal plants from the Tascarara Indians. They later supervised the production of a book about Indian medical knowledge, *Libellus de medicinalibus indorum herbis* (Little Book of the Medicinal Herbs of the Indians, also known as the Badianus Codex, 1522), which was based on research among native communities, and then written, translated into Latin, and illustrated by indigenous scholars and artisans. They were not alone: Spanish doctor Nicolás Monardes crafted a successful career publishing about American materia medica, using information that he gathered from Spaniards in the colonies who queried indigenous informants to learn about plant medicine.

By 1570, King Philip II had decided that botanical data from America were so important that he appointed Francisco Hernández as *protomédico*, or first doctor, of the Indies. Hernández was to spend seven years in New Spain with royal instructions to consult "medicine men, herbalists, Indians, and other persons with knowledge in such matters" to gather information about "herbs, trees, and medicinal plants."[12]

Likewise, in Peru the process of gathering botanical knowledge was highly dependent on indigenous informants. The work of the chroniclers Pedro Cieza de León, Francisco López de Gómara, and Agustín Zarate stressed the botanical expertise of the natives. This collaboration was essential to the 1779–1788 Hipólito Ruiz and José Pavón Crown-sponsored Royal Botanical Expedition to Peru, wherein Spanish botanists surveyed the natural landscape under the guidance of area naturalists. In the Amazonian province of Moxos (today Bolivia), governor Lázaro de Ribera worked with local Indians to illustrate and gather data for two works that he commissioned to describe his region: *Exact and Faithful Descriptions of the Indians, Animals, and Plants of the Province of Moxos in Peru* (1794); and *The Book of Woods* (1790). José Eusebio Llano Zapata's posthumously published *Memorias histórico, físicas, crítico, apologéticas de la América Meridional* tells of how he observed local uses of plants and herbs among native communities. He pointed out that some American specimens, such as the delectable cherimoya fruit, were superior to any similar items known in Europe.[13]

While such use of native languages, informants, and illustrators suggests a fruitful, easy collaboration with native peoples, this relationship cannot be characterized as an exchange between equals. As elsewhere, in the process of generating natural data, most Europeans did not treat Americans as peers. A clear sign of this is that in all the instances of "collaboration" mentioned above, the indigenous informants, assistants, and illustrators—without whose contributions the works would never have materialized—were not recognized by name, and the written works tell very little about their participation in the process. As for indigenous artists creating paintings, their work was thought inferior to that of formally trained Europeans, so it was not worthwhile to give them their due credit.[14] As Neil Safier has shown, this process of obfuscating native participation is especially clear in the case of the French expedition to Peru under Charles Marie de La Condamine from 1735 to 1744. Scholars know that La Condamine used an essentially collaborative method to gather his natural history data, collecting information from wherever he could get it: manuscripts, letters, maps, and missionary histories, as well as discussions with local informants, including Indians and slaves. Yet in order to conform to the conventions of eighteenth-century scientific culture and meet the demands of potential publishers, in final manuscript preparations he smoothed over these disparate data sources, instead emphasizing his own authority through stressing firsthand observation, even when he had not directly observed the events or items in question. Effectively, La Condamine—and many others like him—erased the participation of the indigenous, African, and mixed-race local people who were the very sources of his information.[15]

Understanding the processes that these naturalists used to gather data and then obfuscate evidence of the participation of the Indians, Africans, and mestizos who provided it helps illustrate how and why local participation in natural history projects often went unacknowledged. This is an important addition to our understanding of the dynamics of natural history construction but does not fully explain the critical yet mysterious first phase of early modern American scientific data making: gathering information on the ground. Almost without exception, the archival records do not discuss these earliest phases of data collection: the stages when informants went out into the field to assemble specimens, make images, or gather data for descriptions. Without knowledge of this part of the process, our understanding of the dynamics of natural history remains stunted.

This same practice of cultivating, employing, and ultimately obfuscating local knowledge is reflected in the Trujillo natural history created by Martínez Compañón. It is most immediately apparent in the disparate nature of his natural history documents. Even though the collection and the watercolors were related projects—of the 488 botanical images in volumes 3, 4, and 5 of the watercolors, 198 show specimens also found within the botanical collection inventory—recall that without the written natural history, there was no explanatory link between the two works. But as the *angusacha* example shows, creative analysis can transform this apparent roadblock into a methodological advantage. Such effort might seem laborious to contemporary observers, but this sort of interpretative work was a standard step in the making of natural history in the early modern period. For example, the Royal Botanical Expedition to Peru produced separate sets of plant descriptions, plant illustrations, and dried plant specimens. These categories were never evenly matched, and the expedition's leaders had always planned that upon their return to Spain, they would seek financial support to allow them to edit, compile, and write up their data before publication. Ultimately, they were able to publish only parts of their work. Similarly, under the direction of Martínez Compañón's friend José Mutis, the Royal Botanical Expedition to New Granada (1783–1808) produced separate descriptions, illustrations, and specimens, all to be interpreted and employed by European scientists at home.[16]

Creating distinct sets of illustrations, descriptions, and specimens, and then sending them back across the Atlantic for interpretation, was a standard process throughout the early modern Americas, and a typical but largely unacknowledged side effect of this practice was to further conceal evidence of native involvement in the search.[17] First, plebeians, servants, and low-ranking assistants harvested data in the colonies, picking plant specimens, sketching and painting them, and recording the ways local communities used them. This information was then prepared by elite Creoles and Europeans based in America who sifted it into its most "objective" form: herbariums (collections of dried and pressed plants), written descriptions, and occasionally live specimens that were carefully packaged to survive the transatlantic crossing but rarely did. Finally, the naturalists sent these data to scientific institutions in Europe, where the possible uses and value of the plant would be determined. Scholars have a good understanding of the second and third parts of this process: preparation by elites on the ground in the colonies and reception by another set of elites in European institutions. Frustratingly, we still know almost nothing about the first part of the process—about how the data were actually collected. Without knowledge of this critical piece of making scientific data, the history of natural history in colonial Spanish America is inevitably slanted toward the perspective of Spanish and Creole elites, the political economy goals of the metropolis, and the growing international culture of scientific institutions. But by approaching the making of natural history from a perspective that focuses on how individuals gathered, prepared, and vetted information before it was sent overseas, we can gain a broader understanding of the local contours, uses, and traditions of natural history. The Trujillo case provides a unique starting point from which to examine these dynamics of knowledge making. In particular, the strong visual component of its data provides different ways to imagine what it meant for local peoples to participate in natural history projects. Closer examination of how the natural history work was created helps demonstrate how their participation bolstered the efforts to build a utopia in Trujillo, by providing useful information about the natural world and, at the same time, by demonstrating their advanced intellectual capacity.

Requesting, Gathering, and Depicting

As in any natural history endeavor, the network of participants—from local informants to leading bureaucrats in Lima—made the project possible and inextricably linked it to its place of origin. As countless ecclesiastics, scientists, and bureaucrats had done before him, Martínez Compañón gathered his local knowledge through travel, which afforded him opportunities for first-hand observation and for contact with a wider array of local sources. Most important, it allowed him to cultivate an expansive network of scientific inquiry, including local informants and illustrators (often Indians) with valuable ancestral knowledge of local botanical traditions. His network also included parish priests and local elites who served as collaborators, helping him compile the data from the original sources; and viceregal and imperial officials who served as arbiters who ultimately approved the research and forwarded it to the proper metropolitan institutions. By gathering and displaying the potential riches contained in Trujillo's botanical universe, Martínez Compañón contributed to the debate over American inferiority in yet another fashion—this time, arguing for the value of its environment. Conveniently, such work met his broader goal of defending the Indians of Trujillo by vividly demonstrating that they were the keepers of valuable scientific information and that they were apt enough to learn to display it within the contours of eighteenth-century botanical traditions.

The Bishop's investigation into Trujillo's natural utopia began with his first point of contact in the provinces: his parish priests. The questionnaires that he sent them prior to leaving on his *visita* ask not only about common diseases but also how these were cured with botanical medicines. He inquired about medicinal herbs, branches, and fruits, wanting to know about "their appearance, the virtue of each one of them, and the method of applying and using them." He was interested in balsams and woods. All these areas of interest suggest a diligent Crown functionary seeking to promote the productions of empire through learning about how the local community used them.[18]

The answers that parish priests provided in response likely formed the basis for the collection inventory, and the specimens collected along with this information must have been the ones depicted throughout the nine volumes of *Trujillo del Perú*. Unfortunately, none of the priests' written reports on natural history survive; we know of their existence only because Martínez Compañón referred to them when he discussed the two hundred reports and "unique" maps that he was sending to Viceroy Croix—documents that have long since been lost. But before it was misplaced, where was this information gathered? Mostly likely, as Crown functionaries had done almost two hundred years earlier with the *Relaciones Geográficas* maps and surveys in New Spain, the priests "farmed out" the responsibility to collect plants, balsam, trees, and botanical data to members of their local communities. This same relationship between Spanish functionaries and local informants has been proved for other natural history projects in the colonial period. José Mutis began work as director of the Royal Botanical Expedition in New Granada by going into the field and collecting specimens; but as the prestige of his project grew, he hired local *herbolarios* to do this for him, reasoning that their native knowledge would lead to more specific information on plant uses. It seems likely that Martínez Compañón would have done the same thing, using the parish priests as middle points where locals would send data.[19]

Like his contemporaries in America, Martínez Compañón utilized local connections and friendships to achieve his political goals, even in the case of natural history. It was through these networks that amateur naturalists gained data, expertise, and financial support. Martínez Compañón's network can be partially reconstructed through documentary fragments, allowing us to imagine the chain of data transmission and providing a broader sense of what his project might have meant to local communities. In an age where transatlantic communication remained slow and unreliable, individuals throughout the colonies relied on local relationships even when generating knowledge that could ultimately prove useful for the entire empire. The Bishop's network comprised three distinct but related groups: informants and illustrators, collaborators, and arbiters. The informants and illustrators group is arguably the most essential but is also the hardest to track. Very little documentation survives in which the Bishop discusses his natural history work, and he never directly mentioned the people who helped him gather his information on the ground or who participated in creating the watercolor images. This lack of documentation does not rule out other clues or suggestions about who the informants and illustrators were. For instance, several items in the collection inventory directly mention native participation, revealing that Indian women usually put *huarhuar* leaves in *chicha*, the Andean alcoholic beverage made of fermented corn, because they made the alcohol stronger. The inventory also reveals that natives "told wonders" about how the leaves of the *fresno* tree helped facilitate childbirth.

These are strong suggestions of local involvement, but a closer look at a watercolor image from *Trujillo del Perú* confirms local, specifically indigenous, involvement in this botanical research. Plate 5 from volume 2 shows a "hill Indian" in typical dress. The individual stands near a tree, with a bush and various shrubs; mountains are in the background, and grassy rolling hills are in the foreground. What is remarkable about this image is the freshly picked plant that he holds in his left hand. This man is depicted in the process of "botanizing," or collecting botanical samples. Although one image is far from sufficient to authoritatively confirm local participation in the Bishop's botanical work, it strongly implies that the natural history was created with the help of native peoples. It is an incontrovertible visual confirmation of a long-standing, defining trend of scientific investigation in the New World, something that becomes all the more important upon considering how difficult it is to uncover documentary evidence of this sort of native participation in natural history.[20]

Another telling clue about Indian participation in the project lies in the watercolor illustration of the *añame* plant in volume 3. Beneath the image of the plant, there is small writing that says, "Indians, unguent. . . ." Though the explanation—perhaps written by Martínez Compañón himself?—trails off, it reveals that it was Indians who provided the data about the plant and described what they used it for.[21] Although we must read carefully to see how the native informants sought to cultivate their communal image through the *Trujillo* natural history, we can assume that the local informants who participated in the Bishop's research were eager to show how ancestral botanical knowledge could become information useful to their local communities, the bishopric, the viceroyalty, and the Spanish Empire at large. Like Martínez Compañón, they were proud of the natural utopia in which they lived, and they wanted to display it for audiences in the viceroyalty, the empire, and beyond.

Once locals collected the information, they transferred it to the next group of participants in the project: their parish priests, who were part of the collaborator group. The priests served as liaisons, passing the material on when the *visita* entourage arrived in their parishes. In so doing, they decided what aspects of Trujillo's natural, social, and historical world the Bishop should consider for inclusion in the collections and the watercolors. Their willing participation in the project not only boded well for their relationships with superiors in the Church but also demonstrated the influence and control that they had over their parishioners. Martínez Compañón had every confidence in the ability of parish priests to partner with local informants to produce useful data. The Bishop considered this information to be the real basis of his natural history work, noting that reports on the various *doctrinas* "could serve to make some exact notes for the history of this bishopric, whose work will give me a great deal of satisfaction." He was convinced that they showed that "within the diocese, we have much more than we imagine, and that a clear and exact knowledge of it could be quite useful."[22]

In addition to the *herbolarios* and the priests, the illustrators who completed the watercolor images were key to the first phase of the project. If the Bishop handled the business of natural history illustration as José Mutis did in Bogotá, he may have sponsored or planned a sort of workshop where artists sketched and then painted the specimens he selected for them. While archival records have no indication of a painting workshop or school in Trujillo, we know that he at least considered such an institution. In 1788, he asked a friend for a copy of a "printed museum" by Federico Borromeo, a famous sixteenth-century polymath ecclesiastic who founded a drawing academy in Milan; perhaps Martínez Compañón hoped to follow in his footsteps.[23]

Another exemplar was Martínez Compañón's contemporary José Mutis, who preferred American-trained artists for his workshop in Bogotá because it was easier to inculcate them into an original style of botanical illustration that emphasized saturated color, flatness, and symmetry. He believed that this style more accurately represented American nature, and therefore his visual lexicon of plants would be more useful to those who studied the botanical life of New Granada.[24] Perhaps Martínez Compañón chose indigenous artisans for the same reason. However, Mutis's case is admittedly different from that of Martínez Compañón: his artists' workshop, drawing school, and *herbolarios* all functioned under the auspices of the Spanish Crown and the Royal Botanical Expedition to New Granada. Martínez Compañón, in contrast, received no metropolitan support or funding for his natural history research, which he decided to undertake of his own accord. Whatever funds he put toward the project came from his own salary. Therefore, he would have been even more reliant on local resources and even more apt to promote a local style that shared traits with, but was ultimately distinct from, European natural history techniques.

Even if the drawing workshop never materialized, the botanical illustrations that make up volumes 3, 4, and 5 of the *Trujillo del Perú* watercolors suggest a similar process of *herbolarios* gathering the specimens in the field, artists creating their portraits in a second location, and the Bishop ultimately compiling the work. Many of the plants have dangling roots, suggesting that they were drawn exactly as they arrived in front of their illustrator (see Plate 21). Some images appear to be in intermediate stages of being colorized; parts of them are in pencil sketch only. The "frame" that was drawn around the outside of some images overlaps with the plant itself—suggesting that these lines were added afterward. All this implies that *herbolarios* gathered the specimens and then brought them to a second location, where they were prepared, sketched, and painted. Those involved in the first aspect of this project were most likely locals, since they would have had more intimate knowledge of the area's plants, their locations, and how they could be used. Presumably, the contribution of these individuals is represented in the watercolor of the "hill Indian" depicted in the process of botanizing.

The drawings hold clues about the process of compiling this botanical work. The almost complete lack of volume in many suggests that they were drawn from herbarium specimens that had already been pressed and dried. This was a common practice, since dried plants would last longer and serve as useful substitutes for scientists who could not grow the said specimen outside its natural climate. Such samples were so coveted that Casimiro Gómez Ortega, a senior researcher at the Royal Botanical Garden of Madrid, wrote about compiling them in a 1779 directive. Gómez specified that specimens chosen to be pressed and dried should include all parts of the plant: roots, branches, flowers, seeds, and/or fruits. Once picked, the plants should be pressed and dried as quickly as possible, with extra care being taken that the paper would not cause discoloration. He stressed that during this process, the naturalists should focus on "patiently unwrinkling [the plant's] leaves and other parts, conserving as much as possible their symmetry."[25]

Since Martínez Compañón first requested specimens from parish priests in 1782 and did not return to Trujillo city permanently until 1785, it is inevitable that, in many cases, too much time would have passed to preserve specimens in any way other than pressed in the pages of an herbarium. Therefore, we can assume that when faced with these flattened, dried specimens, instead of trying to imagine what the plant might have looked like when alive, the Trujillo artists chose to represent what they saw before them, drawing a one-dimensional dried specimen. Again, this indicates that the artists were participants in a multiphase process, one that began on the ground with local botanizers and then moved to the workshops of local illustrators and artisans.

Another clue to the local provenance of the images is the fact that they were the work of several different artisans. Iconographic analysis confirms that there were at least five artisans who participated in the *Trujillo del Perú* volumes. One artisan clearly had the benefit of the most formal training, as this individual had superior drawing skills and advanced command of shading, perspective, and dimension. He or she seems to have been tasked with many of the "most important" images, including depicting the bureaucrats and officials in volume 1 and many of the plants portrayed throughout the collection. A second individual, for whom only a small portion of the images of people, animals, and fish can be positively identified, has a different style that is characterized by more cartoon-like eyes. The watery color, undefined shapes, and lack of detail characterizing the third artisan's work is identified in some of the plant illustrations. Wispy coloring, fuzzy, undefined lines, and a perspective that often portrays the subjects from a greater distance are the markers of a fourth individual's work. The fifth illustrator favors heavy brushstrokes and strong black outlines. Together, these individuals composed a team. While we do not know whether they worked side by side in the same physical location, it is clear that they collaborated in making Trujillo's utopia visible to the outside world.

From the lack of any mention of paying or employing artisans in the Martínez Compañón records, we can infer that none were professionals hired or paid explicitly for this purpose. Perhaps the illustrators were assistants who served officially in other capacities, or they were students in the Bishop's schools. The work of the first artisan, who appears to have had the most official training, could compare with the official illustrations generated by the Royal Botanical Expeditions to Peru, New Granada, or elsewhere in the empire; but for the most part, the *Trujillo* images are highly vernacular and do not fare well against those produced by specifically trained, hired, and compensated artists. Yet the Trujillo artisans would have had good reason to produce them nevertheless, because in so doing, they knew that they were recording the natural knowledge of their communities. They may have known that the king was to be the ultimate judge of their work—a unique circumstance that offered them a chance to communicate in images with the ruler of all the Spanish kingdoms. What better opportunity to present Trujillo and its people in a good light?

Though historians and art historians do not often celebrate such informal images, a quick survey of visual reports gathered from around the empire in the Bourbon period suggests that such vernacular illustrations were rather common. The awkward human figures and watery colors recall Joaquín Antonio Basarás's *Origin, Customs, and Present State of the Mexicans and the Philipinos* (1763), which has a familiar color palette, similarly undefined facial features, and simple square buildings recalling those in the Trujillo images. Images produced for Diego Panes's *Theater of New Spain* (created in the 1770s and 1780s but not published until 1820) have similar buildings, blue mountains in the background, and awkward body shapes. Likewise, there are striking iconographical commonalities between the Trujillo images and those produced for Pedro O'Crouley's *Comprehensive Idea of New Spain* (1774). Martínez Compañón could have seen or owned copies of Basarás's and Panes's works, which were quite popular in their time. Furthermore, Basarás, Panes, and O'Crouley were all in some way involved with the Basque Friends of the Country Society—a group to which Martínez Compañón also belonged.[26] All three would have been familiar with the free drawing schools that the Basque Friends sponsored in Spain. Here, children learned and practiced drawing landscapes, urban scenes, figures, and decoration. The society's yearly report from 1780 proclaimed that "drawing is useful for all kinds of people; it is the foundation of the fine arts and the soul of many branches of commerce." The value that the society's members placed on visual data highlights the dominance of visual documentation of useful information in contemporary scientific culture.[27]

Interestingly, there are additional iconographical links between the Trujillo images and some of the most popular books of the time—connections that reveal how the images might have been executed. For instance, a visual comparison of the image of the manatee in José Gumilla's *Orinoco Ilustrado* with the manatee appearing in volume 8 of *Trujillo del Perú* shows an unmistakable link: the two are almost exact copies. Gumilla's work also contains maps and illustrations of machines, both of which are included in the Trujillo watercolors.[28] First published in 1741, the book was widely read in Spain and abroad, and although it is not listed in his library inventory, it is plausible that Martínez Compañón had access to a copy. Likewise, José Quer's *Flora Española*, perhaps the most popular botanical manual of the time, featured several images that look remarkably like those in the watercolors, such as the illustrations of avocados and plantains. By modern standards, it is tempting to see this repetition as pseudo-plagiarism; but in the early modern period, it was common to use printed images as inspiration, and these templates helped local artisans understand what was expected of them.[29] Presumably, this imitation of imagery was something that Martínez Compañón purposely encouraged with his team. By showing the untrained artisans images from similar natural history works, he shared with them a valuable template for inspiration. This indicates that, to some degree, the Bishop wanted his natural history work to dialogue with the standardized and formalized culture of scientific inquiry that dominated the eighteenth-century Atlantic arena.

After the artisans made their illustrations, we can assume that it was up to the Bishop to choose which were to be included (as we shall see, it seems that, at times, he hurried more at this task than he might have). He then determined how to arrange the various books of his "paper museum," changing his mind once or twice about how the volumes should be ordered.[30] Once he finished refining and selecting, the project required the assistance of his elite friends, the second ring of his network—the collaborators who assisted him with sifting and enhancing these data. Their help was especially important given Trujillo's distance from Lima, Arequipa, and the other main population centers of the viceroyalty. Most crucial here is the Bishop's relationship with the Hermenegildo family of Lima—Antonio was a judge, or *oidor*, of the *audiencia*, or high court, with whom the Bishop maintained close relations. Both he and his son Agustín shared the Bishop's affinity for natural history, assisting him with longitudinal measurements of the Peruvian coast, loaning him scientific books, collecting seeds for him, and even sending him reports on the culture and dances of the Afro-Peruvians of the central coast. They were key participants in overseeing the passage of Martínez Compañón's work to Spain, receiving the twenty-four boxes of natural history items, their index, and the maps and reports on Trujillo with the responsibility of passing them on to Viceroy Croix.[31]

The Bishop likewise had an important relationship with the Marqués de Soto Florido, an elite Lima landowner. Soto was a longtime supporter of the *Mercurio Peruano*, Peru's leading Enlightenment periodical, and his library, which included works by Hume, Condillac, and Feijoo, was reputedly one of the best in the viceroyalty.[32] Martínez Compañón likely knew this when he requested that the Hermenegildos relay to Soto his request to borrow copies of Monardes's books on "American herbs," as he called them.[33] Another key collaborator in the natural history research was the Bishop's own nephew, José Ignacio de Lecuanda, who had come with his uncle to Peru in 1768. Lecuanda later accompanied his uncle on the *visita*, charged with collecting demographic and economic statistics. He was a contributor to the *Mercurio Peruano*, a member of Lima's economic society, and a good friend of Viceroy Gil.[34] These collaborators were clearly friends of Martínez Compañón and, as such, would willingly have assisted him with this work, but it is also likely that they participated because they knew that they would benefit from anything that improved the finances of Trujillo. They would gain valuable political advantage by demonstrating their largesse with the influential Bishop. And unlike the projects to found new towns or schools, which might remove the plebeians on which they relied from their influence, they risked nothing by engaging with local botanical research, and likely recognized that they stood only to gain by enhancing the prestige of Trujillo and Peru in the eyes of the world.

After the collaborators helped the Bishop refine his data, the work needed final approval and transportation back to Spain. The group of elite bureaucrats who facilitated this process can be characterized as arbiters because their assent was essential to this last phase of data transmission. An important part of this group was Intendant Fernando de Saavedra, who agreed to assist the Bishop with the natural history project, especially since Spanish *visitador* Jorge Escobedo had said in 1784 that the "lack of geographic information of the entire kingdom" was nothing less than "painful."[35] Likely keeping this in mind, Saavedra and his assessor personally reviewed and approved the collection. Next, the work passed to the ecclesiastical and secular *cabildos* of Trujillo, who both praised the Bishop's scientific investigations "with the profundity and attention that such a work deserves."[36]

With the *cabildos'* approval, the twenty-four boxes and their index passed to the care of the Hermenegildos, who were tasked with getting them to the appropriate authorities in Lima. At some point, they became the responsibility of two men who must have been the Bishop's friends or acquaintances: Pedro Saldeguí, secretary of Lima's Inquisition; and Domingo Estevan de Olza, a merchant from Cádiz, who paid for the cost of their impending passage to Spain. The boxes finally reached Viceroy Croix, whom the Bishop had asked to "take the task of seeing that the said boxes are opened and reviewed," since "these subjects [of natural history are] distant from my principal profession."[37] It was Croix who would ultimately bring the items with him on his return to Spain. Apparently, he gave his blessing because Martínez Compañón later wrote that the intendant, *cabildos*, and especially the viceroy had approved all parts of the project with "exceptional praise." However, they all suggested that he develop the written reports, which, in their current state, did not fully explain some of the images. (Presumably, they referred to the collection inventory, although they may have been discussing the now-lost notes for the intended book. With this accomplished, they recommended that the entire project should immediately be sent to Madrid.)[38] In Spain several months later, Antonio Porlier received the materials and passed them on to the king, who personally reviewed the collection and, through his agents, expressed "effusive thanks for the care and labor that [the Bishop] employed in putting them together."[39]

Reconstructing the three groups of participants in the creation of this work helps highlight how local manpower, initiative, and support were central to the project. Without the local informants, such a comprehensive portrait of Trujillo would have been impossible to create. Although they did not ultimately choose which of the specimens would be included in the collection or the watercolors, it was from the results of their efforts that the Bishop made his selection. This indicates a complex process of refining information to represent Trujillo to the outside world: first, the local informants gathered the information in data, images, and specimens; then the parish priests chose what field specimens should be picked and preserved, and which would be sent to the Bishop. Martínez Compañón made his own refinements to the work, and then turned to his collaborators for assistance in deciding which portions of the work should be further developed and enhanced. The illustrators drew the images. Finally, even the third group in the Bishop's natural history network—the arbiters—had deep local contacts that were central to directing the work to its ultimate destination.

This, unfortunately, is the last that the documents have to say about Martínez Compañón's natural history collection. We can only assume that the contents were dispersed to the appropriate locations: materia medica to the royal pharmacy, botanical specimens to the botanical garden, animals to the natural history museum. Several of the pottery pieces he included are still held today at the Museo de América in Madrid. The watercolors that Martínez Compañón commissioned to accompany the collection were still unfinished when he left Peru to assume his new post as archbishop of Santa Fé in 1790. Three years after his death, they finally arrived in Madrid.[40]

It is obvious why Martínez Compañón relied on travel, questionnaires, and his network of informants, collaborators, and arbiters to compile his natural history work: these were the local resources available to him, and he made the best use of them that he could. Yet one question remains: Why would they assist him? They were unlikely to receive financial returns, since it was improbable that any new medicinal plants or crops uncovered would immediately prove profitable. Others who assisted him knew full well that they did so anonymously. But whatever their reasons for collaborating, everyone who did so participated in creating a utopian vision of Trujillo for the world out-side to see and treasure. We should understand their participation as a way to celebrate the local identity of their town, region, or viceroyalty. Often known as chorography, this type of local study cataloged a region's natural resources and then displayed them for outside viewers. In so doing, the makers of cho-rographies converted simple productions of nature into objects that marked local identity and distinguished their communities from others.[41] The Mar-tínez Compañón natural history performs a similar task for Trujillo. By trans-forming basic data into commodifiable products, it identified a lexicon of natural resources that could sustain the utopia that the Bishop and the people wanted to create.

Productions of Empire

As the watercolor images and collection inventory suggest, Spanish Ameri-can plant resources were big business in the early modern Atlantic world, and the ability to locate, produce, market, and trade them had a serious impact on imperial economies. An outstanding example of commercial uses of plants was the American plant-based drug cascarilla, or *quina*, the key ingredient of fever-combating quinine, the most useful tool for the most pervasive of ill-nesses. Accordingly, by the late eighteenth century, the cascarilla plant had become by weight the most valuable import from Spanish America. Various individuals recognized the potential that it might have to invigorate both local and imperial economies: Antonio Porlier promoted its export from Ecuador, and the Ruiz and Pavón expedition attempted to set up a profitable *quina* monopoly that could serve as a basis for other plant-based commercial mono-polies throughout the empire. One of the main reasons the Crown funded José Mutis's botanical expedition to New Granada was to try to establish a profitable *quina* monopoly in the area.[42] In Trujillo, Martínez Compañón con-tributed to the search for cascarilla. His collection contained a box with seven-teen different samples of the plant, all culled from different climatic areas of Trujillo. In a 1786 letter to King Charles, he insisted that Peruvian cascarilla was of "very good quality."[43] He sent proof of this with his natural history collections, including cascarilla wood (known as *cochana*) in his collection of wood samples from Piura and Jaén. He included cascarilla leaves among the medicinal herbs in box eleven, explaining that the plant would grow in all climates and that the uses of the leaves were "very well known." He began designing plans to cultivate cascarilla on a broader scale throughout the bishopric, in accordance with *visitador* Jorge Escobedo's instructions to develop Piura's official commerce in cascarilla while restricting its contraband trade.[44] The cascarilla example highlights the possibilities of combining local plant-based medical knowledge with the influence of the imperial bureaucracy. Local informants provided the samples from various areas of Trujillo, and the Bishop, as a good Crown functionary, imagined how these could best be employed to improve the finances of Trujillo, Peru, and the Spanish Empire at large. Once products of nature became productions of empire, they could contribute to the utopian project by augmenting viceregal finances, displaying the rich local environment, and confirming the mental abilities of the native peoples who were the keepers of this useful information.

Cascarilla was just the beginning of the materia medica available in Trujillo. In a letter to the king in 1786, the Bishop described Trujillo's plant kingdom as having "an infinity of herbs, roots, and other . . . medicinal simples, many of them very effective."[45] Accordingly, volume 5 of the *Trujillo* watercolors was set apart for medicinal herbs. When cross-read with the collection inventory, we can see how this work is a veritable cornucopia of natural knowledge. The collection inventory confirmed that local plants *mugues* and *palo de chino* could successfully treat syphilis, while herbs such as *llusqui* could cure the large boils caused by venereal diseases that were known as *bubas*. When applied as a paste, *amarrajudio* reed was used to combat tumors. *Pacharrosa*, *sauco*, and *lechugilla* could be used against different types of fevers. Notations on the original watercolors reveal that the *ruibarbo de Guayabamba* plant could be used to heal *mal del valle*, or intestinal gangrene caused by amoebic infection.[46]

Trujillo's materia medica included plants that served more mundane health purposes as well: when its leaves were cooked in water, the infusion of the *chiumba* plant served as a coagulant, while tea from *cuhillo-pico* was useful in healing burns. In fact, the vast majority of the herbs inventoried were homeopathic cures for everyday aches and pains. For cold-like symptoms, the *sanga-rupauran* reed could ease throat inflammation, and a runny nose could be alleviated with the juice of *reuma* leaves. Several plants could assist with tooth pain, including the *salvaje* herb or *conana* resin. For teeth that were beyond palliative care, the sap of the *catahua* tree could ease their removal. Surely this was preferable to visiting the terrifying-looking dentist shown in Plate 22. Other common everyday complaints that could be cured with American herbs were digestive issues. One useful medicine was *huachapurga*, which the Bishop noted was commonly known as the "purgative of the poor." He explained that it should be taken in the form of a stew made with butter, onions, potatoes, and garlic, commonly eaten for breakfast. If such a stew worked too well, the person could always turn to the *pedorrera*, or "farter" herb, which was politely used to "destroy winds." Several other plants addressed health concerns. The *romana* herb was useful for healing wounds, sores, and burns. The juice of the *anatqui* plant could be applied to eyes that had been damaged by a direct blow to the face and were swollen or had clouded vision. A rather gruesome but certainly useful function of the *navarrete* reed was that its bark could be shaved, and "when introduced on sores that have grown worms, [it will] kill them and cure the sore."

Herbs and plants that healed and cured were clearly one of the most valuable potential resources of any locality in the Spanish kingdoms. These are, unsurprisingly, some of the more general cures: *suelda* for broken bones, granadilla for fever, *llanten* for wounds, and *sangre de drago* as a coagulant. With each of these examples, informants offered knowledge that had been part of their local networks for centuries. In sharing this knowledge with the broader community, they were participating in the crucial first step of identifying the information necessary to transform a mere natural specimen, or a product of nature, into a valuable commodity—a production of empire.

Not all botanical items with potential economic benefits were medicinal in nature—some had strictly commercial uses. European trade in dyestuffs was brisk, and the inventory listed many plants used for dye, such as *pul*, which produced a yellow color, and *mihquichilca*, which dyed fabric green. Peru's plant life included potentially valuable fibers. The Bishop noted that the *cambira* plant produced a fiber "similar to the fiber used in the fabrics of China," or silk. Chocolate was a highly desirable product in the luxury market, and Martínez Compañón was somewhat of an aficionado, who fretted when the cacao used to make it was not available in northern Peru. From the provincial town of Lambayeque, he wrote despairingly to friends in Lima that "not one grain of cacao have I been able to find."[47] Perhaps deprivation spurred him to search for a viable substitute because later, he noted that the seed of the *chonta* fruit had the same taste as cacao. These commercial plants all provided alternate methods of transforming local data into imperial profit. They confirm that the Bishop assumed that the data he gathered on the ground could be transformed into something of use to the larger Spanish economy.

While the standard medicinal plants readily fit into the Spanish Bourbons' plans for regenerating the empire's finances through cataloging and harnessing American nature, some plants in the collection inventory tell alternate, more complicated, stories about local knowledge in Trujillo. Some of these stood in opposition to the useful information paradigm of colonial improvement that was the center of the Bishop's utopia. Stories of abortion-inducing herbs, narcotic and hallucinogenic plants, and natural drugs that remedied the consequences of supernatural encounters would all have aroused the suspicion of administrative and ecclesiastical authorities in the colonies. Yet when his informants shared such information with him, in visual mediums and in oral testimony, Martínez Compañón chose not to exclude it from the scientific data that he collected. In these instances, his interest in presenting a truthful, far-reaching survey of data on the natural world seems to have outweighed any moralizing tendencies that were expected of a bishop.

Not surprisingly, some of the potentially inflammatory botanical data revolved around the lives and health of women. Yet not all these were suspect: several plants in the collection were used to facilitate childbirth—an important contribution to medical knowledge in a time when the dangers of delivery were very real. Martínez Compañón's inventory cited the *fresno* plant, which, when cooked and applied over the uterus, facilitated difficult births; "the natives tell wonders about it," he noted. Women who wanted to "stop the curse," or end their menstrual cycle, could boil the leaves of the *siempre viva* plant with water. To induce menstruation, they could try the *culantrillo* leaf or *millma sacha*.[48]

The Bishop does not mention "inducing menstruation" as anything out of the ordinary; but in the eighteenth century, the notion was not without complications. The phrase most typically meant starting the menstrual cycle in order to terminate a pregnancy. Ambiguities in the common understanding of when, exactly, a woman became pregnant and at which moment the pregnancy went from a mere embryo to an actual fetus meant that "taking a menstrual regulator, or emmenagogue, . . . was not necessarily considered 'inducing abortion.' . . . A woman ingesting an emmenagogue might not have been sure whether she was inducting a late period or provoking what would be known today as an early-term abortion—and she had little reason or ability to distinguish between the two." Indeed, the Spanish Royal Academy of Language Dictionary from 1770 defines abortion as a fetus "born before its time," and the verb "to abort" as "bad birth, early birth."[49]

As a pious bishop and the highest-ranked representative of the Spanish Catholic Church for hundreds of miles, Martínez Compañón was in no position to promote or condone abortion, however it happened. He publicly decried it as "contrary to reason" and "abominable even among Gentiles and pagans." He gave his parish priests specific instructions about how they might avoid abortions among their flock. First, the priest should attempt to marry the couple involved in the unwanted pregnancy. If that did not succeed, he should promise to see to the care of the unwanted child. Avoiding abortion was so important that the Bishop even offered to cover the costs of raising the unwanted child himself.[50] But if Martínez Compañón was so opposed to abortion, why would he have included several abortive herbs in his botanical collections? Perhaps here his priorities as a natural historian overtook his piety as a bishop. It might be that since these plants and their uses were so important to local culture, he chose not to censure them. At the same time, the inclusion of abortive herbs highlights how the informants who gathered, prepared, and described the plant specimens did not always depict the same orderly, pious society that Martínez Compañón imagined Trujillo to be.

A close reading of the collection inventory confirms that the very people who elsewhere in the nine volumes and collection inventory seem to be industrious and Hispanicized maintained habits that some Europeans would have found morally reprehensible. In this way, the botanical data in the *Trujillo* natural history provide unsanctioned glimpses into native Peruvian culture. For instance, the Catholic Church had made repeated injunctions against the leaves of the coca plant, which the Bishop included in his collection. The second Lima Church Council in 1567 deemed coca a useless plant that only encouraged Indian superstitions and bad behavior. A royal decree of 1569 claimed that the Devil himself had tricked the Indians into believing that coca fortified them for hard work. Although soon thereafter, the church gave up on official prohibitions, stigma undoubtedly remained.[51] However, instead of thundering with condemnation, Martínez Compañón's inventory calmly described coca as "a small bush that is grown in hot areas, used by those who work in the mines to chew, mixed with some calcium, because they say it gives them strength and takes away the cold."[52] It seems that in his natural history work, at least, he made no moral judgment about its cultural uses.

Neither did the Bishop pass judgment on local botanical practices that he surely knew were, to some degree, superstitious. For instance, the collection inventory noted that locals believed that the *mihquichilca* herb could bring success in amorous ventures. Martínez Compañón wrote that the flowers and leaves of the *mogomogo prieto* plant were crushed in water and used "to bathe the children that suffer from an accident that around here is known as *pachachari*," which his inventory described as "sickness from fright." A modern Peruvian anthropologist refers to the condition with the same name, noting that symptoms are uniform and include "chills, fever, nausea, vomiting, and diarrhea." Treatment is provided by shamans or, in severe cases, witch doctors or *hechiceros* who purify a ritual space by passing a black ear of corn along the walls and the floor while blowing on it, then burning the corn in the middle of the room. The entire process is repeated with a white ear of corn. The burned kernels are then pounded into corn flour, which is sprinkled onto the back of the afflicted person.[53] Certainly, such a treatment would have been outwardly condemned by the Bishop, who referred to *curanderos* and *hechiceros* as "great liars" who would "die of hunger" if they were no longer able to "steal and rob from the people with their deceits and tricks."[54] In his mind, indigenous medicine men were frauds who claimed to have boundless powers but in fact were unable to save even themselves from untimely death. Yet Martínez Compañón still allowed their cures to be included in the collection that he compiled to be sent back to Spain. Although Martínez Compañón was first and foremost a bishop, in certain moments he acted with the detached observation of a natural historian and included useful scientific descriptions even if they might have contradicted religious dogma.

In addition to the herbal remedy for "sickness from fright," the collection discussed another type of specimen that would have been even greater anathema to ecclesiastics. While coca chewing may have been only tacitly condemned, there is no way a bishop would have allowed psychotropic drug use. But a careful examination of an image from volume 6 of the watercolors, labeled an *omeco-machacuai* snake, might prove that he may have overlooked this visual evidence of indigenous drug culture. Plate 23 shows a large furry brown snake wrapped around a tree. It has two heads. A monkey stuffs something into the mouth of the top head; at the bottom head, a goat escapes from the snake's lashing tongue. A cutaway view of one of the leaves highlights the patterns on the leaves of the tree around which the snake is wrapped. The thorns on the tree's trunk and the roots at its bottom are clearly visible. An Indian in Amazonian dress stands next to it, drinking from a gourd and looking up at the entire panorama with an expression of wonder.

This is one of the most compelling and confusing watercolors in all nine volumes. Although it is included with the snakes and animals, it might just as easily have been placed in volume 2, focusing on quotidian life, or in one of the three volumes with botanical illustrations, since the large cutaway of the plant leaf is the central feature of the image. An interpretation of this image begins with its name, which, when translated from Quechua, means the "my head makes me inebriated" snake.[55] Although this is a strange name for a snake, it makes sense, given how the man to the left is drinking something that appears to cause him to hallucinate. Another clue is the prominently displayed leaves of the tree. These bear resemblance to the leaves of the ayahuasca plant, which Peruvians of the Amazonian jungle use to produce hallucinatory visions, much in the same way that certain native groups of North America use peyote.

In the Amazon, the snake is thought to be the animal mother of the ayahuasca plant. Anthropologists have found that ayahuasca visions often include "jungle creatures such as boa constrictors and viperous snakes," sometimes bicephalous ones.[56] Is it possible that the *omeco-machacuai* from the nine volumes is the hallucinatory vision of an Indian who has drunk ayahuasca? If so, how would the Bishop have allowed its inclusion in a work that was destined for the king of Spain? Perhaps the contradiction between official sanctions against *curanderos* and the Bishop's desire to provide empirical natural history data led him to try to disguise the ayahuasca plant illustration by including it with those of the snakes. He may have hoped that the reader would not notice how strange the *omeco* snake was, or might simply believe that Peru was a strange and exotic land where two-headed snakes could be found deep in the Amazonian jungle. But more in keeping with his thoroughness is the notion that he wanted in some way to familiarize audiences on the Peninsula with this important native tradition. For modern scholars, this evidence of ayahuasca use, ceremonies to heal "sickness from fright," and the variety of local plants used to control women's reproductive cycles all suggest just how deeply synchronous native life was with the botanical universe of Trujillo. In recording and preserving this possibly polemical information, the Bishop was following his original stated purpose of informing his audience about the native people of Trujillo. When it came to botany, Martínez Compañón's vision was for a utopia of information that was thorough and diverse. His dedication to scientific inquiry proved to be just as significant as his commitment to founding new towns, building schools, and reforming the Hualgayoc silver mine. Ironically, this same meticulousness may explain why his natural history work was never immortalized in official scientific publications or institutions. In the end, Martínez Compañón's nine volumes never made it beyond the Royal Palace Library, where they sat idle, a mere curiosity from an exotic land. His collection was parsed up and parts of it distributed to the appropriate metropolitan institutions, but even what was saved was cataloged without attribution, leaving almost no definitive trace of the objects that he so carefully selected to represent his utopia.

The Death of Botany?

Although the neglect that met the Bishop's natural history work is a sad fate, it was by no means exceptional. Though the Spanish had begun gathering natural data from locals almost as soon as they had arrived in America, time and again their experiments and research failed to produce the lavish financial windfalls or international medical praise that they sought. The relationships that they forged with indigenous informants while making these projects were complex; most Spanish viewed local informants as sources of raw information to be refined and utilized by those who surely "knew better." Therefore, they failed to properly attribute, discuss, or credit their involvement in creating natural history in America. This process of obfuscating local participation has resulted in a story of early modern natural history that is frustratingly incomplete. Its focus on results, metropolitan institutions, and international standards makes it almost impossible for us to know how scientific culture functioned in the fields, workshops, and drawing rooms of the late Spanish Empire.

In many ways, Martínez Compañón's botanical work in Trujillo followed this flawed model; in essence, it, too, "covered up" native participation, failing to record the dynamics of information exchange and to properly attribute local informants and illustrators. Yet the unique set of sources that the Bishop left behind—specifically, the watercolor images of *Trujillo del Perú*—provides an unprecedented chance to imagine how the informants and illustrators who participated in the project imagined the world they saw around them. The botanical illustrations and collection inventory demonstrate the sheer wealth of local botanical knowledge in terms of materia medica and commercial plants. This useful information conforms to the overall plan of the late eighteenth-century Spanish Crown to increase economic profits through drawing plebeian participants into the larger drama of locating and managing the natural resources of the empire. At the same time, the botanical data enable the careful observer to find unsanctioned glimpses of local plant uses. Neither Bishop nor bureaucrat would have officially approved the use of plant-based stimulants, psychedelics, or abortives. Yet because of the detached scientific context in which this information was gathered and presented, Martínez Compañón allowed it to appear in his natural history work.

In addition to providing new alternatives to understanding local involvement in natural history research, the *Trujillo* botanical project illuminates the complex nature of colonial scientific networks. The Bishop had an unusually diverse and large network that assisted him in this scientific research, and all levels of participants therein stood to gain from participating in the project. Local informants and illustrators recorded invaluable community information about the natural world of Trujillo, demonstrating that the lands of their ancestors were rich with the resources of nature and the human initiative necessary to catalog them and that they had the mental capacity to do such difficult, detail-oriented work. Elite collaborators stood to gain financially from their participation in the research; if they knew what products were desired on the Peninsula, they could focus on developing trade networks that would bring them the most profit. The arbiter group that finally decided whether the Bishop's research should be sent back to Spain benefited from showing their support for this comparably small project that spoke to larger concerns of cataloging information and surveying America's natural world in the Age of Enlightenment.

Analysis of the Bishop's botanical research thus sheds new light on the politics of local involvement in late colonial scientific culture. But what about the fate of the physical objects themselves? This can help explain the dynamics of colonial-metropolitan scientific collaboration and exchange. Documents confirm that, after all the effort it took to compile them, the drawing of the double-headed snake, the herbarium specimens, and the rest of the collection finally made it back to Spain on the frigate *Rosa*. A letter from Charles IV's Escorial palace acknowledged the collection as a "very precious shipment," but thereafter simply expressed the king's "satisfaction" at receiving and viewing them and thanked the Bishop for his promptness in gathering the materials.[57] What was the ultimate fate of all the items that the Bishop had so carefully gathered, observed, and packaged? Documents confirm that the botanical specimens made it to the Royal Botanical Garden, but there is no further evidence of them in that collection today, likely because contemporaries did not place a high value on the vernacular type of botanical information that Martínez Compañón had sent. The archival record shows that the quinine samples arrived at the Royal Pharmacy, where, as was customary, they would have been combined with similar specimens.[58] For their part, the Bishop's own records offer no comment on whether he was disappointed with the relative disregard that met his many years of work cataloging Trujillo's natural world. Had he lived longer, he would have seen that his reports never inspired a series of general studies of American nature, as he had hoped. His images were not publicly circulated beyond a small set of viceregal officials—at least not during his lifetime or in the century thereafter.

If the Trujillo botanical research was so detailed and offered so many products with potential commercial windfalls, and if it described life in the area so well, why did the peninsular authorities basically ignore it? Plausible explanations include the fact that the empire's finances and political situation were in marked decline by 1790; and that the Bishop's proposed materia medica seems to have treated mundane concerns that already had European botanical cures, so it held no real promise of profit. It is true that that the findings and illustrations of the vast majority of scientific expeditions throughout the early modern Atlantic were not immediately published, published only in part, or never published at all. The most quantifiably "successful" royal scientific expedition was that of Ruiz and Pavón, which produced three thousand plant descriptions, and at least two thousand drawings—enough material, scholars surmise, to have published twelve separate volumes. Although the scientists and their team had returned to Spain in 1788, the first (and only) set of data from their expedition did not see publication until 1796. This contained only thirty-seven plates—an infinitesimal portion of all the images produced. And book buyers did not rush to purchase the few copies that were printed: only two-thirds of them were bought. This mirrored what would happen time and again when it came to colonial natural history. Scientists and bureaucrats in Spain and throughout Europe searched for the next tobacco, sugarcane, or cascarilla in their colonies. In the process, they produced thorough catalogs of their natural worlds, bolstering their reputations as colonizers of profitable, useful land. These displays of American nature served as testaments to their benevolence and expertise as colonizers but did not pass to international commercial markets or enter into the official discourse of imperial "science" with a capital S.[59]

Of course, we must consider why these productions of empire never produced the financial windfall that so many had hoped they would. Did the eighteenth-century push to catalog, export, and market American medicinal herbs, woods, and food crops have any real effect on local economies, or those of the empire at large? Despite the feverish interest in botany throughout the eighteenth century, silver remained the most important American export, and the Spanish continued to import the same dyes, animal hides, and large-scale crops, such as tobacco and cotton, that had always interested them. Medicinal plants made up only 5 percent of the trade goods coming from America. One scholar of these efforts has argued that "they must be understood in light of the spirit of observation and experimentation with which they were carried out."[60] The Martínez Compañón case shows that perhaps there is an alternative answer, one that is complexly intertwined with the supposed inferiority of American nature and American people.

The *Trujillo* botanical research is thus poised at a more complicated intersection of colonial science and imperial identity. As Jean-Jacques Rousseau described in his 1785 *Letters on the Elements of Botany*, by the so-called Age of Enlightenment, the science of botany had changed in Europe. Voicing the dominant opinion of the scientific establishment, he explained how the vernacular botanical traditions of the past had one distinct problem: their locally based systems made it impossible to definitively identify specimens or their uses. Naming and recognizing plants in local languages and dialects resulted in a system of materia medica in which random "balsams and ointments quickly disappeared, and soon made room for others, to which newcomers, in order to distinguish themselves, attributed the same effects." The complexity of this scheme only increased once the plants were removed from their immediate contexts and "when their recipes traveled to other countries, it was no longer known which plant they spoke of." Had the science of plants not advanced beyond this cumbersome naming system, he exclaimed dramatically, "it would have been all over for Botany!"[61]

Weighed down by extraneous and confusing information, how did the science of plants survive such adversity? According to Rousseau and the majority of naturalists of the day, it was saved by a heroic figure. In 1735, Swedish naturalist Karl Linnaeus proposed a new nomenclature system that was easily understood. Because this system was based on Latin, it was "universally" intelligible (at least to learned men from European nations). The Linnaean system quickly became the standard for official botany throughout the Atlantic world, with the Spanish Empire mandating that it be used for Crown-sponsored expeditions as early as 1752. Indeed, archival material for the Ruiz and Pavón Royal Botanical Expedition to Peru shows strong official preference for Linnaean standards and methodologies. Royal instructions made clear that Ruiz and Pavón should follow Linnaean methods, classifying plants by the sexual system, providing their Latin names, and discussing the species and varieties of each genus. The botanists were even ordered to read Linnaeus's *Botanical Philosophy* and *Peregrinatores Americani*. Expedition documents indicate that they did indeed follow these guidelines: each inventory entry names the item in Latin, and continues in Latin to discuss the sexual system of the plant. The entries have almost no "vernacular" information. A few discuss local indigenous uses of plants, but for the most part, they provide standardized scientific knowledge. Contoured in this fashion, botanical data became useful information that was more immediately relevant to medicine, trade, and imperial politics. These were the types of scientific data that European governments sought and the type of botanical research that they sponsored.[62]

However, in some parts of the Spanish Empire, local scholars—most often Creoles—who lacked imperial support for their naturalist projects mounted an ideological backlash against Linnaean botany. They argued that the Swedish botanist's method required too many expensive instruments not readily available in America, that the classifications based on sexual parts were obscene, and that the system was inherently incompatible with local natural knowledge. This counterattack was particularly focused in Peru, where popular naturalist Llano Zapata selected an alternative reader-friendly system of organization for his botanical work, one that privileged the physical description, geography, and utility of the plants that he described. Not only did Llano Zapata refuse to give Latin names to the plants that he studied; he also eschewed naming them in Castilian. Instead, he favored names in the indigenous language of Quechua. Eventually, he went so far as to argue that schools should make Quechua a required language for students of natural history. Similarly, Alonso Huerta, a professor at the University of Lima, argued that physicians should study Quechua because it would help them understand the local naming system that Peruvian Indians had already developed for their botanical universe. Hipólito Unanue agreed that the Linnaean system was simply unsuited for the unimaginably immense world of American plant life.[63] Particularly in Peru, the issue of naming and classification seemed to separate the metropolitan scientific establishment from the local, vernacular naturalist tradition. While Peru's naturalists and scholars argued for the superiority of locally based naming systems and botanical research, the Spanish on the Peninsula decided that this information was not readily translatable to European scientific institutions.

As one man straddling this growing epistemological divide, Martínez Compañón might have envisioned that by using Quechua names, he was recording local natural knowledge, something that benefited local communities by demonstrating their facility with plant matter and plant medicine. He believed in the importance of making these essentially local data visible to the broader Spanish Empire and beyond. In so doing, he stressed the local contours of imperial botany and used local knowledge to create a source of data that could serve both the regional community and the empire at large. In this way, it would become a scientific and political source to service his broader utopian agenda. Such an equation was a metanarrative of all his work as a naturalist and illustrates how the watercolors carried a deeper meaning about native peoples and their place in the world. While he may have employed local, untrained artisans for his watercolor collection simply as a matter of convenience, it is likewise plausible that the Bishop purposely chose to use Indians as informants and illustrators in his natural history project. Perhaps he thought that their work would help to prove to the king, his court, and the European scientific community that they were equal to other men. He certainly spoke of his native parishioners within these parameters, arguing that "the Indians are not how those stupid men wish to portray them" and chiding those who "mistake them with beasts to the point of downgrading them from being human." The Indians were not inherently different because of natural causes, he argued. Rather, they had lived under the repressive Inca regime, they had learned bad habits and vices from their Spanish neighbors, and they had not been properly educated or introduced to civil life. For the Bishop, these were all circumstantial causes for difference. He was so sure of this that he informed the king of Spain that "the Indians are equal, or very little different to the other men of their *calidad* [or sociocultural status] in this area."[64] By bringing them on as informants and as illustrators, the Bishop was able not only to record and share their ancestral knowledge about their physical and cultural world but also to prove to their detractors that they were able to understand and contribute to his utopian vision of Trujillo.

CHAPTER 7

The Legacy of Martínez Compañón

The end of this story begins on November 27, 1797, at the San Francisco Church in Bogotá. It was the morning of the final Mass in celebration of the twenty-seventh Bishop of Trujillo and the twenty-eighth Archbishop of Bogotá, Baltasar Jaime Martínez Compañón. His body had been interred in the cathedral three months earlier, and the city had already held four major ceremonies celebrating his life and works. The suitably impressive San Francisco Church that was the site of his final service was dominated by a dazzling gold *retablo* altarpiece that stood behind the presbytery, gleaming from ceiling to floor. Completed in 1622 by renowned Spanish craftsman Ignacio García de Asucha, the *retablo* featured eight life-size figures of saints, a Virgin Mary, and six separate paintings. The entire ensemble was gilded and encrusted with jewels. Smaller carvings and engravings sprinkled throughout the piece highlighted the flora and fauna of the Indies. A coconut palm wavered near an image of Saint Francis. Deer, hummingbirds, dogs, and macaws played nearby. The *retablo* even depicted mythical animals, such as a unicorn and an elephant, which would have arrived in Bogotá only in images in books borne by learned men like Martínez Compañón.[1]

That morning, some of the faithful had brought with them poems composed in honor of the Archbishop, which were to be carried to his tomb in the cathedral after the ceremonies. One was decorated with an image of a cypress tree sprouting from a gravestone, surrounded by four burning hearts pierced with a flaming golden arrow. The image represented a verse from the Song of Solomon, *fortis ut mors dilectio*: strong as death is love. The verses beneath it read:

We are now missing our Father, what sad luck!
We are all penetrated by this wound.

Even though love sustains our lives,
The same love also brings us death.[2]

That day's eulogy was offered by Franciscan friar Fermín Ibañez, who began
somewhat philosophically, reminding the faithful that God gave them "days
that pass with such speed . . . [and] restlessness as a seafaring ship, as much
quickness as the eagle."[3] He consoled the people by reminding them that a
loss such as that of their beloved archbishop was inevitable, given the imper-
manence of life. Nevertheless, he understood that their pain called for the
priests to grieve "the absence of your Teacher, whose affable face you will
never see again." Ibañez said that all the inhabitants of the capital city should
cry for the loss of the man "whom you barely began to love and know, when
death stole him from you." He continued with a series of accolades about the
Archbishop's life and work, describing how, in his university days, Martínez
Compañón had been "like the tall cypress among the tiniest bushes" and
how his work at Lima's cathedral evinced a "knowledge and intelligence rarely
seen." But Ibañez saved his most vivid praise for Martínez Compañón's years
in Trujillo. It was there, he told the people, that the Bishop had traveled to all
corners of his territory, "without being detained by the difficult roads, the
varied climates, the fastness of the rivers, or the inclemency of the weather."
Sometimes he even slept "on the ground with his body covered only by his
cape." The Bishop did all this because he wished "to know his flock, to imitate
somehow the Prince of Shepherds, Jesus Christ."[4]

Although Ibañez's eulogy was just one of several citywide episodes of
mourning, for most who were acquainted with Martínez Compañón, the
Archbishop's death had not come as a surprise. His health had been failing
throughout the summer months; on July 25, he finally resigned himself to
bed, where he maintained a stoic silence, meditating on his life and its impending end. His confidants, friends, and assistants did what they could. One
commentator noted that "the doctors applied all the knowledge of their art to
see if they could preserve his precious life. The holy virgins of all the convents
lifted their hands to the sky, and with the most fervent prayers begged to God
that he not take away their good father."[5] Despite these efforts, Martínez
Compañón mostly refused to take drink or food or even converse with his
visitors, focusing instead on preparing himself to meet his God. On August
14, the doctors were summoned, and they determined that the time of final
rites had arrived. The Archbishop dictated his will, with his friend José Mutis
serving as a witness.[6] He then gave what Fray Fermín Ibañez would later refer

to in his funeral oration as a "humble and simple" confession. It was on the morning of August 17, 1797, when the Archbishop of Bogotá said his final words: "Death is a holy gift; it is a consolation and a joy to me, as I have always lived in Jesus Christ."[7] Then he breathed his last breath.

Legend holds that after his passing, Martínez Compañón's body exhibited the fantastical properties that marked a saintly death. It remained supple and flexible, with so little rigor mortis that when the priests were dressing it in holy garments for his funeral, they were able to sit it up, move its arms, and position its head with ease. Some of the toenails continued to grow—a normal event for dead bodies—but these seemed determined to continue their holy martyrdom, for they reportedly curved into the toes, digging back into the flesh.[8] An "aromatic fragrance" wafted from the corpse. All this suggested that the Archbishop had been so holy that he had passed to a higher spiritual level and had overcome the decrepitude of human physicality. Outside his bedchambers, the news of his death reverberated throughout the city. Chronicler José Maria Caballero Ochoa wrote that afterward, "everyone—even the little boys—went about the city streets crying. The very sky was in pain," he added, "because in the . . . days before his burial the sun did not come out."[9]

The following Wednesday, August 19, the citizens of Bogotá awoke early to attend a "magnificent procession" in honor of their former archbishop. Winding around the city's main plaza, the parade included scores of ecclesiastics, guild members, city authorities, and a "crowd of the people who were very sad and mournful." Once they reached their destination of the cathedral, the Bishop was buried there. Though we have no record of how the solemn occasion proceeded, it must have followed traditional funereal rites for elite churchmen: lavishly attired, the Archbishop's body would have been laid out in a coffin and blessed with holy water. It was then carried in a solemn procession to the cathedral, while psalms and songs were sung. It was placed before the cathedral's main altar, where it remained during requiem Mass. However, this did not mark the end of the public remembrances for the beloved Martínez Compañón. On October 23, Manuel de Andrade, prebend and vicar of the archbishopric, gave his first funeral Mass in the cathedral. The Dominican and Capuchin churches also sponsored services for Martínez Compañón, and on November 18, Fernando Caycedo Florez, rector of Bogotá's cathedral, opened a series of remembrances at a location dear to the Archbishop's heart: the Convent of La Enseñanza. It was there that Martínez Compañón had worked with María Caycedo to support a school for girls in Bogotá. She, her brother Fernando, and Martínez Compañón had been "like family," according to José Mutis, who penned the introduction to the printed version of Caycedo Florez's eulogy. In it, Mutis described Martínez Compañón as "a hero we have loved so tenderly."[10]

At the Convent Church that Saturday in November, Caycedo Florez's tribute began with a quotation from the book of Ecclesiastes, one that Martínez Compañón might have publicly dismissed as hubris while he privately smiled. "The wise man will always be honored among his people," the cathedral canon pronounced, "and his name will live forever in future times." Though Caycedo Florez spoke to a large crowd that filled the church, this eulogy was particularly directed to the nuns, who were "the object of [the Archbishop's] charities and attentions," the women who "most completely enjoyed his benevolence" and were therefore especially bereft at his death. Twice, the Bishop had donated large sums of money to support education efforts at La Enseñanza. But such charity had actually begun during Martínez Compañón's tenure in Trujillo, the Franciscan explained. There he had been "like a benign star that blesses the earth with its influences wherever it goes." In Peru, he had determined to pay for his schools, seminaries, and new towns with his own salary, as "he knew that he could not neglect the magnificent divine promises he had made that he would rescue the poor."[11]

From Trujillo to Bogotá

By the day of his final eulogy, over six years had passed since Martínez Compañón last set foot on Peruvian soil. Despite the many concerns of an archbishop that had occupied him as the summers folded into autumns and the rains turned cold as winter began, he never would have forgotten what he once described as the "unspeakable pain" he felt about leaving his beloved Trujillo.[12] "Every day, the bitterness of my heart is greater," he admitted to Antonio Hermenegildo de Querejazu from Trujillo in 1789, "because of the certain departure I am taking from Peru."[13] Although his promotion to Bogotá was an accomplishment worthy of fanfare and celebration, it came with a healthy dose of melancholy. He regretted leaving behind "my poor diocesans, whose happiness is the central aim of my attentions and cares."[14] The Bishop explained that the move tugged at his heart because of the "deep relationship that for such a long time I have had with [Peru], the reverence . . . and love that its townspeople and inhabitants of all conditions and classes have merited." He was thankful to his diocesans for displaying "general docility in embracing my dispositions and proposals. Certainly," he wrote to Andrés de Achurra, the man who would replace him as bishop of Trujillo, "they are very deserving of eternal remembrance and recognition from me."[15] He wished that Crown administrators would reward his good work by allowing him to retire to Spain, "because from there, without a position or a benefice, I would be able to better promote my efforts on behalf of these unhappy people." He had hoped to make shorter trips back to Peru to "propose, promote, and complete the matters pertaining to my diocese" before returning to Spain, where he could better oversee the necessary bureaucratic processes.[16]

But the move back to Spain was not to be. Instead, he was promoted to an archbishopric in New Granada. The anticipation of the departure must have been made all the more difficult because two and a half years passed between September 1788, when he first received notice of the promotion, and his departure for Bogotá on June 30, 1790. Although normal by the bureaucratic standards of the day, this delay provided ample time for Martínez Compañón to dwell on his fear that "after our time, or our move to another church," the utopian future he had struggled to build for Trujillo would be "exposed to total inobservance and forget." To combat such destruction of his carefully laid plans, he planned to convoke a diocesan synod on July 2, 1789. He hoped that all the bishopric's parish priests would travel to their capital city on this solemn occasion, gathering to create "a body of statutes, or municipal laws . . . that would perpetuate and invigorate the providences of our *visita*."[17] Martínez Compañón knew that this undertaking would be all the more important since Trujillo had never before held its own synod and therefore had no existing code of local church law. In a series of pastoral letters distributed throughout the diocese, he instructed all parish priests of sound health to attend. Concurrently with the synod, he planned to sponsor a competition wherein young priests would compete for positions in the vacant parishes throughout Trujillo, providing them with gainful employment and ensuring that the faithful would not be unattended.[18]

While these designs were typical of church synods, such as the one in Lima in 1772–1773 for which he had served as secretary, Martínez Compañón also hoped that his meeting would advance his secular reform agenda. He instructed his priests to bring with them "clear and specific reports" about whether their parishes had followed the instructions he left them on his *visita*. In particular, he wanted to know if rural communities had built lodging for the faithful to use when attending Mass on festival occasions and whether townspeople had erected separate bedrooms for their male and female children. He also asked for information about each town's primary school—specifically, "its condition and state, and its instruction," as well as "whether people contribute to it with the assigned quota." Most important, he wanted to hear whether "the children attend school every day" and about "their advancement in intellect and the use of the Spanish language." By imagining the synod as an occasion to generate and gather information, the Bishop hoped to promote the "easiest, surest, and broadest reformation of customs: ordering of Christian and ecclesiastical discipline, and the greater splendor of His Majesty and dignity of the Divine Cult."[19]

Although local priests, Intendant Saavedra, and the ecclesiastical *cabildo* all enthusiastically endorsed the synod, bureaucratic wrangling over the creation of new parishes delayed it, and it could not be convoked before his transfer to New Granada. With the advantage of hindsight, we can see that, had the synod taken place, the documentary record of the local reform projects would have been infinitely richer. Scholars would have definitive data about which new towns and parishes were flourishing and which schools were operating and which had never been opened. Such information would have been invaluable in helping to explain the fate of local reform initiatives in Trujillo and the colonies in general.[20]

Back in Trujillo, with the synod seeming increasingly unlikely as his departure drew nearer, Martínez Compañón's letters show that his sadness began to transform into anxiety. He fought to hang on to the hope that he would meet incoming Bishop Andrés de Achurra in person, smoothing the way for his projects to continue uninterrupted. However, the travel schedules of the two men could not be coordinated; although the Bishop wished for them to meet in the northern Peruvian port of Paita, the captain of the ship on which he traveled feared that if they touched ground there, the crew would desert in the rough-and-tumble area notorious for piracy and contraband trading.[21] Martínez Compañón worried more and more that his schools, seminaries, towns, and new churches would be abandoned and forgotten once he left for New Granada. He explained to Achurra how much he would have liked for the two of them to meet in person because this would give him the "satisfaction of suggesting my principal designs and intentions . . . the methods I have found best for their achievement, the state in which they were." He cautioned his successor to pay special attention to the demarcations that he had put into place for new parishes and towns because local hacendados who were convinced "that this would be the ruin of their haciendas" would surely try to block them. Martínez Compañón wanted Achurra to see to the seminaries, assign priests to empty parishes, and monitor the progress of the new primary schools. He worried most about the schools in larger towns because there, parents were more likely to find themselves "busy or distracted" with work or social matters, which increased the "risk of the loss of the children" from school. Among his concerns, he struggled to maintain a positive tone in his correspondence. "I go with the consolation that you will advance much more than I would have advanced," he confided to Achurra in May 1790. "This hope is the only handkerchief for [my] tears at the time of my most painful departure from my bishopric that I have come to love so much for so many different reasons, and whose prosperity will interest me always as much as my own."[22]

In these letters from his final years in Peru, the Bishop repeatedly noted how he was "half convalescent."[23] Yet more careful examination shows that such warnings about his advancing age had been appearing in his correspondence for quite some time. Just one year after he had arrived in his bishopric, he reflected that a friend "would not find believable . . . how much I have aged in this handful of days."[24] In April 1785, a few weeks after returning from his epic travels throughout Trujillo, he admitted that "every day, I feel more and more the results of my travels, and sometimes my limbs hurt so much that I would like to end the suffering."[25] To Viceroy Croix in Lima, he confessed, "I have gotten so old, and so full of gray hairs, that if Your Excellency saw me, you would not recognize me."[26] By June 1789, he was complaining of eye and stomach problems;[27] eight months later, he had a troublesome congestion in his chest.[28] In addition to physical ailments, he suffered sometimes from feelings of loneliness and isolation, once even grumbling that "before I was Bishop, everyone wrote to me, but afterward, I don't get letters from anyone."[29]

Although such complaints were clear signs that he was advancing in age (he was fifty-two years old when he departed for Bogotá), the list of Martínez Compañón's accomplishments since his entrance to Trujillo in May 1779 was, by any standards, dazzling—indeed, what the Bishop did in eleven years could easily amount to an entire lifetime's worth of work. In Trujillo itself, he had orchestrated the rebuilding of the cathedral, which, when he arrived, was still damaged from the disastrous earthquake of 1759. He had added a new neoclassical façade—the same one that adorns the building today—built a crypt, and made space for a *cabildo* meeting room. He had commissioned a series of portraits of the thirty bishops of Trujillo who preceded him and had written an accompanying history of each of their lives. He had rebuilt the city's San Carlos Seminary and opened Trujillo's Seminario de Operarios del Salvador in September 1785. Outside the cathedral city, he had made the most extensive episcopal visitation of northern Peru since Archbishop Toribio's trip there in the sixteenth century. His *visita* totaled over two years and eight months of travel through the mountains, jungles, and plains of his bishopric. During this time, he had ordered the construction of thirty-nine new churches and provided for the rebuilding of twenty-one. He had founded forty-two new parishes and confirmed 162,000 people.[30] He laid the plans for a new road from Motilones de Lamas to Pajatén in Chachapoyas and an irrigation system in the town of Guanscapata. All this was in addition to commissioning and compiling the 1,372 watercolor images that constituted the nine volumes of *Trujillo del Perú* and amassing his twenty-four-crate natural history collection, with its accompanying inventory. He gathered and remitted to Madrid a separate archaeological collection of six boxes of pre-Hispanic tools, pottery, and other items totaling more than six hundred specimens. His archaeological investigations, especially the maps that he had commissioned of the Chan Chan complex outside Trujillo, remained unsurpassed by modern archaeologists until the 1970s Harvard expedition to the Moche Valley.[31]

The nine volumes and collections were particularly lavished with praise from contemporaries in the colonies—the Trujillo *cabildo* commended the "attention to detail" of what they called a "most laudable effort." They were certain that the project had brought great benefit to the diocese, pointing out the "hard work and dedication [the Bishop] had in its composition," as well as "his wishes that he had helped to benefit the bishopric with giving a public knowledge of its riches . . . and society."[32] Their words highlight how Martínez Compañón and his collaborators envisioned the natural history as the crowning achievement of over a decade of hard work—not an abstracted, separate set of investigations that had produced simple curiosities. Explaining who lived in Trujillo, how they occupied themselves, and how they made use of their surroundings, as well as laying out the vast cornucopia of resources that its natural environment offered was a service to the community. On the books' thick pages, the rich utopia of Trujillo's nature was laid out in bright hues and arresting images. The nine volumes could function as a point of pride and of posterity.

Not all Martínez Compañón's work in Trujillo met with such resounding success: though he founded twenty new towns, only four are known to have survived. He had ordered the construction of fifty-four primary schools throughout the diocese and secured viceregal approval for thirty-seven of them, although documentary evidence suggests that only four of these were ever operational. The two Indian colleges that he imagined for Trujillo and a separate school that he had planned to found for girls in Huamachuco never got off the ground. Likewise, the utopian mining town of Los Dos Carlos that he had imagined outside the Hualgayoc silver mine never materialized.

These were admittedly the more ambitious of his projects, those requiring extensive secular collaboration and funding. Although they were not successful, their failure was by no means unusual. The history of colonial Spanish America in the late eighteenth century is replete with stories of futile attempts at reforms and improvements. Despite these disappointments, the news was not all bad. Trujillo's general economic situation improved markedly during and after the Bishop's time there: provincial tax revenues increased by 48 percent between 1780 and 1790; mining income, stalled at zero in the 1760s, skyrocketed to 62,036 eight-reales in the 1770s and 75,659 in the 1780s; Trujillo became the third-largest mining region in Peru during this time. Trade revenue increased over 175 percent in the 1780s, making Trujillo a commercial center that closely rivaled Lima and Cuzco. Monopoly tax revenue more than doubled during the Bishop's years in Trujillo, going from 20,831 eight-reales to 49,393.[33] These trends admittedly reflected a general upswing in economic productivity in Spanish America in the 1780s; but in some very real ways, Trujillo was better off than when the Bishop had found it. For those eleven years, everything he did had contributed to what he referred to as "my only objective": "to make of each one of my diocesans a good man, a good vassal, and a good Christian."[34]

Accordingly, Martínez Compañón believed that his greatest accomplishment was having "been able to declare and maintain peace, discipline, and good order," ultimately securing "greater prosperity and splendor."[35] Indeed, a Spanish expedition to Trujillo in 1795 reported that "the Indians . . . are very docile and obedient, and all of them speak Castilian. Their principal application is agriculture and fishing, [and] they prosper with this." Even more telling was that "they have changed their dress to using that of Spaniards."[36] Had Martínez Compañón heard this, perhaps he would have smiled knowingly, recalling his conviction that "the exterior of the man indicates his interior."[37]

Legacy in Trujillo

Let us circle back to Martínez Compañón in Trujillo, where he was waiting for the final details of his departure. To mark his exit from the place where he had lived what he called the "headiest days of my life,"[38] he must have thought carefully about the material legacy that he would bequeath to the cathedral. Perhaps it did not take him long to realize that he wanted to leave his most precious religious relic in the city that had become his adopted home. He chose to honor the cathedral with a parting gift of a "gold reliquary, adorned with nineteen pearls, large and small among them, and forty-four diamonds." This bejeweled container held a prized remnant "of the glorious Saint Toribio,"[39] Toribio Alfonso de Mogrovejo, the Spaniard who had served as the third archbishop of Lima, from 1579 to 1606. Perhaps Martínez Compañón had acquired this holy relic in 1783, when his *visita* had brought him to the town of Saña, where the saint was buried.[40]

Toribio had arrived in Peru 204 years before Martínez Compañón visited his grave, making landfall in the aftermath of the so-called Toledan reforms of the late sixteenth century. Imposed by Viceroy Francisco de Toledo, these plans sought to maximize Spanish profits from native peoples through relocating them to *reducciones*, where Spaniards could more easily control their labor; establishing the *repartimiento* administrative districts run by *corregidores* responsible for gathering tribute monies and administering justice; and founding the dreaded *mita* labor draft to provide an adequate supply of workers for Peru's silver mines. All this resulted in an unprecedented pressure on the Indian population, one that uprooted traditional communal boundaries, stressed finances to the point of abject poverty, and subjected countless thousands to backbreaking forced labor in the mines.[41]

Archbishop Toribio realized that such demands would alienate Peru's native peoples from Spanish authorities both secular and ecclesiastic. So he set out to transform the Peruvian Catholic Church into a counterforce that would incorporate the Indians into Spanish society while offering them sympathy and support. He knew that to do so most effectively, he needed to collect accurate information about the local situation. Therefore, he set out on what would become one of the most comprehensive official journeys through the rural areas of Peru, making the first—and only, until Martínez Compañón's—*visita* of the northern bishopric of Trujillo.[42] As he traveled through the cragged peaks of the Andes, the lush Chicama Valley, and the Sechura desert, Toribio left in his wake plans to found churches, schools, and hospitals—all specifically for Peru's Indians. Upon returning to Lima, he founded the Saint Toribio Seminary in 1591, mandating that students there study Peru's main indigenous languages of Quechua and Aymara, and pass competency exams proving them capable of ministering to the native population. He took up the study of Quechua so that he could communicate directly with the Indians. In acknowledgment of his efforts, the Catholic Church canonized Toribio in 1679.[43]

While Martínez Compañón did not advance as far in his Quechua studies as his predecessor—it seems he knew only a smattering of Quechua words, including *sonco* (heart), *hanac pacha* (heaven), and *siza* (flower)—he did follow in Toribio's footsteps with his *visita* and its resulting reform agenda.[44] Furthermore, in Lima, he had served as rector of the seminary that still bore Toribio's name in 1770. In important ways, the two men found themselves in analogous historical moments: when Martínez Compañón arrived in Peru, the Spanish Crown was setting out on an unprecedented "reconquest" of the colonies, with extensive agendas of new taxes, improved bureaucracy, and renewed fiscal control. Like the Toledan reforms before them, the Bourbon reforms particularly affected Peru's indigenous communities. When Martínez Compañón began his career as a high prelate in this highly volatile situation, he sought to position himself as a benevolent intermediary between native communities and Spanish authorities, just as Toribio had done two hundred years earlier. Throughout his time in Trujillo, his reform initiatives mirrored Toribio's singular focus on assisting the Indians and the plebeians to develop the broader economy of the bishopric. He hoped to provide an alternative method for a more peaceful and mutually beneficial coexistence and, in so doing, to create a veritable utopia in colonial Peru.

Ultimately, Martínez Compañón's admiration for Saint Toribio drove him to declare Toribio the patron saint of the bishopric, with all the accompanying fanfare of a "first-class fiesta" that every year would grant the day off of work and sponsor a Mass in his honor.[45] He named a new settlement in Moyobamba after him, calling it Santo Toribio de la Nueva Rioja.[46] Doubtless, Martínez Compañón would have been pleased to hear Fernando Caycedo announce in his eulogy that "one same spirit motivated" both archbishop and saint, that "grace endowed them with a similar zeal, an equal vitality and strength [that] they both had to overcome the greatest obstacles, and overlook the greatest hardships when they found them necessary for the good of their people." Although Martínez Compañón was leaving many of his projects in Trujillo in a state of uncertainty, perhaps he took comfort in how he had molded his career after Toribio's. While he never admitted it in writing, maybe he hoped that someday, like Toribio, he would be beatified and even sanctified.[47]

Still, during his final days in Peru, as servants bustled around him packing his possessions while he scribbled his last few letters, we can imagine that a few tears fell from the Bishop's watery eyes when he thought of all he would leave behind. Perhaps he endured a sleepless night before waking up early on June 30, 1790, to head to Huanchaco and the boat that would take him away from his beloved Trujillo, toward a life that he did not yet know. He would turn fifty-three at his next birthday, and, at his advanced age, such a long trip was no easy undertaking. The boat would bring him first to Portobello, Panama, but not before it ran aground twice when traversing the lakes and rivers that striated the thin stretch of land near what is today the country's Soberania national park. These mishaps confirmed the Bishop's fears that the trip would be "even more dangerous through Panama,"[48] but the alternate route of disembarking somewhere in unsettled territory and crossing the Andes on foot was simply untenable. Martínez Compañón was too old for such travels now, something that he was likely forced to remember when during the journey he developed an infection in his right eye that prevented him from reading or writing. He first reached New Granada via the bustling port city of Cartagena. From there, he traveled up the Magdalena River to Mompox, in the Colombian interior, where his failing health and migraine headaches waylaid him for an extra month. During this time, it might have been difficult for him to keep his mind from traveling back across the isthmus of Panama, south along the Pacific coast, past Ecuador and the port city of Paita, back to his beloved Trujillo.[49]

Archbishop of Santa Fé

With his heart likely elsewhere, on Friday, January 28, 1791, Martínez Compañón awoke in the small town of Honda, New Granada. Honda was the main port city for the region, as it was conveniently situated ninety kilometers from Bogotá, at the center of the road network that stretched toward Mariquita and the Antioquia region. Five days earlier, when Martínez Compañón entered the town, he had been "received with the greatest demonstrations of happiness by the inhabitants."[50] Francisco Martínez, dean of the Bogotá cathedral, had traveled downriver to meet the party there. On that morning, Pedro Echevarri—Martínez Compañón's faithful secretary with him since his days as a young man in Spain, recently named a *racionero*, or lower-level dignitary of the cathedral—said Mass to commemorate the solemn occasion. Once the liturgy ended, Martínez Compañón dressed in his archbishop's robes and knelt before Francisco Martínez, who then bestowed upon his new leader the most significant instruments of his power: his archbishop's cape and his miter—the conical hat worn by bishops, archbishops, and cardinals. Echevarri read aloud the royal decree that declared Baltasar Jaime Martínez Compañón the twenty-eighth archbishop of Santa Fé de Bogotá, New Granada. Next, Francisco Martínez took out the Bishop's pallium, a white wool collar adorned with six crosses embroidered in black silk. Once Martínez Compañón finished saying another set of prayers, Echevarri produced three delicate gold pins, "each one encrusted with a precious stone," and affixed the collar to the Archbishop's vestments. As of that moment, Martínez Compañón was no longer bishop of Trujillo.[51]

The newly minted Archbishop of Bogotá spent the next six weeks visiting the Honda and Mariquita areas, confirming large crowds of the faithful and meeting with religious officials wherever he was able. On Saturday, March 12, he made his first public appearance in Bogotá. The city's *Papel Periódico* news-weekly reported of his entrance that "the happiness of the public was great at the view of a pastor that they had so desired because of the news they had heard of his talents and virtues." The occasion was commemorated by a spe-cially composed song that celebrated the Archbishop's "heroic spirit," explaining how "this most blessed day will be the most loved day in the history of the Kingdom of New Granada."[52]

This was an enthusiastic welcome suited to New Granada's biggest city; as of the 1780 census, Santa Fé de Bogotá marked a population of 20,000 inhabitants—almost four times as many as Trujillo. The city's downtown was home to historic stone houses, many of them whitewashed in limestone, as well as a number of churches renowned for their beauty. It was flanked by two great hills named Guadalupe and Montserrate, and the downtown was bisected by little bridges that crossed the Magdalena and Vicachá Rivers. The cathedral that would be Martínez Compañón's spiritual home stood on the city's spacious main plaza. Originally built in 1572, it had been badly dam-aged in an earthquake in 1785 and was still under repair when he arrived. The new façade was in typical neoclassical style, with three entry doors and two bell towers.[53]

Regardless of the state of its renovations, the city cathedral was the reli-gious center for Bogotá's markedly large population of religious men and women—a group that scholars estimate was so large that the city was home to one cleric for every twenty-five to thirty laypeople. The Archbishop must have been equally pleased to learn that his new home supported a vibrant intellectual culture, including several flourishing *tertulias*, or salon gatherings, where intellectuals discussed everything from politics to literature to art and culture. The city was home to the *Papel Periódico*, which reported on local and empire-wide news and often commented on the Archbishop's activities. Despite all this, Trujillo was never far from the Archbishop's mind. From his friend Viceroy José Manuel Ezpeleta, a fellow Navarro, he borrowed copies of the *Mercurio Peruano* newspaper to keep abreast of goings-on in his old home.[54]

As Martínez Compañón struggled to learn the geography of his new hometown—on one occasion, reportedly even missing Mass because he was unable to see the city clock or hear the church bells from the archbishop's palace—he had to come to terms with a world that every day seemed to become a bit less familiar. The physical environment surrounding him was not the only thing that had changed drastically. In December 1788, as Martínez Compañón was organizing his diocesan synod, his beloved monarch Charles III died, leaving the throne to his son Charles IV. Although the new king and his ministers initially believed that they had inherited a stable, productive Spain, fiscal difficulties soon emerged. Charles IV proved to be a weak ruler with little interest in politics, and he left most matters of governance to a revolving cadre of ineffective favorites. Meanwhile, across the Pyrenees, the French Revolution grew increasingly violent toward the Bourbons there. Fearing similar intolerance within Spain, the Spanish Bourbons broke their long-standing family compact with the French in 1793 and declared war on their neighbor nation. When the war ended two years later and Spain restored good relations with France, the reunited allies fought against Britain. Spain fared much worse in this conflict, losing naval dominance of its own territories and being cut off from its main source of wealth: its American possessions. The wars against France and Britain meant that from 1793 to 1808, Spain experienced "almost uninterrupted warfare," resulting in unprecedented fiscal crisis. The cash-strapped Crown sought to gather funds wherever it was able. Even from distant Bogotá, Martínez Compañón contributed what he could, offering eight thousand pesos and "all his facilities and abilities, along with those of his office" to the king.[55]

Although Spain's colonies in America seemed more stable than the metropolis, trouble was nevertheless afoot in New Granada. Despite the Crown's best efforts at censorship and control of the press, the anti-monarchical liberalism of the new United States of America and the French revolutionaries could not be kept out forever. In winter 1793, in Bogotá, a young Creole named Antonio Nariño took it upon himself to translate the 1789 "Declaration of the

Rights of Man." Using his own printing press called La Patriótica, he produced a hundred copies that he intended to distribute throughout the viceroyalty. But once the printing was finished, he thought better of the plan and decided to burn all but two copies, which he kept in his personal files.

These documents lay undiscovered until summer 1794, when the viceroy and *audiencia* members woke up one August morning to learn that six satirical lampoons poking fun at them had been posted throughout the city. Believing that Spanish sovereignty was facing a full-frontal attack, the *audiencia* judges mercilessly sought the perpetrators and before long captured the young men who had affixed the offending broadsides throughout town. The judges may have been slightly disappointed when their interrogations revealed that these young men did have complaints about politics within Bogotá but were decidedly uninvolved in any sort of larger plot to disrupt Spanish rule in the viceroyalty. Yet the judges remained convinced that somewhere, someone in Bogotá was trying to overthrow the Spanish monarchy. Further investigation led them to the circle of intellectuals who frequented the city's *tertulia* gatherings and contributed to weekly publications such as the *Papel Periódico*, which happened to be published by none other than Nariño. It did not take them long to discover his aborted attempt at distributing the "Rights of Man"—a direct challenge to absolute monarchy if there ever was one. Soon they came to believe that he stood at the center of a conspiracy involving plans to seize the city's military barracks, capture up to three hundred armed men, and abscond with large amounts of money. The document had been printed, they argued, to garner further support for this attempted coup. In the aftermath of what scholars now call the "Pasquinades Rebellion," the young men who posted the original pasquinade lampoons were arrested, as were Nariño and his printer, Diego de Espinosa.[56]

Even with these perpetrators in jail, Viceroy Ezpeleta and the *audiencia* could not shake the sense of impending threat to their authority. They nervously initiated a campaign to preempt possible rebellion by fortifying military protection around the city. But not everyone agreed with this agenda. The powerful Creoles of the *cabildo* resented the implication of the Bogotanos' disloyalty; by January 1795, Bogotá seemed divided into a Creole camp, which defended the city's loyalty, and the peninsular one, determined to head off any perceived threat to Spanish sovereignty. Desperate to manage a situation that was quickly spiraling out of his control, Viceroy Ezpeleta sought advice from his closest advisers. This group included Archbishop Martínez Compañón, who, in October 1795, assured him that the rebels did not pose a true threat to the kingdom. The matter had been nothing but a careless mix of "freedom, imprudence, and levity," he wrote. He was certain that the guilty parties were nothing more than "poor young men, from the provinces, without connections or influence."[57] Because the punishment they had already endured had been sufficient—extended jail sentences had even led to the death of one of the offenders—the Archbishop recommended that they be pardoned.[58]

He never retracted this recommendation for clemency for the perpetrators; but the following year, Martínez Compañón seemed to reconsider leniency toward the rebellion in general. He still insisted that "the people of this capital and its provinces are in general peaceful, well meaning . . . [and] obedient to their king and ministers." He continued to recommend religious instruction, primary education, and training in trades to maintain good order. Yet in the months that passed, his correspondence with the viceroy took on darker undertones, especially when it came to his extensive list of suggestions regarding "the methods that seem appropriate to fulfill the goals of Your Excellency's mandates" to govern an orderly kingdom. Several of these mirrored his old reform agenda in Trujillo: he suggested founding two new primary schools, a seminary for *operarios eclesiásticos*, and schools for missionaries. He recommended surveying the local population by making an accurate map of the viceroyalty and compiling a chart listing the population by sex, age, race, and profession. But this was no simple demographic compilation like what he had ordered in Trujillo. This time, the Archbishop reasoned that the information could be used to amass information about defenses and evacuation routes. A final copy, he thought, could be remitted to Madrid—presumably so that officials there could review and approve evacuation programs in advance and keep a copy on file, "for what it was worth." In such a precarious situation, Martínez Compañón thought to use information to ensure state control of the people.[59]

Martínez Compañón never expressed such alarmist thinking in Trujillo, not even when he was called to Otusco to pacify the tax rebellion there. Instead, he had penned an elegant letter explaining the necessity of taxation in the Spanish Empire and the benevolence of the Spanish king. Perhaps events in France since he had arrived in Bogotá—especially the January 1793 guillotine death of French king Louis XVI and Maximilien Robespierre's so-called Reign of Terror—had frightened him, as they had so many Spanish ministers and elites. Maybe this is why he recommended to Ezpeleta that the viceroyalty prohibit the sale, purchase, printing, or reading of any book or manuscript found to be "seditious, or subversive to public tranquillity and good manners." As punishment for cases of violation, the Archbishop suggested six months of banishment from New Granada. He recommended closing the public printing press in the city, as well as rooting out any smaller presses held in private homes or shops. He suggested shutting the doors of the public library, reasoning that "the men of studies and letters of this city all in general have within their houses the necessary books." Furthermore, he recommended that the Inquisition stop distributing licenses to read prohibited books in New Granada, in order to "prevent their introduction." Finally, he thought that the Inquisition should erect a court in Bogotá, as a satellite to the viceroyalty's main Inquisition tribunal in Cartagena.[60]

A few months earlier, Martínez Compañón had dismissed the Pasquinades Rebellion as youthful folly; now his opinion of the city's security had changed drastically. Given local history, his abundance of caution was not unfounded—after all, just thirteen years prior, provincial Colombians had rallied against tax and fiscal reforms, gathering 20,000 troops and threatening to march on a vulnerable Bogotá, standing down only after the viceregal authorities conceded to their desires to return to the financial status quo. We might imagine that as he aged, Martínez Compañón came to feel that the world around him was changing too quickly. The old order in which he had played such a defined part was slipping away before his eyes. But closer investigation into the rebellion and the intellectual culture in Bogotá in the 1790s suggests another explanation. It appears that, like Antonio Nariño and Viceroy Ezpeleta, the Archbishop found himself caught up in a scandal that quickly outgrew its fairly modest beginnings.[61]

Although the brunt of the blame for the Pasquinades Rebellion was clearly laid on Nariño, once he was squirreled away in prison, viceregal authorities began to wonder how he had gotten hold of the forbidden treatise of the French Revolution in the first place. Directly or indirectly, it must have come from someone who had a license to read prohibited material. When questioned on the matter, Nariño admitted that he had found the document in a book that he had managed to obtain from a military guard at the viceregal palace. In a roundabout way, the viceroy himself had been responsible for permitting the young man access to a document that he never should have seen. Even though this mistake was unintentional, its consequences were potentially disastrous. To save face, Ezpeleta desperately needed to demonstrate his loyalty to the Spanish Crown, his opposition to liberal Creoles, and his ability to prevent future such episodes in the city and the viceroyalty.[62]

While Ezpeleta's link to Nariño through the palace guard who "lent" the contentious book explains why the viceroy would have wanted to foster an austere crackdown on insubordination in New Granada, it still leaves unanswered the question of why Martínez Compañón so dramatically altered his own stance on the rebellion and its aftermath. Further investigation reveals that, like Ezpeleta, the Archbishop may have responded so harshly because he felt that his own reputation was in jeopardy. Though his name was never specifically implicated, Martínez Compañón had participated in many of the same social and intellectual activities as Nariño and his coconspirators, most of whom had met through their participation in Bogotá's growing network of public intellectual institutions, including José Mutis's botanical expedition, the *Papel Periódico*, and the city's *tertulias*. The Archbishop had notable links to all of these. Martínez Compañón's friendship with Mutis was so dear that the latter dedicated a plant to him—the *Martinezia granatensis*—and in 1793, the Archbishop tried (unsuccessfully) to persuade the botanist to assume an honorary position within the local church hierarchy. Given their common interest in botany and natural history, Martínez Compañón must have visited the expedition's famed workshop and spoken with the researchers and illustrators it employed. Mutis was one of the few men who stood by as the Archbishop breathed his last breath. Their relatively intimate relationship unmistakably linked him to one of the sites where insubordination had grown. The Archbishop also had connections to the *Papel Periódico*, which was produced by Nariño's press: he was friendly with the paper's editor, Manuel Socorro Rodríguez, and he was a lauded subscriber. Furthermore, Martínez Compañón was known to attend the *tertulia* Eutropélica that Socorro Rodríguez held at his home. However tangential, these connections to a convicted subversive were improper for the highest ecclesiastical authority in the land. Perhaps they explain how his harsh recommendations for censorship were a response to the endangerment of his own reputation.[63]

Whatever the reasoning behind his sudden conservatism, it is important to remember that from the start, Martínez Compañón's agenda in Bogotá plainly differed from what he had done in Trujillo. First, the scope of his activities was greatly limited: he was now an archbishop, with a much larger set of ecclesiastical responsibilities and an even more prominent position within the Spanish Empire. The increased concerns of his office inevitably preempted him from engaging in the type of locally based social improvements that he had worked so hard to effect in Trujillo. He was also older, with less energy and worse health than when he had arrived in northern Peru in 1779. Despite these concerns, he managed to pursue some of the concerns that had busied him in Trujillo: he ordered repairs for local churches that had been damaged in earthquakes and established Bogotá's provincial seminary with funding from his own coffers. He confirmed 25,000 people throughout his time in New Granada. In March 1795, he set out on a pastoral *visita*. But in general, these efforts paled in comparison with the great agenda he had undertaken in Trujillo. It seemed that the Bishop's utopia in Trujillo was so closely tied to the place in which he conceived it and constructed it that it would be impossible to replicate in the context of his new position in New Granada.[64]

Nevertheless, Martínez Compañón continued with one of the causes dearest to his heart in Peru. With Viceroy Ezpeleta's help, he sponsored five primary schools throughout Bogotá, one in each principal neighborhood. But most of his focus was on the school at the Convent of La Enseñanza. He thought that the girls there should learn "reading, writing, and something of math," as well as Christian doctrine and embroidery. He proposed that the attached public school instruct sixty to seventy day students, who would study the same curriculum as the seminary students. He concluded that the convent needed more nuns who would dedicate themselves to teaching. To facilitate these reforms, he donated 41,000 pesos in 1795, endowing twenty-four new nuns at the convent and providing spaces for seventeen students at the day school. When he died, he left an additional 51,000 pesos to the school, endowing twenty-six more nuns and sixteen more day students.[65] Important as they were, these efforts paled in comparison with what he had proposed for Trujillo. Constricted by his advancing age, increased responsibilities of office, the tense political climate, and the more defined administrative hierarchy in Bogotá, Martínez Compañón seemed to have been forced to abandon his utopian vision of plebeian improvement on the thin sandy shore of Trujillo's port of Huanchaco.

Martínez Compañón's Native Utopia

In 1516, an English lawyer named Thomas More penned a canonical literary work that, almost half a millennium later, would be declared by a professor at Paris's Sorbonne to be one of the most seminal publications in the history of the world. In that 2011 editorial in the *New York Times*, Yves Charles Zarka referred to *Utopia* as a book that "inaugurated" the modern era, the time in which man was able to assess the world around him, find it lacking, and "look for an elsewhere" by imagining a better situation for humanity. More's *Utopia* invented a fantastical island of cities all "identical in language, customs, institutions, and laws," with uniformly straight streets and pleasingly similar buildings. Nestled among them were public hospitals to serve the sick and schools where children would learn primary letters in their native language. Outside the cities' protective walls lay farmhouses run by citizens who periodically served two-year agricultural work terms cultivating and harvesting. *Utopia*'s social universe was equally ordered: the people had at first practiced their own religions, worshiping the sun, moon, or the planets; but after they learned of Christianity, according to More, "you would not believe how eagerly they assented to it." Priests in *Utopia* were revered above all others. In general, the justice, peace, and prosperity that prevailed there promoted a hierarchical but fair social order, one in which "wives are subject to their husbands, children to their parents, and generally the young to their elders."[1]

Utopia has long since earned its place on the shelves of libraries around the world; but at the dawn of the twenty-first century, "utopia" has come to mean much more than the specific society that More imagined. It is today a "non-existent good place,"[2] a dream-like alternative to the "immoral, unjust laws which determine politics" in the real world.[3] More's imagined world— and the scores of utopias that have been invented afterward, on paper and in real time—purports to rescue the quotidian from the disorder, disagreement, disaffection, disease, and disenfranchisement of reality. Utopias offer a proposed "transformation of the everyday," one that in its mere existence "envisions a radically different society."[4] Utopias, as Oscar Wilde once wrote, show humankind's best vision of itself.[5]

Like the ship in another utopian story, Francis Bacon's celebrated *New Atlantis*, the utopia that Martínez Compañón imagined "sailed from Peru." But unlike Bacon's fictitious journey, which ended on the mythical island of Bensalem somewhere in the Pacific Ocean, Martínez Compañón's adventure not only began in Peru; it ended there, as well.[6] Outside Trujillo, the Bishop's utopia was unimaginable. It could not have existed without Trujillo's rich pre-Hispanic past, its diverse population, its microclimates, and its abundant natural world. Trujillo was where Martínez Compañón lived what he called the "headiest days of my life,"[7] the place he had dreamed of since he was a boy in Spain. He had "reverence . . . and love" for its people, whom he said he would always remember fondly no matter where he was.[8] Among its valleys, hills, and mountains, he found an "isolated retreat" that held within it "much more than we imagine": a utopia of natural, historical, and human resources.[9]

Martínez Compañón's ultimate testament to this prolific universe was the nine volumes of *Trujillo del Perú*, the books that the *cabildo* celebrated as the "most laudable effort" of his own "hard work and dedication." These were his gift to Trujillo's posterity, forever documenting "public knowledge of its riches . . . and society."[10] The nine volumes revealed a world in miniature, a society inhabited by elegantly attired Spanish gentlemen, humble Indian women who attended church wrapped in modest dark brown *pullu* shawls, and African slaves who labored in sugarcane fields. The people of this paper utopia worked almost ceaselessly at cultivating its rich soil, growing alfalfa, and plowing fields of corn and wheat. They raised horses and tended cattle, while their herds of sheep produced thick fleece that became thread and eventually fabric. They hunted mountain lions, bears, and wild boars, and they fished with intricate nets and *caballito* boats. They produced local manufactures like cheese and *chicha* corn beer. In their free time, they behaved appropriately—attending state-sponsored cockfights and bullfights, playing sports, and mounting elaborate dances during Carnival season. They were respectful and polite—of one another, with neighbors helping neighbors during harvest season, and especially of the authorities who periodically arrived with their staffs of office and tribute lists. They lived in orderly cities, with straight city blocks, central plazas, churches, and hospitals. Their children attended school in sturdy buildings with desks equipped with inkwells, kitchens, and court-yards for playing.

This painted microcosm of daily life in late colonial Trujillo is centered on the very type of activities that historian of utopias Lyman Tower Sargent argues are the most typical. Sargent contends that utopias "show people going about their everyday lives and depict marriage and the family, education, meals, work, and the like. It is this showing of everyday life that characterizes a utopia," he suggests, "and utopianism is about just that transformation of the everyday."[11] At the same time, it is important to remember that the utopia in *Trujillo del Perú* is an imagined one—it is Trujillo presented in the best possible light, with the greatest possible optimism. Like any creative, academic, or even scientific work, it was far from objective; it bore the dreams, hopes, and prejudices of the Bishop and of the artisans and naturalists who created it. Martínez Compañón did not display to his king the grinding poverty, social isolation, and technological backwardness in which so many of his diocesans lived. The *Trujillo del Perú* watercolors were instead his vision of what *could* have been in Trujillo: the best of all possible worlds.

Just as important to how the Bishop chose to visually represent his proposed social utopia in Peru was the natural world in which it existed. He showed a nature that was resoundingly fertile—its plant kingdom, in particular, revealed to the viewer 488 distinct species. It included the granadilla vines, which grew on arbors and produced a luscious fruit that could be used to cure fevers, and the *chamcas* plant, which shepherds added to the salt they left out for their sheep because it would help to combat parasites.[12] Trujillo's animal life was equally vibrant, as the nine volumes reveal the bishopric to be home to everything from the humble guinea pig and the common squirrel to the fearsome mountain lion and the petite brown "Little Friar" monkey. The many birds of the area merited their own separate volume, brimming with detailed portraits of specimens such as the *coto* bird, whose barrel-chested silhouette, spindly legs, and extended tail resembled the dress of fancy gentlemen of the era. Even the humble anchovy found its own place in this natural utopia, alongside other more infamous specimens such as the shark and the swordfish. Perhaps most important, all these plants, animals, birds, and fish served the people who lived among them—as medicine, food, clothing, and even diversion. The natural world of Trujillo was a veritable Eden, a lavish universe brimming with exuberant life, green leaves, iridescent feathers and durable cowhides. As the image of the mestizo curing his leishmaniasis with an unguent from the *angusacha* plant (see Plate 20) made clear, it was a world where people, especially hardworking ones like those the Bishop depicted, could find all they needed to make use of the bountiful environment around them.

Somewhere among all the idealism and optimism that leap off the pages of the *Trujillo* watercolors lies the reality that this imagined future depicts Trujillo as "becoming as opposed to what has become; what is emerging as opposed to what is fixed and static."[13] Yet as astute early modern readers of *Utopia* and *New Atlantis* recognized as they turned the pages in front of them, utopias were not exclusively imaginings of an idealized life; utopias comment equally on the society in which they are produced. They offer a subtle yet pointed critique of imperialism, capitalism, religious dogma, or whatever disturbs their creator most. Their cloak of fiction is the disguise that permitted More and Bacon to confront and criticize their own societies. Though Martínez Compañón did not write a utopian literary text for public consumption, he, too, imagined and envisioned a critique of the world around him. Implicit in his architecture of utopia was the assertion that the machinations of the Spanish Empire were in dire need of repair.

As the infamous Juan de Palafox, bishop of Puebla, had learned in seventeenth-century New Spain, it was clearly beyond the official duties of any high ecclesiastic—or any wise one, at least—to gesture toward critiquing Church policy in the Spanish Empire.[14] Had he ventured to do so in writing, Martínez Compañón would have been summarily demoted and removed from the very place he so loved. But in laying out what he wanted to reform, the Bishop demonstrated what he wanted to change. Clearly, his push to build churches in the wilderness and to have religious men visit rural communities indicates his conviction that outside major population centers, priests did not adequately minister to many of the faithful. His constant pleas for priests to oversee social propriety (such as his concern that male and female children slept in separate bedrooms) suggest that many local communities were regularly left to their own devices when it came to everyday propriety. His incessant tallying of church finances implies that a good part of these were mismanaged.

While disapproving of the Church was risky business, going against the Spanish Crown had potentially more disastrous consequences. Yet, if we look closely, we can see how Martínez Compañón's architecture of reform for Trujillo cleverly disguises his seeds of contention with Spanish imperial policy. At its core, it suggests that the Crown failed to make good use of its greatest resource: the people of America and the world they lived in. The Bishop's insistence on surveying and cataloging Trujillo's human and natural resources implied that the Spanish had yet to capitalize on what was all around them. His focus on spreading knowledge of efficient agricultural techniques suggests that the Crown had work to do in that area. Likewise, had the Spanish already managed to properly harness the commercial and medicinal value of Spanish America's plant life, there would have been no need for three entire books of plant images and countless descriptions of their properties. If they did not yet know what they had, the Spanish would be unable to make use of it or improve upon it. Such deficiencies could throw into question the entire agenda of colonialism in Spanish America. If the Spanish were not bringing benefit to the New World, if their mission of evangelization and civilization had yet to penetrate into so many corners of the empire, how should they measure what they had been doing there for centuries?

Above all, Martínez Compañón's plans to remake Trujillo into an ideal colonial setting depended on better treatment of its native peoples. After all, he had once boldly ventured to King Charles III that the Indians of America were "a miserable people . . . wherever one looks." Specifically noting their lack of spiritual education, he insisted that they lived in "profound ignorance," with "no idea of good, bad, or virtue." Here he implicated the Spaniards, whose neglect had left the Indians without honor for themselves or their work. As a result, the Indians did not understand industriousness and were ill inclined to exert themselves.[15]

But for all their misfortune, Martínez Compañón was sure that the Indians were not inherently irredeemable. Recall that he had characterized as "stupid" his contemporaries who dismissed Native Americans as mentally feeble, insisting instead that the Indians were human and actually "equal, or very little different from, other men of their *calidad* [or sociocultural status] in this area."[16] Their willing involvement in his plans to build new towns in the wilderness demonstrated that, like plebeians elsewhere in the empire, they believed in the utility of living a "civil life" in an organized community. Their overwhelming enthusiasm for town primary schools and Indian colleges showed that they were equally convinced about the importance of education and how it could help their children advance. Just as important, the Bishop's work contended that the Indians' intellect should be valued. Employing native informants and artisans for the natural history research implied that the Bishop valued their knowledge of the world in which they lived. Not only were they able to provide useful information about botanical medicines and potential commercial crops; they were also sophisticated enough to portray these data in a visual medium that could be shared with scholars throughout the world. The Carnival dances, architectural plans, musical notations, woven textiles, and pottery that he included in his collection and portrayed in his nine volumes were vivid proof of the accomplishments of Peru's native peoples. Displaying them to the king indicated that this culture was complex and sophisticated and that it was also worthy of being cataloged, studied, and displayed.

Since it was so focused on improving the lives of the Indians, Martínez Compañón's reform agenda in Peru is highly revealing about the socioeconomic ills to which he believed they were subject. Through reading it critically, we can see his conviction that Indians were not taught proper religious dogma, or shepherded through behavior befitting Catholics, or made to follow a regular schedule of sacraments. Had Martínez Compañón not been convinced of this, he would not have gone to such extremes to carve out new parishes, fill them with priests, and assess how matters were proceeding in areas that were already staffed by religious figures. The Bishop suggested that the Spanish had failed at incorporating a vast portion of their American vassals into town life, with its accompanying institutional structure and social observation—otherwise, he would not have proposed that the Trujillo diocese would benefit from the foundation of twenty new towns and the relocation of four to areas where they would serve a greater population. Indian education was inadequate, his utopia implied, because there were no primary schools or special Indian colleges for the natives to attend. Martínez Compañón's reform agenda also reveals—and this was likely a surprise to no one—his belief that the Indians were mistreated when working in Peru's mines. Whether they were swept up in the *mita* labor draft (which he directly opposed) or simply brought to the mines by their need to fulfill tribute payments, he believed that the Indians were abused, overworked, and underpaid. In his mind, their life conditions in mining areas were untenable—so much so that he envisioned an entirely new type of settlement that would attract voluntary workers to the mines, putting them to work in exchange for plots of land and the tools they would need to work them.

In sum, in imagining his utopia in colonial Peru, the Bishop concurrently pointed out the very things that he believed made Peru a dystopia. While he never would have publicly pronounced his program as criticism of Spanish policy, and likely would never have uttered such sentiments publicly (possibly not even silently to himself), the critique remains. In this way, the Bishop's utopia reveals not only what he imagined that could be but also what he lamented that was.

AFTERWORD

To conclude our story, perhaps we can imagine a chilly afternoon in 1803 made much colder by the granite walls of the Escorial palace nestled in the gently rolling hills outside Madrid. This was the day that the wooden crates from Peru finally arrived at their destination—the palace library.[1] Whoever opened the crates would have found nine books, their pages sewn with red thread into red Moroccan leather covers. Their pages revealed intricate hand-painted watercolors of Indian chiefs lying in state with striking feather headdresses, exquisite orange and black monarch butterflies, and plump shepherdesses tending to puffy white sheep on rolling green hills. Whoever was reviewing them perhaps admired the lush, gilded images of a world so far away and might have paused for a moment, wondering how a tiny place he had never heard of, in a kingdom where he had never been, could contain an entire world in itself.

But as happens with books, the viewer soon tired of them and left the nine red leather tomes forlornly in their wooden crate. They were later repackaged in their tomb-like box and sent to Madrid. There, far from Trujillo's coastal desert and verdant jungles, they would find a new home in the chilly, high-ceilinged chambers of the Library of the Royal Palace in central Madrid. Soon after their arrival, a librarian unceremoniously filed them away. The nine volumes were then largely forgotten, except by one brown book mouse who, on a winter afternoon, made a meager lunch of a small bit of the leather inside the front cover of volume 3.[2] Although the books remained unopened, within their silent pages lay a vision of a distant world, where Carnival dancers adorned as devils twirled in circles with streamers trailing from their rainbow-hued costumes (see Plate 24). Elegantly dressed bishops stood patiently with hands clasped, while light-skinned Indians with European-style clothing obediently refused to gamble with money. Sitting silently with their playing cards and feathers, they waited for a curious soul to peer into their universe again.

SOURCES AND METHODS

One afternoon at the National Archive of Colombia in Bogotá, a fellow researcher asked me what I was working on. "Bishop Martínez Compañón of Trujillo, Peru," I told him. He thought for a minute and then replied that the biggest challenge I would face in this project would be the problem of too much information. "His documents are everywhere. Here, Trujillo, Lima," he trailed off. "Pages and pages, thousands," he cautioned. True to his prediction, I would soon find that there were countless *legajo* files of documents and that the archivists in Bogotá alone had combined this embarrassment of riches into eleven entire rolls of microfilm. Like the vast majority of the Martínez Compañón documents, they were from the epic *visita* that he undertook from June 1782 through March 1785. The papers had arrived in Colombia because after learning that he was to become archbishop of New Granada, Martínez Compañón ordered a complete set of his official papers duplicated and brought with him. Among these were instructions for how to cultivate flax and detailed directions for cesarean operations. Other documents told the story of unruly townspeople dressing up as Franciscans (which appears in Chapter 2 of this volume) and an Inquisition case from the sleepy hamlet of San Pedro de Lloc, in which an elderly Andres Ribera was deemed an "old witch" who had killed his neighbor. It was inevitable that only some of these documents would find their way to becoming part of the story I tell about the Bishop in these pages. However compelling I found them, many had to be pushed aside to make room for those truly central to the project.

While in Colombia, I faced the problem of too much information; in Peru, the problem I encountered more often was difficulty in accessing what I needed. Though I arrived in Lima and Trujillo by plane, the most reasonable way to reach the highland city of Cajamarca was by an eight-hour bus ride on winding country roads so precipitous that my local friends all but promised me that I would become disastrously ill along the way. Transportation was not the only challenge I faced; at a state archive in Lima, a guard refused to allow me into the building because my passport lacked the requisite two last names. At one ecclesiastical archive in the provinces, it took three weeks to secure permission to work in the collection. After gaining access, there were more surprises: large portions of the documents were eaten away by the insidious bookworms whose curlicued paths destroyed chunks of careful handwriting; other pages were partially burned, marred by water stains, or simply disintegrated. The climate and the history of northern Peru—particularly the humidity and the wars for independence, the archivists told me—had taken their toll on the documents that the colonial period had left behind.

As the research trips continued and I learned to anticipate these challenges, I came to grips with what was likely my biggest—and perhaps my only—disappointment in working on Martínez Compañón. As the reader no doubt has noticed, the vast majority of the archival records about the Bishop's reform projects simply drop off after his time in the region. Time and again, we find the story beautifully set up: Martínez Compañón visits; the people are inspired to ask him for a school, a new town, or some other improvement; local officials express their most enthusiastic support; permissions are given, and the bureaucratic groundwork is laid; and then, nothing. The document trail simply ends. It is possible that municipal archives contain documentary indications of how local primary schools or town foundations continued after the initial planning stages; but in my years of archival research, I saw no such evidence, nor have other scholars of the Bishop managed to find them. Perhaps this is because the projects died a languid bureaucratic death once Martínez Compañón moved on to other concerns. Equally possible is that the projects did proceed at the municipal level, but the corresponding documentation was not deemed worthy of preservation. Although it was beyond the scope of this book, I hold out hope that a dedicated investigation through municipal archives in the Trujillo region might produce further documentation about the fate of some of the projects that the Bishop initiated.

Without exact notice of how what I studied had ended, I had to shift my focus from outcome and toward environment—to how the Bishop and his contemporaries would have viewed their efforts and how they were a reflection of the world in which they lived. Martínez Compañón and those who collaborated with him were part of a tireless culture of improvement and reform, one that confronted what was lacking by imagining how to remake it into a better version of colonialism. They were taken by the idea of building a utopia around themselves—or they convincingly presented themselves as such. Though they intended for their utopia to move past the stages of planning and into the realm of reality, its failure to do so made it no different from other utopias of the past—or those of the present or the future. For by their very nature, when utopias become reality, they are no longer utopias.

Methodology

From the beginning of my work on this project, one of the choices I deliberated on the most was how I would handle the disparate set of natural history data that the Bishop left behind. What would I do with images meant to illustrate a book that was never written? How would I read the inventory for a collection that no longer existed? Although the information held within Martínez Compañón's scientific research was rich with promise, it was unrelentingly raw. Had the Bishop had the luxury of time to organize his notes and write the natural history that he had intended, matching it with his nine volumes of watercolors and his collections, my task would have been infinitely easier—and Martínez Compañón likely would have been one of the most studied figures of the early modern Spanish Empire. But I came to see why Martínez Compañón's natural history research had been relegated to the periphery of scholarship about natural histories in the colonial period: it was exasperatingly difficult to match up the different sets of information in order to draw the substantiated conclusions that would make sense of the data.

As I read more about how scientific knowledge was generated in the early modern Atlantic world, I began to understand that Martínez Compañón's system of data organization was little different from that of many of his contemporaries. I learned how in the most celebrated of the botanical expeditions to South America in the eighteenth century, José Mutis compiled separate sets of botanical illustrations and descriptions in his workshop in Bogotá. Farther south in Peru, Hipólito Ruiz and José Pavón gathered the data necessary for a comprehensive history of Peru's plant life but never managed to produce or publish more than a small fraction of the written work that they had intended to complete. Eventually, my task with Martínez Compañón's watercolor images and collection inventory became clear: I would do for the Bishop what Ruiz and Pavón had done for themselves in Madrid, years after their expedition had ended. They gathered their plant illustrations and written descriptions, pairing them with herbarium specimens and reporting on their findings.

Though I had no dried plants to work with, I developed my own methodology of "cross-reading" the botanical images and the collection descriptions, further investigating any compelling connections I found with contemporary natural histories and current ethnobotanical research. Essentially, I did—or tried to do—for Martínez Compañón what he would have done for himself, had his old age played out as he had imagined, with him finally finishing his peripatetic travels between Spain and Trujillo, seated in a comfortable chair in a library, his aching fingers and watery eyes working far into the night in order to make the utopia he had found in Trujillo come alive for the eyes of the world.

This same measured analysis of uncooked data has guided my work with the visual lexicon called *Trujillo del Perú*. Here the idea of "looking at" instead of just "looking through" guided my analysis. This was all the more important because, as students and scholars of colonial Latin America are well aware, the Martínez Compañón images are ubiquitous in the way we retell the colonial past of Peru through scholarship. They appear on the covers of books about disease, science, gender history, agriculture, and race relations. They are used in the pages of monographs and textbooks as illustrations that "add visual interest." Despite their pervasiveness, the images are not analyzed; they are discussed merely as "commissioned by Bishop Martínez Compañón," or described with the even more misleading "by Bishop Martínez Compañón." Yet they, too, have their own story to tell: about their contents, their creators, the world in which they were made, where they were meant to go, and how they would arrive there. Theirs is one of the stories I have told here, through pairing the images with archival documents and secondary literature in order to read them as a type of historical documentation.[1]

I have benefited from some excellent models for this new methodology of cultural history. At the beginning of the 2000s, Carolyn Dean's influential *Inka Bodies and the Body of Christ* was recently published to great interest and praise, Barbara Mundy's *The Mapping of New Spain* had appeared just a few years earlier, and Ilona Katzew's exhaustive study of *casta* painting in Mexico was forthcoming. Though trained as art historians, these scholars worked with visual sources in innovative ways that intrigued their counterparts in history. I was determined to follow their lead and employ the *Trujillo* images as a body of historical documentation in my work. To use them to their fullest capacity, I began thinking more broadly about what images meant in the early modern Spanish Empire. Here I benefited immensely from the rich intellectual environment in Los Angeles, its decided interest in all things visual, and the numerous conferences, exhibitions, and seminars I attended at the Huntington Library, the Getty Museum, and the Los Angeles County Museum of Art. Hearing papers by and conversing with leading innovators in the field such as Daniela Bleichmar, Tom Cummins, Richard Kagan, Ilona Katzew, and Barbara Mundy helped me to flesh out the central role that images played in the life of Martínez Compañón and his contemporaries.

Modern audiences consider paintings and drawings to be creative endeavors, reserving terms such as "objectivity" and "science" for photographs and some computer-generated imagery; but in an age with no technology for photographic reproduction, drawings, paintings, and illustrations were record and evidence. They were eyewitness accounts that stood as fact. Furthermore, drawings and illustrations were durable and movable in a time when information was transmitted over mountains and across oceans at a speed that seems incomprehensibly glacial to those of us who have grown up with a world's worth of data at our fingertips. While specimens—living or preserved—were apt to die in different climates or be ruined by humidity, images on paper could readily be passed from expert to expert, carried by people or horses or even ships. They could be shared with naturalists in the metropolis and could serve as subjects of international scientific inquiry. They were also valuable proof of work accomplished, a key factor in making transatlantic requests for continued patronage or approval. They were essential to the politics of display that were the backbone of knowledge generating in the Age of Enlightenment. As Charles V's efforts to refashion the image on the most commonly circulated currency of his empire demonstrate, it was through images that empires saw themselves and showed themselves to others.[2]

In the Spanish American context, developing a language of images took on a special urgency. The Spaniards who arrived in Mesoamerica in the sixteenth century encountered highly complex native cultures, many of which had developed sophisticated systems of visual record. The Nahua pictographs infuriated and fascinated the Spanish, as they were incontrovertibly troubling evidence that the men they had discovered on the other side of the world had their own vision of history and society, along with the techniques to record it. In the scores of codices and manuscripts produced after the conquest—most often by Indian students supervised by Spanish ecclesiastics—the visual became an epistemological bridge between two worlds that had collided but remained, for the most part, mutually unintelligible. Once Pizarro and the Spanish arrived in the great Inca Empire of Tawatinsuyo, they would find no such connection. The *quipu,* or knotted cords of string that served as mnemonic devices or tally quotas, were some form of recording knowledge but none that could easily be translated to European understandings. But as Felipe Guaman Poma de Ayala's extensively illustrated 1615 *First New Chronicle and Good Government* so aptly demonstrated, colonial Andeans soon recognized how pictures could speak more clearly than the written word, vividly conveying messages that zealous censors would have stripped from text. As I worked with the nine volumes of *Trujillo* watercolors, I became convinced that Martínez Compañón and the native artisans of Trujillo felt similarly about the unique power of images to convey potentially inflammatory information. Their original work to catalog "the arts, society, and culture of the Indians of Peru" is largely why, over two hundred years after the *Trujillo* history was completed, it remains so intriguing today.

Historiographical Connections

Although Martínez Compañón and his diocesans worked to build their utopia in a distant corner of the Kingdom of Peru, their project was inextricably linked to the reform culture of the eighteenth-century Spanish Empire. They drew on broader ideas of urbanity, sociability, and utility that were originally articulated on the other side of the Atlantic by theorists such as José Campillo, Pedro Campomanes, and Bernardo Ward, men whom scholars recognize as the original architects of the reformist policies today known as the Bourbon reforms. To understand the culture that inspired them, I relied on some of the most important syntheses of the eighteenth-century Spanish Empire, especially John Lynch's *Bourbon Spain, 1700–1808* (Oxford, 1989). I found John Elliott's *Empires of the Atlantic World: Britain and Spain in America, 1492–1830* (New Haven, Conn., 2006) helpful in providing background for the Spanish and Spanish American cases and as a comparative model to inspire deeper critical thinking on the processes of colonialism. Other useful studies include Antonio Domínguez Ortiz, *Carlos III y la España de la Ilustración* (Madrid, 1988); Ruth MacKay, *"Lazy, Improvident People": Myth and Reality in the Writing of Spanish History* (Ithaca, N.Y., 2006); Gabriel Paquette, *Enlightenment, Governance, and Reform in Spain and Its Empire, 1759–1808* (New York, 2008); José M. Portillo Valdés, *Crisis atlántica: Autonomía e independencia en la crisis de la monarquía hispana* (Madrid, 2006); Jaime Rodríguez, *The Independence of Spanish America* (Cambridge, 1998); Francisco Sánchez-Blanco, *Europa y el pensamiento español del siglo XVIII* (Madrid, 1991); and *El Absolutismo y las luces en el reinado de Carlos III* (Madrid, 2002). Richard Kagan's *Urban Images of the Hispanic World, 1493–1793* (New Haven, Conn., 2000) helped me to understand the importance of the city in Spanish colonization. I also found several older works useful, such as Nigel Glendinning, *A Literary History of Spain: The Eighteenth Century* (London, 1972); Richard Herr, *The Eighteenth-Century Revolution in Spain* (Princeton, N.J., 1958); and R. J. Shafer, *The Economic Societies in the Spanish World, 1763–1821* (Syracuse, N.Y., 1958).

On the ground in Trujillo, the Bishop and the people worked to fashion their own utopia, willingly adopting the rhetoric of urbane civility, public happiness, and economic utility that Spanish reformers espoused. Using it to envision how to improve their own local communities, they initiated projects to incorporate isolated settlements into towns and to build local primary schools. In so doing, they learned how to manage an incredibly complex bureaucratic process, how to gather and distribute information in ways bureaucrats would accept, and how to ask for what they wanted in terms that would appeal to those in power. Instead of rebelling against colonialism, as their counterparts in the south of the viceroyalty did, they engaged with the culture of reform, endearing themselves to Spanish society. This engendered a drastically different dynamic from the one that interests most scholars of the eighteenth-century Andes. There is an excellent body of recent scholarship on the Túpac Amaru rebellion, when indigenous communities of the central and southern Andes waged war against the Spanish in response to the increased taxation and stricter local governance that characterized the Bourbon reform agenda. For the best work on this subject, see Sergio Serulnikov, *Subverting Colonial Authority: Challenges to Spanish Rule in Eighteenth-Century Southern Andes* (Durham, N.C., 2003); Ward Stavig, *The World of Túpac Amaru: Conflict, Community, and Identity in Colonial Peru* (Lincoln, Neb., 1999); and, especially, Charles Walker, *Smoldering Ashes: Cuzco and the Creation of Republican Peru, 1780–1840* (Durham, N.C., 1999).

More recently, scholars of the second half of the colonial period in Peru have produced focused studies detailing how specific communities and interest groups engaged with the Bourbon reform agenda. By tracing the history of multiple reform initiatives in a single province over a relatively short time span, *The Bishop's Utopia* takes a multileveled approach to this question, highlighting how even though reform agendas differed by project and by region, outcomes were disappointingly similar. This perspective is akin to that taken by Charles Walker in his excellent *Shaky Colonialism: The 1746*

Earthquake-Tsunami in Lima, Peru, and Its Long Aftermath (Durham, N.C., 2008), which details a citywide program of regeneration that met with decidedly mixed results. Similar to my findings with the Trujillo case, Walker uncovers a heavy dose of stonewalling by local elites who opposed rebuilding and resettlement programs that they perceived as jeopardizing their entrenched economic interests. Other studies approach the Bourbon reforms in Peru thematically instead. Adam Warren's *Medicine and Politics in Colonial Peru: Population Growth and the Bourbon Reforms* (Pittsburgh, 2010) demonstrates how elite Creole medical professionals positioned their work as benefiting the greater social good, but privately were more concerned with their own advancement than any public interest. Elites in Trujillo regularly employed these same techniques of disingenuousness when they publicly supported the Bishop's projects, but claimed to be unable to secure the necessary bureaucratic permits to proceed. Bianca Premo's *Children of the Father King: Youth, Authority, and Legal Minority in Colonial Lima* (Chapel Hill, N.C., 2005) illustrates how Bourbon social policies on children, family, and education were imagined at the metropolitan level in ignorance of local circumstance, and therefore often met with resistance from local communities.

Throughout my research and writing, I also relied on generalist works on the late colonial period in Peru, especially the foundational scholarship of John Fisher, including *Bourbon Peru, 1750–1824* (Liverpool, 2003), *Silver Mines and Miners in Colonial Peru* (Liverpool, 1977), and *Government and Society in Colonial Peru: The Intendant System, 1784–1814* (London, 1970). The fact that the Peruvian historiography, in Spanish and in English, still lags so far behind what is available for New Spain makes his work all the more indispensable. I found Patricia Marks's *Deconstructing Legitimacy: Viceroys, Merchants, and the Military in Late Colonial Peru* (University Park, Pa., 2007) useful for thinking about how economic concerns influenced viceregal policy in Lima. It was only after I finished my doctoral studies that the superb *Guide to Documentary Sources for Andean Studies, 1530–1900*, ed. Joanne Pillsbury (Norman, Okla., 2007) appeared, but it made the rest of my work infinitely more expeditious and will surely be an indispensable resource for future generations of historians, archaeologists, literary scholars, and anthropologists.

Several works on the history of native peoples in Spanish Peru were essential to understanding how Martínez Compañón's project both built on past agendas and diverged from them, including Kenneth Andrien, *Andean Worlds: Indigenous History, Culture, and Consciousness Under Spanish Rule, 1532–1825* (Albuquerque, N.M., 2001); Carolyn Dean, *Inka Bodies and the Body of Christ: Corpus Christi in Colonial Cuzco, Peru* (Durham, N.C., 1999); David Garret, *Shadows of Empire: The Indian Nobility of Cuzco, 1750–1825* (Cambridge, 2005); Jeremy Mumford, *Vertical Empire: The General Resettlement of Indians in the Colonial Andes* (Durham, N.C., 2012); and Ann Wightman, *Indigenous Migration and Social Change: The Forasteros of Cuzco, 1570–1720* (Durham, N.C., 1990). Although it focuses on northern New Spain, David Weber's *Bárbaros: Spaniards and Their Savages in the Age of Enlightenment* (New Haven, Conn., 2005) provided a wonderful overview of policy toward Indians on the edges of empire. I also referenced other useful works on colonial governance and native peoples elsewhere in Spanish America, including Woodrow Borah, *Justice by Insurance: The General Indian Court of Colonial Mexico and the Legal Aides of the Half-Real* (Berkeley, Calif., 1983); James Lockhart, *The Nahuas After the Conquest: A Social and Cultural History of the Indians of Central Mexico, Sixteenth Through Eighteenth Centuries* (Stanford, Calif., 1992); Dorothy Tanck Estrada, *Pueblos de indios y educación en el México colonial, 1750–1821* (Mexico City, 1999); and Kevin Terraciano, *The Mixtecs of Colonial Oaxaca: Ñudzahui History, Sixteenth Through Eighteenth Centuries* (Stanford, Calif., 2001). To help me think about what it meant to be Indian in a world obsessed with racial "purity," I used the excellent study of race, religion, and political identity in New Spain by María Elena Martínez, *Genealogical Fictions: Limpieza de Sangre, Religion, and Gender in Colonial Mexico* (Stanford, Calif., 2008).

Economic histories and statistical compilations were important for providing context to understand Trujillo's fiscal backdrop, including Herbert Klein, *The American Finances of the Spanish Empire: Royal Income and Expenditures in Colonial Mexico, Peru, and Bolivia, 1680–1809* (Albuquerque, N.M., 1988); Nils Jacobsen and Hans Jürgen-Puhle, eds., *The Economies of Mexico and Peru During the Late Colonial Period, 1760–1810* (Berlin, 1986); and John TePaske and Herbert Klein, eds., *The Royal Treasuries of the Spanish Empire in America*, vol. 1: *Peru* (Durham, N.C., 1982). Carlos Marichal's admirable *Bankruptcy of Empire: Mexican Silver and the Wars Between Spain, Britain, and France, 1760–1810* (Cambridge, 2010) inspired me to think about how the macro-level fiscal operations of the empire affected regional initiatives. These works offer a solid starting point for scholars to begin to understand the complex economies of the viceroyalty in the colonial period, but there is ample room for further study in the Peruvian case.

In contrast, a related area of inquiry—colonial mining in the Andes— enjoys a more developed body of scholarship. Some of the most important works include Peter Bakewell, *Silver and Entrepreneurship in Seventeenth-Century Potosí: The Life and Times of Antonio López de Quiroga* (Albuquerque, N.M., 1988); Kendall Brown, *A History of Mining in Latin America from the Colonial Era to the Present* (Albuquerque, N.M., 2012); Carlos Contreras, *Los Mineros y el rey: La Economía colonial en los Andes del norte: Hualgayoc, 1770–1824* (Lima, 1995); John Fisher, *Silver Mines and Miners in Colonial Peru* (Liverpool, 1977); Miguel Molina Martínez, *Antonio de Ulloa en Huancavelica* (Granada, 1995); and Arthur Whitaker, *The Huancavelica Mercury Mine: A Contribution to the History of the Bourbon Renaissance in the Spanish Empire* (London, 1971). I turned to David Brading, *Miners and Merchants in Bourbon Mexico, 1760–1810* (Cambridge, 1971) for further background.

Even though the Hualgayoc miners hoped to flatter the Bishop by saying otherwise, the fact remains that Martínez Compañón was far from a mining expert. As a historical figure, he is exceedingly difficult to categorize either as a naturalist or a reformer: his interests and pursuits were too broad and his agenda too locally calibrated to be easily situated in bigger metropolitan categories. However, he was most decidedly a member of the eighteenth-century religious hierarchy, and to properly identify him as such, I relied on a large corpus of scholarship. For a general orientation to ecclesiastical hierarchies, parish culture, and the complex vocabulary of colonial Catholicism, I turned to William Taylor's essential *Magistrates of the Sacred: Priests and Parishioners in Eighteenth-Century Mexico* (Stanford, Calif., 1996). I also utilized David Brading's *Church and State in Bourbon Mexico: The Diocese of Michoacán, 1749–1810* (Cambridge, Mass., 1994) and consulted Nancy Farriss, *Crown and Clergy in Colonial Mexico, 1759–1821: The Crisis of Ecclesiastical Privilege* (London, 1968). For the Spanish case, I turned to William J. Callahan, *Church, Politics, and Society in Spain, 1750–1874* (Cambridge, Mass., 1984).

The most dynamic specialized studies on the Church in eighteenth-century Spanish America focus almost exclusively on New Spain. Most recently, Matthew O'Hara's *A Flock Divided: Race, Religion, and Politics in Mexico, 1749–1857* (Durham, N.C., 2010) examines how the politics of Indianness and religion intersected in reform ideology. Pamela Voekel's *Alone Before God: The Religious Origins of Modernity in Mexico* (Durham, N.C., 2002) considers the religious realm of eighteenth-century reform culture there, as does Brian Larkin's more generalist *The Very Nature of God: Baroque Catholicism and Religious Reform in Bourbon Mexico City* (Albuquerque, N.M., 2010), which treats many of the same subjects. For the Peruvian case, the best scholarship in English revolves around female religious orders and spiritual practices, including Kathryn Burns's excellent first book, *Colonial Habits: Convents and the Spiritual Economy of Cuzco, Peru* (Durham, N.C., 1999); and Nancy van Deusen, *Between the Sacred and the Worldly: The Cultural Practice of Recogimiento in Colonial Lima* (Stanford, Calif., 2001). Dean's *Inka Bodies and the Body of Christ* offers a good orientation on how native peoples were incorporated into Catholic ritual. For background on the early Church in Peru, I used Kenneth Mills, *Idolatry and Its Enemies: Colonial Andean Religion in Extirpation, 1640–1750* (Princeton, N.J., 1997) as well as Sabine MacCormack, *Religion in the Andes: Vision and Imagination in Colonial Peru* (Princeton, N.J., 1991); and Irene Silverblatt, *Modern Inquisitions: Peru and the Colonial Origins of the Civilized World* (Durham, N.C., 2004).

The Bishop's Utopia implies that Martínez Compañón deserves a space next to his more recognized ecclesiastical colleagues who promoted "enlightened" reform in Spanish America in the eighteenth century, most often in New Spain. Although the scholarship has yet to produce a monograph that offers a thoughtful overview of their careers, there are ample studies on the individual lives of the most important reforming archbishops, bishops, and cathedral canons of eighteenth-century Spanish America. On New Granada's commanding Antonio Caballero y Góngora, who served concurrently as viceroy and archbishop, I consulted Marco Antonio Fonseca Truque, *Historia del delito en Colombia: El Veneno del arzobispo* (Bogotá, 1983); and Roberto María Tisnes Jiménez, *Caballero y Góngora y los comuneros* (Bogotá, 1984). I was surprised that such an exceptional figure has not merited a more recent monograph. On José Pérez Calama, cathedral canon of Michoacán and later bishop of Quito, see Germán Cardozo Galue, *Michoacán en el siglo de las luces* (Mexico City, 1973); Juvenal Jaramillo, *José Pérez Calama: Un Clerigo ilustrado del siglo XVIII en la antigua Valladolid de Michoacán* (Morelia, 1990); and Ekkehart Keeding, *Surge la nación: La Ilustración en la audiencia de Quito, 1725–1812* (Quito, 2005). Francisco Fabián y Fuero is the subject of Francisco Rodríguez de Coro's *Fabián y Fuero: Un Ilustrado Molinés en Puebla de los Angeles* (Madrid, 1988). The best of these studies is Luis Sierra Nava Lasa's look at Francisco Lorenzana, archbishop of Mexico, *El Cardenal Lorenzana y la Ilustración* (Madrid, 1973).

Other than these reformers, the ecclesiastic who looms largest in this study is the great "defender of the Indians," Bartolomé de Las Casas. Here the historiography seems to have suffered from the controversy about the contradictions between Las Casas's scholarly arguments and his actual life because there is great need for an updated scholarly look at his influence on the ideas of race and slavery in colonial Spanish America. Although it is dated, Lewis Hanke's *All Mankind Is One: A Study of the Disputation Between Bartolomé de Las Casas and Juan Ginés de Sepúlveda on the Religious and Intellectual Capacity of the American Indians* (DeKalb, Ill., 1974) is the most comprehensive study available. Additional works that touch on Las Casas and his influence include Anthony Pagden, *The Fall of Natural Man: The American Indian and the Origins of Comparative Ethnology* (Cambridge, 1982); and Tzvetan Todorov's *The Conquest of America: The Question of the Other* (New York, 1984). Other Catholic thinkers make appearances in this study as well, with the most important (and interesting) of them being Athanasius Kircher, of whom Martínez Compañón was a dedicated fan. Here Paula Findlen's cleverly titled edited volume, *Athanasius Kircher: The Last Man Who Knew Everything* (New York, 2004), is an excellent starting point. For a study of another cleric interested in matters of nature and science, I looked to the somewhat convoluted literary scholarship of Margaret Ewalt, *Peripheral Wonders: Nature, Knowledge, and Enlightenment in the Eighteenth-Century Orinoco* (Lewisburg, Pa., 2008).

In situating the Bishop's archaeological research, I benefited greatly from the work of Joanne Pillsbury, including *Past Presented: Archaeological Illustration and the Ancient Americas* (Washington, D.C., 2012), and *Palaces of the Ancient New World* (Washington, D.C., 2004), edited with Susan Toby Evans. Also important was the work of Paz Cabello Carro, including *Coleccionismo americano indígena en la España del siglo XVIII* (Madrid, 1989), *Museo de América* (Madrid, 1984), and "Spanish Collections of Americana in the Late Eighteenth Century" (Philadelphia, 2011). Rosa Zeta Quinde's *El Pensamiento ilustrado en el Mercurio Peruano, 1791–1794* (Piura, 2000), and *La Ilustración en América colonial*, ed. Diana Soto Arango et al. (Madrid, 1995) were especially helpful in fleshing out the intellectual culture of Peru and Spanish America in the late eighteenth century. Kathryn Burns's *Into the Archive: Writing and Power in Colonial Peru* (Durham, N.C., 2010) influenced my thinking about the socioeconomic politics of generating documents and reminded me to look beneath the surface of the stories they tell.

While I locate *The Bishop's Utopia* in the broader contexts of the Spanish Empire and the viceroyalty of Peru, it is just as much situated in the distinctive context of the north coast. In this region—where *mita* and tribute duties were less, indigenous communities fared comparatively better, and Spanish-Indian relations were traditionally more peaceable—native groups staged alternative responses to increased pressure from Spanish authorities. Instead of reacting against the Bourbon agendas with violence, the people of Trujillo absorbed the discourse of reform and refashioned it into a locally based vision of improvement that would better suit their needs. Readings here include the influential work of Scarlett O'Phelan, especially *El Perú en el siglo XVIII: La Era borbónica* (Lima, 1999), *Rebellions and Revolts in Eighteenth-Century Peru and Upper Peru* (Cologne, 1984), and *El Norte en la historia regional, siglos XVIII–XIX* (Lima, 1998). I also relied on the excellent body of work that focuses on the Trujillo region in the colonial period, including Karen Graubart, *With Our Labor and Sweat: Indigenous Women and the Formation of Colonial Society in Peru, 1550–1700* (Stanford, Calif., 2007); Susan E. Ramírez, *Provincial Patriarchs: Land Tenure and the Economics of Power in Colonial Peru* (Albuquerque, N.M., 1986), and *The World Upside Down: Cross-Cultural Contact and Conflict in Sixteenth-Century Peru* (Stanford, Calif., 1996); and Alejandro Reyes Flores, *Hacendados y comerciantes: Piura, Chachapoyas, Moyobamba, Lamas, Maynas (1770–1820)* (Lima, 1999).

Following the ways in which local communities dialogued with a reform agenda inspired by the eighteenth-century culture of improvement highlights how local people reimagined these initiatives to suit their particular circumstances and needs. This periphery-center approach to the Bourbon reforms builds on previous scholarship showing how native and plebeian groups turned instruments of imperial exploitation to their advantage, especially Jeremy Baskes, *Indians, Merchants, and Markets: A Reinterpretation of the Repartimiento and Spanish-Indian Economic Relations in Colonial Oaxaca, 1750–1821* (Stanford, Calif., 2000); and Susan Deans-Smith, *Bureaucrats, Planters, and Workers: The Making of the Tobacco Monopoly in Bourbon Mexico* (Austin, Tex., 1992). At the same time, the book's focus on broader ideas of "improving" the Indians through promoting education and managing social behavior contributes to the need for more studies of the social aspects of the Bourbon reforms, as so elegantly called for in Ann Twinam's influential *Public Lives, Private Secrets: Gender, Honor, Sexuality and Illegitimacy in Colonial Spanish America* (Stanford, Calif., 1999).

Although *The Bishop's Utopia* is the first monograph focusing on Martínez Compañón's secular reform agenda and natural history research, I was lucky to have a handful of past studies of his life and work to build upon. The most recent (and most comprehensive) of these is Daniel Restrepo Manrique, *Sociedad y religión en Trujillo (Perú), bajo el episcopado de Baltasar Jaime Martínez Compañón, 1780–1790* (Vitoria-Gasteiz, Spain, 1992), which examines Martínez Compañón's secular and ecclesiastical work. Between 1978 and 1994, the Real Biblioteca de España published beautiful high-quality reproductions of the nine volumes, also titled *Trujillo del Perú* (Madrid, 1978–1994). The Banco Continental de Perú published an illustrated volume of the Peruvian images called *Crónica gráfica del Obispo Martínez Compañón* (Lima, 1993). A conference at the University of Piura resulted in an edited volume of detailed studies on various aspects of the Bishop's work, *Vida y obra del Obispo Martínez Compañón* (Piura, 1991). Carlos Contreras discussed his work at Hualgayoc in *Los Mineros y el rey* (Lima, 1995); and Inge Schjellerup published a book about a second, mostly duplicate set of watercolors that were left behind in Trujillo, *Razón de las especies de la naturaleza del arte del obispado de Trujillo del Peru del Obispo D. Baltasar Jaime Martínez Compañón* (Trujillo, 1991). Pilar Foz y Foz considers his involvement with La Enseñanza schools in *Mujer y educación en Colombia, siglos XVI–XIX: Aportaciones del colegio de la Enseñanza, 1783–1900* (Bogotá, 1997). Older studies of the Bishop include the comprehensive biography by José Manuel Pérez Ayala, *Baltasar Jaime Martínez Compañón y Bujanda, prelado español de Colombia y el Perú* (Bogotá, 1955); and Ruben Vargas Ugarte, *Tres figuras señeras del episcopado americano* (Lima, 1966).

The main intellectual discourse in which I locate Martínez Compañón's utopia, the so-called debate over the New World, has been the subject or theme of several important works. In his seminal text *The Dispute of the New World: The History of a Polemic, 1750–1900* (Pittsburgh, 1973; 2nd ed., 2010), Antonello Gerbi pointed out that the Americans who wrote in defense of their native (or adopted, in the case of the Creoles) territory did not generate any new information to make their claims. Instead, they analyzed pre-Hispanic artifacts already known to scholars and developed complicated dialogues refuting arguments that other Europeans had already printed. This is, of course, much different from the Bishop's approach, which generated original scientific data from collaboration with native communities. Key participants in the debate, including the myriad Jesuits who wrote from Europe after their 1776 expulsion, are the focus of a good part of David Brading's massive intellectual-political history of Spanish colonialism in America, *The First America: The Spanish Monarchy, Creole Patriots, and the Liberal State, 1492–1867* (Cambridge, 1991). Jorge Cañizares-Esguerra revisited "the great debate," pairing it with an admirably broad analysis of science, politics, and racial dynamics in *How to Write the History of the New World: Histories, Epistemologies, and Identities in the Eighteenth-Century Atlantic World* (Stanford, Calif., 2001). As he so elegantly demonstrates, changing scientific epistemologies stood at the center of the controversy over America in the late colonial period. In the Age of Enlightenment, firsthand accounts were no longer thought to be valuable scientific data—unless trained European "experts" made them. Native sources of information—such as the *quipu* in Peru—were discredited as insufficiently objective. Now scientists sought what they conceived of as definitive, verifiable data. Information had to be filtered through European experts, both when it was gathered on the ground—as Neil Safier's *Measuring the New World: Enlightenment Science and South America* (Chicago, 2008) aptly describes—and when it was received in the study halls and museum chambers of the metropolis, only to be sifted and repurposed by men whose degrees and training gave them the true intellectual authority to do so. The conventions that information had to be gathered and recorded on the ground by a European expert, then shipped back to the hallowed halls of "true" science, where it would be examined by another team of experts who would decide on its value, meant that the crucial first phase of natural history making—how data were collected, interpreted, and represented on the ground by local, most often native, informants—was effectively stricken from the record of official scientific knowledge. The dominant paradigm of scientific investigation followed European standards—particularly the Latin-based Linnaean binomial system (described in thoughtful detail in Lisbet Koerner's *Linnaeus: Nature and Nation* [Cambridge, Mass., 1999])—which the Spanish valued dearly because only data that could be easily transmitted and understood would impress the other European powers.

But a smaller, competing scientific methodology was developed and used by some individuals on the ground in America. It privileged native languages, scientific traditions, and ways of understanding the local environment. As Antonio Barrera argues in *Experiencing Nature: The Spanish American Empire and the Early Scientific Revolution* (Austin, Tex., 2006), it had actually been born in the sixteenth century in New Spain, when Spaniards such as Francisco Hernández and Nicolás Monardes, who lacked essential knowledge about the natural world around them, began to collaborate with local populations. Other useful contributions to this literature include David Freedberg, *The Eye of the Lynx: Galileo, His Friends, and the Beginnings of Modern Natural History* (Chicago, 2002); and Cañizares-Esguerra, *How to Write the History of the New World*. But by the eighteenth century, the tradition was most relevant in Peru. Particularly in Lima, Creole naturalists such as José

Eusebio Llano Zapata, Alonso Huerta, and Hipólito Unanue stressed the value of indigenous knowledge of the natural world and sometimes even collaborated with native informants.

My work with natural history was grounded in broad reading on the topic, with other important recent monographs being Daniela Bleichmar, *Visible Empire: Botanical Expeditions and Visual Culture in the Hispanic Enlightenment* (Chicago, 2012); and Maria Portuondo, *Secret Science: Spanish Cosmography and the New World* (Chicago, 2009). I benefited from Daniela Bleichmar et al., eds., *Science in the Spanish and Portuguese Empires, 1500–1800* (Stanford, Calif., 2009); Iris Engstrand, *Spanish Scientists in the New World: The Eighteenth-Century Expeditions* (Seattle, 1981); Marcelo Frias Núñez, *Tras el dorado vegetal: José Celestino Mutis y la Real Expedición Botánica del Nuevo Reino de Granada, 1783–1808* (Seville, 1994); Manuel Selles, José Luis Peset, and Antonio Lafuente, eds., *Carlos III y la ciencia de la Ilustración* (Madrid, 1988); Xavier Lozoya, *Plantas y luces en México: La Real Expedición Científica a Nueva España (1787–1803)* (Barcelona, 1984); and Francisco Puerto Sarmiento, *La Ilusión quebrada: Botánica, sanidad, y política científica en la España ilustrada* (Madrid, 1988). Specifically for the Peruvian context, I relied on Félix Muñoz Garmendia, *La Botánica al servicio de la corona: La Expedición de Ruiz, Pavón y Dombey al Virreinato del Perú (1777–1831)* (Madrid, 2003); and Arthur Robert Steele, *Flowers for the King: The Expedition of Ruiz and Pavón and the Flora of Peru* (Durham, N.C., 1964).

I also read on natural history elsewhere in the early modern world, using Anita Been, *Animals and Authors in the Eighteenth-Century Americas: A Hemispheric Look at the Writing of Natural History* (Providence, R.I., 2004); Lucile Brockway, *Science and Colonial Expansion: The Role of the British Royal Botanic Gardens* (New Haven, Conn., 2002); Alix Cooper, *Inventing the Indigenous: Local Knowledge and Natural History in Early Modern Europe* (Cambridge, 2007); Lorraine Daston and Peter Gailson, *Objectivity* (New York, 2007); James Delbourgo and Nicholas Dew, eds., *Science and Empire in the Atlantic World* (New York, 2008); Richard Drayton, *Nature's Government: Science, Imperial Britain, and the 'Improvement' of the World* (New Haven, Conn., 2000); Richard Grove, *Green Imperialism: Colonial Expansion, Tropical Island Edens, and the Origins of Environmentalism, 1600–1860* (Cambridge, 1995); N. Jardine and E. C. Spary, eds., *Cultures of Natural History* (Cambridge, 1996); Roy Porter, ed., *The Cambridge History of Science: Eighteenth-Century Science* (Cambridge, 2003); Kapil Raj, *Relocating Modern Science: Circulation and the Construction of Knowledge in South Asia and Europe, 1650–1900* (New York,

2007); Londa Schiebinger, *Plants and Empire: Colonial Bioprospecting in the Atlantic World* (Cambridge, 2004); Londa Schiebinger and Claudia Swan, eds., *Colonial Botany: Science, Commerce, and Politics in the Early Modern World* (Philadelphia, 2005); and Emma Spary, *Utopia's Garden: French Natural History from Old Regime to Revolution* (Chicago, 2000). Michel Foucault's *The Order of Things: An Archaeology of the Human Sciences* (New York, 1994) helped frame the epistemological divide upon which Martínez Compañón stood.

Any study of natural history and intellectual culture in the eighteenth-century Atlantic world will necessarily touch on the visual culture that was such an integral part thereof. In thinking about the Bishop's nine volumes, the artisans who made them, the works that influenced them, and their broader meaning in the Spanish world, I made use of a dynamic and growing body of excellent scholarship. The best work includes Bleichmar, *Visible Empire*; Linda Curcio-Nagy, *The Great Festivals of Colonial Mexico City* (Albuquerque, N.M., 2004); Dean, *Inka Bodies and the Body of Christ*; Ilona Katzew, *Casta Painting: Images of Race in Eighteenth-Century Mexico* (New Haven, Conn., 2004); Richard Kagan, *Urban Images of the Hispanic World*; and Barbara Mundy, *The Mapping of New Spain: Indigenous Cartography and the Maps of the Relaciones Geográficas* (Chicago, 1996). Even better than reading books was seeing the brilliantly curated show *The Arts in Latin America, 1492–1820* at the Los Angeles County Museum of Art in 2007. The richly illustrated catalog of the same name, ed. Joseph J. Rishel and Suzanne Stratton-Pritt (New Haven, Conn., 2006), contains breathtaking reproductions of the pieces exhibited in the show, as well as useful essays by experts in the field.

On visual culture in the colonial Andes, I found Teresa Gisbert's classic *Iconografía y mitas indígenas en el arte* (La Paz, 1994) to be useful, as well as *El Paraíso de los pájaros parlantes* (La Paz, 1999). See also Rolena Adorno, *Guaman Poma: Writing and Resistance in Colonial Peru* (Austin, Tex., 2000); Valerie Fraser, *The Architecture of Conquest: Building in the Viceroyalty of Peru, 1535–1635* (Cambridge, 2009); and Pablo Macera, *La Pintura mural andina, siglos XVI–XIX* (Lima, 1993). It was only after much careful thinking that I was able to iron out a good strategy for writing about the indigenous artisans who were so essential to the project. Samuel Edgerton's *Theaters of Conversion: Religious Architecture and Indian Artisans in Colonial Mexico* (Albuquerque, N.M., 2001) elegantly pointed out the dangers of arguing for an "indigenous" style that was inherently antithetical to mainstream European art and visual culture. Good general orientations to visual culture in the

Spanish Empire and Spanish America include Gauvin Bailey, *Art of Colonial Latin America* (London, 2005); Jonathan Brown, *Painting in Spain, 1500–1700* (New Haven, Conn., 1991); Kelly Donahue-Wallace, *Art and Architecture of Viceregal Latin America, 1521–1821* (Albuquerque, N.M., 2008); Diana Fane, ed., *Converging Cultures: Art and Identity in Spanish America* (New York, 1996); John F. Moffit, *The Arts in Spain* (London, 1999); Marjorie Trusted, *The Arts of Spain: Iberia and Latin America, 1400–1700* (University Park, Pa., 2007); and John F. Scott, *Latin American Art: Ancient to Modern* (Gainesville, Fla., 1999). George Kubler and Martin Soria's *Art and Architecture in Spain and Portugal and Their American Dominions, 1500 to 1800* (New York, 1959) is dated but remains a useful reference.

For colonial visual lexicons that provided points of comparison for the *Trujillo* volumes, I looked at Martinus de la Cruz, *The Badianus Manuscript: An Aztec Herbal of 1552* (Baltimore, 1940); Juan de la Cruz Cano y Holmedilla, *Colección de trajes de España: Tanto antiguos como modernos* (Madrid, 1988); Francisco Hernández, *Cuatro libros de la naturaleza y virtudes de plantas y animales que están recaídos en el uso de medicina en la Nueva España* (Mexico City, 1615); Ilona Katzew, *Una Visión del México del siglo de las luces: La Codificación de Joaquín Antonio Basarás* (Mexico City, 2006); Pedro O'Crouley, *Idea compendiosa del reino de Nueva España* (Mexico City, 1975); and Mercedes Palau and Blanca Saíz, eds., *Moxos: Descripciones exactas y historia fiel de los indios, animales, y plantas de la provincia de Moxos en el Virreinato del Perú por Lázaro de Ribera, 1786–1794* (Madrid, 1989).

Outside the Hispanic context, I read Mildred Archer, *Company Paintings: Indian Paintings of the British Period* (Middletown, N.J., 1992); Peter Mason, *Infelicities: Representations of the Exotic* (Baltimore, 1998); Pamela H. Smith, *The Body of the Artisan: Art and Experience in the Scientific Revolution* (Chicago, 2004); Pamela Smith and Paula Findlen, eds., *Merchants and Marvels: Commerce, Science, and Art in Early Modern Europe* (New York, 2002); Nicholas Thomas, *Licensed Curiosity: Cook's Pacific Voyages* (Cambridge, 1994), and *Possessions: Indigenous Art / Colonial Culture* (London, 1999); and Beth Fowkes Tobin, *Picturing Imperial Power: Colonial Subjects in Eighteenth-Century British Painting* (Durham, N.C., 1999).

On museums and collecting, I used Daniela Bleichmar and Peter Mancall, eds., *Collecting Across Cultures: Material Exchanges in the Early Modern Atlantic World* (Philadelphia, 2011); Paz Cabello Carro, *Coleccionismo americano indígena en la España del siglo XVIII* (Madrid, 1989); Fernando Checa and Miguel Morán, *El Coleccionismo en España: De la cámara de maravillas a la galería de pinturas* (Madrid, 1985); John Elsner and Roger Cardinal, eds., *Telling Objects: A Narrative Perspective on Collecting* (Cambridge, 1994); Sharon Macdonald, *The Politics of Display: Museums, Science, Culture* (London, 1998); Susan M. Pearce, *On Collecting: An Investigation into Collecting in the European Tradition* (London, 1995); and Krystof Pomian, *Collectors and Curiosities: Paris and Venice, 1500–1800* (Oxford, 1990).

In considering how the Bishop's vision for Trujillo was a utopia, I turned to the seminal work of Alberto Flores Galindo on Andean Indians and utopias, *Buscando un Inca: Identidad y utopia en los Andes* (Lima, 1987), later translated into English as *In Search of an Inca: Identity and Utopia in the Andes* (Cambridge, 2010). I read Thomas More's *Utopia* (New York, 2011); and Francis Bacon's *New Atlantis* (Oxford, 1974). On More, I used Silvio Zavala, *Sir Thomas More in New Spain: A Utopian Adventure of the Renaissance* (London, 1955). For Vasco de Quiroga's efforts to make his imagined society into reality in sixteenth-century New Spain, I used Warren B. Fintan, *Vasco de Quiroga and His Pueblo-Hospitales of Santa Fé* (Berkeley, Calif., 1963); and Bernardino Verástique, *Michoacán and Eden: Vasco de Quiroga and the Evangelization of Western Mexico* (Austin, Tex., 2000) but in general found that the historiography in both Spanish and English lacks a good modern study on such an important early colonial figure. The literature on utopias in America includes Francisco Fernández Buey, *Utopia e ilusiones naturales* (Granada, 2007); Frank Graziano, *The Millennial New World* (Oxford, 1999); Pedro Henríquez Ureña, *La Utopia de América* (Caracas, 1925); and Beatríz Pastor, *El Jardín y el peregrino: El Pensamiento utópico en América Latina* (Amsterdam, 1999). Among other useful writings on utopia are Gregory Claeys, ed., *Utopias of the British Enlightenment* (Cambridge, 1994); Frank E. and Fritzie P. Manuel, *Utopian Thought in the Western World* (Cambridge, 1979); Lyman Tower Sargent, *Utopianism: A Very Short Introduction* (Oxford, 2010); and Roland Schaer, Gregory Claeys, and Lyman Tower Sargent, eds., *Utopia: The Search for the Ideal Society in the Western World* (Oxford, 2001). Although it traces a young man's journey through awakening to the dystopia that surrounds him, over the years of writing this book, I thought repeatedly of Voltaire's beautifully phrased notion of "the best of all possible worlds" (*Candide; Or All the Best*, 1759), for this was what Martínez Compañón had hoped to make of his beloved Trujillo.

Ecclesiastical Questionnaire Sent to Priests
Prior to the *Visita* Party's Arrival

1. If the said priest knows or has news of the matter about whether they are going to do exams; and if they follow the dictates of the law [in doing so].
2. If every one of the priests, according to the information he has received, receives a *synodo* [priests' salary], and if he does, whether it is royal, comes from an endowment, or both, and what amount it is.
3. If there are any *primicias* [first fruits of church taxes], and of what kind, and what is the amount of each one of them, and their total value given in currency.
4. If there is any chaplaincy annexed to the *curato* [parish], which would be its capital, where it pays taxes to, and how much it produces each year.
5. If there is any report of Masses, or any *anniversario* [yearly] reports; what their assets and annual revenue would be.
6. How many *cofradías* there might be; how many Masses each of them celebrate, what the *limosna* charity donation is, and the total this brings in.
7. If there are any religious holidays, which they would be, and how much is given to the priest for each of them, and the total amount as well.
8. If there are any *obvenciones* [periodic fee collections] or baptisms, marriages, or burials; how much they charge for each one of them, and in which cases, and how much these total every year.
9. If [the priest] keeps any assistant, in which town, and how much he is paid annually.

Transcribed from "Decree and Questionnaire of Martínez Compañón, Trujillo, 26 May 1782" (Bogotá: ANC, Virreyes 14, 356–358).

10. What family members [the priest] maintains; and how much he spends on this per day on average, and throughout the year.
11. How much does the priest get paid every year, [both] quarterly and monthly.
12. If the said town is healthy or sick; and where they turn for medicines in case of sickness; and how much these cost.
13. If there are any poor people unable to work in the matrix or in its *añejos* [annex or ancillary churches].
14. How many *añejos* there are, what is the true location of each of them, the distance between them, and their distance from the capital.

Natural History Questionnaire Sent to Priests Prior to the *Visita* Party's Arrival

1. What is the character and natural inclination of the natives of this *doctrina*, and if they understand, and speak Castilian. If they are applied to their work or not. If there is any noticeable difference between Indians, Spanish, and other *castas*, as much in this or in their customs. And if this is attributed to differences in their education, or to some other natural or accidental principle. And what is the education they usually give to their children.

2. If the weather and climate is beneficial, and if . . . the . . . [territories] . . . of your jurisdiction are reputed to be healthy or sick, and to what they attribute whichever of these two qualities . . . are prevalent. Which are the most common sicknesses, and their causes, and the common medicines used to cure them, and [what is] the age to which its inhabitants typically live.

3. If there might be news that any of the towns belonging to this *doctrina* have been abandoned, [have] disappeared, or moved to another place, and the cause of the one or the other.

4. At what age they usually marry . . . in this *doctrina*. By which hand they usually arrange marriages. If there are any celibates, and [where] this virtue is most frequently found, both in terms of the *castas* and in terms of the sexes.

Transcribed from "Pastoral Letter of Martínez Compañón, Trujillo, 14 April 1782" (Seville: AGI, Cartas y expedientes: Curiosidades para el Jardín Botánico, Lima 798).

5. If one finds increased or not the number of landowners and city residents, both in this capital and in its annexes, with respect to the information in the censuses and old books, or the traditions of the towns. And what is the total of this augmentation or diminution, and if it is of Indians or other *castas*, and to what cause they attribute it.

6. If either within this principal town or its annexes, or surrounding areas begin any sources [of water], if these are the waters that serve for the common use of the people, and if in these they might have noted any particular quality, and what it might be.

7. If a river runs through its land or its borders, what they call it, where it has its beginnings, if they make use of its waters, and if they are known to be healthy. If it is navigable and if it has a bridge, and if not having a bridge if it would be possible to build one, and how much, more or less, its construction would cost.

8. What crops they harvest, and their quality, how much the fields produce, and what is the method, form, and season of doing their planting, cultivating, and harvesting.

9. If they keep any commerce . . . and of what kind, with towns or provinces, and what utilities it produces, and whether there might be some method or means of advancing it.

10. If there are any sugar mills, cattle ranches, workshops, or agricultural plantations, what are their profits, if tribute is given to them, how much they are given and how many workers they maintain. And if among them there are any *mitayos*, what salaries they pay them, and how they are paid.

11. If there are any minerals, which they are, how they mine them, and what they yield.

12. If there are any medicinal herbs, branches, or fruits, which they are, what are their shape, and the virtue of each one of them, and the mode of applying and using them.

13. If there are any mineral waters, and . . . if they are hot or temperate, sulfurous, nitrous, ferrous, or of another quality, what use they made of them, and to what effect.

14. If there are any resins or fragrant balsams, which they are, and what virtue they attribute to them.

15. If there are any strange birds or carnivorous animals, or any poisonous animals or insects, and if there are any of these, what precautions those who live around them take.

16. If there are any woods, their abundance, and qualities, the use they make of them, or might be able to make of them.

17. If there are any structures from the times before the conquest that are notable for their material, form, grandness, or any vestiges of that. If at any time they have found any huge bones that seem to be human. And whether they have any tradition that in some time there might have been giants, and in the places where they might have had them, for what time, when did they become extinct and for what reason, and what support the people have for the said legend.

18. If in the Indians one sees anything that smells of superstition, about what points and which are the reasons to distrust, or believe it, and what methods would be the most effective to extirpate them with respect to [the Indians'] character, inclinations, ideas, and customs.

ARCHIVES AND SPECIAL
COLLECTIONS CONSULTED

Colombia

ANC   Archivo Nacional de Colombia, Bogotá
BNC   Biblioteca Nacional de Colombia, Bogotá

Peru

AAL   Archivo Arzobispal, Lima
AAT   Archivo Arzobispal, Trujillo
ACE   Archivo del Cabildo Eclesiástico, Lima
AEC   Archivo Episcopal, Cajamarca
ADL   Archivo Departamental de la Libertad, Trujillo
ALMR   Archivo Histórico de Límites, Ministerio de Relaciones
                Exteriores, Lima
AGNP   Archivo General de la Nación, Peru
ARC   Archivo Regional, Cajamarca

Spain

AGI   Archivo General de Indias, Seville
AMNCN   Archivo del Museo Nacional de Ciencias Naturales, Madrid
AMN   Archivo del Museo Naval de España, Madrid
ARJB   Archivo del Real Jardín Botánico, Madrid
BNE   Biblioteca Nacional de España, Madrid
BPR   Biblioteca del Palacio Real, Madrid

United States

BLAC	Benson Latin American Collection, University of Texas at Austin
JHL	John Hay Library, Brown University, Providence
HEH	Henry E. Huntington Library, San Marino
JCB	John Carter Brown Library, Providence

NOTES

INTRODUCTION

1. Diego de Landa's atrocities in the Yucatán are the subject of Inga Clendinnen, *Ambivalent Conquests: Maya and Spaniard in Yucatán, 1517–1570* (Cambridge: Cambridge University Press, 1987). Sepúlveda and his theory of "natural slavery" are discussed in Lewis Hanke, *All Mankind Is One: A Study of the Disputation Between Bartolomé de Las Casas and Juan Ginés de Sepúlveda on the Religious and Intellectual Capacity of the American Indians* (DeKalb: Northern Illinois University Press, 1974); and Anthony Pagden, *The Fall of Natural Man: The American Indian and the Origins of Comparative Ethnology* (Cambridge: Cambridge University Press, 1982).

2. "Martínez Compañón to Antonio Porlier, Trujillo, 2 December 1788" (Seville: Archivo General de Indias [hereafter, AGI], Lima 978, Cartas y Expedientes: Curiosidades para el Jardín Botánico).

3. On Martínez Compañón's collections, see *Museo de América*, ed. Paz Cabello Carro et al. (Madrid: Ministerio de Cultura, 1984); Paz Cabello Carro, *Coleccionismo americano indígena en la España del siglo XVIII* (Madrid: Ediciones de Cultura Hispánica, 1989), and "Spanish Collections of Americana in the Late Eighteenth Century," in *Collecting Across Cultures: Material Exchanges in the Early Modern Atlantic World*, ed. Daniela Bleichmar and Peter C. Mancall (Philadelphia: University of Pennsylvania Press, 2011); Joanne Pillsbury and Lisa Trever, "The King, the Bishop, and the Creation of an American Antiquity," *Ñawpa Pacha: Journal of Andean Archaeology* 29 (2008): 191–219, and "Martínez Compañón and His Illustrated 'Museum,'" in Bleichmar and Mancall, *Collecting Across Cultures*, 236–254.

4. "Martínez Compañón to Viceroy Croix, Trujillo, 25 July 1785" (Bogotá: Archivo Nacional de Colombia [hereafter, ANC], Virreyes 17, 432–433).

5. In a 1788 letter to a friend in Lima, the Bishop requested copies of works by Kircher and Borromeo, "Martínez Compañón to Agustín Hermenegildo de Querejazu, Trujillo, 1788" (Lima: Archivo General de la Nación de Peru [hereafter, AGNP], Correspondencia D1-25-727). See also Athanasius Kircher, *China Monumentis: Qua Sacris Qua Profanis, Nec Non Variis* (Amsterdam: Joannem Janssonium, 1667); and Federico Borromeo, "Museum," in *Sacred Painting: Museum*, I. Tatti Renaissance Library, ed. Kenneth S. Rothwell, Jr. (Cambridge, Mass.: Harvard University Press, 2010). For modern scholarship

on paper museums, see David Freedberg, *The Eye of the Lynx: Galileo, His Friends, and the Beginnings of Modern Natural History* (Chicago: University of Chicago Press, 2002); Susan Owens, Martin Clayton, and Rea Alexandratos, *Amazing Rare Things: The Art of Natural History in the Age of Discovery* (New Haven, Conn.: Yale University Press, 2007); and Rebecca Zorach, ed., *Paper Museums: The Reproductive Print in Europe, 1500–1800* (Chicago: University of Chicago Press, 2005).

6. Jorge Escobedo, "Instrucción Práctica que para adaptar la nueva Real Ordenanza de Intendencias se da por el Tribunal de Visita al Señor Don Fernando Saavedra que va a servir la de Truxillo, 1784" (Seville: AGI, Lima 117). Arturo Jiménez Borja suggests that the topographical map was most likely the work of parish priest Clemente de Castillo: "Arte Popular en Martínez Compañón," in *Trujillo del Perú: Baltasar Jaime Martínez Compañón: Acuarelas, siglo XVIII*, ed. Pablo Macera (Lima: Fundación del Banco Continental, 1997), 51.

7. The definitive work on the Spanish American ethnographic genre of *casta* painting is Ilona Katzew, *Casta Painting: Images of Race in Eighteenth-Century Mexico* (New Haven, Conn.: Yale University Press, 2004).

8. Martínez Compañón approved of card playing but recommended that people use "imaginary coins made of grains of corn" for fictitious bets: "Disposiciones sobre el culto Católico para las distintas parroquías de su diócesis, dictadas por el Excelentisimo Baltasar Jaime Martínez Compañón" (Bogotá: ANC, Virreyes 10, doc. 15, 525–594). Along with tobacco, alcohol, and paper, playing cards were a profitable component of the Bourbon state monopoly system, and their purchase helped fill Crown coffers. On Bourbon monopolies, see Susan Deans-Smith, *Bureaucrats, Planters, and Workers: The Making of the Tobacco Monopoly in Bourbon Mexico* (Austin: University of Texas, 1992). Card playing also promoted European-style manners because, in the words of David Shields, the card table had become "the great altar of sociability," a signifier and promoter of "conversation, courtship, and conviviality" in the Atlantic world: *Civil Tongues and Polite Letters in British America* (Chapel Hill: University of North Carolina Press, 1997), 159.

9. On Martínez Compañón's botany, see Rainer W. Bussmann and Douglas Sharon, "Shadows of the Colonial Past: Diverging Plant Use in Northern Peru and Southern Ecuador," *Journal of Ethnobiology and Ethnomedicine* 5:4 (2009) (http://www.ethnobiomed.com/content/5/1/4). For archaeology, see Pillsbury and Trever, "The King, the Bishop, and the Creation of an American Antiquity." Ethnomusicologists who praise the Bishop's work include Gisela Kánepa Koch, James M. Vreeland, and Leonida Casas Roque, in *Danzas y máscaras en los Andes*, ed. Raul F. Romero (Lima: Instituto Riva-Agüero, 1993). For a good introduction to natural history collecting in the eighteenth-century Spanish Empire, as well as a basic orientation to Martínez Compañón's role therein, see Paula De Vos, "The Rare, the Singular, and the Extraordinary: Natural History and the Collection of Curiosities in the Spanish Empire," in *Science in the Spanish and Portuguese Empires, 1500–1800*, ed. Daniela Bleichmar (Stanford, Calif.: Stanford University Press, 2009), 271–289. Martínez Compañón discussed his collection in "Martínez Compañón to Viceroy Croix, Trujillo, 25 July 1785."

10. "Martínez Compañón to Antonio Porlier, Trujillo, 2 December 1788."

11. "Martínez Compañón to Viceroy Croix, Trujillo, 25 July 1785."

12. Martínez Compañón, "Santa Visita de Piura, 19 Julio 1783" (Trujillo: Archivo Arzobispal [hereafter, AAT], Colegios y Universidades: Erección y fundación de dos colegios de cholos y cholas en Trujillo).

13. This fate stands in contrast to the more concerted attempts to publish data from the Crown-sponsored natural history expeditions to America, such as the extensive (though troubled) effort to make public data and illustrations from the Ruiz and Pavón expedition to Peru, as detailed in Arthur Robert Steele, *Flowers for the King: The Expedition of Ruiz and Pavón and the Flora of Peru* (Durham, N.C.: Duke University Press, 1964).

14. "Martínez Compañón to King Charles III, Trujillo, 15 May 1786" (AAT, Colegios y Universidades: Erección y fundación de dos colegios de cholos y cholas en Trujillo).

15. For more on racial diversity in northern colonial Peru, see Rachel O'Toole, *Bound Lives: Africans, Indians, and the Making of Race in Colonial Peru* (Pittsburgh: University of Pittsburgh, 2012).

16. "Martínez Compañón to Don Juan José Urteaga, Cura y Vicario de la Provincia de Chachapoyas, Trujillo, 26 June 1785" (AAT: Colegios y Universidades: Erección y fundación de dos colegios de cholos y cholas en Trujillo).

17. The nine volumes were beautifully reproduced, along with three appendixes of commentary, analysis, and documents, by the Spanish Ministry of Culture. See Baltasar Jaime Martínez Compañón y Bujanda, *Trujillo del Perú* (Madrid: Ediciones Cultura Hispánica, 1978–1994). The images are also available online as part of the "American Manuscripts in the Royal Collections" division at the Biblioteca Virtual Miguel Cervantes, funded by the University of Alicante: http://bib.cervantesvirtual.com/portal/patrimonio/catalogo.shtml.

18. "Expediente sobre la remisión de 24 cajones de curiosidades de la naturaleza y del arte, recogidos por el obispo de Trujillo (hoy arzobispo de Santa Fé) y remitidas por el Virrey de Lima, venidas en la Fragata Rosa" (Seville: AGI, Lima 798).

19. "Martínez Compañón to Agustín Hermenegildo de Querejazu, Trujillo, 10 August 1780" (Lima: AGNP, Correspondencia D1-25-727).

20. "Martínez Compañón to Viceroy Croix, 29 July 1789, Trujillo" (Bogotá: ANC, Virreyes 17: Documentos de Visita, #19).

21. "Carta de Cristóbal Colón a los Reyes Católicos, acerca de la población y negociación de la Española y de las otras islas descubiertas y por descubrir"; "Carta del almirante Cristóbal Colón escrita al escribano de ración de los Señores Reyes Católicos"; and "Carta del almirante Cristóbal Colón al Sr. Rafael Sánchez, tesorero de los Serenísimos Monarcas, 4 de Marzo de 1493," in *Cartas de relación de la conquista de América*, ed. Julio de Riverend (Mexico City: Editorial de Nueva España, 1945).

22. On Columbus, see Kirkpatrick Sale, *The Conquest of Paradise: Christopher Columbus and the Columbian Legacy* (New York: Alfred A. Knopf, 1990); and Nicolás Wey Gómez, *The Tropics of Empire: Why Columbus Sailed South to the Indies* (Cambridge, Mass.: MIT Press, 2008). For the distribution of his letters, see Rudolf Hirsch, "Printed

Reports on the Early Discoveries and Their Reception," and Thomas R. Adams, "Some Bibliographical Observations on and Questions About the Relationship Between the Discovery of America and the Invention of Printing," in *First Images of America: The Impact of the New World on the Old*, ed. Fredi Chiapelli (Berkeley: University of California Press, 1976), 2:537–561 and 529–536. A book that colorfully illustrates the European belief that the unknown world was populated by monsters is Sebastian Münster, *Cosmographiae universales* (Basel, 1552), bk. 6.

23. On utopias in the early modern European psyche, see J. C. Davis, "Utopia and the New World, 1500–1700," in *Utopia: the Search for the Ideal Society in the Western World*, ed. Roland Schaer, Gregory Claeys, and Lyman Tower Sargent (New York: New York Public Library / Oxford University, 2000). Athanasius Kircher mapped Atlantis in his *Burning and Fire-Vomiting Mountains Famous in the World* (London: J. Darby, 1669).

24. Thomas More, *Utopia*, ed. George M. Logan (New York: W. W. Norton, 2011), 11–40.

25. See Francisco Fernandez Buey, *Utopia e ilusiones naturales* (Barcelona: Viejo Topo, 2007); and Pedro Henríquez Ureña, *La Utopia de América* (Caracas: Biblioteca Ayacucho, 1925).

26. The eight-real coin is discussed in "Eight-Piece," in *Dictionary of Political Economy*, ed. Sir Robert Harry Inglis Palgrave (London: Macmillan, 1894), 1:687. On *plus ultra*, see Earl Rosenthal, "*Plus Ultra, Non Plus Ultra*, and the Columnar Device of Emperor Charles V," *Journal of the Warburg and Courtauld Institutes* 34 (1971): 204–228. For a discussion of this symbol's importance in the early modern Atlantic culture of scientific innovation, see "Introduction: The Far Side of the Ocean," in *Science and Empire in the Atlantic World*, ed. James Delbourgo and Nicholas Dew (New York: Routledge, 2008). Michael R. Huber discusses the Pillars of Hercules in *Mythematics: Solving the 12 Labors of Hercules* (Princeton, N.J.: Princeton University Press, 2009), 106–108.

27. Rosenthal, "*Plus Ultra*," 204–208.

28. Bartolomé de Las Casas, *A Brief Account of the Destruction of the Indies* (Middlesex: Echo Library, 2007), 45–57.

29. For a short bibliographical study of Las Casas's work, see John F. Moffit and Santiago Sebastián, *O Brave New People: The European Invention of the American Indian* (Albuquerque: University of New Mexico Press, 1996), 291–302.

30. On the reducciones and their articulation in 1512 as part of the Laws of Burgos, see Margarita Durán Estragó, "The Reductions," in *The Church in Latin America, 1492–1992*, ed. Enrique Dussel (London: Burns & Oates, 1992). Tribute is explained succinctly in Leslie Bethell, *The Cambridge History of Latin America*, vol. 2: *Colonial Latin America* (Cambridge: Cambridge University Press, 1984), 399.

31. Bernardino Verástique, *Michoacán and Eden: Vasco de Quiroga and the Evangelization of Western Mexico* (Austin: University of Texas Press, 2000), 119–131.

32. For a description of the towns, see Warren B. Fintan, *Vasco de Quiroga and His Pueblo-Hospitals of Santa Fé* (Washington, D.C.: Academy of American Franciscan History, 1963).

33. Campillo's work circulated in manuscript form and was later plagiarized in a widely available text by Bernardo Ward, the *Economic Project* (1762). For discussion of the relationship between the two works, see Eduardo Arcila Farias, "Campillo y Cosio en el pensamiento económico español," in Joseph del Campillo, *Nuevo sistema de gobierno económico para la América* (Mérida, Venezuela: Universidad de los Andes, 1971).

CHAPTER 1. THE BOOKS OF A BISHOP

1. The *Cámara de Indias* recommended Martínez Compañón to become *chantre* of the Lima cathedral on December 21, 1765: "Relación de los méritos y servicios del Doctor D. Baltasar Jayme Martínez Compañón," in *Trujillo del Perú: Appendice III*, ed. Manuel Ballesteros Gaibrois (Madrid: Ediciones de Cultura Hispánica, 1994), 43–45. Special thanks to Mariano Barriendos Vallvé of the University of Barcelona, who helped me locate sources on historical meteorology in Cádiz. I also consulted Ricardo García-Herrera, Luis Gimeno, Pedro Ribero, and Emiliano Hernández, "New Records of Atlantic Hurricanes from Spanish Documentary Sources," *Journal of Geophysical Research* 110 (2005), http://onlinelibrary.wiley.com/doi/10.1029/2005JD005955/abstract; and María Jesús Arazola Corvera, *Hombres, barcos y comercio de la ruta Cádiz–Buenos Aires (1737–1757)* (Seville: Diputación de Seville, 1998), 145–146.

2. On Cádiz and its cathedral, see Fernando Marías, "From Madrid to Cádiz: The Last Baroque Cathedral for the New Economic Capital of Spain," *Studies in the History of Art* 66 (2005): 139–141; and Manuel Bustos Rodríguez, *Cádiz en el sistema atlántico: La Ciudad, sus comerciantes, y la actividad mercantil (1650–1830)* (Cádiz: Universidad de Cádiz, 2005). For early modern European urban population statistics, see Paul M. Hohenberg and Lynn Hollen Lees, *The Making of Urban Europe, 1000–1950* (Cambridge, Mass.: Harvard University Press, 1985), 227.

3. On canon law curriculum and the education of high clergy in the Spanish Empire, see William B. Taylor, *Magistrates of the Sacred: Priests and Parishioners in Eighteenth-Century Mexico* (Stanford, Calif.: Stanford University Press, 1996), 88–90. Students of the Bishop know almost nothing about his time serving the Holy Office, as the records have not been located. For basic biographical details on Martínez Compañón, see the older studies of José Manuel Pérez Ayala, *Baltasar Jaime Martínez Compañón y Bujanda, prelado Español de Colombia y el Perú* (Bogotá: Imprenta Nacional, 1955); and Rubén Vargas Ugarte, *Tres figuras señeras del episcopado americano* (Lima: Charles Milla Batres, 1966). For an authoritative, recent ecclesiastical and social history of Martínez Compañón's work with the Church in Trujillo, see Daniel Restrepo Manrique, *Sociedad y religión en Trujillo (Peru) bajo el episcopado de Baltasar Jaime Martínez Compañón, 1780–1790* (Vitoria-Gasteiz: Servicio Central de Publicaciones, Gobierno Vasco, 1992).

4. "Información y licencia de pasajero a Indias del Dr. Baltasar Jaime Martínez Compañón, con sus criados, a Lima, 1768" (Seville: AGI, Contratación 5511B, N. 2, R. 12).

5. "Pedro Echevarri and Fausto Sodupe to Antonio de Solar, Santa Fé de Bogotá, 15 September 1797" (Seville: AGI, Estado 57, #23).

6. For routes to the southern portions of Spanish America, see Bustos Rodríguez, *Cádiz en el sistema atlántico*, 66. Daniel Restrepo discusses Martínez Compañón's library in "Vida y hechos de Martínez Compañón," in *Trujillo del Perú: Appendice II*, ed. Ballesteros Gaibrois, 42. For the Bishop's inventory, see "Inventario de bienes de Baltasar Jaime Martínez Compañón, Obispo de Trujillo, 1779" (Trujillo: Archivo Departamental de la Libertad [hereafter, ADL], Protocolos Notariales Siglo XVIII, Antonio del Solar, leg. 385, fols. 221v–301). Because of the damage sustained after several fires in the Cathedral Archive in Bogotá, this is the only existing documentation on what books the Bishop owned.

7. On Mabillon, see Joseph Urban Bergkamp, "Dom Jean Mabillon and the Benedictine School of Saint-Maur" (Ph.D. thesis, Catholic University, 1928).

8. Kenneth S. Rothwell, ed., *Federico Borromeo: Sacred Painting/Museum* (Cambridge, Mass.: Harvard University Press, 2010), xv. Martínez Compañón requested a copy of "any printed museum like that of Vormio [*sic*] [or] Kircher" from his friend Agustín Hermenegildo in 1788: "Martínez Compañón to Agustín Hermenegildo de Querejazu, Lima, 1788" (Lima: AGNP, Correspondencia D1-25-727, fol. 414).

9. Alonso de la Peña Montenegro, *Itinerario para parrocos de indios* (Madrid: Pedro Marin, 1771), 188. William Taylor discusses the popularity of Montenegro's work in *Magistrates of the Sacred*, 153.

10. Athanasius Kircher, *Burning and Fire-Vomiting Mountains Famous in the World* (London: J. Darby, 1669), 35. On volcanic activity at Sabancaya, see Fred Bullard, "Volcanoes of Southern Peru," *Bulletin of Volcanology* 24:1 (1962): 449; and Mauro Rosi et al., *Volcanoes* (Richmond Hill, Ontario: Firefly, 2003), 297.

11. Gabriel Alonso de Herrera, *Agricultura general de Gabriel Alonso de Herrera, corregida según el testo original de la primera edición publicada en 1513 por el mismo autor, y adicionada por la Real Sociedad Económica Maritrense* (Madrid: Imprenta Real, 1819). The prints were H. C. Verdussen, *Theatro moral de la vida humana en cien emblemas* (Amberes: Henrico y Cornelio Verdussen, 1701).

12. Lewis Hanke, "Statement Concerning the Contents of the *Historia de la Villa Imperial de Potosí*," *Journal de la Société des Américanists* 28:2 (1936): 402.

13. The river Tercero and the city of Cuzco are described in Concolorcorvo (Calixto Bustamante Charles Inca), *El Lazarillo de ciegos caminantes: Desde Buenos Aires hasta Lima* (Buenos Aires: Stockero, 2005), 14–22. On Potosí, see Hanke, "Statement Concerning the Contents of the *Historia de la Villa Imperial de Potosí*."

14. Martínez Compañón to Viceroy Croix, Trujillo, 15 May 1786" (Trujillo: AAT: Colegios y Universidades, Erección y fundación de dos colegios de cholos y cholas en Trujillo).

15. For more on the early chronicles and the Tiwanaku culture, see Paul S. Goldstein, *Andean Diaspora: The Tiwanaku Colonies and the Origins of South American Empire* (Gainesville: University Press of Florida, 2004); Weston La Barre Source, "The Uru of

the Rio Desaguadero," *American Anthropologist* 43:4 (1941): 493–522; and Bartolomé de Las Casas, *A Brief Account of the Destruction of the Indies* (Gutenberg E-book), http://www.gutenberg.org/ebooks/20321, 4–6.

16. Gregorio García, *Origen de los indios de el nuevo mundo, e Indias Occidentales* (Valencia: Pedro Patricia Mey, 1607).

17. "Martínez Compañón to Antonio Porlier, Cartagena, 13 December 1790" (Seville: AGI, Lima 798: "Expediente sobre la remisión de 24 cajones de curiosidades de la naturaleza y del arte, recogidos por el obispo de Trujillo (hoy arzobispo de Santa Fé) y remitidas por el Virrey de Lima, venidas en la Fragata Rosa."

18. Joseph François Lafitau, *Customs of the American Indians Compared with Customs of Primitive Times* (Toronto: Champlain Society, 1977), 56.

19. For some commentary on how Lafitau's work was received by his contemporaries, see William N. Fenton and Elizabeth L. Moore, "J. F. Lafitau, Precursor of Scientific Anthropology," *Southwestern Journal of Anthropology* 25:2 (1969): 173–187. Surprisingly, the scholarly literature lacks a larger body of work on such an important figure in the history of European understandings of native peoples.

20. See Jorge Cañizares-Esguerra, *How to Write the History of the New World: Histories, Epistemologies, and Identities in the Eighteenth-Century Atlantic World* (Stanford, Calif.: Stanford University Press, 2001), esp. 60–130.

21. Ibid., 130–204.

22. Alexander Jardine, *Letters from Barbary, France, Spain, Portugal &c.* (London: T. Cadell, 1790), 133. There is a good discussion of Buffon's place in the debate in David A. Brading, *The First America: The Spanish Monarchy, Creole Patriots, and the Liberal State, 1492–1867* (Cambridge: Cambridge University Press, 1991), 429–430. Along with Cañizares, Brading offers a mainstay of the literature on the so-called debate over the New World. Also foundational is Antonello Gerbi, whose *The Dispute of the New World: The History of a Polemic, 1750–1900* has recently been reprinted: Jeremy Moyle, trans. (Pittsburgh: University of Pittsburgh Press, 2010).

23. Cornelius de Pauw, *A General History of the Americans, of Their Customs, Manners, and Colors . . . Selected from M. Pauw*, ed. Daniel Webb (Rochdale: T. Wood, 1806), 8–9.

24. Guillaume-Thomas de Raynal, *A Philosophical and Political History of the Settlement and Trade of the Europeans in the East and West Indies* (Glasgow: Mundell and Son, 1804), 25.

25. William Robertson, *The History of America* (Philadelphia: Robert and Thomas Desilver, 1822), 1:162.

26. Cañizares-Esguerra, *How to Write the History of the New World*, 165.

27. Francisco Saviero Clavigero, *Historia antigua de Megico* (London: R. Ackerman, Strand, 1826), 76. Cañizares-Esguerra also covers the Spanish Royal Academy of History in *How to Write the History of the New World*, 165.

28. Juan Ignacio Molina, *Compendio de la historia geográfica, natural, y civil del reyno de Chile* (Madrid: Antonio de Sancha, 1788), xv.

29. Juan de Velasco, *Historia de reino de Quito* (Ayacucho: Biblioteca Ayacucho, 1981), 320.

30. On the idea of "lettered cities," see Angel Rama, *The Lettered City* (Durham, N.C.: Duke University Press, 1996); and Joanne Rappaport and Tom Cummins, eds., *Beyond the Lettered City: Indigenous Literacies in the Andes* (Durham, N.C.: Duke University Press, 2011).

31. Matthew D. O'Hara, *A Flock Divided: Race, Religion, and Politics in Mexico, 1759–1857* (Durham, N.C.: Duke University Press, 2010), 55.

32. "Martínez Compañón to Don Juan José Urteaga, Trujillo, 26 June 1785" (Erección y fundación de dos colegios de cholos y cholas en Trujillo).

33. "Santa Visita de Piura, 19 Julio 1783" (Erección y fundación de dos colegios de cholos y cholas en Trujillo). Martínez Compañón fits easily into the trend of Spanish bishops serving in America who promoted a patriotic epistemology, as identified by Cañizares-Esguerra, *How to Write the History of the New World*, 209.

34. "Martínez Compañón to Don Juan José Urteaga, Trujillo, 26 June 1785."

35. "Pastoral Letter of Martínez Compañón, Trujillo, 14 April 1782" (Seville: AGI, Cartas y expedientes: Curiosidades para el Jardín Botánico, Lima 798).

36. "Expediente sobre la remisión de 24 cajones de curiosidades de la naturaleza y del arte."

37. Ricardo A. Alegre and M. Colon, "Male Pseudohermaphroditism Caused by Enzymatic Deficiency of 17-Alpha-Hydroxlase: First Case Reported in Puerto Rico," *Boletín: Asociación Médica de Puerto Rico* 89 (1997): 10–12.

38. On Huaylas, see "Descripción del gigante que acaba de ser conducido a esta ciudad de la de Ica," *Mercurio Peruano* 4:138 (April 29, 1792): 293. On Pedro O'Crouley, see *A Description of the Kingdom of New Spain* (San Francisco: John Howell, 1794), chap. 26. Lorenzana's interest in giants is discussed in Luis Sierra Nava-Lasa, *El Cardenal Lorenzana y la Ilustración* (Madrid: Fundación Universitaria Española, 1973), 159. Robertson's *History of America* discusses giants, 2:168. Gerbi mentioned the importance giants in the great eighteenth-century debate in his 1973 *The Dispute of the New World*, 114.

39. Lima population statistics from José Hipólito Unanue, *Observaciones sobre el clima de Lima y sus influencias en los seres organizados en especial el hombre* (Lima: Imprenta Real de los Huerfanos, 1806), 100. Viceregal fanfare and ceremonies are described in Rafael Ramos Sosa, *Arte festivo en Lima virreinal (siglos XVI–XVII)* (Andalucía: Junta de Andalucía, 1992), 32; and Jorge Juan and Antonio Ulloa, *A Voyage to South America* (New York: Knopf, 1964), 183.

40. For descriptions of leisure activities in late eighteenth-century Lima, see the following editions of the *Mercurio Peruano*: 13 January 1791, 20 January 1791, 10 February 1791, and 9 February 1792. As for chocolate, the Bishop was somewhat of an aficionado who fretted when the cacao used to make it was not available. From the provincial town of Lambayeque, he wrote despairingly to friends in Lima that "not one grain of cacao have I been able to find. . . . [I]f it is not possible to find some in this town quickly, we will have to be patient this year." Perhaps deprivation spurred him to search for a viable

substitute, for later he noted in the collection inventory that the seed of the *chonta* fruit had the same taste as cacao. "Martínez Compañón to Augustín Hermenegildo de Querejazu, Lambayeque, 22 December 1783" (Lima: AGNP, Colección Francisco Moyrera Matute, #564). On chocolate customs, see Marcy Norton, "Conquests of Chocolate," *OAH Magazine of History* 18:3 (2004): 16.

41. For relevant background on the scientific community in late eighteenth-century Lima, see Arthur Robert Steele, *Flowers for the King: The Expedition of Ruíz and Pavón and the Flora of Peru* (Durham, N.C.: Duke University Press, 1964); Jorge Cañizares-Esguerra, "La Utopia de Hipólito Unanue: Comercio, naturaleza, y religión en el Perú," in *Saberes andinos: Ciencia y tecnología en Bolivia, Ecuador, y Perú*, ed. Marcos Cueto (Lima: Instituto de Estudios Peruanos, 1995), 91–109; José Eusebio Llano Zapata, *Memorias histórico, físicas, crítico, apologéticas de la America Meridional*, ed. Charles Walker et al. (Lima: Instituto Francés de Estudios Andinos, 2005); and Diana Soto Arango, "La enseñanza ilustrada en las universidades de América colonial: Estudio historiográfico," in *La Ilustración en América colonial* (Madrid: Doce Calles, 1995), 91–121.

42. *Cabildo* functions are described in Taylor, *Magistrates of the Sacred*, 121. For the Lima cathedral, see Emilio Harth-Terré, "Tesoros de la catedral de Lima," *Anales*, Instituto de Investigaciones Estéticas, Universidad Nacional Autónoma de México 11 (1944): 5–18.

43. For the Bishop's musical activities, see Guillermo J. Marchant E., "The Musical Legacy of Martínez Compañón," in *Codex Martínez Compañón (Trujillo, Perú, 1783–1785)* Paris: Harmonia Mundi, 2005), 34; and R. Stevenson, *The Music of Peru: Aboriginal and Viceroyal Epochs* (Washington, D.C.: Pan American Union, General Secretariat of the Organization of American States, 1959), 159–170. The tambourine is described in "Expediente sobre la remisión de 24 cajones de curiosidades de la naturaleza y del arte."

44. Martínez Compañón, "Capellanías y Otras Obras Pias, vol. 16, 1769" (Lima: Archivo del Cabildo Eclesiástico [hereafter, ACE].

45. Martínez Compañón, "Solicitud a fin de que se conceda la licéncia necesária para la construcción y fábrica de un cuarto más para los colegiales y obras para conducir el agua al traspatio del colegio, 1775" (Lima: Archivo Arzobispal [hereafter, AAL], Seminario de Santo Toribio, 1606–1921; V:47; 1775); "Martínez Compañón to Antonio Hermenegildo de Querejazu, Trujillo, November 1781" (Lima: AGNP, Colección Francisco Moyrera Matute, #564).

46. Rubén Vargas Ugarte, S. J., *Concilios limenses, 1551–1772* (Lima: Arzobispado de Lima, 1952), 12.

47. On the RSBAP, see Julian Martínez Ruiz, Maria Camino Urdiain, and Juan Ignacio Tellechea Igidoras, *Catálogo género de individuos de la Real Sociedad Bascongada de los Amigos del País* (San Sebastián: Sociedad Guipúzcoana de Ediciones y Publicaciones [RSBAP], 1985); R. J. Shafer, *The Economic Societies in the Spanish World, 1763–1821* (Syracuse, N.Y.: Syracuse University, 1968); and *Ensayo de la Sociedad Bascongada de los Amigos del País* (Vitoria: Thomás de Robles, 1766). See also Teresa Recarte Barriola, *Ilustración vasca y renovación educativa: La Real Sociedad*

Bascongada de los Amigos del País (Salamanca: Universidad Pontificia, 1990); and María Cristina Torales Pacheco, *Ilustrados en la Nueva España: Los Socios de la Real Sociedad Bascongada de los Amigos del País* (Mexico City: Universidad Iberoamericana, 2001). The manifesto is reprinted in D. Javier Aizarna Azula and José Ignacio Tellechea Igidoras, eds., *Plan de una sociedad económica o academia de agricultura, ciencias, y artes utiles; y comercio* (San Sebastián: Donostia, 1985), 18. The 1780 ordinances are available in Marian J. Ruiz de Ael, *Ilustración artística en el País Vasco: La Real Sociedad Bascongada de Amigos del País y las artes* (Vitoria-Gasteiz: Diputación Foral de Alava, 1993), 31–33.

48. "Martínez Compañón to Antonio Hermenegildo de Querejazu, Trujillo, 25 March 1790" (Lima: AGNP, Colección Francisco Moyrera Matute, #564).

49. "El fiat de S.V. Santidad, Real Cedula de S.V. Majestad, por la que presenta a Illustrisimo Sr. Dr. Don Baltasar Jaime Martínez Compañón a Obispo de Esta Santa Iglesia Catedral de Trujillo, 1777" (Bogotá: ANC, Curas y Obispos, doc. 17, 789–816).

50. "Actas de Cabildo Eclesiástico: Las Vidas de los obispos de Trujillo, 1790" (Trujillo: AAT, Actas del Cabildo Eclesiástico).

CHAPTER 2. PARISH PRIESTS AND USEFUL INFORMATION

1. "Inventario de bienes de Baltasar Jaime Martínez Compañón, Obispo de Trujillo, Trujillo, 1779" (Trujillo: ADL, Protocolos notariales siglo XVIII, Antonio de Solar, leg. 385, fols. 221v–301).

2. The *rancherías* are described by Katharine Coleman in "Provincial Urban Problems: Trujillo, Peru, 1600–1784," in *Social Fabric and Spatial Structure in Colonial Latin America*, ed. David Robinson (Syracuse, N.Y.: Syracuse University Press, 1979), 405.

3. Estuardo Núñez and Georg Peterson, eds., *Alexander von Humboldt en el Perú: Diario de viaje y otros escritos* (Lima: Banco Central de Reserva, 2002), 74.

4. "Martínez Compañón to Amados Hijos Míos, Los Indios de Este Obispado de Trujillo, Piura, 19 July 1783" (Trujillo: AAT, Colegios y Universidades, legajo 1).

5. The most recent population statistics by race for colonial Peru can be found in John R. Fisher, *Bourbon Peru, 1750–1824* (Liverpool: Liverpool Latin American Studies, 2003), 82. For free blacks and slaves in Bourbon Trujillo, see Paul Rizo-Patrón Boylan and Cristóbal Aljovín de Losada, "La élite nobilaria de Trujillo de 1700 a 1830," in *El Norte en la historia regional: Siglos XVIII–XIX*, ed. Scarlett O'Phelan Godoy and Yves Saint-Geours (Lima: Instituto de Estudios Andinos, 1998), 241–293. Regarding Tomás Rodríguez, I am indebted to field communications I had with Trujillan historian Ricardo Morales, a specialist on the topic. See Ricardo Morales, "Los Pardos libres en el arte virreinal de Trujillo del Perú (siglos XVIII y XIX)," in *A Propósito de Raúl Porras Barrenechea: Viejos y nuevos temas de cultura andina*, ed. Antonio Garrido Aranda (Córdoba: Universidad de Córdoba, 2001), 406–407, and "Arquitectura virreynal:

Don Evaristo, un alarife negro en Trujillo," *ArkInca* 11 (1996): 74–80. For more on why Spanish reformers so closely concentrated on Indians and ignored people of African descent, see my second book project, first outlined in Emily Berquist, "Early Anti-Slavery Sentiment in the Spanish Atlantic World, 1765–1817," *Slavery & Abolition* 31:2 (2010): 181–205.

6. Teodoro de Croix, "Relación en que se manifiesta con toda expecificación y claridad al estado que tenía el virreynato del Perú" (Madrid: Biblioteca del Palacio Real [hereafter, BPR], BPRII-26 Croix, 144).

7. Don Miguel Feyjoo, *Relación descriptiva de la ciudad, y provincia de Truxillo del Perú con noticias exactas de su estado político según el real orden dirigido al Excelentisimo Señor Virrey Conde de Super-Unda* (Madrid: Imprenta del Real Consejo Suprema de las Indias, 1763).

8. William J. Callahan, *Church, Politics, and Society in Spain, 1750–1874* (Cambridge, Mass.: Harvard University Press, 1984), 5.

9. For Bourbon-era changes in managing the clergy and the faithful, see David Brading, *Church and State in Bourbon Mexico: The Diocese of Michoacán, 1749–1810* (Cambridge: Cambridge University Press, 1994); Callahan, *Church, Politics, and Society in Spain*; Margaret Chowning, *Rebellious Nuns: The Troubled History of a Mexican Convent, 1752–1863* (Oxford: Oxford University Press, 2006); Nancy Farris, *Crown and Clergy in Colonial Mexico, 1759–1821: The Crisis of Ecclesiastical Privilege* (London: Athlone, 1968); Brian Larkin, *The Very Nature of God: Baroque Catholicism and Religious Reform in Bourbon Mexico City* (Albuquerque: University of New Mexico Press, 2010); Matthew D. O'Hara, *A Flock Divided: Race, Religion, and Politics in Mexico, 1749–1857* (Durham, N.C.: Duke University Press, 2010); William Taylor, *Magistrates of the Sacred: Priests and Parishioners in Eighteenth-Century Mexico* (Stanford, Calif.: Stanford University Press, 1996); and Pamela Voekel, *Alone Before God: The Religious Origins of Modernity in Mexico* (Durham, N.C.: Duke University Press, 2002). Martínez Compañón's religious reforms are detailed in Daniel Restrepo Manrique's exhaustive study, *La Iglesia de Trujillo (Perú) bajo el episcopado de Baltasar Jaime Martínez Compañón (1780–1790)* (Vitoria-Gasteiz: Servicio Central de Publicaciones, Gobierno Vasco, 1992).

10. See O'Hara, *A Flock Divided*, 55–91.

11. The Bishop's plans to afford certain Indians with markers of noble status are discussed at length in Chapter 4 of this volume. His "Chart of 43 Castilian Words Translated" appears in vol. 2 of *Trujillo del Perú*.

12. "Plan de la bóveda subterránea construido al costado . . . sur de la Santa Iglesia Cathedral . . . en el año pasado de 1782, en la que se entierran los cadáveres que antes se enterraban en la dicha iglesia y eran los de todos los habitantes, a reserva de los Indios": *Trujillo del Perú*, vol. 1. The portraits are discussed in "Las Vidas de los Obispos de Trujillo, 1790" (Trujillo: AAT: Actas de Cabildo Eclesiástico).

13. Restrepo, *La Iglesia de Trujillo*, 324–325.

14. "Martínez Compañón to the *cabildo* of Piura, Villa de Cajamarca, 2 August 1784" (Bogotá. ANC, Virreyes 7:13, Visita a Cajamarca). On *Propaganda Fide*, see Peter

Guilday, "The Sacred Congregation de *Propaganda Fide* (1622–1922)," *Catholic Historical Review* 6:4 (January 1921): 479–494.

15. "Martínez Compañón to Agustín Hermenegildo de Querejazu, November 1782" (Lima: AGNP, Colección Francisco Moyrera Matute, #564).

16. "Martínez Compañón to Viceroy Jáuregui, Expedientes sobre la fundación del Seminario de Operarios de Trujillo" (Bogotá: ANC, Virreyes 7, 971–976). For more on the outcome of these projects, see Restrepo, *La Iglesia de Trujillo*, 255.

17. See Sabine Patricia Hyland, "Illegitimacy and Racial Hierarchy in the Peruvian Priesthood: A Seventeenth-Century Dispute," *Catholic Historical Review* 84:3 (July 1998): 431–454; O'Hara, *A Flock Divided*, 72–79; and Robert Ricard, *The Spiritual Conquest of Mexico: An Essay on the Apostolate and the Evangelizing Methods of the Mendicant Orders in New Spain, 1532–1572* (Berkeley: University of California Press, 1966).

18. For a thorough description of the state of the lower clergy in late colonial Trujillo, see Restrepo, *La Iglesia de Trujillo*, 241–243.

19. See Dorothy Tanck de Estrada, *Pueblos de indios y educación en México colonial, 1750–1821* (Mexico City: El Colegio de México, 1999).

20. The Virgin of Guadalupe had, in fact, been popular in the area since the mid-sixteenth century, when a son of one of the original founders of Trujillo had built a chapel to her. See Kenneth Mills, "Diego de Ocaña's Hagiography of New and Renewed Devotion in Colonial Peru," in *Colonial Saints: Discovering the Holy in the Americas, 1500–1800*, ed. Alan Greer and Jodi Bilinkoff (New York: Routledge, 2003), 53; and "Información sobre la profamación de la imágen de la Virgen, en unas fiestas, 1786" (Bogotá: ANC, Virreyes 17, #20).

21. The square miles figure is in Restrepo, *La Iglesia de Trujillo*, 253. One of the most important calls for *visitas* was first issued by Campillo in *Nuevo sistema de gobierno económico para la América* (Mérida, Venezuela: Universidad de los Andes, 1971), 84. For Charles III's mandate to prelates, see Jesús Paniagua Pérez, *España y América: Entre el Barroco y la Ilustración (1722–1804)* (León: Universidad de León, 2005), 123–155.

22. Martínez Compañón to Viceroy Croix, Trujillo, 29 May 1786" (Bogotá: ANC, Miscelánea 46, doc. 20, 602–627).

23. Gabriel B. Paquette, *Enlightenment, Governance, and Reform in Spain and Its Empire, 1759–1808* (New York: Palgrave Macmillan, 2008), 57.

24. José Palafox y Mendoza, *Virtudes del indio* (Madrid: Imprenta de Tomás Minuesa de los Rios, 1893), 73.

25. "Inventario de bienes de Baltasar Jaime Martínez Compañón."

26. "Pastoral Letter of Martínez Compañón, Trujillo, 14 April 1782" (Seville: AGI, Cartas y expedientes: Curiosidades para el Jardín Botánico, Lima 798).

27. "Inventario de bienes de Baltasar Jaime Martínez Compañón."

28. Such modest rhetoric was not exclusive to Martínez Compañón. In 1766 and in 1775, respectively, Lorenzana and his successor as archbishop of Mexico, Alonso Núñez de Haro, sent similar letters to parish priests requesting no special fanfare greet the arrival of their *visita* parties. See O'Hara, *A Flock Divided*, 66.

29. Rachel O'Toole argues that in Trujillo's urban areas, Indians owned property and could achieve *vecino* status: "Fitting In: Urban Indians, Migrants, and Muleteers in Colonial Peru," in *City Indians in Spain's American Empire: Urban Indigenous Society in Colonial Mesoamerica and Andean South America, 1530–1810*, ed. Dana Velasco Murillo, Mark Lentz, and Margarita R. Ochoa (Brighton: Sussex Academic Press, 2012), 148–172.

30. "Decree and Questionnaire of Martínez Compañón, Trujillo, 26 May 1782" (Bogotá: ANC, Virreyes 14, 356–358). Jesús Paniagua Pérez discusses the 1776 decree to the bishops in Paniagua Pérez, *España y América*, 123–155. The only two existing responses to the ecclesiastical questionnaire came from local officials in the *doctrina* of Jayanca. In 1789 in the parish of San Carlos, priests Francisco Collantes and Alvaro Valdés wrote their own answers to their prelate's questionnaires. Valdés revealed that the people there venerated a wooden image of the Virgin of Guadalupe and that the Virgin had "many devotees" throughout the province of Chachapoyas. Collantes explained that in his church, burials and marriages were paid by a group fund to which all community members contributed. Each was also careful to note that he had complied with Martínez Compañón's request to provide the account books of their parish finances: "Martínez Compañón to Viceroy Croix, Trujillo, 25 July 1785" (Bogotá: ANC, Virreyes 17, 432–433).

31. "Pastoral Letter of Martínez Compañón, Trujillo, 14 April 1782."

32. "Martínez Compañón to Viceroy Croix, Trujillo, 25 July 1785."

33. For a good explanation of how the *Codex* was created, see Donald Robertson, *Mexican Manuscript Painting of the Early Colonial Period: The Metropolitan Schools* (Norman: University of Oklahoma Press, 1994), 25–34. See also Antonio Barrera, "Empire and Knowledge: Reporting from the New World," *Colonial Latin American Review* 15:1 (June 2006): 39–54. The outstanding study of the *relaciones* is Barbara E. Mundy, *The Mapping of New Spain: Indigenous Cartography and the Maps of the Relaciones Geográficas* (Chicago: University of Chicago Press, 1996). Maria M. Portuondo makes an eloquent argument about the intellectual importance of changing scientific epistemologies in the Spanish world in *Secret Science: Spanish Cosmography and the New World* (Chicago: University of Chicago Press, 2009), 211.

34. "Pastoral Letter of Martínez Compañón, Trujillo, 14 April 1782."

35. Alonso Carrio, *El Lazarillo: A Guide for Inexperienced Travelers Between Buenos Aires and Lima, 1773*, ed. Walter Kline (Bloomington: Indiana University Press, 1965), 229.

36. On this practice, see Richard Price, "Trial Marriage in the Andes," *Ethnology* 4:3 (July 1965): 310–322.

37. On balsams in Spanish America, see Antonio Barrera-Osorio, *Experiencing Nature: The Spanish American Empire and the Early Scientific Revolution* (Austin: University of Texas Press, 2006), 13–29.

38. On leprosy in colonial Peru, see Adam Warren, *Medicine and Politics in Colonial Peru: Population Growth and the Bourbon Reforms* (Pittsburgh: University of Pittsburgh Press, 2010), 118 157.

39. "Martínez Compañón to Jorge Escobedo, Trujillo, 23 January 1784" (Bogotá: ANC, Virreyes 7, 522–523).

40. On the market for American wood in Europe, see Antonio Lafuente and Nuria Valverde, "Linnaen Botany and Spanish Imperial Biopolitics," in *Colonial Botany: Science, Commerce, and Politics in the Early Modern World*, ed. Londa Schiebinger and Claudia Swan (Philadelphia: University of Pennsylvania, 2005), 143.

41. "Pastoral Letter of Martínez Compañón, Trujillo, 14 April 1782."

42. Martínez Compañón to Antonio Porlier, Cartagena, 13 December 1790, "Expediente sobre la remisión de 24 cajones de curiosidades de la naturaleza y del arte."

43. Teodoro de Croix, "Relación," 69–70.

44. "Libro de bautismos de Celendín" (Cajamarca: Archivo Episcopal [hereafter, AEC], Celendín, Bautismos, book 4, 1782–1789).

45. These appear in vol. 9 of the *Trujillo* watercolors.

46. Daniel Restrepo Manrique, "Plan reformador del Obispo Martínez Compañón," in *La Obra de Obispo Martínez Compañón sobre Trujillo del Perú en el siglo XVIII: Appendice II* (Madrid: Ediciones Cultural Hispánica del Centro Iberoamericano de Cooperación, 1994), 108.

47. Ibid., 65.

48. "Actas del Cabildo de 22 Junio 1790: Oficios que dirigó Martínez Compañón antes de su partida" (Trujillo: AAT, Actas de Cabildo Eclesiástico).

49. "Autos de Visita a Santiago de Cao" (Bogotá: ANC, Virreyes 10, #15).

50. "Expediente sobre la remisión de 24 cajones."

51. "Martínez Compañón to Antonio Hermenegildo de Querejazu, Trujillo, 10 April 1785" (Lima: AGNP, Correspondencia D1-25-727).

52. "Martínez Compañón to Viceroy Croix, Trujillo, 25 July 1785."

CHAPTER 3. IMAGINING TOWNS IN TRUJILLO

1. I would like to extend grateful thanks to Joanne Pillsbury for her bibliographic and editorial suggestions for this chapter. For an introduction to Chan Chan, see Joanne Pillsbury and Banks L. Leonard, "Identifying Chimú Palaces: Elite Residential Architecture in the Late Intermediate Period," in *Palaces of the Ancient New World*, ed. Susan Toby Evans and Joanne Pillsbury (Washington, D.C.: Dumbarton Oaks, 2004), 248. The 1602 episode is recounted in Don Miguel Feyjoo, *Relación descriptiva de la ciudad, y provincia de Truxillo del Peru, con noticias exactas de su estado político, según el real orden dirigido al Excelentisimo Señor Virrey Conde de Super-Unda* (Madrid: Imprenta del Real Consejo Suprema de las Indias, 1763), 25. For an excellent retelling of the Antonio Zarco incident, see Susan E. Ramírez, *The World Upside Down: Cross-Cultural Contact and Conflict in Sixteenth-Century Peru* (Stanford, Calif.: Stanford University Press, 1996), 121–151.

2. For early north coast archaeological investigations, see José Alcina Franch, *Arqueólogos o anticuarios: Historia antigua de la arqueología en la América española* (Barce-

lona: Ediciones del Serbal, 1995). On La Condamine in the region, see Monica Barnes, "Charles-Marie de La Condamine (1701–1774)," in *Guide to Documentary Sources for Andean Studies, 1530–1900,* ed. Joanne Pillsbury (Norman: University of Oklahoma Press, 2008), 2:336–342. On Spanish investigations at Pompeii, see Alicia M. Canto, *La Arqueología española en la época de Charles IV y Godoy: Los Dibujos de Mérida de Don Manuel de Villena Moziño, 1791–1794* (Madrid: Ministerio de Educación, Cultura, y Deporte, 2001), 18–19. Joanne Pillsbury and Lisa Trever discuss the call for antiquities in their article on Martínez Compañón's archaeological investigations, "The King, the Bishop, and the Creation of an American Antiquity," *Ñawpa Pacha: Journal of Andean Archaeology* 29 (2008): 191–219.

3. For the first 24 crates sent in 1788, see "Expediente sobre la remisión de 24 cajones de curiosidades de la naturaleza y del arte, recogidos por el obispo de Trujillo (hoy arzobispo de Santa Fé) y remitidas por el Virrey de Lima, venidas en la Fragata Rosa" (Seville: AGI, Lima 798). The inventory of the second shipments totaling six crates of artifacts remitted from Cartagena in 1790 and 1791 is "Expediente sobre la remisión a España por el Arzobispo de Santa Fé de 6 cajones de huacos o barros de la gentilidad del obispado de Trujillo" (Seville: AGI, Indiferente General 1545).

4. The shells and the *ciudadelas* are discussed in Joanne Pillsbury, "The Thorny Oyster and the Origins of Empire: Implications of Recently Uncovered Spondylus Imagery from Chan Chan, Peru," *Latin American Antiquity* 7:4 (December 1996): 313–340. The contents of the storage areas are discussed in Pillsbury and Leonard, "Identifying Chimú Palaces," 248–255.

5. "Expediente sobre la remisión de 24 cajones de curiosidades." For more on Chimú whistling jugs, see Cecilia Bákula, "The Art of the Late Intermediate Period," in *The Inca World: The Development of Pre-Columbian Peru, A.D. 1000–1534,* ed. Laura Larencich Minelli (Norman: University of Oklahoma Press, 2000), 111–121.

6. "Expedientes de remisiónes de maderas, plantas, semillas y otras producciones de America" (Seville: AGI, Indiferente General, 1545).

7. "Expediente sobre la remisión de 24 cajones de curiosidades."

8. "Pastoral Letter of Martínez Compañón, Trujillo, 14 April 1782" (Seville: AGI, Cartas y expedientes: Curiosidades para el Jardín Botánico, Lima 798).

9. This detail about the *huaca* is mentioned in the key to the corresponding image. Paz Cabello Carro points out that Feyjoo and Martínez Compañón lived in Lima at the same time, so it is likely that they conversed about these explorations before the latter became bishop of Trujillo: "Spanish Collections of Americana in the Late Eighteenth Century," in *Collecting Across Cultures: Material Exchanges in the Early Modern Atlantic World,* ed. Daniela Bleichmar and Peter C. Mancall (Philadelphia: University of Pennsylvania Press, 2011), 219. Marcahuamachuco is discussed in John R. Topic, "A Sequence of Monumental Architecture from Huamachuco," in *Perspectives on Andean Prehistory and Protohistory: Papers from the Third Annual Northeast Conference on Andean Archaeology and Ethnohistory,* ed. Daniel H. Sandweiss and D. Peter Kvietok (Ithaca, N.Y.: Cornell Latin American Studies Program, 1986), 63. See also the pertinent website of the Global Heritage Fund, http://global

heritagefund.org/images/uploads/projects/ghf_marcahuamachuco_peru.pdf. Some archaeologists assume that the Chimú irrigation canals were never completed because of tectonic
movement below. See Charles R. Ortloff, Michael E. Moseley, and Robert E. Feldman,
"Hydraulic Engineering Aspects of the Chimu Chicama-Moche Intervalley Canal," *American Antiquity* 47:3 (July 1982): 593. Lisa Trever characterizes the *Trujillo* burial portraits as
"disarmingly lifelike" images that defied archaeological convention by depicting their subjects "as perfectly preserved and lifelike, as if not deceased but perhaps just sleeping": Lisa
Trever, "The Uncanny Tombs in Martínez Compañón's *Trujillo del Perú*," in *Past Presented*
(Washington, D.C.: Dumbarton Oaks, 2012), 112.

　　10. For Martínez Compañón's archaeological work, see Philip Ainsworth Means,
"A Great Prelate and Archaeologist," in *Hispanic American Essays: A Memorial to James
Alexander Robertson*, ed. A. Curtis Wilgus (Chapel Hill: University of North Carolina
Press, 1942), 67. For the denigrating narrative on Inca history and material culture, see
José Mariano Millán de Aguirre, "Discurso sobre la falsa religión y costumbres super-
sticiosas de los Indios de Peru," *Mercurio Peruano* (December 11, 1791). Guillaume-
Thomas de Raynal wrote dismissively about Inca ruins in *A Philosophical and Political
History of the Settlement and Trade of the Europeans in the East and West Indies* (Glasgow:
Mundell and Son, 1804), 25. There is an excellent discussion of how pre-Hispanic monu-
ments and antiquities were involved in the debate over the inferiority of the Americas
in Franch, *Arqueólogos o anticuarios*, chap. 4. See also Jorge Cañizares-Esguerra, *How
to Write the History of the New World: Histories, Epistemologies, and Identities in the
Eighteenth-Century Atlantic World* (Stanford, Calif.: Stanford University Press, 2001),
chap. 1.

　　11. Richard Kagan with Fernando Marias, *Urban Images of the Hispanic World, 1493–
1793* (New Haven, Conn.: Yale University Press, 2000), 21.

　　12. Zelia Nuttall, "Royal Ordinances Concerning the Laying Out of New Towns,"
Hispanic American Historical Review 4 (1921): 743–753.

　　13. Ibid.

　　14. Margarita Durán Estragó, "The Reductions," in *The Church in Latin America
1492–1992*, ed. Enrique Dussel (London: Burns & Oates, 1992), 355.

　　15. D. Juan Tejeda y Ramiro, *Colección de cánones y de todos los concilios de la iglesia
de España y de América* (Madrid: Imprenta de D. Pedro Montero, 1859), 317.

　　16. "Visita a Piura, 3 June 1783" (Bogotá: ANC, Virreyes 13, #33).

　　17. For a good overview of the town foundation projects, see Restrepo Manrique,
Sociedad y religión en Trujillo, 184–194.

　　18. "Carta topográfica de la Provincia de Piura," *Trujillo del Perú*.

　　19. "Martínez Compañón to Viceroy Croix, Trujillo, 1 December 1785" (Bogotá:
ANC, Virreyes 13, #33).

　　20. José Campillo, *Nuevo sistema de gobierno económico para la América* (Merida,
Venezuela: Universidad de los Andes, 1971), 98.

　　21. "Representación de los Españoles y Mixtos Oriundos, y residentes en el Partido
de Tambogrande, Anexo de la Ciudad de Piura, sobre reducirse en población, Tambo-

grande, n.d." (Bogotá: ANC, Virreyes 13, #33). The date Martínez Compañón received (or inventoried) the letter is listed in the following notation, "Santa Visita de Piura, 24 May, 1783" (Bogotá: ANC, Virreyes 13, #33).

22. "Otra representación de los Indios del dicho partido, sobre el mismo intento, Piura, n.d." (Bogotá: ANC, Virreyes 13, #33). The date Martínez Compañón received (or inventoried) the letter is listed in the following notation, "Santa Visita de Piura, 24 May, 1783" (Bogotá: ANC, Virreyes 13, #33).

23. "José Luis Freyre Orbegoso to Martínez Compañón, Piura, 17 June 1783" (Bogotá: ANC, Virreyes 7, #13).

24. "Don José Vizente de Zavala to Martínez Compañón, Piura, 6 July 1783" (Bogotá: ANC, Virreyes 13, #33).

25. "Martínez Compañón to Señores Don Silvestre, Doctor Don Diego, Don Miguel, y Doña Mariana del Castillo, Dueños de las Haciendas de Tambogrande, Piura, 3 June 1783" (Bogotá: ANC, Virreyes 7, #13).

26. "Silvestre Antonio del Castillo, Doctor Diego del Castillo, Miguel Serafín del Castillo and Doña Maria Ana del Castillo to Martínez Compañón, San Miguel de Piura, n.d." (Bogotá: ANC, Virreyes 13, #33).

27. "Visita a Piura, 15 June 1783" (Bogotá: ANC, Virreyes 7, #13).

28. "Martínez Compañón to Viceroy Croix, Trujillo, 1 December 1785."

29. "Martínez Compañón to the Marqués de Salinas, Trujillo, 10 March 1786" (Bogotá: ANC, Virreyes 13, #33).

30. "Viceroy Croix to Martínez Compañón, Lima, 5 April 1786" (Bogotá: ANC, Virreyes 13, #33).

31. "Marqués de Salinas to Martínez Compañón, Lima, 5 April 1786" (Bogotá: ANC, Virreyes 13, #32).

32. "Martínez Compañón to Intendant Saavedra, Trujillo, 7 December 1789" (Bogotá: ANC, Virreyes 13, #33).

33. "Intendant Saavedra to Martínez Compañón, Trujillo, 11 December 1789" (Trujillo: AAT, Comunicaciones Eclesiásticas, Expediente K-1-17).

34. Restrepo Manrique, *Sociedad y religión en Trujillo*, 169.

35. "Bernardino Cuccha to Martínez Compañón, San Carlos, July 1784" (Trujillo: AAT, Curatos).

36. "Miguel Sarmiento, Pedro Nolasco Castillo, Jazinto Merchena et al. to Martínez Compañón, n.d." (Bogotá: ANC, Virreyes 13, #32).

37. "Don Vicente Fernández Otero to Martínez Compañón, n.d." (Bogotá: ANC, Virreyes 13, #32).

38. "Vicente Fernández Otero to Apolinario Herrera, Piura, 20 June 1783" (Bogotá: ANC, Virreyes 13, #32).

39. "Antonio Alvarado y Astudillo, Justo Roberto, Juan Jazinto Ortiz et al. to Martínez Compañón, n.d." (Bogotá: ANC, Virreyes 13, #32).

40. "Fray Apolinario Herrera to Luis José Freyre Orbegoso, Chipillico, 17 August 1783" (Bogotá: ANC, Virreyes 13, #32).

41. "Fray Apolinario Herrera to Martínez Compañón, Tambogrande, 13 September 1783" (Bogotá: ANC, Virreyes 13, #32).

42. "Don Pedro Rafael Castillo a Vicente Fernández Otero, Piura, 27 June 1785" (Bogotá: ANC, Virreyes 13, #32).

43. "Don Vicente Fernández Otero to Rafael Castillo, Piura, 30 June 1785" (Bogotá: ANC, Virreyes 13, #32).

44. "Martínez Compañón to Viceroy Croix, Trujillo, 1 December 1785."

45. "Juan José Pinillos to Martínez Compañón, Chachapoyas, 25 April 1783" (Lima: Ministerio de Relaciones Exteriores, Archivo Histórico de Limites [hereafter, ALMR], legajo 90, #LEB-4-13).

46. The figure about town foundations is taken from "Estado que demuestra el número de pueblos nuevos, y trasladados," *Trujillo del Perú*, vol. 1. For the history of Sullana, see Miguel Arturo Seminario Ojeda, *Historia de Sullana* (Peru: Municipalidad Provincial de Sullana, 1994). On Tambogrande, Miguel Arturo Seminario Ojeda, *Historia de Tambogrande: Una aproximación socio-económica del medio Piura, 1532–1932* (Peru: Municipalidad de Tambogrande, 1995). The letter about Celendín is mentioned in Manuel Ballesteros Gaibrois, introduction to *Trujillo del Perú: Appendice II* (Madrid: Ediciones de Cultura Hispánica, 1994). The Bishop wrote about the town in "Martínez Compañón to Viceroy Croix, Trujillo, 25 July 1785" (Bogotá: ANC, Virreyes 17, 432–433).

CHAPTER 4. IMPROVEMENT THROUGH EDUCATION

1. "Santa Visita de Piura, 19 July 1793" (Trujillo: AAT, Colegios y Universidades, Erección y fundación de dos colegios).

2. On card playing and sociability in the eighteenth-century Atlantic world, see David S. Shields, *Civil Tongues and Polite Letters in British America* (Chapel Hill: University of North Carolina, 1997), 159. For more on Bourbon monopolies, see Susan Deans-Smith, *Bureaucrats, Planters, and Workers: The Making of the Tobacco Monopoly in Mexico* (Austin: University of Texas, 1992). Martínez Compañón's decree on the morally upstanding way to make wagers in card playing is discussed in "Disposiciones sobre el culto Católico para las distintas parroquías de su diócesis, dictadas por el Excelentisimo Baltasar Jaime Martínez Compañón" (Bogotá: ANC, Virreyes 10, #15, 525–594).

3. "Disposiciones sobre el culto Católico para las distintas parroquías de su diócesis, dictadas por el Excelentisimo Baltasar Jaime Martínez Compañón."

4. José del Campillo, *Nuevo sistema de gobierno económico para la América* (Merida, Venezuela: Universidad de los Andes, 1971), 74.

5. "Martínez Compañón to José Urteaga, Trujillo, 26 June 1785" (Trujillo: AAT, Colegios y Universidades, Erección y fundación de dos colegios).

6. For this retelling of events, I relied mostly on the excellent work of Charles Walker, *Smoldering Ashes: Cuzco and the Creation of Republican Peru, 1780–1840* (Durham, N.C.: Duke University Press, 1999). See also Sergio Serulnikov, *Subverting Colonial*

Authority: Challenges to Spanish Rule in Eighteenth-Century Southern Andes (Durham, N.C.: Duke University Press, 2003); and Ward Stavig, *The World of Túpac Amaru: Conflict, Community, and Identity in Colonial Peru* (Lincoln: University of Nebraska Press, 1999). Stavig also coedited a document reader about the rebellions that was published posthumously: *The Tupac Amaru and Catarista Rebellions: An Anthology of Sources*, ed. Ward Stavig and Ella Schmidt (Indianapolis: Hackett, 2008).

7. For a good synthesis of the three different rebellions, see Sergio Serulnikov, *Subverting Colonial Authority: Challenges to Spanish Rule in the Eighteenth-Century Southern Andes* (Durham, N.C.: Duke University Press, 2003).

8. Stavig, *The World of Túpac Amaru*, 216–224.

9. The figure of the number killed is provided by Stavig in *The Túpac Amaru and Catarista Rebellions*, xiii. For documentation on the cultural restrictions put into place after the rebellion, see "Sentence Pronounced in Cuzco by the *Visitador* D. José Antonio de Areche against José Gabriel Túpac Amaru, His Wife, Children, and Other Principal Prisoners (Defendants)," ibid., 134.

10. The documents from this rebellion are reproduced in José Manuel Pérez Ayala, *Baltasar Jaime Martínez Compañón y Bujanda: Prelado español de Colombia y el Perú, 1737–1797* (Bogotá: Imprenta Nacional, 1955), 169–221. The best work on these Northern Peruvian rebellions is by Scarlett O'Phelan, esp. *Rebellions and Revolts in Eighteenth-Century Peru and Upper Peru* (Cologne: Bohlau, 1984).

11. "Sentence Pronounced in Cuzco by the *Visitador* D. José Antonio de Areche against José Gabriel Túpac Amaru," ed. Stavig and Schmidt, 135.

12. "Real cédula para que los Indios sean admitidos en las religiones, educados en los colegios y promovidos, según su mérito y capacidad, a dignidades y oficios públicos, San Ildefonso, 11 de Septiembre 1776," in *Colección de documentos para la historia de la formación social de Hispanoamérica, 1493–1820*, vol. 3, *Primer Tomo, 1661–1779*, ed. Richard Konetzke (Madrid: Consejo Superior de Investigaciones Científicas, 1962), 333–334; "Real cédula sobre establecimiento de escuelas del idioma Castellano en los pueblos de Indios, El Pardo, 22 February 1778," ibid., 436–437; and "Real cédula sobre dotación de maestros para las escuelas del idioma Castellano en los pueblos de Indios, San Lorenzo, 5 November 1782," ibid., 500–501.

13. Campillo, *Nuevo sistema*, 73–74, 114–115.

14. "Martínez Compañón to Intendant Saavedra, Trujillo, 1 November 1785" (Trujillo: AAT: Colegios y Universidades, "Sobre la Fundación de Escuelas de Primeras Letras en Trujillo").

15. For excellent background information on Indian education in Spain and New Spain, see Dorothy Tanck de Estrada, *Pueblos de indios y educación en el México colonial, 1750–1821* (Mexico City: El Colegio de México, 1999). For Peru, Robert D. Wood's *Teach Them Good Customs* (Culver City, Calif.: Labyrinthos, 1986) is a starting point, but the literature lacks a good scholarly survey on the topic.

16. Rubén Vargas Ugarte, *Concilios Limenses, 1551–1772* (Lima: Arzobispado de Lima, 1952), 12.

17. The most comprehensive work on primary education in colonial Spanish America remains Tanck de Estrada, *Pueblos de indios*. See also Julio Ruiz Berrio, "La Educación del pueblo español en el proyecto de los ilustrados," *Revista de Educación* (1988): 165–191. The Lima Council is examined in Rubén Vargas Ugarte, *Concilios limenses, 1551–1772* (Lima: Arzobispado de Lima, 1952), 2:18. For more on the state of late colonial education in Peru, see Luis Martin, *The Intellectual Conquest of Peru: The Jesuit College of San Pablo, 1568–1767* (New York: Fordham University, 1968); Bianca Premo, *Children of the Father King: Youth, Authority, and Legal Minority in Colonial Lima* (Chapel Hill: University of North Carolina, 2005); and Daniel Valcárcel Esparza, *Historia de la educación colonial* (Lima: Editorial Universo, 1968), vol. 2.

18. Ibid. In eighteenth-century Spanish usage, *colegio* denoted an educational house of primary and secondary education—not a university, as it means in English; see *Diccionario de la Real Academia Española* (Madrid: Joachín Ibarra, 1783).

19. On elite Indian education in Cuzco, see David T. Garrett, *Shadows of Empire: The Indian Nobility of Cuzco, 1750–1825* (Cambridge: Cambridge University Press, 2005).

20. "Martínez Compañón to Charles III, Trujillo, 15 May 1786" (Trujillo: AAT, Colegios y Universidades, Erección y fundación de dos colegios).

21. "Martínez Compañón to Amados hijos mios, los Indios de este Obispado de Trujillo, 31 July 1783" (Trujillo: AAT, Colegios y Universidades, Erección y fundación de dos colegios).

22. "Martínez Compañón to Don Juan José Urteaga, Cura y Vicario de la Provincia de Chachapoyas, Trujillo, 26 June 1785" (Trujillo: AAT, Colegios y Universidades, Erección y fundación de dos colegios de cholos y cholas en Trujillo).

23. In early modern Spanish, *vos* was used more commonly than the better-known contemporary *usted*. Today throughout much of South America, *vos* has replaced *tu* but no longer carries the same deference.

24. "Martínez Compañón to Charles III, Trujillo, 15 May 1786."

25. "Town of Cajabamba to Martínez Compañón, n.d." (Trujillo: AAT, Colegios y Universidades, Erección y fundación de dos colegios).

26. "Santa Visita de Etén, 7 June 1784" (Lima: ALMR, legajo 90, #LEB-4-13, 110).

27. "Martínez Compañón to King Charles III of Spain, Trujillo, 15 May 1786."

28. Ibid. The process of funding Indian schools is discussed for the case of colonial New Spain in Tanck de Estrada, *Pueblos de indios*, esp. chap. 3.

29. "Teodoro de Croix to Martínez Compañón, Lima, 20 January 1786" (Lima: ALMR: Documentos de fundación de escuelas por el Obispo Martínez de Compañón de Trujillo, legajo 90, #LEB-4-13).

30. See James Axtell, *The Invasion Within: The Contest of Cultures in Colonial North America* (New York: Oxford University Press, 1985), esp. chap. 8.

31. "Don Gabriel Carillo to Martínez Compañón, Etén, 14 June 1784" (Lima: ALMR, Documentos de fundación de escuelas por el Obispo Martínez de Compañón de Trujillo, legajo 90, #LEB-4-13).

32. "Cabildo y Ayuntamiento de Chachapoyas to Martínez Compañón, Chachapoyas, 6 December 1782" (Lima: ALMR, Documentos de fundación de escuelas por el Obispo Martínez de Compañón de Trujillo, legajo 90, #LEB-4-13).

33. "Don Juan Fernando Coronado to Martínez Compañón, Morrope, n.d." (Lima: ALMR, Documentos de fundación de escuelas por el Obispo Martínez de Compañón de Trujillo, legajo 90, #LEB-4-13, 98r).

34. "Los Alcaldes Ordinarios de Naturales de Santa Cruz to Martínez Compañón, Santa Cruz, n.d." (Lima: ALMR, Documentos de fundación de escuelas por el Obispo Martínez de Compañón de Trujillo, legajo 90, #LEB-4-13, 80r).

35. "Don Pedro Llontop Chumbisino to Martínez Compañón, Chiclayo, 7 June 1784" (Lima: ALMR, Documentos de fundación de escuelas por el Obispo Martínez de Compañón de Trujillo, legajo 90, #LEB-4-13, 102v).

36. "Capítulos y ordenanzas generales de las escuelas fundadas y por fundar en esta diócesis de Truxillo del Perú" (Lima: ALMR, Documentos de fundación de escuelas por el Obispo Martínez de Compañón de Trujillo, legajo 90, #LEB-4-13, 121r).

37. Martínez Compañón, "Decretos de visita, Trujillo, 3 November 1785" (Seville: AGI, Estado 75, no. 109).

38. "José de Urteaga to Martínez Compañón, Chachapoyas, 9 December 1782" (Lima: ALMR, #LEB-4-13, 123r).

39. "Gregorio de Guinea to Martínez Compañón, Chachapoyas, 10 December 1782" (Lima: ALMR, #LEB-4-13, 11v).

40. "Visita a Ferreñafe, Ferreñafe, 24 November 1783" (Trujillo: AAT, Visitas).

41. Martínez Compañón, "Decretos de visita, Trujillo, 3 November 1785."

42. Thomas A. Kempis, *The Imitation of Christ* (Boston: Lincoln & Edmands, 1829), 39.

43. The inventory taken of Martínez Compañón's possessions when he arrived in Trujillo in 1779 listed several of these titles as already in his possession. He owned the nine-volume set of Granada's *Works*, two folio-size volumes of Luis Vive's *Works*, as well as copies of his *Dialogues* both in Latin and Spanish, and a copy of his Latin work *Coloquia*. He had three volumes of Plutarch's *De Viris Illustribus*, a collection of moralistic biographies of classical and biblical figures. He owned a thirty-four-volume collection of small hardbacks with speckled covers of Cicero's *Works*. "Inventario de bienes de Baltasar Jaime Martínez Compañón, Obispo de Trujillo, 1779" (Trujillo: ADL, Protocolos Notariales Siglo XVIII, Antonio del Solar, leg. 385, fols. 221v–301).

44. "Martínez Compañón to Intendant Saavedra, Trujillo, 1 November 1785" (Trujillo: AAT, Colegios y Universidades, legajo 1).

45. "Decretos de visita a Trujillo, Trujillo, 3 November 1785," 4r.

46. "Capítulos y ordenanzas generales de las escuelas fundadas y por fundar en esta diócesis de Trujillo del Perú, Trujillo, 1 December 1785" (Lima: ALMR, #LEB-4-13, 123r).

47. "Decretos de visita a Ferreñafe, Ferreñafe, 24 November 1784" (Lima: ALMR, #LEB-4-13, 91v).

48. "Advertencias particulares al nuevo maestro mayor y director de las escuelas de primeras letras de la villa de Cajamarca, Cajamarca, 20 October 1784" (Lima: ALMR, #LEB-4-13, 51r).

49. "Martínez Compañón to the Intendant of Lamas, Lamas, 28 August 1782" (Lima: ALMR, #LEB-4-13, 2r).

50. "Marqués de Salinas to Martínez Compañón, Lima, 28 May 1786" (Trujillo: AAT, Colegios y Universidades, legajo 1: "Sobre la fundación de escuelas de primeras letras en Trujillo").

51. "Fiscal Gálvez to Martínez Compañón, Lima, 20 February 1783" (Trujillo: AAT, Colegios y Universidades, legajo 1: "Sobre la fundación de escuelas de primeras letras en Trujillo," 28r).

52. "Viceroy Croix to Martínez Compañón, Lima, 9 June 1786" (Trujillo: AAT, Colegios y Universidades, legajo 1).

53. Susan E. Ramírez, "To Serve God and King: The Origins of Public Schools for Native Children in Eighteenth-Century Northern Peru," *Colonial Latin American Review* 17:1 (June 2008): 73–99. Of course, it is also possible that more extensive research in municipal archives would produce evidence of others that were successful.

54. In 1784, the plan to found a girls' school outside Cajamarca in Huamachuco began when the Bishop received a letter from the powerful Indian cacique of the area, Patricio Astopilco. Astopilco sought the Bishop's help in founding a primary school for local Indian, mestiza, and Spanish girls. He was confident that the Indian community could raise most of the necessary funding, except for the more expensive doors and windows for the building. Once Bishop Martínez Compañón came on board, the community's initial response to the proposal seemed positive: the parish priests supported it, and offers of help poured in. A Spanish militia captain offered to donate two hundred head of cattle, and two aging *beatas* said that they were available to teach classes. Martínez Compañón designated two Spaniards to oversee the project after he departed from the area. It seems that they had a difficult time persuading the Spanish majority of the area to go along with the plan: in July 1784, the Spaniards and mestizos of Cajamarca sent the Bishop a letter expressing concern about funding the project, which, in their opinion (even though this had not been part of the original plan), would require the appointment of an additional ecclesiastic to run it. Soon thereafter, the school fell from the archival records. Perhaps the Bishop had made a fatal error in placing two Spaniards in charge of a project initiated by—and largely intended to benefit— the Indian community. For documentation of this episode, see "De la erección de una beatería para niñas en la capital de Huamachuco" (Trujillo: AAT, Colegios y universidades).

55. David Weber, *Bárbaros: Spaniards and Their Savages in the Age of Enlightenment* (New Haven, Conn.: Yale University Press, 2005), 157.

56. For a good explanation of political events at the time, see John Fisher, *Bourbon Peru, 1750–1824* (Liverpool: Liverpool University Press, 2003), esp. chap. 2.

57. "Cartas de Francisco Paula Collantes y Alvaro Vietano Llanos Valdes a Martínez Compañón, Chachapoyas, June 1789" (Bogotá: ANC, Miscelánea de la Colonia III, SC-39, 210–213).

58. "Expediente sobre la remisión de 24 cajones de curiosidades de la naturaleza y del arte, recogidos por el obispo de Trujillo (hoy arzobispo de Santa Fé) y remitidas por el Virrey de Lima, venidas en la Fragata Rosa" (Seville: AGI, Lima 798).

59. "Martínez Compañón to Viceroy Croix, Lima, 9 June 1786" (Lima: ALMR, #LEB-4-13, 147r).

60. "Martínez Compañón to Andrés de Achurra, Trujillo, 26 May 1790" (Bogotá: ANC, Virreyes 7, 559–560).

61. I borrow the phrase "moral capital" from Christopher Brown's essential work on early abolitionism in the British Empire. He defines it as a "resource" that "is employed in a way that sustains the moral prestige of the actor": Christopher Leslie Brown, *Moral Capital: Foundations of British Abolitionism* (Chapel Hill: University of North Carolina Press, 2006), 457.

62. The definitive scholarship on conquest plays and religious theater in colonial Spanish America is by Louise Burkhardt: *Aztecs on Stage: Religious Theater in Colonial Mexico* (Norman: University of Oklahoma, 2011); *Nahuatl Theater*, vol. 1: *Life and Death in Colonial Mexico* (Norman: University of Oklahoma, 2004); and *Holy Wednesday: A Nahua Drama from Early Colonial Mexico* (Philadelphia: University of Pennsylvania, 1996).

CHAPTER 5. THE HUALGAYOC SILVER MINE

1. Alexander von Humboldt wrote about the frigid climate at Hualgayoc in *Views of Nature* (New York: Arno, 1975), 45.

2. Much of this chapter's background information on Hualgayoc and mining in colonial Peru is from John Fisher, *Silver Mines and Silver Miners in Colonial Peru, 1776–1824* (Liverpool: Centre for Latin American Studies, 1977). Conditions inside silver mines were described by José de Acosta, in *Natural and Moral History of the Indies*, ed. Jane Mangan (Durham, N.C.: Duke University Press, 2002), 173–181, as well as by the eighteenth-century reformer Francisco X. de Gamboa, in *Comentarios a las ordenanzas de minas, dedicados al Cathólico Rey, Nuestro Señor, Don Carlos III* (Madrid: Joachin Ibarra, 1771), later translated as *Commentaries on the Mining Ordinances of New Spain*, vol. 1 (London: Longman, Rees, Orme, Brown & Green, 1830), and by Kendall Brown, "Workers' Health and Colonial Mercury Mining at Huancavelica, Peru," *The Americas* 57:4 (April 2001): 467–496.

3. Brown, "Workers' Health," 476.

4. "Martínez Compañón to Viceroy Croix, Trujillo, 29 May 1786" (Bogotá: ANC, Miscelánea 46, doc. 20).

5. The work of the *barreteros* is described in Fisher, *Silver Mines*, 9; and Gamboa, *Commentaries*, 136. Indian terms for silver are described in Joaquín Pérez Melero, "From Alchemy to Science: The Scientific Revolution and Enlightenment in Spanish American Mining and Metallurgy," in *The Revolution in Geology from the Renaissance to the Enlightenment*, ed. Gary D. Rosenberg (Boulder, Colo.: Geological Society of America, 2009), 53. Humboldt discussed the wooden mine supports used in Peru in *Alexander von Humboldt en el Perú: Diario de viaje y otros escritos*, ed. Estuardo Núñez and Georg Petersen (Lima: Banco Central de Reserva, 2002), 57. For an excellent discussion of the tasks of various mine workers, see Carlos Contreras, *Los Mineros y el rey: Los Andes del norte: Hualgayoc, 1770–1825* (Lima: Instituto de Estudios Peruanos, 1995), chap. 3. Gamboa's quotation on the difficulty of mine work is from Gamboa, *Commentaries*, 280.

6. For an excellent general introduction to the importance of the mining sector in the imperial Spanish economy and the labor practices therein, see J. H. Elliott, *Empires of the Atlantic World: Britain and Spain in America, 1492–1830* (New Haven, Conn.: Yale University Press, 2006), 95–100; and Kendall W. Brown, *A History of Mining in Latin America from the Colonial Era to the Present* (Albuquerque: University of New Mexico Press, 2012).

7. Miners' continued requests for *mita* laborers are discussed in Fisher, *Silver Mines*, 11. It should also be noted that Potosí had not been part of Peru since the Spanish created the viceroyalty of Río de la Plata in 1776. The Bishop's quotation is from "Martínez Compañón to Viceroy Croix, Trujillo, 29 May 1786."

8. Gamboa, *Commentaries*, 110.

9. "Martínez Compañón to Viceroy Croix, Trujillo, 29 May 1786."

10. For studies of how local communities attempted to manipulate various reform efforts in Peru, see Bianca Premo, *Children of the Father King: Youth, Authority, and Legal Minority in Colonial Lima* (Chapel Hill: University of North Carolina Press, 2005); Adam Warren, *Medicine and Politics in Colonial Peru: Population Growth and the Bourbon Reforms* (Pittsburgh: University of Pittsburgh Press, 2010); and Charles Walker, *Shaky Colonialism: The 1746 Earthquake-Tsunami in Peru and Its Long Aftermath* (Durham, N.C.: Duke University Press, 2008).

11. Bartolomé Arzáns de Orsua y Vela, *Historia de la Villa Imperial de Potosí*, ed. Lewis Hanke and Gunnar Mendoza (Providence, R.I.: Brown University Press, 1965), 255.

12. "Los Mineros del asiento real de minas de Micuypampa . . . solicitan reunirse con el Obispo de Trujillo" (Bogotá: ANC, Virreyes 14, #27, 839–842).

13. "Don Joseph Thadeo Ordones to José de Gálvez, San Ildefonso, 24 September 1776" (Seville: AGI, Lima, 1130).

14. John Fisher discusses the shortage of mine workers in "Mining and the Peruvian Economy in the Late Colonial Period," in *The Economies of Mexico and Peru During the Late Colonial Period, 1760–1810*, ed. Nils Jacobsen and Hans Pulhe (Berlin: Colloquium, 1986). A watercolor image of Ignacio Amoroto's barrel-refining machine appears in *Trujillo del Perú*, vol. 2.

15. On the scarcity of mercury, see Fisher, *Silver Mines*, 20. Uralde's report can be found in "Francisco Uralde to José de Gálvez, Cerro de Hualgayoc, 24 November 1778" (Seville: AGI, Lima 1130).

16. When Areche requested the right to appoint the alcalde mayor at Hualgayoc, Jáuregui refused him the right to do so. Areche complained to José Gálvez about this matter on at least four occasions. John Fisher has determined that to Areche, "the issue was important only because it provided a further opportunity for a general attack upon excessive viceregal authority in Peru"; Fisher, *Silver Mines*, 20. The Bishop described the situation at Micuypampa in "Martínez Compañón to Viceroy Croix, Trujillo, 29 May 1786."

17. John Fisher, *Bourbon Peru, 1750–1824* (Liverpool: Liverpool University Press, 2003), 51.

18. Ibid.

19. On the process of refining silver, see Daniel Restrepo, *Sociedad y religion en Trujillo (Peru), bajo el episcopado de Baltasar Jaime Martínez Compañón, 1780–1790* (Vitoria-Gasteiz: Servicio Central de Publicaciones del Gobierno Vasco, 1992), 103. Selling it to silver merchants is described in Contreras, *Los Mineros y el rey*, 39.

20. On how production costs varied in New Spain and Peru, see Richard L. Garner, "Long-Term Silver Mining Trends in Spanish America: A Comparative Analysis of Peru and Mexico," in *Mines of Silver and Gold in the Americas*, ed. Peter Bakewell (Brookfield, Vt.: Variorum, 1997), 223. José Campillo covered mining in his *Nuevo sistema de gobierno económico para la América* (Merida, Venezuela: Universidad de los Andes, 1971), 139–140.

21. Private merchants usually offered six pesos, two reales. Though this was less than the 8.5 pesos that the miners would receive if they sold their silver at the royal mint in Lima, it saved them the risks and costs of transporting the bullion more than 500 miles down the coast; Fisher, *Silver Mines*, 41.

22. "Martínez Compañón to Viceroy Croix, Trujillo, 29 May 1786."

23. Carlos Contreras defines *quinteros* as *forastero* Indians or mestizos who made their living as smallholders or day laborers in the country. They were not *yanaconas* assigned to a large estate or *indios originarios* enrolled in a communal or corporate economic complex; Contreras, *Los Mineros y el rey*, 109.

24. For more on *habilitadores*, see ibid., 31–65.

25. "Martínez Compañón to Viceroy Croix, Trujillo, 29 May 1786."

26. Ibid.

27. Ibid.

28. "Informe sobre el sitio donde debe trasladarse la población de Los Dos Carlos (Perú)" (Bogotá: ANC, Virreyes 15).

29. Ibid.

30. For background on Azereto, see Contreras, *Los Mineros y el rey*, 102.

31. For Espinach's holdings in Cajamarca, see Julio Sarmiento Gutiérrez and Tristán Ravines Sánchez, *Cajamarca: Historia y cultura* (Camajarca: Municipalidad Provincial de Cajamarca, 2004), 84.

32. "Juan de Azereto to Martínez Compañón, Cajamarca, 1 September 1784" (Bogotá: ANC, Curas y Obispos 9, Santa Visita de Cajamarca).

33. "Miguel Espinach to Martínez Compañón, Cajamarca, 30 August 1784" (Bogotá: ANC, Curas y Obispos 9, Santa Visita de Cajamarca).

34. "Martínez Compañón to Juan de Azereto and Miguel Espinach, 3 September 1784" (Bogotá: ANC, Curas y Obispos 9, Santa Visita de Cajamarca).

35. "Juan de Azereto to Martínez Compañón, 28 September 1784" (Bogotá: ANC, Curas y Obispos 9, Santa Visita de Cajamarca).

36. "Miguel Espinach to Martínez Compañón, 10 September 1784" (Bogotá: ANC, Curas y Obispos 9, Santa Visita de Cajamarca).

37. "Juan de Azereto to Martínez Compañón, 28 September 1784."

38. "Marcelo Hernández de Villanueva to Martínez Compañón, Cajamarca, n.d." (Bogotá: ANC, Curas y Obispos 9, Santa Visita de Cajamarca).

39. "Antonio Bernal y Castro to Martínez Compañón, n.d." (Bogotá: ANC, Curas y Obispos 9, Santa Visita de Cajamarca).

40. "Juan de Azereto to Martínez Compañón, Cajamarca, 1 September 1784" (Bogotá: ANC, Curas y Obispos 9, Santa Visita de Cajamarca).

41. "Don Francisco Xavier de Villanueva to Martínez Compañón, n.d." (Bogotá: ANC, Curas y Obispos 9, Santa Visita de Cajamarca).

42. "Don Juan Pérez Prieto et al. to Martínez Compañón, n.d." (Bogotá: ANC, Curas y Obispos 9, Santa Visita de Cajamarca).

43. "Don Marcos Carhuajulca to Martínez Compañón, n.d." (Bogotá: ANC, Curas y Obispos 9, Santa Visita de Cajamarca).

44. "Antonio Bernal to Martínez Compañón, Cajamarca, n.d." (Bogotá: ANC, Curas y Obispos 9, Santa Visita de Cajamarca).

45. See Contreras, *Los Mineros y el rey*, 102.

46. For Cajamarca's bid to become a city, see "Asuntos de Gobierno #2365, 13 January 1798" (Trujillo: ADL, Intendencia, Tomo 2); and Fernando Silva Santisteban, *Cajamarca: Historia y paisaje* (Lima: Antares, 2000), 148. On various categories of civic status, see Jay Kinsbruner, *The Colonial Spanish-American City: Urban Life in the Age of Atlantic Capitalism* (Austin: University of Texas Press, 2005), 1–13.

47. "Martínez Compañón to Viceroy Croix, Trujillo, 29 May 1786."

48. K. P. Companje, R. H. M. Hendriks, K. F. E. Veraghtert, and B. E. M. Widdershoven, *Two Centuries of Solidarity: German, Belgian, and Dutch Social Health Care Insurance, 1770–2008* (Amsterdam: Aksant, 2009), 30; and C. R. Phillips, "'The Life Blood of the Navy': Recruiting Sailors in Eighteenth-Century Spain," *The Mariner's Mirror* 87:4 (November 2001): 427. For Campomanes, see discussion of his *Discurso sobre la legislación gremial de los artesanos*, in Antonio Rumeu de Armas, *Historia de la previsión social en España: Cofradías, gremios, hermandades, montepíos* (Madrid: Editorial Revista de Derecho Privado, 1944), 331.

49. Susan E. Ramírez, *Provincial Patriarchs: Land Tenure and the Economics of Power in Colonial Peru* (Albuquerque: University of New Mexico Press, 1986), 48.

50. Campillo pointed out that "precarious possession is not a possession that encourages man to work like a certain possession would; because in this way he works with the certainty that whatever improvements are made to the land, they will undoubtedly be to the benefit of his children and grandchildren"; Campillo, *Nuevo sistema*, 105.

51. "Martínez Compañón to Viceroy Croix, Trujillo, 29 May 1786."

52. "Decretos de visita a Cajamarca" (Bogotá: ANC, Virreyes 15, 83–92).

53. For additional background on Gamboa, see Christopher Albi, "Contested Legalities in Colonial Mexico: Francisco Xavier Gamboa and the Defense of Derecho Indiano" (Ph.D. thesis, University of Texas at Austin, 2009); and Doris M. Ladd, *The Making of a Strike: Mexican Silver Workers' Struggles in Real del Monte, 1766–1775* (Lincoln: University of Nebraska Press, 1988), 60–65. Almadén is described by José Parés y Franqués, *Catástrofe morboso de las minas mercuriales de la Villa de Almadén del azogue, 1778*, ed. Alfredo Menéndez Navarro (Cuenca: Ediciones de la Universidad de Castilla–La Mancha, 1998).

54. Contreras, *Los Mineros y el rey*, 84.

55. "Los Mineros del asiento real de minas de Micuypampa."

56. "Martínez Compañón to Viceroy Croix, Trujillo, 29 May 1786."

57. "Martínez Compañón to Charles III, Trujillo, 15 May 1786."

58. "Los Mineros del asiento real de minas de Micuypampa."

59. "Martínez Compañón to Viceroy Croix, Trujillo, 29 May 1786."

60. Ibid.

61. Ibid.

62. Ibid.

63. Arzáns de Orsúa y Vela, *Historia de la Villa Imperial de Potosí*, 73.

64. "Martínez Compañón to Viceroy Croix, Trujillo, 29 May 1786."

65. "Pedro Ventura de Orbegoso to Martínez Compañón, Cajamarca, 23 September 1784" (Bogotá: ANC, Curas y Obispos 9, Santa Visita de Cajamarca).

66. "Pedro de Orbegoso to Martínez Compañón, Cajamarca, 16 September 1784" (Bogotá: ANC, Curas y Obispos 9, Santa Visita de Cajamarca).

67. "Martínez Compañón to Viceroy Croix, Trujillo, 29 May 1786."

68. Ibid.

69. Ibid.

70. Ibid.

71. Contreras, *Los Mineros y el rey*, 107.

72. For *caja* income, see John J. TePaske and Herbert S. Klein, *The American Finances of the Spanish Empire: Royal Income and Expenditures in Colonial Mexico, Peru, and Bolivia, 1680–1809* (Albuquerque: University of New Mexico Press, 1998), 38–44. It should be mentioned that at least part of these increases can be explained by the combination of the Trujillo *caja* with other smaller, area *cajas*: Saña in 1776; Piura and Paita in 1779. See also Fisher, *Bourbon Peru*, 70–71.

73. John Lynch, *Bourbon Spain, 1700–1808* (Oxford: Basil Blackwell, 1989), 348.

74. For a superb study of Spanish imperial tax structures at the end of the colonial period, see Carlos Marichal, *Bankruptcy of Empire: Mexican Silver and the Wars Between Spain, Britain, and France, 1760–1810* (Cambridge: Cambridge University Press, 2007).

75. Contreras, *Los Mineros y el rey*, 62.

76. "Descripción geográfica del partido de Cajamarca en la Intendencia de Trujillo, por Don Joseph Ignacio Lecuanda, Contador de la Real Aduana de Lima," *Mercurio Peruano* 333 (30 March 1794): 210.

77. Núñez and Petersen, *Alexander von Humboldt en el Perú*, 57.

78. Miguel Molina Martínez, *El Real tribunal de minería de Lima (1785–1821)* (Seville: Diputación Provincial, 1986), 276–289.

79. "Martínez Compañón to Viceroy Croix, Trujillo, 29 May 1786."

80. The viceroy and the miners' guild soon turned against him, complaining that the new method did not offer significant improvements. Nordenflicht and his men languished, forgotten by the viceregal powers, from 1795 to 1797. See Fisher, *Bourbon Peru*, 69–70.

81. Molina Martínez, *El Real tribunal*, 87–88.

82. "Descripción geográfica del partido de Cajamarca en la Intendencia de Trujillo, por Don Joseph Ignacio Lecuanda."

83. Jorge Escobedo, "Instrucción Práctica de . . . Intendencias . . . de Truxillo" (Seville: AGI, Lima 117).

84. "Teodoro Croix to Martínez Compañón, Lima, 20 June 1786" (Bogotá: ANC, Virreyes 17, doc. 11, fol. 132).

CHAPTER 6. LOCAL BOTANY: THE PRODUCTS OF UTOPIA

1. "Expediente sobre la remisión de 24 cajones de curiosidades de la naturaleza y del arte, recognidos por el obispo de Trujillo (hoy arzobispo de Santa Fé) y remitidas por el Virrey de Lima, venidas en la Fragata Rosa" (Seville: AGI, Lima 798).

2. "Martínez Compañón to Antonio Porlier, Cartagena, 13 December 1790" (Seville: AGI, Lima 798).

3. Ibid.

4. Paula De Vos, "Natural History and the Pursuit of Empire in Eighteenth-Century Spain," *Eighteenth-Century Studies* 40:2 (2007): 209.

5. A 1789 letter to Antonio Porlier proves that the specimens were shipped to the garden: "Manuel González Guisal to Antonio Porlier, Cádiz, 14 August 1789" (Seville: AGI, Lima 978). A 2010 research trip to the Archive and Herbarium of the Garden confirmed that there is no extant record of them.

6. "Martínez Compañón to Antonio Porlier, Cartagena, 13 December 1790."

7. "Expediente sobre la remisión de 24 cajones de curiosidades de la naturaleza y del arte."

8. Visceral leishmaniasis, an internal infection of the organs caused by the same parasite, is not typically found in Latin America. Susan Campbell, "Insect-Borne Diseases and Their Prevention," *Primary Health Care* 18:6 (2008): 25. For general information about the disease, see Arfan ul Bari, "Chronology of Cutaneous Leishmaniasis: An Overview of the History of the Disease," *Journal of Pakistan Association of Dermatologists* 16 (2006): 24–27; Bertha Pareja and Ana Maria Muñoz, "Dermofarmacia: Plantas medicinales empleadas en el tratamiento de la leishmaniasis," *Folia Dermatológia Peruana* 14 (2003): 10–14; and Kenneth Wener, "Leishmaniasis" (U.S. National Library of Medicine and the National Institutes of Health), http://www.nlm.nih.gov/medlineplus/ency/article /001386.htm.

9. Gender distribution of leishmaniasis cases is discussed in Carmen M. Lucas et al., "Geographic Distribution and Clinical Description of Leishmaniasis Cases in Peru," *American Journal of Tropical Medicine and Hygiene* 59:2 (1998): 316. The ethnopharmacological work in the Loreto region is the subject of L. P. Kvist et al., "Identification and Evaluation of Peruvian Plants Used to Treat Malaria and Leishmaniasis," *Journal of Ethnopharmacology* 106 (2006): 394. Here the plant is referred to by an alternate spelling: *ajo sacha*.

10. See Robert E. Sniden, "Malaria, Mosquitoes, and the Legacy of Ronald Ross," *Bulletin of the World Health Organization* 85:11 (2007): 894–896; and J. Erin Staples and Thomas P. Monath, "Yellow Fever: 100 Years of Discovery," *Journal of the American Medical Association* 300:8 (2008): 960–962.

11. Much of the most important work on Creole science in Spanish America is by Jorge Cañizares-Esguerra, including the collection of his essays, *Nature, Empire, and Nation: Explorations in the History of Science in the Iberian World* (Stanford, Calif.: Stanford University Press, 2006), and *How to Write the History of the New World: Histories, Epistemologies, and Identities in the Eighteenth-Century Atlantic World* (Stanford, Calif.: Stanford University Press, 2001). See also Antonio Lafuente, "Enlightenment in an Imperial Context: Local Science in the Late-Eighteenth-Century Hispanic World," *Osiris* 15 (October 2000): 155–174; and Antonio Lafuente and Nuria Valverde, "Linnaean Botany and Spanish Imperial Biopolitics," in *Colonial Botany: Science, Commerce, and Politics in the Early Modern World*, ed. Londa Schiebinger and Claudia Swan (Philadelphia: University of Pennsylvania, 2005). For José Eusebio Llano Zapata, see *Memorias histórico, físicas, crítico, apologéticas de la América Meridional*, ed. Charles Walker et al. (Lima: Instituto Francés de Estudios Andinos, 2005), which includes a good selection of critical essays. On Huerta, see Cañizares-Esguerra, "Spanish America: From Baroque to Modern Colonial Science," in *Nature, Empire, and Nation*, 46–64. For Hipólito Unanue, see his *Guia política, ecclesiastica y militar del virreynato del Perú, para el año de 1793*, ed. José Durand (Lima: Academia Nacional de la Historia, 1985). For secondary literature, see Joseph Alva Dager, *Hipólito Unanue, o el cambio en la continuidad* (Lima: Convenio Hipólito Unanue, 2000); Jorge Cañizares-Esguerra, "La Utopia de Hipólito Unanue: Comercio, naturaleza, y religión en el Perú," in *Saberes andinos: Ciencia y tecnología en Bolivia, Ecuador, y Perú*, ed. Marcos Cueto (Lima: Instituto de Estudios Peruanos, 1995).

The *Mercurio Peruano*, Amantes del País society, and the intellectual culture of late eighteenth-century Peru are the subjects of Rosa Zeta Quinde, *El Pensamiento ilustrado en el Mercurio Peruano, 1791–1794* (Piura: Universidad de Piura, 2000). *La Ilustración en América colonial*, ed. Diana Soto Arango et al. (Madrid: Ediciones Doce Calles, 1995), touches on many of the same matters, with a broader focus on different regions of Spanish America.

12. On the Badianus Codex, see Antonio Barrera-Osorio, "Knowledge and Empiricism in the Sixteenth-Century Spanish Atlantic World," in *Science in the Spanish and Portuguese Empires, 1500–1800*, ed. Daniela Bleichmar et al. (Stanford, Calif.: Stanford University Press, 2009), 228; Martinus de la Cruz, *The Badianus Manuscript: An Aztec Herbal of 1552 (Codex Barberini, Latin 241) Vatican Library*, trans. Emily Walcott Emmart (Baltimore: Johns Hopkins University Press, 1940); and Donald Robertson, *Mexican Manuscript Painting of the Early Colonial Period: The Metropolitan Schools* (Norman: University of Oklahoma Press, 1959). For Monardes, see Agnes Arber, *Herbals: Their Origin and Evolution: A Chapter in the History of Botany, 1470–1670* (Cambridge: Cambridge University Press, 1938); Charles Boxer, "Two Pioneers of Tropical Medicine: Garcia d'Orta and Nicolás Monardes" (paper presented at the Wellcome Historical Medical Library, 1963); Francisco Guerra, *Nicolás Bautista Monardes: Su vida y su obra* (Mexico City: Compañia Fundadora de Fierry y Acerro de Monterrey, 1961); Nicolás Monardes, *Todas las cosas que traen de nuestras Indias Occidentales* (Seville: Hernando Díaz, 1569); and Nicolás Monardes, *Joyfull Newes Out of the Newe Founde Worlde. Written in Spanish by Nicholas Monardes . . . 1577*, ed. Charles Whibley (London: Constable, 1925). The king's instructions to Hernández can be found in "Letter to Francisco Hernández from King Philip II, 11 January 1570," quoted in *The Mexican Treasury: The Writings of Dr. Francisco Hernández*, ed. Simon Varey (Stanford, Calif.: Stanford University Press, 2000), 46.

13. Lázaro de Ribera, *Moxos: Descripciones exactas e historia fiel de los indios, animales y plantas de la provincia de Moxos en el virreinato del Perú por Lázaro de Ribera, 1786–1794*, ed. Mercedes Palau and Blanca Sáiz (Madrid: Ministerio de Agricultura, Pesca, y Alimentación, 1989); and Llano Zapata, *Memorias histórico*, ed. Walker et al., 77.

14. Often art historians of colonial Spanish America believe that unsigned images indicate that the individuals who created them were indigenous and therefore not considered "true" artists worthy of commemoration. For this issue, see Carolyn Dean, *Inka Bodies and the Body of Christ: Corpus Christi in Colonial Cuzco, Peru* (Durham, N.C.: Duke University Press, 1999), 63–97.

15. This is a central argument of Neil Safier, *Measuring the New World: Enlightenment Science and South America* (Chicago: University of Chicago Press, 2008).

16. On Ruiz and Pavón, see F. Muñoz Garmendia, ed., *La Botánica al servicio de la corona: La Expedición de Ruiz, Pavón, y Dombey al virreinato del Perú (1777–1788)* (Madrid: Caja Madrid Obra Social y Lunwerg Editores, 2003); and Arthur Robert Steele, *Flowers for the King: The Expedition of Ruiz and Pavón and the Flora of Peru* (Durham, N.C.: Duke University Press, 1964). For Mutis, see Daniela Bleichmar, *Visible Empire:*

Botanical Expeditions and Visual Culture in the Hispanic Enlightenment (Chicago: University of Chicago Press, 2012), and "Painting as Exploration: Visualizing Nature in Eighteenth-Century Colonial Science," *Colonial Latin American Review* 15:1 (2006): 81–104. See also Marcelo Frías Núñez, *Tras el dorado vegetal: José Celestino Mutis y la Real Expedición Botánica del Nuevo Reino de Granada (1783–1808)* (Seville: Diputación de Seville, 1994); and Antonio González Bueno, *Plantas americanas para la España ilustrada: Genésis, desarollo, y ocaso del proyecto español de expediciones botánicas* (Madrid: Editorial Complutense, 2000).

17. This is a major theme of Susan Scott Parrish, *American Curiosity: Cultures of Natural History in the Colonial British Atlantic World* (Chapel Hill: University of North Carolina Press, 2006).

18. "Pastoral Letter of Martínez Compañón, Trujillo, 14 April 1782" (Seville: AGI, Cartas y expedientes: Curiosidades para el Jardín Botánico, Lima 798).

19. For more information on the *Relacíones*, see Barbara Mundy, *The Mapping of New Spain: Indigenous Cartography and the Maps of the Relacíones Geográficas* (Chicago: University of Chicago Press, 1996). For Mutis's workshop, see Bleichmar, *Visible Empire*, 79–123.

20. While he might have turned to local healers (*curanderos*) for information on materia medica, the Bishop presumably would not have contacted the men he referred to as "witch doctors" (*hechiceros*), as he dismissed these individuals as "lazy, drunk, lascivious, lying, and abandoned to all types of vice." He declared that they had no training in medicine and lacked medical knowledge. "Martínez Compañón to Amados Hijos Mios, Los Indios de Este Obispado de Trujillo, Trujillo, 31 July 1783" (Trujillo: AAT, Colegios y Universidades, Erección y fundación de dos colegios).

21. This notation has been omitted in the reproductions of the watercolors available from the Biblioteca Cervantes and the set of nine volumes published by the Spanish Ministry of Culture, but it remains on the original held in the Royal Palace Library in Madrid.

22. "Pastoral Letter of Martínez Compañón, Trujillo, 14 April 1782."

23. Martínez Compañón made a common spelling error (confusing a *V* for a *B*) when he wrote *Vormio* instead of *Borromeo*. "Martínez Compañón to Agustín Hermenegildo de Querejazu, Trujillo, 1788" (Lima: AGNP, Correspondencia D1-25-727). On Borromeo's workshop, see *Federico Borromeo: Sacred Painting/Museum*, ed. Kenneth S. Roswell (Cambridge, Mass.: Harvard University Press, 2010), 207.

24. Bleichmar, *Visible Empire*, 103–122.

25. Casimiro Gómez Ortega, "Instrucción sobre el modo más seguro y económico de transportar plantas vivas por mar y tierra á los países más distantes," Biblioteca Virtual Miguel Cervantes, http://www.cervantesvirtual.com/FichaObra.html?Ref=1066.

26. Julián Martínez Ruíz et al., *Catálogo género de individuos de la Real Sociedad Bascongada de los Amigos del País* (San Sebastian: RSBAP, 1985), 77.

27. Real Sociedad Bascongada de los Amigos del País, "Extractos del año, 1780," quoted in Maria Theresa Barrola Recarte, *Ilustración vasca y renovación educativa. La Real*

Sociedad Bascongada de los Amigos del País (Salamanca: Universidad Pontificia, 1990), 106–107.

28. José Gumilla, *El Orinoco ilustrado* (Madrid: M. Aguilar, 1945), 2:129. For background on the text, see Margaret R. Ewalt, *Peripheral Wonders: Nature, Knowledge, and Enlightenment in Eighteenth-Century Orinoco* (Lewisburg, Pa.: Bucknell University Press, 2008), 17–24. Joseph Quer, *Continuación de la flora española, o historia de las plantas de España, que escribió Don Joseph Quer . . . con encargo y dirección de su Real Protomedicato, por el Dr. Don Casimiro Gómez de Ortega*, vol. 6 (Madrid: Joachim Ibarra, Impresor de Cámara de S.M., 1774); see, esp., the avocado tree on 77 and the *queria hispanica* on 334. About Quer's work, see Antonio González Bueno and F. J. Puerto Sarmiento, "Ciencia y farmácia durante la Ilustración," in *Carlos III y la ciencia de la Ilustración*, ed. Manuel Selles, José Luis Peset, and Antonio Lafuente (Madrid: Alianza Editorial, 1988).

29. Kapil Raj, *Relocating Modern Science: Circulation and the Construction of Knowledge in South Asia and Europe, 1650–1900* (New York: Palgrave Macmillan, 2007), 48.

30. A note in pencil on the inside cover of vol. 5 says, "volume nine, medicinal plants." This suggests that the Bishop changed his mind about the importance of the plant volumes; he had originally intended for them to appear at the end of the set but moved them up so that they appeared third, following the volume introducing Trujillo's ecclesiastics and royal functionaries and the volume pertaining to quotidian life in Trujillo.

31. "Martínez Compañón to Agustín Hermenegildo de Querejazu, Trujillo, 29 April 1790" (Lima: AGNP, Correspondencia D1-25-727).

32. Guillermo Lohman Villena, ed., *Un Tríptico del Perú virreinal: El Virrey Amat, el Marqués de Soto Florido y la Perricholi: El Drama de dos palanganas y su circunstancia* (Chapel Hill: University of North Carolina Press, 1976), 43–47.

33. "Martínez Compañón to Antonio Hermenegildo de Querejazu, Trujillo, 25 July 1788" (Lima: Archivo Histórico Nacional, Colección Francisco Moyrera Matute, #564).

34. Víctor Peralta Ruíz, "Lecuanda y Escarsaga, José Ignacio," in *Diccionario biográfico español* (Madrid: Real Academia Histórica, forthcoming). Lecuanda appears to have made use of his uncle's research to write his "Geographical Description of the City and Partido of Trujillo," which appeared in the *Mercurio Peruano* on May 16, 1793. He later published similar descriptions of Piura and Cajamarca, discussing geography, cities, the outfits, occupations, and customs of local inhabitants, flora, fauna, and the same themes as Martínez Compañón's nine volumes. For a discussion of his artistic activities after his return to Spain, see Bleichmar, *Visible Empire*, 174–184.

35. Jorge Escobedo, "Instrucción práctica que para adaptar la nueva Real Ordenanza de Intendencias se da por el Tribunal de Visita al Senor Don Fernando Saavedra que va a servir la de Trujillo" (Seville: AGI, Lima 117).

36. "Martínez Compañón to Antonio Porlier, Cartagena, 13 December 1790." See also "Oficios que dirigió Martínez Compañón antes de su partida, Actas del Cabildo Eclesiástico, Trujillo, 22 June 1790" (Trujillo: AAT, Actas del Cabildo Eclesiástico).

37. Martínez Compañón to Viceroy Croix, Trujillo, 2 December 1788." See also "Expediente sobre la remisión de 24 cajones de curiosidades de la naturaleza y del arte."

38. Martínez Compañón to Antonio Porlier, Cartagena, 13 December 1790."

39. "Letter from El Escorial to Martínez Compañón, San Lorenzo, 29 October 1789" (Seville: AGI, Lima 798).

40. We know that the botanical specimens did arrive at the Royal Botanical Garden. See "Manuel González Guisal to Antonio Porlier, Cádiz, 14 August 1789" (Seville: AGI, Lima 978, Cartas y Expedientes: Curiosidades para el Jardín Botánico). The quinine samples made it to the Royal Pharmacy, where, as was customary, they would have been mixed with other similar specimens. See "Letter to Marqués de Valdecaranza, Escorial Palace, 15 December 1789" (Seville: AGI, Lima 798, Cartas y Expedientes: Curiosidades para el Jardín Botánico).

41. Chorographies became popular in the Renaissance when early modern scholars looked back to the works of Pliny and Herodotus. The genre was based on maps that showed cityscapes or focused on regions. These maps were thought to complement traditional geographical ones, and Philip II commissioned both chorographic and geographical maps as part of the *Relaciones Geográficas* project. In early modern Germany, academics surveyed regional flora and published botanical chorographies that cataloged and depicted the productions of nature in order to share them with the outside world. For the roots of chorography as a discipline, see Stan Mendyk, "Early British Chorography," *The Sixteenth Century Journal* 17:4 (winter 1986): 459–481. On Philip II and the complementary nature of chorographic and geographic maps, see Mundy, *The Mapping of New Spain*, 3–5. On Germany, see Alix Cooper, *Inventing the Indigenous: Local Knowledge and Natural History in Early Modern Europe* (Cambridge: Cambridge University Press, 2007).

42. On cascarilla, see Londa Schiebinger, "Prospecting for Drugs: European Naturalists in the West Indies," in *Colonial Botany*, ed. Schiebinger and Swan, 127. For Porlier's cascarilla initiative, see Marcos Guimera Peraza, "Don Antonio Porlier, Marqués de Bajamar," *Anuario de Estudios Atlánticos* 27 (1981): 152. Mutis and cascarilla are discussed in Antonio González Bueno, "Deseos y realidades: De la América apetecida a la materialidad americana," in *La Botánica al servicio de la corona: La Expedición de Ruiz, Pavón, y Dombey al virreynato del Perú (1777–1831)*, ed. Félix Muñoz Garmendia (Madrid: Caja Madrid Obra Social y Lunwerg Editores, 2003), 125; and Enrique Pérez Arbeláez, *José Celestino Mutis y la Real Expedición Botánica del Nuevo Reino de Granada* (Bogotá: Antares, 1967), 12.

43. For Martínez Compañón's work with cascarilla, see "Expediente sobre la remisión de 24 cajones de curiosidades de la naturaleza y del arte" and "Martínez Compañón to Charles III, Trujillo, 1 October 1786," as printed in *Mercurio Peruano* 11 (1 May 1794): 1–7.

44. "Las Vidas de los Obispos de Trujillo" (Trujillo: AAT, Actas del Cabildo Eclesiástico, 1790). See also Escobedo, "Instrucción Práctica."

45. "Martínez Compañón to Charles III, Trujillo, 1 October 1786."

46. Susanne Alchon defines *mal del valle* in *Life and Death in Early Colonial Ecuador* (Norman: University of Oklahoma Press, 1995), 366.

47. "Martínez Compañón to Agustín Hermenegildo de Querejazu, Lambayeque, 22 December 1783" (Lima: AGNP, Colección Francisco Moyrera Matute, #564).

48. Londa Schiebinger, *Plants and Empire: Colonial Bioprospecting in the Atlantic World* (Cambridge, Mass.: Harvard University Press, 2004), 129.

49. Ibid., 118–119. See *Diccionario de la Real Academia Española de la Lengua*, s.v. "aborto," 1770, www.drae.es.

50. "Disposiciones sobre el culto Católico para las distintas parroquías de su diócesis, dictadas por el Excelentisimo Baltasar Jaime Martínez Compañón" (Bogotá: ANC, Virreyes 10, doc. 15, 525–594).

51. On coca, see Hipólito Unanue, "Disertación sobre el aspecto, cultivo, comercio, y virtudes de la famosa planta del Perú nombrada COCA," *Mercurio Peruano* 11 (1794); and Catherine J. Allen, *The Hold Life Has: Coca and Cultural Identity in an Andean Community* (Washington, D.C.: Smithsonian Books, 1988).

52. "Expediente sobre la remisión de 24 cajones de curiosidades de la naturaleza y del arte."

53. Aurelio Carmona Cruz, "Etiología y tratamiento de la [sic] enfermedades psicosomáticas en la cultura Andina," online publication (http://www.ciberjure.com.pe/index.php?option=com_content&task=view&id=2355&Itemid=9).

54. "Martínez Compañón to Amados Hijos Mios, los Indios de Este Obispado de Trujillo, Trujillo, 31 July 1783" (Trujillo: AAT, Colegios y Universidades, Erección y fundación de dos colegios).

55. As it is a predominantly oral language with significant regional variations, orthography in Quechua remains unstandardized to this day. This means that *cs* and *ks* are interchangeable, as are *us* and *hs*; and vowels can be reduced to *u*, *a*, and *e* sounds. Spanish or Creole commentators from the viceregal period were quite liberal with their spellings of Quechua words, a fact that has caused no small degree of confusion. Thus, while all the snakes shown in this section of volume 4 are labeled as different species of *machacuai* ("snakes"), a careful interpretation of the *omeco-machacuai* image explores the various meanings of different spellings. One alternate spelling of *omeco* is *umayku*, which sounds quite similar to *omeco* when verbalized but actually means "my head." *Machacuai* is a personalized form of the verb *machay*, "to become inebriated." Therefore, the name of the snake may be interpreted as the "my head makes me inebriated" snake.

56. For more on snakes and ayahuasca visions, see Marlene Dobkin de Rios, *Visionary Vine: Psychedelic Healing in the Peruvian Amazon* (San Francisco: Chandler, 1972), and "Plant Hallucinogens and the Religion of the Mochica, an Ancient Peruvian People," *Economic Botany* 31 (April–June 1977): 189–203; and Angelika Gebhart-Sayer, "Una Terapia estética: Los Diseños visionarios del ayahuasca entre los Shipibo-Conibo," *América Indígena* 46:1 (1986): 189–218.

57. "Letter from El Escorial to Martínez Compañón, San Lorenzo, 29 October 1789."

58. "Manuel González Guisal to Antonio Porlier, Cádiz, 14 August 1789." The shipment is acknowledged in "Letter to Marqués de Valdecaranza, Escorial Palace, 15 December 1789" (Seville: AGI, Lima, 798, Cartas y Expedientes: Curiosidades para el Jardín Botánico).

59. For information on the expedition and the publications of its results, I relied on Steele, *Flowers for the King*, esp. 225–240.

60. Paula De Vos, "Research, Development, and Empire: State Support of Science in the Later Spanish Empire," *Colonial Latin American Review* 15:1 (June 2006): 70.

61. Jean Jacques Rousseau, *Letters on the Elements of Botany* (London: n.p., 1785), 2–9.

62. On the "universality" of the Linnaean system, see Lisbet Koerner, *Linnaeus: Nature and Nation* (Cambridge, Mass.: Harvard University Press, 1999); and Lafuente and Valverde, "Linnaean Botany," 136. The Ruiz and Pavón orders: "Instrucción a que deberán arreglarse los sugetos destinados por S.M. para pasar a la América meridional en compañia del Médico Don Josef Dombey a fin de reconocer las plantas, y yerbas y de hacer observaciones botánicas en aquellos países," repr. in A. J. Barreiro, *Relación del viaje hecho a los reynos del Perú y Chile por los botánicos y dibuxantes enviados para aquella expedición, extractado de los diarios por el orden que llevó en estos su autor Don Hipólito Ruiz* (Madrid: n.p., 1931), 365–378. The archival records containing the Ruiz and Pavón descriptions can be found at "Descripciones originales por J. Tafalla y Y. Manzanilla de la Flora Peruana y Guayaquilense" (Madrid: Archivo del Real Jardín Botánico [hereafter, ARJB], Expedición de Ruiz y Pavón, RJB04/0013/0004). For related secondary analysis, see Lafuente and Valverde, "Linnaean Botany," 138.

63. On local manifestations of scientific culture in Peru, see the recent edition of Llano Zapata's *Memorias histórico*, ed. Walker et al.; Jorge Cañizares-Esguerra, "Spanish America: From Baroque to Modern Colonial Science," in *The Cambridge History of Science*, vol. 4: *Eighteenth-Century Science*, ed. Roy Porter (Cambridge: Cambridge University Press, 2003); and Lafuente and Valverde, "Linnaean Botany," 139.

64. "Martínez Compañón to Don Juan José Urteaga, Cura y Vicario de la Provincia de Chachapoyas, Trujillo, 26 June 1785" (Trujillo: AAT, Colegios y Universidades 1, Erección y fundación de dos colegios de cholos y cholas en Trujillo).

CHAPTER 7. THE LEGACY OF MARTÍNEZ COMPAÑÓN

1. The *retablo* of San Francisco is described in Julián Vargas Lesmes, *Historia de Bogotá: Conquista y colonia* (Bogotá: Villegas Editores, 2007), 104; and Santiago Sebastián, *Estudios sobre el arte y arquitectura coloniales en Colombia* (Bogotá: Corporación la Candelaria, 2006), 89.

2. Padre Fray Fermín Ibañez, *Oración funebre que, en las solemnes exequias dedicadas en el convento máximo de San Francisco de Santa Fé de Bogotá a la feliz memoria del Ilmo. Señor D. Baltasar Jayme Martínez Compañón, Arzobispo que fue de esta Metropoli* (Bogotá: Imprenta Patriotica, 1797).

3. Ibid., 1.

4. Ibid., 3–17.

5. Fernando Caycedo y Florez, "Oración funebre, que en las solemnes exequias funerales hechas por el monasterio de la Enseñanza de Santa Fé de Bogotá; a su insigne benefactor y padre, el ilustrísimo Señor Arzobispo de esta metropolitana, D. Baltasar Jaime Martínez Compañón, de gloriosa memoria. Dixo el D.D. Fernando Caycedo y Flórez, cura rector de dicha Santa Iglesia Cathedral, el día 18 de Noviembre de 1797," in *Fundación del Monasterio de la Enseñanza, de Monjas Benitas, llamadas esclavas de la Virgen, establecidas en la ciudad de Santafé de Bogotá el año de MDCCLXXXIII* (Bogotá: Monasterio de la Enseñanza, 1802), 111.

6. Antón M. Pazos and Daniel Restrepo Manrique, "Acción de Martínez Compañón en Perú y Nueva Granada," in *Los Vascos y América: Ideas, hechos, hombres*, ed. Ignacio Pérez Arana (Madrid: Espasa-Calpe, 1990), 341.

7. José Manuel Pérez Ayala, *Baltasar Jaime Martínez Compañón y Bujanda, prelado español de Colombia y el Peru* (Bogotá: Imprenta Nacional, 1955), 131.

8. Ibid., 133.

9. José Maria Caballero, *Diario* (Bogotá: Fundación Editorial Epígrafe Ebook, 2006), 31.

10. Caballero described the archbishop's funeral procession: ibid., 31. In 1805, an earthquake so badly damaged Bogotá's cathedral that it had to be demolished. Presumably, the Bishop's body was lost at this time, as cathedral staff today do not know its location. See also Julián Vargas Lesmes, *Historia de Bogotá: Conquista y colonia* (Bogotá: Villegas Editores, 2007), 106. For Catholic funeral traditions, see *New Catholic Encyclopedia* (New York: McGraw Hill, 1967), s.v. "funeral," 6:225–226. José Celestino Mutis's introduction to Florez's eulogy, "Censura del Señor Doctor Don Joseph Celestino Mutis . . . Bogotá, 20 December 1797," can be found in Caycedo y Florez, "Oración funebre," 85.

11. Caycedo y Florez, "Oración funebre," 107.

12. "Martínez Compañón to Agustín Hermenegildo de Querejazu, Trujillo, 10 June 1790" (Trujillo: AAT, Comunicaciones Eclesiásticas, 1778–1790, "La Despedida").

13. "Martínez Compañón to Antonio Hermenegildo de Querejazu, Trujillo, 10 October 1789" (Lima: AGNP, Colección Francisco Moyrera Matute, #564).

14. "Martínez Compañón to Viceroy Croix, Trujillo, 25 July 1785" (Bogotá: ANC, Virreyes 17, 432–433).

15. "Martínez Compañón to Andrés de Achurra, Trujillo, 12 April 1790" (Trujillo: AAT, Comunicaciones Eclesiásticas, 1778–1790, "La Despedida").

16. "Martínez Compañón to Viceroy Croix, Trujillo, 25 July 1785."

17. "Informe hecho acerca de las conclusiones que ha sacado de la visita general personal que realizó, 1789" (Lima: AAL, Papeles Importantes 1559–1924, legajo 23, doc. 22, 1789).

18. "Decretos de visita, Trujillo, 3 August 1786" (Trujillo: AAT, Comunicaciones Eclesiásticas, K:1:15).

19. "Pastoral Letter of Martínez Compañón, Trujillo, 22 April 1799" (Trujillo: AAT, Comunicaciones Eclesiásticas, K:1:15).

20. "Informe Hecho acerca de las conclusiones que ha sacado de la visita general personal que realizó . . . Trujillo, 28 April 1789" (Lima: AAL, Papeles Importantes 1559–1924, legajo 23, doc. 22: 30, 1789).

21. Patricia H. Marks, *Deconstructing Legitimacy: Viceroys, Merchants, and the Military in Late Colonial Peru* (University Park: Pennsylvania State University Press, 2007), 25.

22. "Martínez Compañón to Andrés de Achurra, Trujillo, 27 May 1790" (Trujillo: AAT, Communicaciones Eclesiásticas, "La Despedida").

23. "Martínez Compañón to Agustín Hermenegildo de Querejazu, Trujillo, 25 May 1789" (Lima: AGNP, Colección Francisco Moyrera Matute, #564).

24. "Martínez Compañón to Antonio Hermenegildo de Querejazu, Trujillo, 10 May 1780" (Lima: AGNP, Correspondencia, D1-25-727).

25. "Martínez Compañón to Agustín Hermenegildo de Querejazu, Trujillo, 10 April 1785" (Lima: AGNP, Colección Francisco Moyrera Matute, #564).

26. "Martínez Compañón to Viceroy Croix, Trujillo, 25 July 1785."

27. Martínez Compañón to Agustín Hermenegildo de Querejazu, Trujillo, 10 June 1789" (Lima: AGNP, Colección Francisco Moyrera Matute, #564).

28. "Martínez Compañón to Agustín Hermenegildo de Querejazu, Trujillo, 25 March 1790" (Lima: AGNP, Colección Francisco Moyrera Matute, #564).

29. "Martínez Compañón to Agustín Hermenegildo de Querejazu, Trujillo, 10 August 1780" (Lima: AGNP, Colección Francisco Moyrera Matute, #564).

30. Pérez Ayala, *Baltasar Jaime Martínez Compañón y Bujanda*, 20.

31. Joanne Pillsbury and Lisa Trever, "The King, the Bishop, and the Creation of an American Antiquity," *Ñawpa Pacha* 29 (2008): 193.

32. "Actas de Cabildo, 22 June 1790, Oficios que Dirigió Martínez Compañón antes de su partida" (Trujillo: AAT, Actas de Cabildo Eclesiástico).

33. Herbert Klein, *The American Finances of the Spanish Empire: Royal Income and Expenditures in Colonial Mexico, Peru, and Bolivia, 1680–1809* (Albuquerque: University of New Mexico, 1988), 38–43.

34. "Martínez Compañón to Viceroy Croix, Trujillo, 25 July 1785."

35. "Actas de Cabildo: Las Vidas de los Obispos" (Trujillo: AAT, Actas de Cabildo Eclesiástico).

36. "Descripción de la Intendencia de Trujillo, por la Expedición Hidrográfica" (Madrid: Archivo del Museo Naval de España [hereafter, AMN], Peru, Chile 7/Buenos Aires 1: ms. 119, doc. 6.9, pp. 244–254).

37. Martínez Compañón, "Decretos de visita, Trujillo, 3 November 1785" (Seville: AGI, Estado 75, no. 109).

38. "Martínez Compañón to Agustín Hermenegildo de Querejazu, Trujillo, 25 March 1790. (Lima: AGNP, Colección Francisco Moyrera Matute, #564).

39. "Actas de Cabildo, 22 June 1790, Oficios que Dirigó Martínez Compañón antes de su partida."

40. As discussed in Chapter 2 of this volume.

41. For a good description of the Toledan reforms and their negative effects on the native population, see Kenneth Andrien, *Andean Worlds: Indigenous History, Culture, and Consciousness Under Spanish Rule, 1532–1825* (Albuquerque: University of New Mexico Press, 2001), chap. 3. A more recent interpretation is Jeremy Mumford, *Vertical Empire: The General Resettlement of Indians in the Colonial Andes* (Durham, N.C.: Duke University Press, 2012).

42. Daniel Restrepo Manrique, *Sociedad y religión en Trujillo (Perú) bajo el episcopado de Baltasar Jaime Martínez Compañón, 1780–1790* (Vitoria-Gasteiz: Servicio Central de Publicaciones, Gobierno Vasco, 1992), 49–53.

43. Roberto Levillier, *Santo Toribio Alfonso Mogrovejo: Arzobispo de los reyes (1581–1606): Organizador de la iglesia en el virreinato del Perú* (Madrid: Sucesores de Rivadeneyra, 1920), 5.

44. See vol. 2 of *Trujillo del Perú*, "Plan que Contiene 43 Voces Castellanas traducidas a las ocho lenguas que hablan los Indios de la Costa, Sierras, y Montañas del Obispado del Trujillo del Perú."

45. "Actas de Cabildo: Las Vidas de los Obispos."

46. Daniel Restrepo Manrique, "Plan Reformador del Obispo Martínez Compañón," in "La Obra de Obispo Martínez Compañón sobre Trujillo del Perú en el siglo XVII," in Baltasar Jaime Martínez Compañón y Bujanda, *Trujillo del Perú: Appendice II* (Madrid: Ediciones Cultural Hispánica del Centro Iberoamericano de Cooperación, 1994), 108.

47. Caycedo y Florez, "Oración funebre," 97.

48. "Martínez Compañón to Agustín Hermenegildo de Querejazu, Trujillo, 25 July 1789" (Trujillo: Archivo Histórico Nacional, Colección Francisco Moyrera Matute, #564).

49. Information on this trip available in Pazos and Restrepo, "Acción de Martínez Compañón," 338.

50. On the Honda region, see Ángela Inés Guzmán, *La Ciudad del río Honda* (Bogotá: Unibiblios, 2002), 57. The Archbishop's entrance is described in "Noticias Particulares," *Papel Periódico de Santa Fé de Bogotá* 1:1 (February 9, 1791): 4.

51. "Noticias Particulares," *Papel Periódico de Santa Fé de Bogotá* 1:1 (February 9, 1791): 4.

52. "Noticias Particulares," *Papel Periódico de Santa Fé de Bogotá* 1:6 (March 8, 1791): 47–48.

53. Francisco Silvestre, *Descripción del reyno de Santa Fé de Bogotá*, ed. Ricardo S. Pereira (Bogotá: Ministerio de Educación Nacional, 1950), 40.

54. For background on Bogotá, see Anthony McFarlane, *Colombia Before Independence: Economy, Society, and Politics Under Bourbon Rule* (New York: Cambridge University Press, 1993). See also "Martínez Compañón to Viceroy Ezpeleta, Santa Fé, 9 August 1791" (Bogotá: ANC, Curas y Obispos #0037, caja 51, carpeta 1, fols. 78–82).

55. The story about Martínez Compañón missing Mass is from Pérez Ayala, *Baltasar Jaime Martínez Compañón y Bujanda*, 56. To remedy the troublesome distance of his official residence from the cathedral, the Bishop eventually purchased another house that would serve as his home until he died. He then ceded the old archbishop's palace to the city mint, which needed the space to expand. Pazos and Restrepo, "Acción de Martínez Compañón," 338. On the incessant warfare of the period, see John Lynch, *Bourbon Spain, 1700–1808* (Oxford: Basil Blackwell, 1989), 395. Martínez Compañón's pledge to the war effort appears in "Lista Donativo," *Papel Periódico de Santa Fé de Bogotá*, 3:100 (26 July 1793): 379.

56. For general information on the Pasquinades Rebellion, see McFarlane, *Colombia Before Independence*, chap. 10.

57. Quoted in Pérez Ayala, *Baltasar Jaime Martínez Compañón y Bujanda*, 111–112.

58. Ezpeleta eventually followed his suggestion, and by June 1799, the young men had been released from prison; Pazos and Restrepo, "Acción de Martínez Compañón," 339.

59. Pérez Ayala, *Baltasar Jaime Martínez Compañón y Bujanda*, 111–112.

60. "Martínez Compañón al Virrey de Santa Fé sobre Tumultos, Bogotá" (Seville: AGI, Estado 52, no. 25, doc. 3).

61. See McFarlane, *Colombia Before Independence*, 214–216.

62. The Pasquinades Rebellion and the link between Ezpeleta and Nariño are described in McFarlane, *Colombia Before Independence*, 285–290.

63. These relationships were retraced using the "Lista de Subscriptores," *Papel Periódico* 1:20 (24 June 1791): 171, and a letter from "José Celestino Mutis to Martínez Compañón, Bogotá, 12 January 1793," in *Archivo epistolar del sabio naturalista don José Celestino Mutis*, Tomo 11, ed. Guillermo Hernández de Alba (Bogotá: Editorial Kelly, 1968), 77–81. I also used the pertinent secondary sources: McFarlane, *Colombia Before Independence*; and Pazos and Restrepo, "Acción de Martínez Compañón."

64. Martínez Compañón's activities in Bogotá are described in Pérez Ayala, *Baltasar Jaime Martínez Compañón y Bujanda*, 103–130.

65. Pilar Foz y Foz, *Mujer y educación en Colombia, siglos XVI–XIX: Aportaciones del colegio de La Enseñanza, 1783–1900* (Bogotá: Academia Colombiana de Historia, 1997), 204–224.

CONCLUSION

1. Yves Charles Zarka, "The Meaning of Utopia," *New York Times,* August 28, 2011, "The Opinionator" blog. See also Thomas More, *Utopia*, ed. George M. Logan (New York: Norton, 2011), 38–97.

2. Lyman Tower Sargent, *Utopianism: A Very Short Introduction* (Oxford: Oxford University Press, 2010), 2.

3. Zarka, "The Meaning of Utopia."

4. Sargent, *Utopianism*, 5.

5. Oscar Wilde, "The Soul of Man Under Socialism," Gutenberg ebooks #1017, http://www.gutenberg.org/ebooks/1017.

6. Francis Bacon, *The Advancement of Learning* and *New Atlantis*, ed. Arthur Johnston (Oxford: Clarendon, 1974), 215.

7. "Martínez Compañón to Agustín Hermenegildo de Querejazu, Trujillo, 25 March 1790" (Lima: AGNP, Colección Francisco Moyrera Matute, #564).

8. "Martínez Compañón to Andrés de Achurra, Trujillo, 12 April 1790" (Trujillo: AAT, Comunicaciones Eclesiásticas, "La Despedida").

9. "Martínez Compañón to Agustín Hermenegildo de Querejazu, 10 March 1780" (Lima: AGNP, Correspondencia D1-25-727). See also "Pastoral Letter of Martínez Compañón, Trujillo, 14 April 1782" (Seville: AGI, Cartas y expedientes: Curiosidades para el Jardín Botánico, Lima 798).

10. "Actas de Cabildo, 22 June 1790, Oficios que dirigió Martínez Compañón antes de su partida" (Trujillo: AAT, Actas de Cabildo Eclesiástico).

11. Sargent, *Utopianism*, 4.

12. "Expediente sobre la remisión de 24 cajones de curiosidades de la naturaleza y del arte, recogidos por el obispo de Trujillo (hoy arzobispo de Santa Fé) y remitidas por el virrey de Lima, venidas en la Fragata Rosa" (Seville: AGI, Lima 798).

13. Zarka, "The Meaning of Utopia."

14. D. A. Brading, *The First America: The Spanish Monarchy, Creole Patriots, and the Liberal State, 1492–1867* (Cambridge: Cambridge University Press, 1991), 228–253.

15. "Martínez Compañón to King Charles III, Trujillo, 15 May 1786" (Trujillo: AAT, Colegios y Universidades: Erección y fundación de dos colegios de cholos y cholas en Trujillo).

16. "Martínez Compañón to Don Juan José Urteaga, cura y vicario de la Provincia de Chachapoyas, Trujillo, 26 June 1785" (Trujillo: AAT, Colegios y Universidades: Erección y fundación de dos colegios de cholos y cholas en Trujillo).

AFTERWORD

1. Records of the Palacio Real state that the nine volumes arrived there in 1803, delayed by various bureaucratic matters and by Spain's tumultuous international relations. See Manuel Ballesteros Gaibros, introduction to Baltasar Jaime Martínez Compañón, *Trujillo del Perú: Appendice II* (Madrid: Ediciones de Cultura Hispánica, 1994), 14.

2. This can be seen on the original copy at the Royal Palace Library.

SOURCES AND METHODS

1. Books with the Martínez Compañón images on their covers include David Cook, *Born to Die: Disease and the New World Conquest, 1492–1650* (Cambridge: Cambridge Uni-

versity Press, 1998); John Fisher, *El Perú borbónico*, trans. Javier Flores (Lima: Instituto de Estudios Peruanos, 2000); Marcos Cueto, ed., *Saberes andinos: Ciencia y tecnología en Bolivia, Ecuador, y Peru* (Lima: Instituto de Estudios Peruanos, 1995); Alejandro Reyes Flores, *Hacendados y comerciantes: Piura, Chachapoyas, Moyobamba, Lamas, Maynas (1770–1820)* (Lima: Universidad Nacional Mayor de San Marcos, 1999); Karen Graubart, *With Our Labor and Sweat: Indigenous Women and the Formation of Society in Colonial Peru, 1550–1700* (Stanford, Calif.: Stanford University Press, 2007); and Rachel O'Toole, *Bound Lives: Africans, Indians, and the Making of Race in Colonial Peru* (Pittsburgh: University of Pittsburgh Press, 2012).

2. Here I am especially indebted to the work of Daniela Bleichmar and her concept of the Spanish Empire as an "image machine." See her *Visible Empire: Botanical Expeditions and Visual Culture in the Hispanic Enlightenment* (Chicago: University of Chicago Press, 2012).

INDEX

Achurra, Andrés de, 184–186
alcabala sales tax, 93, 94
alcohol, 67, 103, 158, 200; royal monopoly
  on, 91, 236n8
Almagro, Diego de, 40
amoebiasis, 168
Amoroto, Ignacio, 118, 258n14
Andrade, Manuel de, 182
añejo churches, 48, 52, 73
angusacha plant, 149–151, 155, 201
anteater, 4, 8, 9
Antoninus, Marcus Aurelius, 123
arancel (fee for sacraments), 43, 52
archival material, 207–209, 233–234
Areche, Antonio de, 93–95, 101, 118, 119,
  259n16
Aristotle, 70
Arriaga, Antonio de, 92–93
Astopilco, Patricio, 64, 256n54
Atahualpa, Inca emperor, 64, 112
Augustine, Saint, 22, 70–71
Axtell, James, 103–104
ayahuasca plant, 173
Aymara language, 189
Azereto, Juan de, 125–126, 128
Aztecs, 15; writings of, 28, 30, 211

Bacon, Francis, 13, 23, 27, 200, 202
balsams, 59, 157–158, 177. *See also* herbal
  medicines
Basarás, Joaquín Antonio, 163
Basque Friends of the Country Society, 38,
  163
Basque provinces, 20
Bernal, Antonio, 128, 129
Black Legend, 15, 25, 111
Bleichmar, Daniela, 211
Bogotá. *See* Santa Fé de Bogotá
Borromeo, Federico, 3, 22–23, 160

Botanical Expedition to New Granada, 156,
  158, 162, 167, 197
Botanical Expedition to Peru, 154, 155–156,
  162, 177
Bourbon reforms, 18, 190, 212; ecclesiastical,
  43–44, 50; of slave trade, 42
Boyle, Robert, 23
Brazil, 14, 42
Brown, Christopher, 257n61
Bueno, Cosme, 36
Buffon, Georges Louis Leclerc de, 28–29, 69
Buque, Pedro José, 98
Burgos, Laws of, 16

Caballero, Bernabé Antonio, 95
Caballero Ochoa, José María, 182
Caballero y Góngora, Antonio, 44, 217
Cabello Carro, Paz, 249n9
Cádiz, Spain, 19–20
Cajamarca, 57, 62–64, 207; Huaca Tantalluc
  in, 68; incorporation of, 130; map of, xi;
  Martínez Compañón's plans for, 116–117,
  130–38; schools at, 36, 46, 47, 102, 256n54.
  See also Hualgayoc silver mines
Calancha, Antonio de la, 65–66
Campanella, Tomasso, 13
Campillo y Cossío, José del, 212; on Indian
  education, 44, 91, 96; political theories of,
  17–18, 121, 132, 239n33
Campomanes, Pedro, 24, 131, 212
Cañizares-Esguerra, Jorge, 28, 263n11
capellanías (religious endowments), 37, 129
Capitán, Basilio, 98
card playing, 112, 236n8, 252n2; and
  gambling, 3, 91, 205, 236n8; and royal
  paper monopoly, 3, 91, 236n8
Carhuajulca, Marcos, 129
Carillo, Gabriel, 105
Carmen, José, 76

ACKNOWLEDGMENTS

The final years of writing this book were generously funded by two separate yearlong fellowships: one from the American Council of Learned Societies; and one from the Huntington Library and the Dibner program in the History of Science. My research in Colombia and a portion of my research in Peru were funded by a Fulbright fellowship. I am thankful for further funding from the American Historical Association, the John Carter Brown Library, the American Society for Eighteenth-Century Studies, the Seminar on the History of the Atlantic World at Harvard University, the Spanish Ministry of Culture/Hispanex, the Consejo Superior de Investigaciones Científicas, the University of Texas at Austin, California State University at Long Beach, and Cornell University and the Foreign Language Area Studies program in Quechua Language in Bolivia. I also extend my generous thanks to the archivists, research staff, and librarians at the various institutions that have housed and assisted me over the years.

I have benefited immensely from the help and advice of various mentors and friends throughout my work on this project, and I express my heartfelt thanks to all of them. I am tremendously grateful to my editor, Peter Mancall, for his friendship and counsel on this project since I arrived in Los Angeles; under his guidance, it has surpassed what I ever hoped it could be. At the Huntington Library, I thank the former director of research, Roy Ritchie, for his mentorship. Carole Shammas invited me to workshop an early draft of my chapter on the Bishop's botanical research at the American Origins Seminar, cosponsored by the University of Southern California and the Early Modern Studies Institute at the Huntington Library. At California State University at Long Beach, my colleagues in the Department of History and, above all, my department chair, Nancy Quam-Wickham, gave unwavering support to my research program. I also am grateful to the dean's office at the College of Liberal Arts, which allowed me to enjoy two years of research-grant leave and funded a final research trip to Madrid. This project would not be what it is without the thoughtful input of Jorge Cañizares-Esguerra, Susan Deans-Smith, and Ann Twinam. Many years ago, Jim Merrell got me thinking about Indians in colonial history. I am grateful for the professional guidance of my editor at the University of Pennsylvania Press, Bob Lockhart, who read several versions of the manuscript, made valuable suggestions about how to improve it, and wisely shepherded me through the rights and permissions process. Many thanks to the rest of the team who worked on my book, including Rachel Taube, Erica Ginsburg, and especially my outstanding copy editor Janice Meyerson, who tackled two languages with meticulous regard for detail. Any remaining errors in the work are due to my own oversight. I am indebted to the thoughtful comments and critiques of my readers, Charles Walker—a leading figure in Andean history and a congenial colleague who has graciously assisted in Peru and at other critical junctions over the years—and Neil Safier, whose excellent scholarship and exacting standards pushed me to produce what I hope is, in the end, a much better book. I am grateful to the Mellon Art History Publication Initiative, the Spanish Ministry of Culture, and the College of Liberal Arts at California State University at Long Beach for their generous assistance in acquiring the *Trujillo del Perú* images published here.

My work on the Bishop has been greatly improved by consultations I had at various points with other scholars and specialists. Joanne Pillsbury of the Metropolitan Museum of Art generously offered invaluable advice for the discussions of Martínez Compañón's archaeological investigations, and I am thankful for the assistance of Lisa Trever here as well. Christopher Albi helped me through eighteenth-century mining. Ken Ward, curator of Latin American books at the John Carter Brown Library, was a much valued resource. In my foray into historical meteorology, I was aided by the expertise of Mariano Barriendos Vallvé of the University of Barcelona. My research in Peru was greatly facilitated by Scarlett O'Phelan, Juan Castañeda, Marco Curatola, Henry Harmon, and Ricardo Morales. I am most grateful to Margot Beyersdorff, Daniela Bleichmar, Kristen Block, Eva Botella, Steve Bourget, Jim Boyden, Jonathan Brown, Ernie Capello, Matt Childs, Kaja Cook, Helen Cowie, Matthew Crawford, Greg Cushman, Paula De Vos, Rebecca Earle, Mary Fuller, Karen Graubart, Steve Hackel, Dana Leibsohn, Pablo Mijangos, Ricardo Morales, Leslie Offutt, Christopher Parsons, Frances Ramos, Jaime Rodríguez, Susanah Shaw Romney, Karen Spalding, Gary Urton, Tamara Walker, and Sean Wilentz for various consultations and suggestions over the years. Thanks go to my research assistants in Peru who helped in retrieving some of my documents and in transcribing others: Nelly Graciela Cardenas Goya, Carolina Ponce, Deynes Salinas Pérez, and Marina Souza. The Palacios family (Bettza, Nico, and Oscar) and Laura Balbuena gave me welcoming and warm homes away from home in Trujillo and Lima. Finally, my deepest gratitude to my family, especially my parents for their support over the years and above all in the final phases of completing the book, and to my uncle Dennis for outstanding contributions to my education. Leo was a most supportive writing partner and office-mate. Most important, all my love and gratitude to my husband, Bill, who continues to inspire me to be creative, brave, and patient. This book is dedicated to our daughter, Zoey, and to all the adventures that await her as her own story unfolds.